· HOMER ·

THE ILIAD

In every century since the Renaissance, English speakers have felt compelled to possess a translation written especially for their own time of this great epic poem, the earliest and most central literary text of Western culture. That need has now been most thoroughly met in our century by the distinguished poet and classicist Robert Fitzgerald, whose version does justice in every way to the fluent vigor and gravity of the Homeric original.

EVERYMAN,
I WILL GO WITH THEE,
AND BE THY GUIDE,
IN THY MOST NEED
TO GO BY THY SIDE

HOMER

The Iliad

Translated by Robert Fitzgerald

with an Introduction by
Gregory Nagy

EVERYMAN'S LIBRARY

Alfred A. Knopf New York Toronto

60

THIS IS A BORZOI BOOK

PUBLISHED BY ALFRED A. KNOPF, INC.

First included in Everyman's Library, 1910
This translation first published in Everyman's Library, 1992, by
arrangement with Doubleday, a division of Bantam Doubleday
Dell Publishing Group, Inc.
Copyright © 1974 by Robert Fitzgerald
Introduction and Bibliography Copyright © 1992 by David
Campbell Publishers Ltd.
Fifth printing

ISBN 0-679-41075-9
LC 91-53222

Library of Congress Cataloging-in-Publication Data
Homer.
[Iliad. English]
The Iliad / Homer.
p.   cm.——(Everyman's library)
ISBN 0-679-41075-9
1. Achilles (Greek mythology)—Poetry.   2. Trojan War—Poetry.
I. Fitzgerald, Robert. 1910-   . II. Title.
PA4025.A2F5   1992   91-53222
883'.01——dc20   CIP

Book Design by Barbara de Wilde and Carol Devine Carson

Printed and bound in Germany
by Graphischer Grossbetrieb Pössneck GmbH

THE ILIAD

INTRODUCTION

Admired through the ages as the ultimate epic, Homer's *Iliad*, along with its companion-piece *The Odyssey*, was venerated by the ancient Greeks themselves as a cornerstone of their civilization. By force of its prestige, *The Iliad* sets the standard for the very definition of the word *epic*: an expansive poem of enormous scope, composed in an archaic and superbly elevated style of language, concerning the wondrous deeds of heroes. That these deeds were meant to arouse a sense of wonder or marvel is difficult for the modern mind to comprehend, especially in a time when even such words as *wonderful* or *marvellous* have lost much of their evocative power. Nor is it any easier to grasp the ancient Greek concept of *hero* (the English word is descended from the Greek), to go beyond the word's ordinary levels of meaning in casual contemporary usage.

What, then, were the heroes of *The Iliad*? In ancient Greek myth, heroes were humans, male or female, of the remote past, endowed with superhuman abilities and descended from the immortal gods themselves. The prime example is Akhilleus, more commonly known as Achilles in the English tradition. This, the greatest hero of *The Iliad*, was the son of Thetis, a sea-goddess known for her far-reaching cosmic powers.

It is clear in the epic, however, that the father of Akhilleus is mortal, and that this greatest of heroes must therefore be mortal as well. So also with all ancient Greek stories of the heroes: even though they are all descended in some way or another from the gods, however many generations removed, they are mortals, subject to death. No matter how many immortals you find in a family tree, the intrusion of even a single mortal will make all successive descendants mortal. Mortality, not immortality, is the dominant gene.

In some stories, true, the gods themselves can bring it about that the hero becomes miraculously restored to life after death – a life of immortality. The story of Herakles, who had been sired by Zeus, foremost of all the gods, is perhaps the most celebrated instance. But even in such a case, the hero has to die first. It is only after the most excruciating pains, culminating in his death at the funeral pyre on the peak of Mount Oeta, that Herakles is at long last admitted to the company of immortals. In short, although the hero can be *immortalized*, the fundamental painful fact remains: the hero is not by nature *immortal*.

The gods, of course, are exempt from this ultimate pain. When the god Ares goes through the motions of death after he is taken off guard and wounded by the mortal Diomedes in Book 5 of *The Iliad*, we detect a touch of humor in the Homeric treatment of the scene, owing to the fact that this particular 'death' is a mock death. In the world of epic, the dead seriousness of death can be experienced only by humans.

Mortality is the dominant theme in the stories of ancient Greek heroes, and *The Iliad* is no exception. It is *the* burning question for the heroes of Homer's epic, and for Akhilleus in particular. The human condition of mortality, with all its ordeals, defines heroic life itself in *The Iliad*. The certainty that one day we will die makes us human, distinct from animals who are unaware of their future death and from immortal gods. To the warrior-hero all the ordeals of the human condition culminate in the ultimate ordeal of violent death in battle, detailed in all its ghastly varieties by the poet of *The Iliad*.

This deep preoccupation with the primal experience of violent death in war has several possible explanations. Some argue that the answer has to be sought in the simple fact that ancient Greek society accepted war as an important and even necessary part of life. Others seek a deeper answer by pointing to the poet's awe-struck sense of uncontrollable forces at work in the universe, even of a personified concept of Force itself, which then becomes, through the poet's own artistic powers, a kind of eerie esthetic presence.

But there are other answers as well, owing to approaches that delve deeply into the role of religion and, more specifically, into the religious practices of hero-worship and animal-sacrifice in ancient Greece. Of particular interest is the well-attested Greek custom of worshipping a hero precisely by way of slaughtering a sacrificial animal, ordinarily a ram.

There is broad cultural evidence suggesting that hero-worship in ancient Greece was not created out of stories like that of *The Iliad*, but was in fact independent of them. The stories, on the other hand, were based on religious practices, though not always directly. (There are even myths that draw into a parallel the violent death of a hero and the sacrificial slaughter of an animal.) For example, the description of the death of the hero Patroklos in Book 18 of *The Iliad* parallels in striking detail the stylized description, documented elsewhere in Homeric poetry (*Odyssey*, Book 3), of the slaughter of a sacrificial bull: in both cases, the victim is first stunned and disoriented by a fatal blow from behind, then struck frontally by another fatal blow, and then finally administered the *coup de grâce*. An ancient Greek vase-painting represents the same heroic warrior Patroklos in the shape of a sacrificial ram lying supine with its legs in the air and its throat slit open (lettering next to the painted figure specifies Patroklos).

Evidence locates these practices of hero-worship and animal-sacrifice precisely during the era when the story of *The Iliad* took shape. Yet, curiously enough, we find practically no mention there of hero-worship and very little detailed description of animal-sacrifice. Homeric poetry, as a medium that achieved its general appeal to the Greeks by virtue of avoiding the parochial concerns of specific locales and regions, tended to avoid realistic descriptions of any ritual, not just ritual sacrifice. This pattern of avoidance is to be expected, given that any ritual tended to be a localized phenomenon in ancient Greece.

What sacrificial scenes we do find in the epics are markedly stylized, devoid of the kinds of details that characterize real sacrifices as documented archaeologically and historically. In real sacrifice, the parts of the animal victim's body corresponded to the members of the body politic. The ritual dismemberment of the animal in sacrifice set a mental pattern for the idea of the reassembly of the hero in myths of immortalization. Given, then, that Homeric poetry avoids delving into the details of dismemberment as it applies to animals, in that it avoids the details of sacrificial practice, we may expect a parallel avoidance of the topic of immortalization for the hero. The local practices of hero-worship, contemporaneous with the evolution of these epics as we know them, are on the other hand clearly founded on religious notions of heroic immortalization.

While personal immortalization is too localized in orientation for Homeric poetry, the hero's death in battle, in all its stunning varieties, is universally acceptable. *The Iliad* seems to make up for its avoidance of details concerning the sacrifices of animals by dwelling on details concerning the martial deaths of heroes. In this way, the epic poetry of the Greeks, with its staggering volume of minutely detailed descriptions of the deaths of warriors, can serve as a compensation for sacrifice itself.

Such deep concerns about the human condition are organized by *The Iliad* in a framework of heroic portraits, with that of Akhilleus serving as centerpiece. Here is a monolithic and fiercely uncompromising man who actively chooses violent death over life in order to win the glory of being remembered forever in epic poetry. Here is a man of unbending principle who cannot allow his values to be compromised – not even by the desperate needs of his near and dear friends who are begging him to bend his will, bend it just enough to save his own people. Here is a man of constant sorrow, who can never forgive himself for having unwittingly allowed his nearest and dearest friend, Patroklos, to take his place in battle and be killed in his stead, slaughtered like a sacrificial animal – all on account of his own refusal to bend his will by coming to the aid of his fellow warriors. Here is a man, finally, of unspeakable anger, an anger so intense that the poet words it the same way that he words the anger of the gods, even of Zeus himself.

The gods of Homer's *Iliad* take out their anger actively, as in the poet's descriptions of the destructive fire unleashed by the thunderbolt of Zeus. The central hero of *The Iliad* at first takes out his anger passively, by withdrawing his vital presence from his own people. His anger is directed away from the enemy and toward his own people, whose king, Agamemnon, has insulted Akhilleus' honor and demeaned his sense of self. Akhilleus' passive anger translates into the active success of the enemy in the hero's absence. This success is compared, ironically, to the destructive fire unleashed by the thunderbolt of

Zeus. In this way, the passive anger of the hero translates symbolically into the active anger of the god. Then, in response to the death of Patroklos, Akhilleus' anger modulates into an active phase – active no longer in a symbolic but in a real sense. The hero's anger is redirected, away from his own people and back toward his enemy.

This new phase of Akhilleus' anger consumes the hero in a paroxysm of self-destructiveness. His fiery rage plunges him to the depths of brutality as he begins to view the enemy as the ultimate Other, to be hated with such an intensity that Akhilleus can even bring himself in a moment of ultimate fury to express that most ghastly of desires, to eat the flesh of Hektor, the man he is about to kill. *The Iliad* is the story of a hero's pain, culminating in an anger that degrades him to the level of a savage animal, to the depths of bestiality. This same pain, however, this same intense feeling of loss, will ultimately make the savage anger subside in a moment of heroic self-recognition that elevates Akhilleus to the highest realms of humanity, of humanism. At the end of *The Iliad*, as he begins to recognize the pain of his deadliest enemy, of the Other, he begins to achieve a true recognition of the Self. The anger is at an end. And the story can end as well.

We find the poet's own statement about the subject of *The Iliad* in the original Greek poem's first word: Anger. The song of *The Iliad* – for at the time the poets were singers, performers, and their poems were sung – is about the anger, the doomed and ruinous anger, of the hero Akhilleus. The singer was following the rules of his craft in summing up the whole song, all 100,000 or so words, in one single word, the first word of the song. So also in *The Odyssey*, the first word, Man, tells the subject of the song. There the singer calls upon the Muse, goddess of the special Memory that makes him a singer, to tell him the story of the Man, the many-sided man, the hero Odysseus, who wandered so many countless ways in his voyages at sea after his heroic exploit of masterminding the capture and destruction of Troy. The Muse is imagined as telling the singer his song, so that the singer can then sing this song to others. In the same way, here in *The Iliad*, the singer calls upon the goddess to

tell the story of the Anger, the doomed and ruinous anger, of
the hero Akhilleus, which caused countless losses and woes for
Greeks and Trojans alike in the war that later culminated in
the destruction of Troy.

We see from this paraphrase of the beginnings of *The Iliad*
and *The Odyssey* that the rules of the singer's craft extend
beyond the naming of the main subject with the first word. In
the original Greek of the twin epics, the first word announcing
the subject – Anger, Man – is followed by a specially chosen
adjective setting the mood – doomed anger, many-sided man –
to be followed in turn by a relative clause that frames the story
by outlining the plot – the doomed anger that caused count-
less losses and woes, the many-sided man who wandered
countless ways.

The symmetry of these two monumental compositions goes
beyond their strict adherence to the rules of introducing an
ancient Greek song, for they counterbalance each other
throughout their vast stretches of narrative, in a steady,
rhythmic flow of verses, lines called dactylic hexameter (*The
Iliad* contains over 15,000 lines and *The Odyssey* over 12,000).
The counterbalancing focuses on the central plot and the
characterization of the principal hero in each. Akhilleus'
monolithic personality, that of the mightiest warrior of his era
who was monumentally proud of his martial exploits and his
physical prowess, is matched against the many-sidedness of
Odysseus, famed for his crafty stratagems and cunning
intelligence.

The symmetry of *The Iliad* and *The Odyssey* goes even further:
between the two of them, these songs give the impression of
incorporating most of whatever was worth retelling about the
heroic age – at least from the standpoint of the Greeks in the
Classical period of the fifth century B.C.E. and thereafter. The
staggering comprehensiveness of these two songs is apparent
even from a cursory glance. For example, *The Iliad* not only
tells the story that it says it will tell, about Akhilleus' anger
and how it led to countless woes as the Greeks went on fighting
it out with the Trojans in their life-and-death struggle beneath
the walls of Troy. It also manages to retell and even relive,
though with varying degrees of directness or fullness of narra-

tive, the entire Tale of Troy, including from earlier points of the story-line such memorable moments as the Judgment of Paris, the Abduction of Helen, and the Assembly of Ships. More than that: *The Iliad* foreshadows the death of Akhilleus, which does not occur within the bounds of its own plot. In short, although the story of *The Iliad* directly covers only a brief stretch of the whole story of Troy, thereby resembling the compressed time-frame of a Classical Greek tragedy (Aristotle makes this observation in his *Poetics*), it still manages to mention something about practically everything that happened at Troy, then known as Ilion. Hence the epic's title: the Tale of Ilion, *The Iliad*.

For the Greeks of the fifth century B.C.E. and thereafter, these two seemingly all-inclusive and symmetrical songs were the creation of the Master Singer, Homer, reputed to have lived centuries earlier. He was presumed to have been contemporaneous with another Master Singer, Hesiod, who was credited with two other definitive symmetrical songs, the *Theogony* and the *Works and Days*. About the real Homer, there is next to nothing that we can recover from the ancient world. Nor do we have much better luck with Hesiod, except perhaps for whatever the singer says about himself in his own songs. In the case of Homer, we do not even have this much to start with, at least not in *The Iliad* or *The Odyssey*: in neither song does the singer say anything about himself that could be construed as historical information. It can even be said that there is no evidence for the existence of a Homer – and hardly that much more for the existence of a Hesiod.

What we do know, however, is that the Greeks of the Classical period thought of Homer and Hesiod as their first authors, their primary authors. So it is not just for the modern reader that Homer and Hesiod represent the earliest phase of Greek literature. It is moreover a historical fact that Homer and Hesiod were eventually credited by the ancient Greeks with the very foundation of Greek literature. Our primary authority for this fact is none other than the so-called Father of History himself, Herodotus, who observes in Book II of his *Histories* that Homer and Hesiod, by way of their songs, had given the Greeks their first definitive statement about the gods. In a traditional society like that of the ancient Greeks, where the very idea of defining the gods is the equivalent of defining the society itself, this observation by Herodotus amounts to a claim that the songs of Homer and Hesiod are the basis of Greek civilization.

Who, then, was Homer? It is no exaggeration to answer that, along with Hesiod, he had become the prime culture hero of Greek civilization in the Classical period of the fifth century B.C.E. and thereafter. It was a common practice of the ancient Greeks to attribute any major achievement of society, even if this achievement may have taken place through a lengthy period of social evolution, to the personal break-through of a culture hero who was pictured as having made his monumental contribution in the earliest imaginable era of the culture. Greek myths about lawgivers, for example, tended to reconstruct these figures, whether or not they ever really existed, as the originators of the sum total of customary law as it evolved through time. The same sort of evolutionary model may well apply to the figure of Homer as an originator of heroic song.

This model can even be extended from Homer to Homeric song. There is evidence that a type of story, represented in a wide variety of cultures where the evolution of a song tradition moves slowly ahead in time until it reaches a relatively static phase, reinterprets itself as if it resulted from a single event. There were many such stories about Homer in ancient Greece, and what matters most is not so much the stories themselves but what they reveal about society's need to account for the evolution of Homeric song. The internal evidence of the Homeric verses, both in their linguistic development and in their datable references, points to an ongoing evolution of Homeric song embracing a vast stretch of time that lasted perhaps as long as a thousand years, extending from the second millennium B.C.E. This period culminated in a static phase that lasted about two centuries, framed by a *formative stage* in the later part of the eighth century B.C.E., where the epic was taking on its present shape, and a *definitive stage* in the middle of the sixth, where the epic reached its final form.

The basic historical fact remains, in any case, that the figure of Homer had become, by the Classical period of the fifth century B.C.E., a primary culture hero credited with the creation of *The Iliad* and *The Odyssey*. Little wonder, then, that so many Greek cities – Athens included – claimed to be his birthplace. Such rivalry for the possession of Homer points to the increasingly widespread refinement of his identity through the cultural significance of Homeric song.

Of course, the subject of Homeric song is not just the anger of Achilles and the age of heroes. *The Iliad* purports to say everything that is worth saying about the Greeks – the Hellenes, as they called themselves in the Classical period. Not that *The Iliad* calls them Greeks. The Greeks in this song are a larger-than-life cultural construct of what they imagined themselves to have been in the distant age of heroes. These Greeks are retrojected Greeks, given such alternative Homeric names as *Akhaians, Argives, Danaans*, all three of which are used interchangeably to refer to these heroic ancestors whose very existence in song is for the Greeks the basis for their own self-definition as a people. It is as if *The Iliad*, in mirroring for the Greeks of the time an archetypal image of themselves in the past, served as an autobiography of a people.

On the surface these ancestral Greeks of *The Iliad* are on the offensive, attacking Troy. Underneath the surface, they are on the defensive, trying desperately to ward off the fiery on-slaught of Hektor, the leading Trojan hero. At a climactic point of the battle, Hektor shouts out to his men:

> Fire now! Bring it up,
> and all together raise a battle shout!
> Zeus gave this day to us as recompense
> for everything: now we may burn the ships
> that came against the gods' will to our shore ...
>   15.718-20

With all their ships beached on the shores of the Hellespont, marked for destruction by the threatening fire of Hektor, the ancestral Greeks are vulnerable to extinction. *The Iliad* makes it quite clear: if their ships burn, the Greeks will never return home to become the seafaring nation who are the present audience of *The Iliad*. In *The Iliad*, the very survival of this seafaring nation is at stake.

But what exactly is this Greek nation? For the very idea of nationhood is an incongruity if we apply it to the era when *The Iliad* and *The Odyssey* took shape. From the eighth through the fifth centuries B.C.E., the geographical area that we now recognize as ancient Greece was an agglomerate of territories controlled by scores of independent and competing city-states. The most important and prestigious of these were Athens, Sparta, Argos, Thebes and Corinth. Each city-state, or *polis*, was a social entity unto itself, with its own government, customary laws, religious practices, dialect.

The fragmentation of Greece in this era was so pronounced that, looking back, it is hard to find genuine instances of cultural cohesion. One early example is the Olympic Games; another is the Oracle of Apollo at Delphi; still another, and the most obvious, is the poetic legacy of Homer and Hesiod. The Homeric *Iliad* in particular can be viewed as a marvel of cultural synthesis, integrating the diverse institutional heritage of this plurality of city-states, this kaleidoscopic Greek-speaking world, into a unified statement of cultural identity, of civilization.

The cultural universalism of *The Iliad* can best be appreciated when we consider the extent of the diversity that separated the Greek city-states from each other. Nowhere is this diversity more apparent than in the realm of religious practices. How people worshipped any given god, as we know from the historical evidence of the Classical era and thereafter, differed dramatically from one city-state to another. Yet *The Iliad* spoke of the gods in a way that united the varied cultural perceptions and sensitivities of a vast variety of city-states, large and small. The religious dimensions of these gods, with Zeus, Hera, Poseidon, Athena and Apollo in the forefront, were destined to be shaded over by this Homeric process of synthesis, but their divine reality became highlighted as a cultural permanence in the same process. The modern reader may be struck by what seems on the surface to be a distinctly irreligious attitude of Homeric song towards the gods, but the universal cultural edifice of these gods' lofty abode on Mount Olympus was in fact built up from a diversity of unspoken religious foundations. When Herodotus says that Homer and Hesiod, by way of their songs, had given the Greeks their first definitive statement about the gods, he is in effect acknowledging the Olympian synthesis that had been bestowed on civilization by Homeric and Hesiodic song in general and by *The Iliad* in particular. It is the history of Greek civilization, then, that the Homeric *Iliad* defines.

To say that *The Iliad* is about the Greeks and what it is to be a Greek is not far from saying that *The Iliad* is about Akhilleus. We have seen how this hero, as the very first words of the song make clear, is the focal point of *The Iliad*. Given the importance of *The Iliad* to the Greeks, we can also see by virtue of this single fact that Akhilleus is in turn a focal point of Greek civilization. Just how important he is, however, can be illustrated beyond the testimony of Homeric song. Let us take for example an inherited custom connected with the premier social event for all Greeks, the Olympic Games. We know from ancient sources that the traditional ceremony inaugurating this seasonally recurring pan-Hellenic event centers on Akhilleus: on an appointed day when the Games are to begin, the local women of Elis, the place where the Olympics were held, fix their gaze on the sun as it sets into the Western horizon – and begin ceremonially to weep for the hero.

The prestige accorded by ancient Greek civilization to the figure of Akhilleus, and the strong emotional attachment that goes with it, is worthy of our attention especially because modern readers, both men and women, young and old, often find themselves relatively unresponsive to this sullen and darkly brooding hero. Few today feel empathy for his sorrow, which the hero of *The Iliad* himself describes as an everlasting one. The modern reader finds it much easier to feel empathy for Hektor, the champion hero of the Trojans, whose heart-wrenching farewell (in Book 6) to his wife and small son, soon to become his widow and orphan, is often singled out by modern readers as the most memorable scene of *The Iliad*. For the ancient Greeks as well, we may be sure, the figure of Hektor evoked empathy. The difference, however, is that for them, the pathos of Hektor resembles most closely the pathos of Akhilleus himself. Just as Hektor's death evokes the sorrow of unfulfilled promise, even more so does the death of Akhilleus.

While Hektor is the idealized husband and father cut down in his prime, Akhilleus is the idealized bridegroom, sensual in his heroic beauty and likewise doomed to an untimely death. In the songs of Sappho, it is Akhilleus who figures as the ultimate bridegroom. The very mention of him in song conjures up the picture of a beautiful flower cut down at the peak of its bloom. This is how his own mother sings of Akhilleus in Book 18 of *The Iliad*, in a beautiful song of lament that prefigures the hero's untimely death:

> ... how sore my heart is! Now my life is pain
> for my great son's dark destiny! I bore
> a child flawless and strong beyond all men.
> He flourished like a green shoot, and I brought him
> to manhood like a blossoming orchard tree,
> only to send him in the ships to Ilion
> to war with Trojans. Now I shall never see him
> entering Peleus' hall, his home, again.
>
> 18.53-60

All the wistful beauty of sorrow for a life cut short comes back to life in song, and that song of the hero's mother extends into a song that becomes *The Iliad* itself, for the culture of the Greeks was, and still is, a song culture. For them, to weep is to sing a lament, and the sorrow, in all its natural reality of physically crying and sobbing, is not at all incompatible with the art of the song: it flows into it.

If we consider the evocative power that we can sometimes find in even the simplest contemporary popular tunes about the sorrows of war and death, we will have at least something to compare with the emotional and esthetic response to Akhilleus in the song culture of the ancient Greek world. Thinking of Akhilleus led to beautiful sad songs. As we recall the detail about the ritualized weeping of the local women at the commencement of the Olympics, we may note that this act of weeping was considered an act of singing, or of keening. In the words of the fifth-century poet Pindar, the mourning of the Muses, the 'Maidens of Helicon', over the dead Akhilleus, extends into the song of the present:

When he died, the songs did not leave him, but the Maidens of Helicon stood by his funeral pyre and his funeral mound, and they poured forth a lament that is very renowned. And so the gods decided to hand over that worthy man, dead as he was, to the songs of the goddesses.

(*Isthmian*, 8.56-60)

The sadness of Akhilleus' song is of course a necessity of tradition, just as the hero's death, his mortality, is necessary. The hero cannot be complete, his story cannot be complete, if he lives on, for in death the hero wins the ultimate prize of eternal life in song. As Akhilleus himself declares, his heroic death will transcend the fleeting beauty of the earthly cycle:

> ... if ... I remain to fight
> around Troy town, I lose all hope of home
> but gain unfading glory

9.412-13

The Greek word *kleos*, which translates here as 'glory', conventionally refers to the glory of song, while *aphthiton* or 'unfading' evokes the vitality of a plant. Akhilleus' glory in song, then, unlike the beauty of a flower, will never fade. And the song of *kleos* will remain forever alive in the civilization that sings his glorious epic.

In Plato's *Ion*, which gives us a portrait of a virtuoso performer of Homeric song in the Classical era, there is a vivid reference to performances of *The Iliad* and *The Odyssey* before an audience of more than 20,000 at a seasonally recurring festival in Athens. What is particularly arresting about this reference is the image of the audience, all of them, breaking down and weeping as they hear the saddest moments of the song. The performer describes himself as he gazes down upon a sea of faces, all reacting simultaneously to the Homeric song he sings, eyes tear-filled or terror-stricken, or simply wide in sheer amazement as the poem flows from one emotion to another:

As I look down at them from the podium on high, I see them, each and every time, crying or looking terrified, filled with a sense of wonder at what is being retold.

(Plato, *Ion*, 535e)

The song of Akhilleus was ever being retold, nurtured by the song culture that had generated it. And the wonder of it all is that the hero himself foretold it: beyond the song culture, beyond Greek civilization, the epic continues to flourish in our time.

Gregory Nagy

SELECT BIBLIOGRAPHY

ALEXIOU, MARGARET, *The Ritual Lament in Greek Tradition*, Cambridge University Press, Cambridge and New York, 1974. Explores the connections between women's songmaking traditions and epic traditions as perpetuated by male singers.

BLOOM, HAROLD, ed., *Modern Critical Views: Homer*, Chelsea House, New York, 1986. A variety of influential essays on Iliadic topics. Among the authors are Milman Parry, Bruno Snell, Eric Havelock, Norman Austin and Rachel Bespaloff. A particularly striking contribution is Simone Weil's *The Iliad, or the Poem of Force*.

EDWARDS, MARK W., *Homer, Poet of the Iliad*, Johns Hopkins University Press, Baltimore, 1987. Both a general introduction to Homer and a commentary on *The Iliad*. The commentary runs book by book, though not line by line, still managing to cover most of the high points in a clear style of presentation.

FITZGERALD, ROBERT, 'Some General Considerations', the second half of his Postscript (1962) to his translation of *The Odyssey* (Everyman's Library edition, 1992). The translator's essay evolves from a discussion of Homer's oral poetic practice to the relationship of *The Iliad* and *The Odyssey* to an insightful reading of Odysseus and Penélopê's reunion.

FOLEY, JOHN M., *Oral-Formulaic Theory and Research: An Introduction and Annotated Bibliography*, Garland Publishers, New York, 1985.

GOLDHILL, SIMON, *The Poet's Voice: Essays on Poetics and Greek Literature*, Cambridge University Press, Cambridge and New York, 1991. Chapter 2 assesses the importance of song as the key to the hero's achievement of fame and glory, with special reference to the *Iliad*.

GRIFFITHS, ALAN, 'A Ram Called Patroklos', *Bulletin of the Institute of Classical Studies 32*, 1985, 49–50. Plate 4 shows the painting with a picture of a sacrificial ram lying supine with its legs in the air and its throat slit open (lettering next to the painted figure specifies Patroklos).

LORD, ALBERT B., *The Singer of Tales*, Harvard University Press, Cambridge, Mass., 1960. Along with Milman Parry, Lord stands in the forefront of research on living oral poetic traditions. This book gives a definitive account of oral poetics, with special reference to South Slavic and ancient Greek epic. Chapter 9 concerns *The Iliad* in particular.

, *Epic Singers and Oral Tradition*, Cornell University Press, Ithaca,

THE ILIAD

N.Y., 1991. Contains some of Lord's most influential papers, including 'Homer's Originality: Oral Dictated Texts'.

MARTIN, RICHARD P., *The Language of Heroes: Speech and Performance In the Iliad*, Cornell University Press, Ithaca, N. Y., 1989. Argues that the special characteristics of Akhilleus' discourse in *The Iliad*, which make him sound superior to all other heroes, are parallel to the special characteristics of Homeric discourse, which make 'Homer' sound superior to the rest of archaic Greek epic poetry.

MILLER, D. GARY., *Improvisation, Typology, Culture, and the 'New Orthodoxy'. How Oral is Homer?*, University Press of America, Lanham, Md., Washington, 1982. A spirited reassessment of the evidence for the oral poetic heritage of *The Iliad* and *The Odyssey*.

MUELLER, MARTIN, *The Iliad*, Unwin Hyman, London, 1984. A forceful restatement of the evidence for the artistic unity of *The Iliad*.

NAGLER, MICHAEL N., *Spontaneity and Tradition: A Study in the Oral Art of Homer*, University of California Press, Berkeley and Los Angeles, 1974. Describes the mechanics and esthetics of artistic creativity within the oral traditions of epic song.

NAGY, GREGORY, *The Best of the Achaeans: Concepts of the Hero in Archaic Greek Poetry*, Johns Hopkins University Press, Baltimore, 1979. Highlights the religious dimension of the hero in ancient Greek society, exploring how this dimension is reflected in song and poetry, especially in *The Iliad*.

—, *Pindar's Homer: The Lyric Possession of an Epic Past*, Johns Hopkins University Press, Baltimore, 1990. Integrates the study of Homeric song with an overall view of ancient Greek 'song culture'.

—, *Greek Mythology and Poetics*, Cornell University Press, Ithaca, N.Y., 1990. Chapter 1 examines the role of myth in *The Iliad*; Chapter 2 reassesses the definition of the Homeric formula; Chapters 4 and 5 address the topic of heroic immortalization in *The Iliad*, and Chapter 8 interprets the symbolism of the hero's tomb in *Iliad*, Book 23, and elsewhere.

OKPEWHO, ISIDORE, *The Epic in Africa: Toward a Poetics of the Oral Performance*, Columbia University Press, New York, 1979. Keen comparative insights on the *Iliad*.

PARRY, ADAM, ed., *The Making of Homeric Verse: The Collected Papers of Milman Parry*, Clarendon Press, Oxford, 1971. The premier point of reference for the oral poetic heritage of *The Iliad* and *The Odyssey*.

REDFIELD, JAMES M., *Nature and Culture in the Iliad: The Tragedy of Hector*, University of Chicago Press, Chicago, 1975. *The Iliad* viewed from the perspectives of social anthropology.

SELECT BIBLIOGRAPHY

SCHEIN, SETH L., *The Mortal Hero: An Introduction to Homer's Iliad*, University of California Press, Berkeley and Los Angeles, 1984. An articulate synthesis.

SEGAL, CHARLES P., *The Theme of the Mutilation of the Corpse in the Iliad*, Leiden, 1971. A forthright examination of the moral problem of the hero's capacity for brutality in war, which *The Iliad* itself juxtaposes with the hero's ideals of enlightened humanism.

SLATKIN, LAURA M., *The Power of Thetis: Allusion and Interpretation in the Iliad*, University of California Press, Berkeley and Los Angeles, 1991. Demonstrates the evocative power of Homeric mythmaking and relates the narrative masterplan of *The Iliad* to such key passages as Thetis's song of lament in Book 18 of the epic.

TAPLIN, OLIVER I., *Homeric Soundings. The Shaping of the Iliad*, Oxford University Press, Oxford, 1992. 'Sample explorations' of the detail of particular passages lead to larger issues. Interconnections emerge when the poem is *heard*.

THALMANN, WILLIAM G., *Conventions of Form and Thought in Early Greek Epic Poetry*, Johns Hopkins University Press, Baltimore, 1984. A judiciously framed guide to the epic traditions that govern the making of *The Iliad* and *The Odyssey*.

VERMEULE, EMILY, *Aspects of Death in Early Greek Art and Poetry*, University of California Press, Berkeley and Los Angeles, 1979. Describes the cultural context for the ancient Greek understanding of heroic death in epic song.

WHITMAN, CEDRIC H., *Homer and the Heroic Tradition*, Harvard University Press, Cambridge, Mass., 1958. A definitive statement on heroic humanism in *The Iliad*.

For Sarah, and for
Ughetta, Benedict,
Maria, Michael,
Barnaby, and Caterina

CONTENTS

BOOK ONE

Quarrel, Oath, and Promise

Anger be now your song, immortal one,
Akhilleus' anger, doomed and ruinous,
that caused the Akhaians loss on bitter loss
and crowded brave souls into the undergloom,
leaving so many dead men—carrion
for dogs and birds; and the will of Zeus was done.
Begin it when the two men first contending
broke with one another—

                        the Lord Marshal
Agamémnon, Atreus' son, and Prince Akhilleus.

Among the gods, who brought this quarrel on?
The son of Zeus by Lêto. Agamémnon

angered him, so he made a burning wind
of plague rise in the army: rank and file
sickened and died for the ill their chief had done
in despising a man of prayer.
This priest, Khrysês, had come down to the ships
with gifts, no end of ransom for his daughter;
on a golden staff he carried the god's white bands
and sued for grace from the men of all Akhaia,
the two Atreidai most of all:

                                                    "O captains

Meneláos and Agamémnon, and you other
Akhaians under arms!
The gods who hold Olympos, may they grant you
plunder of Priam's town and a fair wind home,
but let me have my daughter back for ransom
as you revere Apollo, son of Zeus!"

Then all the soldiers murmured their assent:

"Behave well to the priest. And take the ransom!"

But Agamémnon would not. It went against his desire,
and brutally he ordered the man away:

"Let me not find you here by the long ships
loitering this time or returning later,
old man; if I do,
the staff and ribbons of the god will fail you.
Give up the girl? I swear she will grow old
at home in Argos, far from her own country,
working my loom and visiting my bed.
Leave me in peace and go, while you can, in safety."

So harsh he was, the old man feared and obeyed him,
in silence trailing away
by the shore of the tumbling clamorous whispering sea,
and he prayed and prayed again, as he withdrew,
to the god whom silken-braided Lêto bore:

"O hear me, master of the silver bow,
protector of Ténedos and the holy towns,
Apollo, Sminthian, if to your liking

ever in any grove I roofed a shrine
or burnt thighbones in fat upon your altar—
bullock or goat flesh—let my wish come true:
your arrows on the Danáäns for my tears!"

Now when he heard this prayer, Phoibos Apollo
walked with storm in his heart from Olympos' crest,
quiver and bow at his back, and the bundled arrows
clanged on the sky behind as he rocked in his anger,
descending like night itself. Apart from the ships
he halted and let fly, and the bowstring slammed
as the silver bow sprang, rolling in thunder away.
Pack animals were his target first, and dogs,
but soldiers, too, soon felt transfixing pain
from his hard shots, and pyres burned night and day.
Nine days the arrows of the god came down
broadside upon the army. On the tenth,
Akhilleus called all ranks to assembly. Hêra,
whose arms are white as ivory, moved him to it,
as she took pity on Danáäns dying.
All being mustered, all in place and quiet,
Akhilleus, fast in battle as a lion,
rose and said:

                                            "Agamémnon, now, I take it,
the siege is broken, we are going to sail,
and even so may not leave death behind:
if war spares anyone, disease will take him . . .
We might, though, ask some priest or some diviner,
even some fellow good at dreams—for dreams
come down from Zeus as well—
why all this anger of the god Apollo?

Has he some quarrel with us for a failure
in vows or hekatombs? Would mutton burned
or smoking goat flesh make him lift the plague?"

Putting the question, down he sat. And Kalkhas,
Kalkhas Thestórides, came forward, wisest
by far of all who scanned the flight of birds.
He knew what was, what had been, what would be,

Kalkhas, who brought Akhaia's ships to Ilion
by the diviner's gift Apollo gave him.
Now for their benefit he said:

                     "Akhilleus,
dear to Zeus, it is on me you call
to tell you why the Archer God is angry.
Well, I can tell you. Are you listening? Swear
by heaven that you will back me and defend me,
because I fear my answer will enrage
a man with power in Argos, one whose word
Akhaian troops obey.

            A great man in his rage is formidable
for underlings: though he may keep it down,
he cherishes the burning in his belly
until a reckoning day. Think well
if you will save me."

Said Akhilleus:

                     "Courage.
Tell what you know, what you have light to know.
I swear by Apollo, the lord god to whom
you pray when you uncover truth,
never while I draw breath, while I have eyes to see,
shall any man upon this beachhead dare
lay hands on you—not one of all the army,
not Agamémnon, if it is he you mean,
though he is first in rank of all Akhaians."

The diviner then took heart and said:

                     "No failure
in hekatombs or vows is held against us.
It is the man of prayer whom Agamémnon
treated with contempt: he kept his daughter,
spurned his gifts: for that man's sake the Archer
visited grief upon us and will again.
Relieve the Danáäns of this plague he will not
until the girl who turns the eyes of men
shall be restored to her own father—freely,
with no demand for ransom—and until

we offer up a hekatomb at Khrysê.
Then only can we calm him and persuade him."

He finished and sat down. The son of Atreus,
ruler of the great plain, Agamémnon,
rose, furious. Round his heart resentment
welled, and his eyes shone out like licking fire.
Then, with a long and boding look at Kalkhas,
he growled at him:

                                                    "You visionary of hell,
never have I had fair play in your forecasts.
Calamity is all you care about, or see,
no happy portents; and you bring to pass
nothing agreeable. Here you stand again
before the army, giving it out as oracle
the Archer made them suffer because of me,
because I would not take the gifts
and let the girl Khrysêis go; I'd have her
mine, at home. Yes, if you like, I rate her
higher than Klytaimnestra, my own wife!
She loses nothing by comparison
in beauty or womanhood, in mind or skill.

For all of that, I am willing now to yield her
if it is best; I want the army saved
and not destroyed. You must prepare, however,
a prize of honor for me, and at once,
that I may not be left without my portion—
I, of all Argives. It is not fitting so.
While every man of you looks on, my girl
goes elsewhere."

Prince Akhilleus answered him:

"Lord Marshal, most insatiate of men,
how can the army make you a new gift?
Where is our store of booty? Can you see it?
Everything plundered from the towns has been
distributed; should troops turn all that in?
Just let the girl go, in the god's name, now;
we'll make it up to you, twice over, three

times over, on that day Zeus gives us leave
to plunder Troy behind her rings of stone."

Agamémnon answered:

                                        "Not that way

will I be gulled, brave as you are, Akhilleus.
Take me in, would you? Try to get around me?
What do you really ask? That you may keep
your own winnings, I am to give up mine
and sit here wanting her? Oh, no:
the army will award a prize to me
and make sure that it measures up, or if
they do not, I will take a girl myself,
your own, or Aías', or Odysseus' prize!
Take her, yes, to keep. The man I visit
may choke with rage; well, let him.
But this, I say, we can decide on later.

Look to it now, we launch on the great sea
a well-found ship, and get her manned with oarsmen,
load her with sacrificial beasts and put aboard
Khryseîs in her loveliness. My deputy,
Aías, Idómeneus, or Prince Odysseus,
or you, Akhilleus, fearsome as you are,
will make the hekatomb and quiet the Archer."

Akhilleus frowned and looked at him, then said:

"You thick-skinned, shameless, greedy fool!
Can any Akhaian care for you, or obey you,
after this on marches or in battle?
As for myself, when I came here to fight,
I had no quarrel with Troy or Trojan spearmen:
they never stole my cattle or my horses,
never in the black farmland of Phthía
ravaged my crops. How many miles there are
of shadowy mountains, foaming seas, between!
No, no, we joined for you, you insolent boor,
to please you, fighting for your brother's sake
and yours, to get revenge upon the Trojans.
You overlook this, dogface, or don't care,

and now in the end you threaten to take my girl,
a prize I sweated for, and soldiers gave me!

Never have I had plunder like your own
from any Trojan stronghold battered down
by the Akhaians. I have seen more action
hand to hand in those assaults than you have,
but when the time for sharing comes, the greater
share is always yours. Worn out with battle
I carry off some trifle to my ships.
Well, this time I make sail for home.
Better to take now to my ships. Why linger,
cheated of winnings, to make wealth for you?"

To this the high commander made reply:

"Desért, if that's the way the wind blows. Will I
beg you to stay on my account? I will not.
Others will honor me, and Zeus who views
the wide world most of all.

                                                        No officer

is hateful to my sight as you are, none
given like you to faction, as to battle—
rugged you are, I grant, by some god's favor.
Sail, then, in your ships, and lord it over
your own battalion of Myrmidons. I do not
give a curse for you, or for your anger.
But here is warning for you:

                                                        Khryseis

being required of me by Phoibos Apollo,
she will be sent back in a ship of mine,
manned by my people. That done, I myself
will call for Briseis at your hut, and take her,
flower of young girls that she is, your prize,
to show you here and now who is the stronger
and make the next man sick at heart—if any
think of claiming equal place with me."

A pain like grief weighed on the son of Pêleus,
and in his shaggy chest this way and that
the passion of his heart ran: should he draw

longsword from hip, stand off the rest, and kill
in single combat the great son of Atreus,
or hold his rage in check and give it time?
And as this tumult swayed him, as he slid
the big blade slowly from the sheath, Athêna
came to him from the sky. The white-armed goddess,
Hêra, sent her, being fond of both,
concerned for both men. And Athêna, stepping
up behind him, visible to no one
except Akhilleus, gripped his red-gold hair.

Startled, he made a half turn, and he knew her
upon the instant for Athêna: terribly
her grey eyes blazed at him. And speaking softly
but rapidly aside to her he said:

"What now, O daughter of the god of heaven
who bears the stormcloud, why are you here? To see
the wolfishness of Agamémnon?
Well, I give you my word: this time, and soon,
he pays for his behavior with his blood."

The grey-eyed goddess Athêna said to him:

"It was to check this killing rage I came
from heaven, if you will listen. Hêra sent me,
being fond of both of you, concerned for both.
Enough: break off this combat, stay your hand
upon the sword hilt. Let him have a lashing
with words, instead: tell him how things will be.
Here is my promise, and it will be kept:
winnings three times as rich, in due season,
you shall have in requital for his arrogance.
But hold your hand. Obey."

                                              The great runner,
Akhilleus, answered:

                                              "Nothing for it, goddess,
but when you two immortals speak, a man
complies, though his heart burst. Just as well.
Honor the gods' will, they may honor ours."

On this he stayed his massive hand
upon the silver pommel, and the blade
of his great weapon slid back in the scabbard.
The man had done her bidding. Off to Olympos,
gaining the air, she went to join the rest,
the powers of heaven in the home of Zeus.

But now the son of Pêleus turned on Agamémnon
and lashed out at him, letting his anger ride
in execration:

                                                    "Sack of wine,
you with your cur's eyes and your antelope heart!
You've never had the kidney to buckle on
armor among the troops, or make a sortie
with picked men—oh, no; that way death might lie.
Safer, by god, in the middle of the army—
is it not?—to commandeer the prize
of any man who stands up to you! Leech!
Commander of trash! If not, I swear,
you never could abuse one soldier more!

But here is what I say: my oath upon it
by this great staff: look: leaf or shoot
it cannot sprout again, once lopped away
from the log it left behind in the timbered hills;
it cannot flower, peeled of bark and leaves;
instead, Akhaian officers in council
take it in hand by turns, when they observe
by the will of Zeus due order in debate:
let this be what I swear by then: I swear
a day will come when every Akhaian soldier
will groan to have Akhilleus back. That day
you shall no more prevail on me than this
dry wood shall flourish—driven though you are,
and though a thousand men perish before
the killer, Hektor. You will eat your heart out,
raging with remorse for this dishonor
done by you to the bravest of Akhaians."

He hurled the staff, studded with golden nails,
before him on the ground. Then down he sat,
and fury filled Agamémnon, looking across at him.
But for the sake of both men Nestor arose,
the Pylians' orator, eloquent and clear;
argument sweeter than honey rolled from his tongue.
By now he had outlived two generations
of mortal men, his own and the one after,
in Pylos land, and still ruled in the third.
In kind reproof he said:

                                        "A black day, this.
Bitter distress comes this way to Akhaia.
How happy Priam and Priam's sons would be,
and all the Trojans—wild with joy—if they
got wind of all these fighting words between you,
foremost in council as you are, foremost
in battle. Give me your attention. Both
are younger men than I, and in my time
men who were even greater have I known
and none of them disdained me. Men like those
I have not seen again, nor shall: Peiríthoös,
the Lord Marshal Dryas, Kaineus, Exádios,
Polyphêmos, Theseus—Aigeus' son,
a man like the immortal gods. I speak
of champions among men of earth, who fought
with champions, with wild things of the mountains,
great centaurs whom they broke and overpowered.
Among these men I say I had my place
when I sailed out of Pylos, my far country,
because they called for me. I fought
for my own hand among them. Not one man
alive now upon earth could stand against them.
And I repeat: they listened to my reasoning,
took my advice. Well, then, you take it too.
It is far better so.

                                        Lord Agamémnon,
do not deprive him of the girl, renounce her.
The army had allotted her to him.
Akhilleus, for your part, do not defy
your King and Captain. No one vies in honor

with him who holds authority from Zeus.
You have more prowess, for a goddess bore you;
his power over men surpasses yours.

But, Agamémnon, let your anger cool.
I beg you to relent, knowing Akhilleus
a sea wall for Akhaians in the black waves of war."

Lord Agamémnon answered:

                                        "All you say

is fairly said, sir, but this man's ambition,
remember, is to lead, to lord it over
everyone, hold power over everyone,
give orders to the rest of us! Well, one
will never take his orders! If the gods
who live forever made a spearman of him,
have they put insults on his lips as well?"

Akhilleus interrupted:

                                        "What a poltroon,

how lily-livered I should be called, if I
knuckled under to all you do or say!
Give your commands to someone else, not me!
And one more thing I have to tell you: think it
over: this time, for the girl, I will not
wrangle in arms with you or anyone,
though I am robbed of what was given me;
but as for any other thing I have
alongside my black ship, you shall not take it
against my will. Try it. Hear this, everyone:
that instant your hot blood blackens my spear!"

They quarreled in this way, face to face, and then
broke off the assembly by the ships. Akhilleus
made his way to his squadron and his quarters,
Patróklos by his side, with his companions.

Agamémnon proceeded to launch a ship,
assigned her twenty oarsmen, loaded beasts
for sacrifice to the god, then set aboard

Khrysêis in her loveliness. The versatile
Odysseus took the deck, and, all oars manned,
they pulled out on the drenching ways of sea.
The troops meanwhile were ordered to police camp
and did so, throwing refuse in the water;
then to Apollo by the barren surf
they carried out full-tally hekatombs,
and the savor curled in crooked smoke toward heaven.

That was the day's work in the army.

                                        Agamémnon

had kept his threat in mind, and now he acted,
calling Eurýbatês and Talthýbios,
his aides and criers:

                              "Go along," he said,

"both of you, to the quarters of Akhilleus
and take his charming Brisêis by the hand
to bring to me. And if he balks at giving her
I shall be there myself with men-at-arms
in force to take her—all the more gall for him."
So, ominously, he sent them on their way,
and they who had no stomach for it went
along the waste sea shingle toward the ships
and shelters of the Myrmidons. Not far
from his black ship and hut they found the prince
in the open, seated. And seeing these two come
was cheerless to Akhilleus. Shamefast, pale
with fear of him, they stood without a word;
but he knew what they felt and called out:

                                        "Peace to you,

criers and couriers of Zeus and men!
Come forward. Not one thing have I against you:
Agamémnon is the man who sent you
for Brisêis. Here then, my lord Patróklos,
bring out the girl and give her to these men.
And let them both bear witness before the gods
who live in bliss, as before men who die,
including this harsh king, if ever hereafter
a need for me arises to keep the rest
from black defeat and ruin.

Lost in folly,
the man cannot think back or think ahead
how to come through a battle by the ships."
Patróklos did the bidding of his friend,
led from the hut Briseis in her beauty
and gave her to them. Back along the ships
they took their way, and the girl went, loath to go.

Leaving his friends in haste, Akhilleus wept,
and sat apart by the grey wave, scanning the endless sea.
Often he spread his hands in prayer to his mother:

"As my life came from you, though it is brief,
honor at least from Zeus who storms in heaven
I call my due. He gives me precious little.
See how the lord of the great plains, Agamémnon,
humiliated me! He has my prize,
by his own whim, for himself."

Eyes wet with tears,
he spoke, and her ladyship his mother heard him
in green deeps where she lolled near her old father.
Gliding she rose and broke like mist from the inshore
grey sea face, to sit down softly before him,
her son in tears; and fondling him she said:

"Child, why do you weep? What grief is this?
Out with it, tell me, both of us should know."
Akhilleus, fast in battle as a lion,
groaned and said:

"Why tell you what you know?
We sailed out raiding, and we took by storm
that ancient town of Eëtíôn called Thêbê,
plundered the place, brought slaves and spoils away.
At the division, later,
they chose a young girl, Khrysêis, for the king.
Then Khrysês, priest of the Archer God, Apollo,
came to the beachhead we Akhaians hold,
bringing no end of ransom for his daughter;
he had the god's white bands on a golden staff
and sued for grace from the army of Akhaia,

mostly the two Atreidai, corps commanders.
All of our soldiers murmured in assent:
'Behave well to the priest. And take the ransom!'
But Agamémnon would not. It went against his desire,
and brutally he ordered the man away.
So the old man withdrew in grief and anger.
Apollo cared for him: he heard his prayer
and let black bolts of plague fly on the Argives.

One by one our men came down with it
and died hard as the god's shots raked the army
broadside. But our priest divined the cause
and told us what the god meant by the plague.

I said, 'Appease the god!' but Agamémnon
could not contain his rage; he threatened me,
and what he threatened is now done—
one girl the Akhaians are embarking now
for Khrysê beach with gifts for Lord Apollo;
the other, just now, from my hut—the criers
came and took her, Briseus' girl, my prize,
given by the army.

                              If you can, stand by me:

go to Olympos, pray to Zeus, if ever
by word or deed you served him—
and so you did, I often heard you tell it
in Father's house: that time when you alone
of all the gods shielded the son of Krónos
from peril and disgrace—when other gods,
Pallas Athêna, Hêra, and Poseidon,
wished him in irons, wished to keep him bound,
you had the will to free him of that bondage,
and called up to Olympos in all haste
Aigaion, whom the gods call Briareus,
the giant with a hundred arms, more powerful
than the sea-god, his father. Down he sat
by the son of Krónos, glorying in that place.
For fear of him the blissful gods forbore
to manacle Zeus.

                              Remind him of these things,
cling to his knees and tell him your good pleasure

if he will take the Trojan side
and roll the Akhaians back to the water's edge,
back on the ships with slaughter! All the troops
may savor what their king has won for them,
and he may know his madness, what he lost
when he dishonored me, peerless among Akhaians."

Her eyes filled, and a tear fell as she answered:

"Alas, my child, why did I rear you, doomed
the day I bore you? Ah, could you only be
serene upon this beachhead through the siege,
your life runs out so soon.
Oh early death! Oh broken heart! No destiny
so cruel! And I bore you to this evil!

But what you wish I will propose
To Zeus, lord of the lightning, going up
myself into the snow-glare of Olympos
with hope for his consent.

                                                        Be quiet now

beside the long ships, keep your anger bright
against the army, quit the war.

                                                        Last night

Zeus made a journey to the shore of Ocean
to feast among the Sunburned, and the gods
accompanied him. In twelve days he will come
back to Olympos. Then I shall be there
to cross his bronze doorsill and take his knees.
I trust I'll move him."

                                                        Thetis left her son

still burning for the softly belted girl
whom they had wrested from him.

                                                        Meanwhile Odysseus

with his shipload of offerings came to Khrysê.
Entering the deep harbor there
they furled the sails and stowed them, and unbent
forestays to ease the mast down quickly aft
into its rest; then rowed her to a mooring.
Bow-stones were dropped, and they tied up astern,

and all stepped out into the wash and ebb,
then disembarked their cattle for the Archer,
and Khrysêis, from the deepsea ship. Odysseus,
the great tactician, led her to the altar,
putting her in her father's hands, and said:

"Khrysês, as Agamémnon's emissary
I bring your child to you, and for Apollo
a hekatomb in the Danáäns' name.
We trust in this way to appease your lord,
who sent down pain and sorrow on the Argives."

So he delivered her, and the priest received her,
the child so dear to him, in joy. Then hastening
to give the god his hekatomb, they led
bullocks to crowd around the compact altar,
rinsed their hands and delved in barley baskets,
as open-armed to heaven Khrysês prayed:

"Oh hear me, master of the silver bow,
protector of Ténedos and the holy towns,
if while I prayed you listened once before
and honored me, and punished the Akhaians,
now let my wish come true again. But turn
your plague away this time from the Danáäns."

And this petition, too, Apollo heard.
When prayers were said and grains of barley strewn,
they held the bullocks for the knife, and flayed them,
cutting out joints and wrapping these in fat,
two layers, folded, with raw strips of flesh,
for the old man to burn on cloven faggots,
wetting it all with wine.

                                    Around him stood
young men with five-tined forks in hand, and when
the vitals had been tasted, joints consumed,
they sliced the chines and quarters for the spits,
roasted them evenly and drew them off.
Their meal being now prepared and all work done,
they feasted to their hearts' content and made
desire for meat and drink recede again,

then young men filled their winebowls to the brim,
ladling drops for the god in every cup.
Propitiatory songs rose clear and strong
until day's end, to praise the god, Apollo,
as One Who Keeps the Plague Afar; and listening
the god took joy.

                              After the sun went down
and darkness came, at last Odysseus' men
lay down to rest under the stern hawsers.

When Dawn spread out her finger tips of rose
they put to sea for the main camp of Akhaians,
and the Archer God sent them a following wind.
Stepping the mast they shook their canvas out,
and wind caught, bellying the sail. A foaming
dark blue wave sang backward from the bow
as the running ship made way against the sea,
until they came offshore of the encampment.
Here they put in and hauled the black ship high,
far up the sand, braced her with shoring timbers,
and then disbanded, each to his own hut.

Meanwhile unstirring and with smoldering heart,
the godlike athlete, son of Pêleus, Prince
Akhilleus waited by his racing ships.
He would not enter the assembly
of emulous men, nor ever go to war,
but felt his valor staling in his breast
with idleness, and missed the cries of battle.

Now when in fact twelve days had passed, the gods
who live forever turned back to Olympos,
with Zeus in power supreme among them.

                                     Thetis
had kept in mind her mission for her son,
and rising like a dawn mist from the sea
into a cloud she soared aloft in heaven
to high Olympos. Zeus with massive brows
she found apart, on the chief crest enthroned,
and slipping down before him, her left hand

placed on his knees and her right hand held up
to cup his chin, she made her plea to him:

"O Father Zeus, if ever amid immortals
by word or deed I served you, grant my wish
and see to my son's honor! Doom for him
of all men came on quickest.

                              Now Lord Marshal
Agamémnon has been highhanded with him,
has commandeered and holds his prize of war.
But you can make him pay for this, profound
mind of Olympos!

                              Lend the Trojans power,
until the Akhaians recompense my son
and heap new honor upon him!"

                              When she finished,
the gatherer of cloud said never a word
but sat unmoving for a long time, silent.
Thetis clung to his knees, then spoke again:

"Give your infallible word, and bow your head,
or else reject me. Can you be afraid
to let me see how low in your esteem
I am of all the gods?"

                              Greatly perturbed,
Lord Zeus who masses cloud said:

                              "Here is trouble.
You drive me into open war with Hêra
sooner or later:
she will be at me, scolding all day long.
Even as matters stand she never rests
from badgering me before the gods: I take
the Trojan side in battle, so she says.

Go home before you are seen. But you can trust me
to put my mind on this; I shall arrange it.
Here let me bow my head, then be content
to see me bound by that most solemn act
before the gods. My word is not revocable
nor ineffectual, once I nod upon it."

He bent his ponderous black brows down, and locks
ambrosial of his immortal head
swung over them, as all Olympos trembled.
After this pact they parted: misty Thetis
from glittering Olympos leapt away
into the deep sea; Zeus to his hall retired.
There all the gods rose from their seats in deference
before their father; not one dared
face him unmoved, but all stood up before him,
and thus he took his throne.

                              But Hêra knew
he had new interests; she had seen
the goddess Thetis, silvery-footed daughter
of the Old One of the sea, conferring with him,
and, nagging, she inquired of Zeus Kroníon:

"Who is it this time, schemer? Who has your ear?
How fond you are of secret plans, of taking
decisions privately! You could not bring yourself,
could you, to favor me with any word
of your new plot?"

                         The father of gods and men
said in reply:

                            "Hêra, all my provisions
you must not itch to know.
You'll find them rigorous, consort though you are.
In all appropriate matters no one else,
no god or man, shall be advised before you.
But when I choose to think alone,
don't harry me about it with your questions."
The Lady Hêra answered, with wide eyes:

"Majesty, what a thing to say. I have not
'harried' you before with questions, surely;
you are quite free to tell what you will tell.
This time I dreadfully fear—I have a feeling—
Thetis, the silvery-footed daughter
of the Old One of the sea, led you astray.
Just now at daybreak, anyway, she came
to sit with you and take your knees; my guess is

you bowed your head for her in solemn pact
that you will see to the honor of Akhilleus—
that is, to Akhaian carnage near the ships."

Now Zeus the gatherer of cloud said:

                                        "Marvelous,
you and your guesses; you are near it, too.
But there is not one thing that you can do about it,
only estrange yourself still more from me—
all the more gall for you. If what you say
is true, you may be sure it pleases me.
And now you just sit down, be still, obey me,
or else not all the gods upon Olympos
can help in the least when I approach your chair
to lay my inexorable hands upon you."
At this the wide-eyed Lady Hêra feared him,
and sat quite still, and bent her will to his.
Up through the hall of Zeus now all the lords
of heaven were sullen and looked askance. Hêphaistos,
master artificer, broke the silence,
doing a kindness to the snowy-armed
lady, his mother Hêra.

                                        He began:

"Ah, what a miserable day, if you two
raise your voices over mortal creatures!
More than enough already! Must you bring
your noisy bickering among the gods?
What pleasure can we take in a fine dinner
when baser matters gain the upper hand?
To Mother my advice is—what she knows—
better make up to Father, or he'll start
his thundering and shake our feast to bits.
You know how he can shock us if he cares to—
out of our seats with lightning bolts!
Supreme power is his. Oh, soothe him, please,
take a soft tone, get back in his good graces.
Then he'll be benign to us again."
He lurched up as he spoke, and held a winecup

out to her, a double-handed one,
and said:

                    "Dear Mother, patience, hold your tongue,
no matter how upset you are. I would not
see you battered, dearest.

                                    It would hurt me,
and yet I could not help you, not a bit.
The Olympian is difficult to oppose.
One other time I took your part he caught me
around one foot and flung me
into the sky from our tremendous terrace.
I soared all day! Just as the sun dropped down
I dropped down, too, on Lemnos—nearly dead.
The island people nursed a fallen god."

He made her smile—and the goddess, white-armed Hêra,
smiling took the winecup from his hand.
Then, dipping from the winebowl, round he went
from left to right, serving the other gods
nectar of sweet delight.

                            And quenchless laughter
broke out among the blissful gods
to see Hêphaistos wheezing down the hall.
So all day long until the sun went down
they spent in feasting, and the measured feast
matched well their hearts' desire.
So did the flawless harp held by Apollo
and heavenly songs in choiring antiphon
that all the Muses sang.

                            And when the shining
sun of day sank in the west, they turned
homeward each one to rest, each to that home
the bandy-legged wondrous artisan
Hêphaistos fashioned for them with his craft.
The lord of storm and lightning, Zeus, retired
and shut his eyes where sweet sleep ever came to him,
and at his side lay Hêra, Goddess of the Golden Chair.

BOOK TWO

Assembly and Muster of Armies

Now slept the gods, and those who fought at Troy—
horse-handlers, charioteers—the long night through,
but slumber had no power over Zeus,
who pondered in the night how to exalt
Akhilleus, how in his absence to destroy
Akhaians in windrows at the ships.
He thought it best to send to Agamémnon
that same night a fatal dream.
Calling the dream he said:

                                              "Sinister Dream,
go down amid the fast ships of Akhaia,
enter Lord Agamémnon's quarters, tell him
everything, point by point, as I command you:
Let him prepare the long-haired carls of Akhaia

to fight at once. Now he may take by storm
the spacious town of Troy. The Olympians, tell him,
are of two minds no longer: Hêra swayed them,
and black days overhang the men of Troy."

The dream departed at his word, descending
swift as wind to where the long ships lay,
and sought the son of Atreus. In his hut
he found him sleeping, drifted all about
with balm of slumber. At the marshal's pillow
standing still, the dream took shape
as Nêleus' son, old Nestor. Agamémnon
deferred to Nestor most, of all his peers;
so in his guise the dream spoke to the dreamer:

"Sleeping, son of Atreus, tamer of horses?
You should not sleep all night, not as a captain
responsible for his men, with many duties,
a great voice in the conferences of war.
Follow me closely: I am a messenger
from Zeus, who is far away but holds you dear.
'Prepare the troops,' he said, 'to take the field
without delay: now may you take by storm
the spacious town of Troy. The Olympian gods
are of two minds no longer: Hêra's pleading
swayed them all, and bitter days from Zeus
await the Trojans.' Hold on to this message
against forgetfulness in tides of day
when blissful sleep is gone."

On this the dream
withdrew into the night, and left the man
to envision, rapt, all that was not to be,
thinking that day to conquer Priam's town.
Oh childish trust! What action lay ahead
in the mind of Zeus he could not know—what grief
and wounds from shock of combat in the field,
alike for Trojans and Akhaians.

Waking,
he heard the dream voice ringing round him still,
and sat up straight to pull his tunic on,

a fresh one, never worn before. He shook
his cloak around him, tied his shining feet
in fitted sandals, hung upon his shoulder
baldric and long sword, hilted all in silver,
and, taking his dynastic staff in hand,
he made his way among the ships.

                                              Pure Dawn

had reached Olympos' mighty side,
heralding day for Zeus and all the gods,
as Agamémnon, the Lord Marshal, met
his clarion criers and directed them
to call the unshorn Akhaians to full assembly.
The call sang out, and quickly they assembled.
But first, alongside Nestor's ship, he held
a council with his peers—there he convened them
and put a subtle plan before them, saying:

"Hear me, friends. A vision in a dream
has come to me in the starry night—a figure
in height and bearing very close to Nestor,
standing above my pillow, saying to me:
'Sleeping, son of Atreus, tamer of horses?
You should not sleep all night, not as a captain
responsible for his men, with many duties,
a great voice in the conferences of war.
Follow me closely: I am a messenger
from Zeus, who is far away but holds you dear.
"Prepare the troops," he said, "to take the field
without delay: now may you take by storm
the spacious town of Troy. The Olympian gods
are of two minds no longer: Hêra's pleading
swayed them all, and bitter days from Zeus
await the Trojans." Hold on to this message.'
When he had said all this, the phantasm
departed like a bird, and slumber left me.
Look to it then, we arm the troops for action—
but let me test them first, in that harangue
that custom calls for. What I shall propose
is flight in the long ships! You must hold them back,
speaking each one from where he stands."

                                                       How curtly

he told his curious plan, and took his seat!
Now stood Lord Nestor of the sandy shore
of Pylos, in concern for them, and spoke:

"Friends, lord and captains of the Argives,
if any other man had told this dream,
a fiction, we should call it; we'd be wary.
But he who saw the vision is our king.
Up with you, and we'll put the men in arms."

On this he turned and led the way from council,
and all the rest, staff-bearing counselors,
rose and obeyed their marshal.

                                                  From the camp

the troops were turning out now, thick as bees
that issue from some crevice in a rock face,
endlessly pouring forth, to make a cluster
and swarm on blooms of summer here and there,
glinting and droning, busy in bright air.
Like bees innumerable from ships and huts
down the deep foreshore streamed those regiments
toward the assembly ground—and Rumor blazed
among them like a crier sent from Zeus.
Turmoil grew in the great field as they entered
and sat down, clangorous companies, the ground
under them groaning, hubbub everywhere.
Now nine men, criers, shouted to compose them:

"Quiet! Quiet! Attention! Hear our captains!"

Then all strove to their seats and hushed their din.
Before them now arose Lord Agamémnon,
holding the staff Hêphaistos fashioned once
and took pains fashioning: it was a gift
from him to the son of Krónos, lordly Zeus,
who gave it to the bright pathfinder, Hermês.
Hermês handed it on in turn to Pélops,
famous charioteer, Pélops to Atreus,
and Atreus gave it to the sheepherder
Thyestês, he to Agamémnon, king
and lord of many islands, of all Argos—

the very same who leaning on it now
spoke out among the Argives:

"Friends, fighters, Danääns, companions of Arês,
the son of Krónos has entangled me
in cruel folly, wayward god! He promised
solemnly that I should not sail
before I stormed the inner town of Troy.
Crookedness and duplicity, it is clear!
He calls me to return to Argos beaten,
after these many losses.

                                                    That must be

his will and his good pleasure, who knows why?
Many a great town's height has he destroyed
and will destroy, being supreme in power.
Shameful indeed that future men should hear
we fought so long here, with such weight of arms,
all uselessly! We made long war for nothing,
never an end to it, though we had the odds.
The odds—if we Akhaians and the Trojans
should hold a truce and tally on both sides,
on one side native Trojans, on the other
Akhaian troops drawn up in squads of ten,
and each squad took one Trojan for a steward,
then many squads would go unserved. I tell you,
Akhaian men so far outnumber those
whose home is Troy!

                                                    But the allies are there.

From many Asian cities came these lances,
and it is they who hedge me out and hinder me
from plundering the fortress town of Troy.
Under great Zeus nine years have passed away,
making ship timbers rot, old tackle fray,
while overseas our wives and children still
await us in our halls. And yet the mission
on which we came is far from being done.
Well and good; let us act on what I say:
Retreat! Embark for our own fatherland!
We cannot hope any longer to take Troy!"

He made their hearts leap in their breasts, the rank
and file, who had no warning of his plan,

and all that throng, aroused, began to surge
as ground swells do on dark Ikarian deeps
under the south and east wind heeling down
from Father Zeus's cloudland—

                                                    or a field
of standing grain when wind-puffs from the west
cross it in billows, and the tasseled ears
are bent and tossed: just so moved this assembly.
Shouting confusedly, they all began
to scramble for the ships. High in the air
a dust cloud from their scuffling rose, commands
rang back and forth—to man the cables, haul
the black ships to the salt immortal sea.
They cleared the launching ways, their hearts on home,
and shouts went up as props were pulled away.

Thus, overriding their own destiny,
the Argives might have had their voyage homeward,
had Hêra not resorted to Athêna
and cried:

                                "Can you believe it? Tireless
daughter of Zeus who bears the shield of cloud,
will they put out for home this way, the Argives,
embarking on the broad back of the sea!
How could they now abandon Helen,
princess of Argos—leave her in Priam's hands,
the boast of every Trojan? Helen, for whom
Akhaians died by thousands far from home?
Ah, go down through the ranks of men-at-arms;
in your mild way dissuade them, one by one,
from hauling out their graceful ships to sea!"

The grey-eyed goddess Athêna obeyed her, diving
swifter than wind, down from the crests of Olympos,
to earth amid the long ships. There she found
Odysseus, peer of Zeus in stratagems,
holding his ground.

                                He had not touched the prow
of his black ship, not he, for anguish filled him,
heart and soul; and halting near him now,
the grey-eyed goddess made her plea to him:

"Son of Laërtês and the gods of old,
Odysseus, master mariner and soldier,
must all of you take oars in the long ships
in flight to your old country? Leaving Helen
in Priam's hands—that Argive grace, to be
the boast of every Trojan? Helen, for whom
Akhaians died by thousands, far from home?
No, no, take heart, and go among the men;
in your mild way dissuade them, one by one,
from hauling out their graceful ships to sea."

Knowing the goddess' clear word when he heard it,
Odysseus broke into a run. He tossed
his cloak to be picked up by his lieutenant,
Eurýbatês of Ithaka, and wheeling
close to the silent figure of Agamémnon
relieved him of his great dynastic staff,
then ran on toward the ships.

                                                        Each time he met

an officer or man of rank he paused
and in his ear he said:

                                                        "Don't be a fool!
It isn't like you to desert the field
the way some coward would! Come, halt, command
the troops back to their seats. You don't yet know
what Agamémnon means.

                                                        He means to test us,
and something punitive comes next. Not everyone
could hear what he proposed just now in council.
Heaven forbid he cripple, in his rage,
the army he commands. There's passion in kings;
they hold power from Zeus, they are dear to Zeus!"

But when Odysseus met some common soldier
bawling still, he drove him back; he swung
upon him with his staff and told him:

                                                        "Fool,
go back, sit down, listen to better men—
unfit for soldiering as you are, weak sister,
counting for nothing in battle or in council!

Shall we all wield the power of kings? We cán not,
and many masters are no good at all.
Let there be one commander, one authority,
holding his royal staff and precedence
from Zeus, the son of crooked-minded Krónos:
one to command the rest."

                                        So he himself
in his commanding way went through the army,
and back to the assembly ground they streamed
from ships and huts with multitudinous roar,
as when a comber from the windy sea
on a majestic beach goes thundering down,
and the ebb seethes offshore.

                                        So all subsided,
except one man who still railed on alone—
Thersítês, a blabbing soldier,
who had an impudent way with officers,
thinking himself amusing to the troops—
the most obnoxious rogue who went to Troy.
Bowlegged, with one limping leg, and shoulders
rounded above his chest, he had a skull
quite conical, and mangy fuzz like mold.
Odious to Akhilleus this man was,
and to Odysseus, having yapped at both,
but this time he berated Agamémnon—
at whom in fact the troops were furious—
lifting his voice and jeering:

                                        "Agamémnon!
What have you got to groan about? What more
can you gape after? Bronze fills all your huts,
bronze and the hottest girls—we hand them over
to you, you first, when any stronghold falls.
Or is it gold you lack? A Trojan father
will bring you gold in ransom for his boy—
though I—or some foot soldier like myself—
roped the prisoner in.

                                        Or a new woman
to lie with, couple with, keep stowed away
for private use—is that your heart's desire?
You send us back to bloody war for that?

Comrades! Are you women of Akhaia?
I say we pull away for home, and leave him
here on the beach to lay his captive girls!
Let him find out if we troops are dispensable
when he loses us! Contempt is all he shows
for a man twice his quality, by keeping
Akhilleus' woman that he snatched away.
But there's no bile, no bad blood in Akhilleus;
he lets it go.

                     Sir, if he drew his blade,
you'd never abuse another man!"

                               So boldly

Thersítês baited Marshal Agamémnon,
till at his side, abruptly,
Odysseus halted, glaring, and grimly said:

"You spellbinder! You sack of wind! Be still!
Will you stand up to officers alone?
Of all who came here to beleaguer Troy
I say there is no soldier worse than you.
Better not raise your voice to your commanders,
or rail at them, after you lie awake
with nothing on your mind but shipping home.
We have no notion, none, how this campaign
may yet turn out. Who knows if we sail homeward
in victory or defeat? Yet you bleat on,
defaming the Lord Marshal Agamémnon
because our Danáän veterans award him
plentiful gifts of war. You sicken me!

Here is my promise, and it will be kept:
if once again I hear your whining voice,
I hope Odysseus' head may be knocked loose
from his own shoulders, hope I may no longer
be called the father of Telémakhos,
if I do not take hold of you and strip you—
yes, even of the shirt that hides your scut!
From this assembly ground I'll drive you howling
and whip you like a dog into the ships!"

At this he struck him sharply with his staff
on ribs and shoulders. The poor devil quailed,
and a welling tear fell from his eyes. A scarlet
welt, raised by the golden-studded staff,
sprang out upon his back. Then, cowering down
in fear and pain, he blinked like an imbecile
and wiped his tears upon his arm.

                                        The soldiers,

for all their irritation, fell to laughing
at the man's disarray. You might have heard
one fellow, glancing at his neighbor, say:

"Oh, what a clout! A thousand times Odysseus
has done good work, thinking out ways to fight
or showing how you do it: this time, though,
he's done the best deed of the war,
making that poisonous clown capsize. By god,
a long, long time will pass before our hero
cares to call down his chief again!"

                                        The crowd

took it in this way. But the raider of cities,
Odysseus, with his staff, stood upright there,
and at his side grey-eyed Athêna stood
in aspect like a crier, calling: "Silence!"
that every man, front rank and rear alike,
might hear his words and weigh what he proposed.
Now for their sake he spoke:

                                        "Lord Agamémnon,

son of Atreus, king, your troops are willing
to let you seem disgraced in all men's eyes;
they will not carry through the work they swore to
en route from Argos, from the bluegrass land,
never to turn back till they plundered Troy.
No, now like callow boys or widowed women
they wail to one another to go home!

I grant this hardship wearying to everyone.
I grant the urge to go. Who can forget,
one month at sea—no more—far from his wife
will make a raider sick of the rowing bench,

sick of his ship, as gales and rising seas
delay him, even a month! As for ourselves,
now is the ninth year that we keep the siege.
No wonder at it, then: I cannot blame
you men for sickening by the beaked ships!
Ah, but still it would be utter shame
to stay so long and sail home empty-handed.
Hold on hard, dear friends!
Come, sweat it out, until at least we learn
if Kalkhas made true prophecy or not.
Here is a thing we cannot help remembering,
and every man of you whom death has spared
can testify:

                     One day, just when the ships
had staged at Aulis, loaded, every one,
with woe for Priam and the men of Troy,
we gathered round a fountain by the altars,
performing sacrifices to the gods
under a dappled sycamore. The water
welled up shining there, and in that place
the great portent appeared.

                           A blood-red serpent
whom Zeus himself sent gliding to the light,
blood-chilling, silent, from beneath our altar,
twined and swiftly spiraled up the tree.
There were some fledgling sparrows, baby things,
hunched in their downy wings—just eight of these
among the leaves along the topmost bough,
and a ninth bird, the mother who had hatched them.
The serpent slid to the babies and devoured them,
all cheeping pitifully, while their mother
fluttered and shrilled in her distress. He coiled
and sprang to catch her by one frantic wing.

After the snake had gorged upon them all,
the god who sent him turned him to an omen:
turned him to stone, hid him in stone—a wonder
worked by the son of crooked-minded Krónos—
and we stood awed by what had come to pass.

Seeing this portent of the gods had visited
our sacrifices, Kalkhas told the meaning
before us all, at once. He said:

'Dumbfounded, are you, gentlemen of Akhaia?
Here was a portent for us, and a great one,
granted us by inscrutable Zeus—a promise
long to be in fulfillment—but the fame
of that event will never die.

Consider:

the snake devoured fledglings and their mother,
the little ones were eight, and she made nine.
Nine are the years that we shall wage this war,
and in the tenth we'll take the spacious town.'

That was his explanation of the sign.
Oh, see now, how it all comes true! Hold out,
Akhaians with your gear of war, campaigners,
hold on the beachhead till we take the town!"

After the speech a great shout from the Argives
echoed fiercely among the ships: they cried
"Aye" to noble Odysseus' words. Then Nestor,
lord of Gerênia, charioteer, addressed them:

"Lamentable, the way you men have talked,
like boys, like children, strangers to stern war.
What will become of our sworn oaths and pacts?
'To the flames,' you mean to say, 'with battle plans,
soldierly calculations, covenants
our right hands pledged and pledged with unmixed wine'?
Once we could trust in these. But wrangling now
and high words dissipate them, and we cannot
turn up a remedy, though we talk for days.

Son of Atreus, be as you were before,
inflexible; commit the troops to combat;
let those go rot, those few, who take their counsel
apart from the Akhaians. They can win
nothing by it. They would sail for Argos
before they know if what the Lord Zeus promised
will be proved false or true.

I think myself the power above us nodded
on that day when the Argives put to sea
in their fast sailing ships, with death aboard
and doom for Trojans.

                              Forking out of heaven,
he lightened on the right—a fateful sign.
Therefore let no man press for our return
before he beds down with some Trojan wife,
to avenge the struggles and the groans of Helen.

If any man would sooner die than stay,
let him lay hand upon his ship—
he meets his death and doom before the rest.
My lord, yourself be otherwise persuaded.
What I am going to say is not a trifle
to toss aside: marshal the troops by nations
and then again by clans, Lord Agamémnon,
clan in support of clan, nation of nation.
If you will do this, and they carry it out,
you may find out which captains are poltroons
and which are valorous; foot soldiers, too;
as each will fight before his clansmen's eyes
when clans make up our units in the battle.
You can discern then if your siege has failed
by heaven's will or men's faintheartedness
and foolishness in war."

                                   Lord Agamémnon
made reply:

                             "Believe me, sir, once more
you win us all with your proposals here.
O Father Zeus, Athêna, and Apollo,
give me ten more to plan with me like this
among the Akhaians! Priam's fortress then
falls in a day, our own hands' prey and spoil.
But Zeus the stormking sent me misery,
plunging me into futile brawls and feuds.
I mean Akhilleus and myself. We fought
like enemies, in words, over a girl—
and I gave way to anger first.

We two—
if we could ever think as one, the Trojans'
evil day would be postponed no longer.

Take your meal, now; we prepare for combat.
Let every man be sure his point is whetted,
his shield well slung. Let every charioteer
give fodder to his battle team, inspect
his wheels and car, and put his mind on war,
so we may bear ourselves as men all day
in the grim battle. There will be no respite,
no break at all—unless night coming on
dissolve the battle lines and rage of men.
The shield strap will be sweat-soaked on your ribs,
your hand will ache and stiffen on the spearshaft,
and sweat will drench the horses' flanks that toil
to pull your polished car.

But let me see
one man of you willing to drop out—one man
skulking around the ships, and from that instant
he has no chance against the dogs and kites!"

Being so dismissed, the Argives roared, as when
upon some cape a sea roused by the south wind
roars on a jutting point of rock, a target
winds and waves will never let alone,
from any quarter rising. So the soldiers
got to their feet and scattered to the ships
to send up smoke from campfires and be fed.
But first, to one of the gods who never die,
each man resigned his bit and made his prayer
to keep away from death in that day's fighting.
As for Lord Agamémnon, their commander,
a fattened ox he chose for sacrifice
to Zeus the overlord of heaven—calling round him
the senior captains of the Akhaian host:
Nestor, then Lord Idómeneus, then those
two lords who bore the name of Aías, then
the son of Tydeus and, sixth, Odysseus,
the peer of Zeus in warcraft. Meneláos,
lord of the warcry, needed no summoning;

he knew and shared the duties of his brother.
Around the ox they stood, and took up barley,
and Agamémnon prayed on their behalf:

"O excellency, O majesty, O Zeus
beyond the stormcloud, dwelling in high air,
let not the sun go down upon this day
into the western gloom, before I tumble
Priam's blackened rooftree down, exploding
fire through his portals! Let me rip
with my bronze point the shirt that clings on Hektor
and slash his ribs! May throngs around him lie—
his friends, head-down in dust, biting dry ground!"

But Zeus would not accomplish these desires.
He took the ox, but added woe on woe.

When prayers were said and grains of barley strewn,
they held the bullock for the knife and flayed him,
cutting out joints and wrapping these in fat,
two layers, folded, with raw strips of flesh,
to burn on cloven faggots, and the tripes
they spitted to be broiled. When every joint
had been consumed, and kidneys had been tasted,
they sliced the chines and quarters for the spits,
roasted them evenly and drew them off.
The meal being now prepared and all work done,
they feasted royally and put away
desire for meat and drink.

                                        Then Nestor spoke:

"Excellency, Lord Marshal Agamémnon,
we shall do well to tarry here no longer,
we officers, in our circle. Let us not
postpone the work heaven put into our hands.
Let criers among the Akhaian men-at-arms
muster our troops along the ships. Ourselves,
we'll pass together down the Akhaian lines
to rouse their appetite for war."

                                        And Agamémnon,
marshal of the army, turned at once,

telling his criers to send out shrill and clear
to all Akhaian troops the call to battle.
The cry went out, the men came crowding, officers
from their commander's side went swiftly down
to form each unit—and the grey-eyed goddess
Athêna kept the pace behind them, bearing
her shield of storm, immortal and august,
whose hundred golden-plaited tassels, worth
a hekatomb each one, floated in air.
So down the ranks that dazzling goddess went
to stir the attack, and each man in his heart
grew strong to fight and never quit the mêlée,
for at her passage war itself became
lovelier than return, lovelier than sailing
in the decked ships to their own native land.

As in dark forests, measureless along
the crests of hills, a conflagration soars,
and the bright bed of fire glows for miles,
now fiery lights from this great host in bronze
played on the earth and flashed high into heaven.

And as migrating birds, nation by nation,
wild geese and arrow-throated cranes and swans,
over Asïa's meadowland and marshes
around the streams of Kaystrios, with giant
flight and glorying wings keep beating down
in tumult on that verdant land
that echoes to their pinions, even so,
nation by nation, from the ships and huts,
this host debouched upon Skamánder plain.
With noise like thunder pent in earth
under their trampling, under the horses' hooves,
they filled the flowering land beside Skamánder,
as countless as the leaves and blades of spring.
So, too, like clouds of buzzing, fevered flies
that swarm about a cattle stall in summer
when pails are splashed with milk: so restlessly
by thousands moved the fighters of Akhaia
over the plain, lusting to rend the Trojans.
But just as herdsmen easily divide

their goats when herds have mingled in a pasture,
so these were marshaled by their officers
to one side and the other, forming companies
for combat.

                              Agamémnon's lordly mien
was like the mien of Zeus whose joy is lightning;
oaken-waisted as Arês, god of war,
he seemed, and deep-chested as Lord Poseidon,
and as a great bull in his majesty
towers supreme amid a grazing herd,
so on that day Zeus made the son of Atreus
tower over his host, supreme among them.
Tell me now, Muses, dwelling on Olympos,
as you are heavenly, and are everywhere,
and everything is known to you—while we
can only hear the tales and never know—
who were the Danáän lords and officers?
The rank and file I shall not name; I could not,
if I were gifted with ten tongues and voices
unfaltering, and a brazen heart within me,
unless the Muses, daughters of Olympian
Zeus beyond the stormcloud, could recall
all those who sailed for the campaign at Troy.
Let me name only captains of contingents
and number all the ships.

                              Of the Boiotians,
Pêneleôs, Lêitos, Arkesílaôs,
Prothoênor, and Klónios were captains.
Boiotians—men of Hyria and Aulis,
the stony town, and those who lived at Skhoinos
and Skólos and the glens of Eteônos;
Thespeia; Graia; round the dancing grounds
of Mykalessos; round the walls of Harma,
Eilésion, Erythrai, Eleôn,
Hylê and Peteôn, and Okaléa,
and Medeôn, that compact citadel,
Kôpai, Eutrêsis, Thisbê of the doves;
those, too, of Korôneia, and the grassland
of Haliartos, and the men who held
Plataia town and Glisas, and the people
of Lower Thebes, the city ringed with walls,

and great Ongkhêstos where Poseidon's grove
glitters; and people, too, of Arnê, rich
in purple winegrapes, and the men of Mideia,
Nisa the blest, and coastal Anthêdôn.
All these had fifty ships. One hundred twenty
Boiotian fighters came in every ship.

Their neighbors of Asplêdon, then, and Minyan
Orkhómenos, Askálaphos their captain
with Iálmenos, both sons of Arês, both
conceived in Aktor's manor by severe
Astýokhê, who kept a tryst with Arês
in the women's rooms above, where secretly
the strong god lay beside her. Thirty ships
these Minyans drew up in line of battle.

Phôkians in their turn were led by Skhedios
and by Epístrophos, the sons of Íphitos
Naubólidês, that hero; Phôkians
dwelling in Kyparíssos, rocky Pythô,
Krisa the holy, Panopeus and Daulis,
near Anemôreia, Hyámpolis,
and by the side of noble Kêphisos,
or in Lilaia, where that river rises.
Forty black ships had crossed the sea with these,
who now drew up their companies on the flank
of the Boiotians, and armed themselves.

The Lokrians had Aías for commander,
Oïleus' son, that Aías known as the Short One
as being neither tall nor great compared
with Aías Telamônios. A corselet
all of linen he wore, and could outthrow
all Hellênes and Akhaians with a spear.
His were the Lokrians who lived at Kynos
and Opoeis and Kallíaros,
Bêssa and Skarphê and the pretty town
Augeiai; Tarphê and Thronion that lie
on both sides of the stream Boágrios.
Aías led forty black ships of the Lokrians
who lived across the channel from Euboia.

Men of that island, then, the resolute
Abantês, those of Khalkis, Eiretria,
and Histiaia, of the laden vines,
Kêrinthos by the sea, the crag of Dion,
those of Karystos, those of Styra—all
who had young Elephênor Khalkodóntiadês,
the chief of the Abantês, for commander.
Quick on their feet, with long scalp locks, those troops
enlisted hungering for body armor
of enemies to pierce with ashen spears;
and Elephênor's black ships numbered forty.

Next were the men of Athens, that strong city,
the commonwealth protected by Erékhtheus.
He it was whom Athêna, Zeus's daughter,
cared for in childhood in the olden time—
though he was born of plowland kind with grain.
She placed him in her city, in her shrine,
where he receives each year, with bulls and rams,
the prayers of young Athenians. Their commander
here at Troy was Péteôs' son, Menéstheus.
No soldier born on earth could equal him
in battle at maneuvering men and horses—
though Nestor rivaled him, by grace of age.
In his command were Athens' fifty ships.

Great Aías led twelve ships from Sálamis
and beached them where Athenians formed for battle.

Then there were those of Argos, those of Tiryns,
fortress with massive walls, Hermíonê
and Asinê that lie upon the gulf,
Troizên, Eíonai, the vineyard country
of Epidauros, Aigina and Masês:
these Diomêdês, lord of the battlecry,
commanded with his comrade, Sthénelos,
whose father was illustrious Kapanéus,
and in third place Eurýalos, a figure
godlike in beauty, son of Mêkisteus,
Lord Talaönidês. Over them all

ruled Diomêdês, lord of the battlecry,
and eighty black ships crossed the sea with these.

Next were the men who held the well-built city,
Mykênai, and rich Korinth, and Kleônai,
and Orneiai and fair Araithyréa
and Sikyôn where first Adrêstos ruled;
Hyperêsia, hilltop Gonoéssa,
Pellênê, and the country round Aigíon,
and those who held the north coast, Aígialos,
with spacious Helikê. Their hundred ships
were under the command of Agamémnon,
son of Atreus: he it was who led
by far the greatest number and the best,
and glorying in arms he now put on
a soldier's bronze—distinguished amid heroes
for valor and the troops he led to war.

Next, those of Lakedaimôn, land of gorges,
men who had lived at Pharis, Sparta, Messê
haunted by doves, Bryseiai, fair Augeiai,
Amyklai, too, and Helos by the sea,
and Laäs and the land around Oitylos:
these Meneláos, Agamémnon's brother,
lord of the warcry, led with sixty ships,
and drawn up separately from all the rest
they armed, as Meneláos on his own
burned to arouse his troops to fight. He burned
to avenge the struggles and the groans of Helen.

Next came the men of Pylos and Arênê,
that trim town, and Thryon where they ford
Alpheios river, Aipy high and stony,
Kyperissêeis, Amphigéneia,
and Ptéleos and Helos—Dorion, too,
where once the Muses, meeting Thamyris,
the Thracian, on his way from Oikhalía—
from visiting Eurýtos, the Oikhalian—
ended his singing. Pride had made him say
he could outsing the very Muses, daughters
of Zeus who bears the stormcloud for a shield.

For this affront they blinded him, bereft him
of his god-given song, and stilled his harping.
The countrymen of Pylos were commanded
by Nestor of Gerênia, charioteer,
whose ninety decked ships lined the shore.

                                              Then came
the troops who had their homes in Arkadía
under Kyllênê crag: close-order fighters
who lived around the tomb of Aipytos,
at Pheneos, and at Orkhómenos
where there are many flocks; at Rhipê, too,
at Stratiê, and in the windy town
Enispê; men of Tegeê and lovely
Mantinea; men of Stymphalos
and Parrhasíê, all of whom were led
by Agapênôr, son of Angkhaios,
and he commanded sixty ships. Arkadians
able in war had thronged to go aboard,
for the Lord Marshal Agamémnon lent
those ships in which they crossed the winedark sea,
as they had none, nor knowledge of seafaring.

Next were the soldiers from Bouprásion
and gracious Elis—all that plain confined
by Hyrminê and Myrsinos, and by
Alesion and the Olenian Rock.
These had four captains with ten ships apiece,
on which the Epeioi had embarked in throngs.
Some served under Amphímakhos and Thálpios,
grandsons of Aktor, sons of Ktéatos
and of Eurýtos. Powerful Diorês
Amaryngkleïdês commanded others,
and Polyxeinos led the fourth division—
son of Agásthenês Augêiadês.

Then came the islanders from Doulíkhion
and the Ekhínadês, all those who dwelt
opposite Elis, over the open sea,
Megês their captain, Megês Phyleïdês
begotten by that friend of Zeus, the horseman
Phyleus, who withdrew to Doulíkhion

in anger at his father long ago.
Forty black ships had crossed the sea with Megês.

Odysseus, then, commanded the brave men
of Kephallênia: islanders of Ithaka
and Nêritos whose leafy heights the seawind
ruffles, and the men of Krokyleia,
of Aigilips the rocky isle, and those
of Samos and Zakynthos: those as well
who held the mainland eastward of the islands.
Odysseus, peer of Zeus in forethought, led them
in twelve good ships with cheek-paint at the bows.

Thoas, Andraimôn's son, led the Aitôlians,
inhabitants of Pleurôn, Ôlenos,
Pylênê, seaside Khalkis, Kalydôn
of rocky mountainsides: Thoas their leader
because the sons of Oineus were no more,
and red-haired Meleágros too was dead.
Command of all had thus devolved on Thoas,
and forty black ships crossed the sea with him.

Idómeneus, famed as a spear-fighter,
led the Kretans: all who came from Knossos,
Gortyn, the town of many walls, and Lyktos,
Milêtos and Lykastos, gleaming white,
Phaistos and Rhytion, those pleasant towns—
all from that island of a hundred cities
served under Idómeneus, the great spearman,
whose second in command, Meríonês,
fought like the slaughtering god of war himself.
Eighty black ships had crossed the sea with these.

Tlêpólemos, the son of Hêraklês,
had led nine ships from Rhodes: impetuous men,
the Rhodians, in three regional divisions:
Lindos, Iêlysos, and bright Kameiros,
serving under Tlêpólemos, the spearman,
whose mother, Astyokheia, had been taken
by Hêraklês, who brought her from Ephyra
out of the Sellêeis river valley,

where he had plundered many noble towns.
No sooner was Tlêpólemos of age
than he had killed his father's uncle, old
Likymnios, Alkmênê's warrior brother,
and fitting out his ships in haste, he sailed
over the deep sea, taking many with him
in flight from other descendants of Hêraklês.
Wandering, suffering bitter days at sea,
he came at last to Rhodes. The island, settled
in townships, one for each of three great clans,
was loved by Zeus, ruler of gods and men,
and wondrous riches he poured out upon them.

Nireus had led three well-found ships from Symê—
Nireus, Aglaia's child by Lord Kharópos—
Nireus, of all Danáäns before Troy
most beautifully made, after Akhilleus,
a feeble man, though, with a small contingent.

Then those of Nísyros and Kárpathos
and Kasos and the island town of Kos,
ruled by Eurýpylos, and the Kalydnai,
islands ruled by Pheídippos and Ántiphos,
the sons of Thessalos, a son of Hêraklês.
Thirty long ships in line belonged to these.

Tell me now, Muse, of those from that great land
called Argos of Pelasgians, who lived
at Alos, at Alopê, and at Trekhis,
and those of Phthía, those of Hellas, lands
of lovely women: all those troops they called
the Myrmidons and Hellênes and Akhaians,
led by Akhilleus, in their fifty ships.
But these made no advances now to battle,
since he was not on hand to dress their lines.
No, the great runner, Prince Akhilleus, lay
amid the ships in desolate rage
for Brisêis, his girl with her soft tresses—
the prize he captured, fighting all the way,
from Lyrnessos after he stormed that town
and stormed the walls of Thêbê, overthrowing

the spearmen, Mynês and Epístrophos,
sons of Euênos Selêpíades.
For her his heart burned, lying there,
but soon the hour would come when he would rouse.

Next were the men of Phylakê, and those
who held Pyrásos, garden of Dêmêtêr,
Itôn, maternal town of grazing flocks,
Antrôn beside the water, and the beds
of meadow grass at Pteleos: all these
were under Prôtesílaos' command
when that intrepid fighter lived—
but black earth held him under now, and grieving
at Phylakê with lacerated cheeks
his bride was left, his house unfinished there.
Plunging ahead from his long ship to be
first man ashore at Troy of all Akhaians,
he had been brought down by a Dardan spear.
By no means were his troops without a leader,
though sorely missing him: they had Podárkês,
another soldier son of Íphiklos
Phylákidês, master of many flocks—
Podárkês, Prôtesílaos' blood brother,
a younger man, less noble. But the troops
were not at all in want of a commander,
though in their hearts they missed the braver one.
Forty black ships had sailed along with him.

Next were the soldiers who had lived at Pherai
by the great lake: at Glaphyrai and Boibê,
and in the well-kept city, Iaôlkos.
Of their eleven ships Admêtos' son
Eumêlos had command—the child conceived
under Admêtos by that splendid queen,
Alkestis, Pelias' most beautiful daughter.

Next, those of Methonê and Thaumakiê,
of rugged Olizôn and Meliboia.
These in their seven ships had been commanded
at first by Philoktêtês, the great archer.
Fifty oarsmen in every ship, they came

as expert archers to the Trojan war.
But he, their captain, lay on Lemnos isle
in anguish, where the Akhaians had marooned him,
bearing the black wound of a deadly snake.
He languished there, but soon, beside the ships,
the Argives would remember and call him back.
Meanwhile his men were not without a leader
though missing Philoktêtês: Medôn led them,
Oïleus' bastard son, conceived
by Rhênê under Oïleus, raider of cities.

Next were the men of Trikê and Ithômê,
that rocky-terraced town, and Oikhalía,
the city of Eurýtos: over these
two sons of old Asklêpios held command—
both skilled in healing: Podaleírios
and Makhaôn. Thirty decked ships were theirs.

Next were the soldiers from Orménios
and from the river source at Hypereia;
those of Asterion and those below
Titanos' high snow-whitened peaks. Eurýpalos,
Euaimôn's shining son, led all of these,
with forty black ships under his command.

Then those who held Argissa and Gyrtônê,
Orthê, Elônê, and the limestone city
Oloösôn, led by a dauntless man,
Polypoitês, the son of Peiríthoös,
whom Zeus, the undying, fathered. Polypoitês
had been conceived by gentle Hippodameia
under Peiríthoös, that day he whipped
the shaggy centaurs out of Pêlion—
routed them, drove them to the Aithikês.
Polypoitês as co-commander had
Leonteus, son of Korônos Kaineïdês.
Forty black ships had crossed the sea with these.

Gouneus commanded twenty-two from Kyphos.
The Eniênes and the brave Peraiboi
served under him: all who had had their homes

around Dôdôna in the wintry north
and in the fertile vale of Titarêssos.
Lovely that gliding river that runs on
into the Pêneios with silver eddies
and rides it for a while as clear as oil—
a branch of Styx, on which great oaths are sworn.

The Magnêtês were led by Prothoös,
Tenthrêdôn's son: by Pêneios they lived
and round Mount Pêlion's shimmering leafy sides.
Forty black ships had come with Prothoös.

These were the lords and captains of the Danáäns.
But tell me, Muse, of all the men and horses
who were the finest, under Agamémnon?
As for the battle horses, those were best
that came from Phêrês' pastures, and Eumêlos
drove those mares, as fleet as birds—a team
perfectly matched in color and in age,
and level to a hair across the cruppers.
Apollo of the silver bow had bred them
in Pêreiê as fearsome steeds of war.
Of all the fighting men, most formidable
was Aías Telamônios—that is
while great Akhilleus raged apart. Akhilleus
towered above them all; so did the stallions
that drew the son of Pêleus in the war.
But now, amid the slim seagoing ships
he lay alone and raged at Agamémnon,
marshal of the army. And his people,
along the shore above the breaking waves,
with discus throw and javelin and archery
sported away the time. Meanwhile their teams
beside the chariots tore and champed at clover
and parsley from the marshes; the war-cars
shrouded in canvas rested in the shelters;
and, longing for their chief, beloved in war,
the Myrmidons, idly throughout the camp,
drifted and took no part in that day's fighting.

But now the marching host devoured the plain
as though it were a prairie fire; the ground

beneath it rumbled, as when Zeus the lord
of lightning bolts, in anger at Typhôeus,
lashes the earth around Einárimos,
where his tremendous couch is said to be.
So thunderously groaned the earth
under the trampling of their coming on,
and they consumed like fire the open plain.

Iris arrived now, running on the wind,
as messenger from Zeus beyond the stormcloud,
bearing the grim news to the men of Troy.
They were assembled, at the gates of Priam,
young men and old, all gathered there, when she
came near and stood to speak to them: her voice
most like the voice of Priam's son Polítês.
Forward observer for the Trojans, trusting
his prowess as a sprinter, he had held
his post mid-plain atop the burial mound
of the patriarch Aisyêtês; waiting there
to see the Akhaians leave their camp and ships.
In his guise, she who runs upon the wind,
Iris, now spoke to Priam:

                                        "Sir, old sir,
will you indulge inordinate talk as always,
just as in peacetime? Frontal war's upon us!
Many a time I've borne a hand in combat,
but never have I seen the enemy
in such array, committed, every man,
uncountable as leaves, or grains of sand,
advancing on the city through the plain!
Hektor, you are the one I call on: take
action as I direct you: the allies
that crowd the great town speak in many tongues
of many scattered countries. Every company
should get its orders from its own commander;
Let him conduct the muster and the sortie!"

Hektor punctiliously obeyed the goddess,
dismissed the assembly on her terms, and troops
ran for their arms. All city gates, wide open,

yawned, and the units poured out, foot soldiers,
horses and chariots, with tremendous din.

Rising in isolation on the plain
in face of Troy, there is a ridge, a bluff
open on all sides: Briar Hill they call it.
Men do, that is; the immortals know the place
to be the Amazon Myrinê's tomb.
Anchored on this the Trojans and allies
formed for battle.

                      Tall, with helmet flashing,
Hektor, great son of Priam, led the Trojans,
largest of those divisions and the best,
who drew up now and armed, and hefted spears.

The Dardans were commanded by Aineías,
whom ravishing Aphrodítê had conceived
under Ankhísês in the vales of Ida,
lying, immortal, in a man's embrace.
His co-commanders were Antênor's sons,
both battle-wise, Arkhélokhos and Akámas.

Then those from Zéleia, the lower slope
of Ida—Trojans, men of means who drank
the waters of Aisêpos dark and still—
they served under Lykáôn's shining son,
Pándaros, whom Apollo taught the bow.

Adrêsteia's men, those of the hinterland
of Apaisós, Pitýeia, the crag
of Trêria—all these Adrêstos led
with Amphios of the linen cuirass, both
sons of Mérops Perkôsios, the seer
profoundest of all seers: he had refused
to let them take the path of war—
man-wasting war—but they were heedless of him,
driven onward by dark powers of death.

Then, too, came those who lived around Perkótê,
at Práktion, at Sestos and Abýdos,
and old Arísbê: Ásïos their captain,

Asïos Hyrtákidês—who drove
great sorrel horses from Sellêeis river.

Hippóthoös led the tough Pelasgians
from Lárisa's rich plowland—Hippóthoös
and the young soldier Pylaios, both sons
of the Pelasgian Lêthos Teutamídês.

Then Thracians from beyond the strait, all those
whom Hellê's rushing water bounded there,
Akámas led, and the veteran Peíroös.

Son of Troizênos Keadês, Euphêmos
led the Kikonês from their distant shore;
and those more distant archers, Paíonês,
Pyraíkhmês led from Ámydôn,
from Axios bemirroring all the plain.
The Paphlagonians followed Pylaiménês,
shaggy, great-hearted, from the wild mule country
of the Enétoi—men who held Kytôros
and Sésamos and had their famous homes
on the Parthénios riverbanks, at Krômna,
Aigialós, and lofty Erythínoi.

Odíos and Epístrophos were captains
of Halizônês from Alýbê, far
eastward, where the mines of silver are.

The Mysians Khrómis led, with Énnomos,
reader of birdflight; signs in flurrying wings
would never save him from the last dark wave
when he went down before the battering hands
of the great runner, Akhilleus, in the river,
with other Trojans slain.

                                        The Phrygians

were under Phorkys and Askánios
from distant Askaníê—ready fighters.

The Lydians, then, Mêionês, had for leaders
Mésthlês and Ántiphos; these were the sons

born by Gygaíê lake to Talaiménês.
They led men bred in vales under Mount Tmôlos.
Nástês commanded Karians in their own tongue,
men of Milêtos, Phthirôn's leafy ridge,
Maiandros' rills and peaks of Mýkalê.
All these Amphímakhos and Nástês led,
Nomíôn's shining children. Wearing gold,
blithe as a girl, Nástês had gone to war,
but gold would not avail the fool
to save him from a bloody end. Akhilleus
Aiákidês would down him in the river,
taking his golden ornaments for spoil.

Sarpêdôn led the Lykians, with Glaukos,
from Lykiê afar, from whirling Xánthos.

BOOK THREE

Dueling for a Haunted Lady

The Trojan squadrons flanked by officers
drew up and sortied, in a din of arms
and shouting voices—wave on wave, like cranes
in clamorous lines before the face of heaven,
beating away from winter's gloom and storms,
over the streams of Ocean, hoarsely calling,
to bring a slaughter on the Pygmy warriors—
cranes at dawn descending, beaked in cruel attack.
The Akhaians for their part came on in silence,
raging under their breath, shoulder to shoulder sworn.

Imagine mist the south wind rolls on hills,
a blowing bane for shepherds, but for thieves
better than nightfall—mist where a man can see
a stone's throw and no more: so dense the dust

that clouded up from these advancing hosts
as they devoured the plain.

                              And near and nearer
the front ranks came, till one from the Trojan front
detached himself to be the first in battle—
vivid and beautiful, Aléxandros,
wearing a cowl of leopard skin, a bow
hung on his back, a longsword at his hip,
with two spears capped in pointed bronze. He shook them
and called out to the best men of the Argives
to meet him in the mêlée face to face.

Meneláos, watching that figure come
with long strides in the clear before the others,
knew him and thrilled with joy. A hungry lion
that falls on heavy game—an antlered deer
or a wild goat—will rend and feast upon it
even though hunters and their hounds assail him.
So Meneláos thrilled when he beheld
Aléxandros before his eyes; he thought
I'll cut him to bits, adulterous dog!

                                      —and vaulted
down from his car at once with all his gear.

But when Aléxandros caught sight of him
emerging from the ranks, his heart misgave,
and he recoiled on his companions, not
to incur the deadly clash.

                          A man who stumbles
upon a viper in a mountain glen
will jump aside: a trembling takes his knees,
pallor his cheeks; he backs and backs away.
In the same way Aléxandros paced backward
into the Trojan lines and edged among them,
dreading the son of Atreus. Hektor watched
and said in scorn:

                              "You bad-luck charm!
Paris, the great lover, a gallant sight!
You should have had no seed and died unmarried.
Would to god you had!

Better than living this way in dishonor,
in everyone's contempt.

                    Now they can laugh, Akhaians
who thought you were a first-rate man, a champion,
going by looks—and no backbone, no staying
power is in you.

                       Were you this way then
when you made up your crews and crossed the sea
in the long ships, for trafficking abroad?
And when you then brought home a lovely woman
from a far land: a girl already married
whose brother-in-law and husband were great soldiers?
Ruin for your father and all his realm,
joy for our enemies, and shame for you!
Now could you not stand up to Meneláos?
You'd find out what a fighting man he is
whose flower-like wife you hold. No charm would come
of harping then, or Aphrodíte's favors—
the clean-limbed body and the flowing hair—
when you lay down to make love to the dust!
What slaves these Trojans are! If not, long since
you might have worn a shirt of cobblestones
for all the wrong you've done!"

                          The beautiful prince,
Aléxandros, replied to him:

                            "Ah, Hektor,
this harshness is no more than just. Remember, though,
your spirit's like an ax-edge whetted sharp
that goes through timber, when a good shipwright
hews out a beam: the tool triples his power.
That is the way your heart is in your breast.
My own gifts are from pale-gold Aphrodíte—
do not taunt me for them. Glorious things
the gods bestow are not to be despised,
being as the gods will: wishing will not bring them.
Now, if what you want from me is fighting,
make all the other Trojans and Akhaians
down their arms; let Meneláos alone
and me, between the lines, in single combat,

duel for Helen and the Spartan gold.
Whoever gets the upper hand in this
shall take the treasure and the woman home;
let the rest part as friends, let all take oath,
that you may live in peace in Troy's rich land
while they make sail for Argos and its pastures
and the land of lovely womankind, Akhaia."

Listening, Hektor felt his heart grow lighter,
and down the Trojan center, with his lance
held up mid-haft, he drove, calling "Battalions
halt!" till he brought them to a stand-at-ease.

The long-haired Akhaian soldiers bent their bows,
aiming with arrows and with stones. But high
and clear they heard a shout from Agamémnon:

"Hold on, Argives! Men, don't shoot! This means
he has in mind some proclamation,
Hektor, there in the flashing helmet!"

                                                    Archers
lowered their bows, and all fell silent now,
as Hektor to both armies made appeal:

"Hear me, Trojans, Akhaians under arms,
hear the proposal of Aléxandros
because of whom this quarrel began. He asks
all other Trojans and Akhaian soldiers
to put their arms aside upon the ground,
while he and Meneláos fight it out
between the lines alone
for Helen and her Spartan gold—the winner
to take the treasure home, and take the woman,
the rest, with solemn oaths, to part as friends."

The armies were now hushed. Across the field,
Meneláos, clarion in war, addressed them:

"Hear me also, as the iron enters
deepest in me. Yet I agree, the Trojans
and Argives should withdraw in peace; you've borne
so many hardships, taking part with me

in the quarrel Aléxandros began.

                                                     So death

to him for whom the hour of death has come!
The rest of you part peacefully and soon!
Bring down a black ewe and a snow-white ram
for sacrifice to Earth and Hêlios;
we here shall dedicate a third to Zeus.
And lead down Priam in his power, that he
himself may swear to peace.

                                  Reckless, untrustworthy

sons he has, but no man's overweening
should break the peace of Zeus. The younger men
are changeable; he in his age among them,
looking before and after, can see clearly
what shall be in the interests of all."

Now all hearts lifted at his words, for both sides
hoped for an end of miserable war;
and backing chariots into line, the men
stepped out, disarmed themselves, and left their weapons
heaped at close intervals on open ground.
Hektor meanwhile had sent two runners back
to bring the sheep and summon the Lord Priam.
Agamémnon at the same time dispatched
Talthýbios to the ships, bidding him bring
a sheep as well, and he obeyed.

                                           Now Iris

made her way to inform the Lady Helen,
appearing as her sister-in-law, Laódikê,
loveliest of Priam's daughters and the wife
of Helikáon, a son of Lord Antênor.
She found her weaving in the women's hall
a double violet stuff, whereon inwoven
were many passages of arms by Trojan
horsemen and Akhaians mailed in bronze—
trials braved for her sake at the wargod's hands.
Approaching her, swift Iris said:

                                         "Come, dearest,

come outside and see the marvelous change
in Trojans and Akhaians! Up to now

they have made war till we were dead with weeping,
war unending, in the cruel plain.
No more now: they are resting on their shields,
each with his tall spear thrust in earth beside him.
It seems Aléxandros and the great soldier,
Meneláos, will meet in single combat
with battle spears, for you! The man who wins
shall win you as his consort."

                                                And the goddess,
even as she spoke, infused in Helen's heart
a smoky sweetness and desire
for him who first had taken her as bride
and for her parents and her ancient town.
Quickly she cloaked herself in silvery veils
and let a teardrop fall and left her chamber,
not unaccompanied, but as became
a princess, with two maids-in-waiting—one
Aithrê, child of Pittheus, and the other
wide-eyed Klýmenê.
Soon these three women neared the Skaian Gates.

There Priam and his counselors were sitting—
Thymoítês, Pánthoös, Lampós, Klytíos,
the soldier Hiketáôn, and those two
clearheaded men, Antênor and Oukálegon—
peers of the realm, in age strengthless at war
but strong still in their talking—perching now
above the Skaian Gates on the escarpment.

They sounded like cicadas in dry summer
that cling on leafy trees and send out voices
rhythmic and long—

                              so droned and murmured these
old leaders of the Trojans on the tower,
and watching Helen as she climbed the stair
in undertones they said to one another:

"We cannot rage at her, it is no wonder
that Trojans and Akhaians under arms
should for so long have borne the pains of war
for one like this."

                                    "Unearthliness. A goddess
the woman is to look at."

                                                "Ah, but still,
still, even so, being all that she is, let her go in the ships
and take her scourge from us and from our children."

These were the old men's voices. But to Helen
Priam called out:

                              "Come here, dear child, sit here
beside me; you shall see your onetime lord
and your dear kinsmen.

                              You are not to blame,
I hold the gods to blame for bringing on
this war against the Akhaians, to our sorrow.
Come, tell me who the big man is out there,
who is that powerful figure? Other men
are taller, but I never saw a soldier
clean-cut as he, as royal in his bearing:
he seems a kingly man."

                                        And the great beauty,
Helen, replied:

                                        "Revere you as I do,
I dread you, too, dear father.

                                        Painful death
would have been sweeter for me, on that day
I joined your son, and left my bridal chamber,
my brothers, my grown child, my childhood friends!
But no death came, though I have pined and wept.
Your question, now: yes, I can answer it:
that man is Agamémnon, son of Atreus,
lord of the plains of Argos, ever both
a good king and a formidable soldier—
brother to the husband of a wanton . . .

                              or was that life a dream?"

The old man gazed and mused and softly cried:

"O fortunate son of Atreus! Child of destiny,
O happy soul! How many sons of Akhaia
serve under you!

In the old days once I went
into the vineyard country of Phrygia
and saw the Phrygian host on nimble ponies,
Otreus' and Mygdôn's people. In those days
they were encamped on Sangaríos river.
And they allotted me as their ally
my place among them when the Amazons
came down, those women who were fighting men;
but that host never equaled this,
the army of the keen-eyed men of Akhaia."

Still gazing out, he caught sight of Odysseus,
and then the old man said:

                              "Tell me, dear child,
who is that officer? The son of Atreus
stands a head taller, but this man appears
to have a deeper chest and broader shoulders.
His gear lies on the ground, but still he goes
like a bellwether up and down the ranks.
A ram I'd call him, burly, thick with fleece,
keeping a flock of silvery sheep in line."

And Helen shaped by heaven answered him:

"That is Laërtês' son, the great tactician,
Odysseus. He was bred on Ithaka,
a bare and stony island—but he knows
all manner of stratagems and moves in war."

Antênor, the alert man, interposed:

"My lady, there indeed you hit the mark.
Once long ago he came here, great Odysseus,
with Meneláos—came to treat of you.
They were my guests, and I made friends of both,
and learned their stratagems and characters.
Among us Trojans, in our gatherings, Meneláos,
broad in the shoulders likewise, overtopped him;
seated, Odysseus looked the kinglier man.
When each of them stood up to make his plea,
his argument before us all, then Meneláos

said a few words in a rather headlong way
but clearly: not long-winded and not vague;
and indeed he was the younger of the two.
Then in his turn the great tactician rose
and stood, and looked at the ground,
moving the staff before him not at all
forward or backward: obstinate and slow
of wit he seemed, gripping the staff: you'd say
some surly fellow, with an empty head.
But when he launched the strong voice from his chest,
and words came driving on the air as thick
and fast as winter snowflakes, then Odysseus
could have no mortal rival as an orator!
The look of him no longer made us wonder."

Observing a third figure, that of Aías,
the old man asked:

                                        "Who is that other one,
so massive and so strongly built, he towers
head and shoulders above the Argive troops?"

Tall in her long gown, in her silver cloak,
Helen replied:

                                        "That is the giant soldier,
Aías, a rugged sea wall for Akhaians.
Opposite him, among the Kretans, there,
is tall Idómeneus, with captains round him.
Meneláos, whom the wargod loves,
received him often in our house in Sparta
when he crossed over out of Krete.

                                                                I see
all the Akhaians now
whom I might recognize and name for you,
except for two I cannot see, the captains
Kastor, breaker of horses,

                                        and the boxer, Polydeukês,
both my brothers; mother bore them both.
Were these not in the fleet from Lakedaimôn?
Or did they cross in the long ships, but refrain
from entering combat here because they dread
vile talk of me and curses on my head?"

So Helen wondered. But her brothers lay
motionless in the arms of life-bestowing earth,
long dead in Lakedaimôn of their fathers.

Meanwhile by lane and wall the criers came
with sacrificial sheep and bearing wine
that warms the heart, gift of the vineyard ground—
a goatskin ponderous with wine.

                    And one, Idaios,
carrying golden goblets and a winebowl
shining, reached the side of the aged king
and called upon him:

                        "Son of Laomédôn,
arise: the master soldiers of both armies,
Trojan breakers of horses, Akhaians mailed in bronze,
request that you be present in the plain
for peace offerings and oaths.

                        Aléxandros
and Meneláos, whom the wargod loves,
will fight with battle spears over the lady.
She and the treasure go to him who wins.
As for the rest, by solemn pact, thereafter
in this rich land of Troy we dwell in peace
while they return to the grazing land of Argos
and to Akhaia, country of fair women."

At this announcement by the crier, a tremor
shook the old king, head to foot.

                        He said:

"Harness the team."

                        And hastily they did so.
Stepping into his car, Lord Priam took
the reins and leaned back, tugging at the horses
until Antênor mounted at his side.
Then to the Skaian Gates and out they drove,
keeping the swift team headed for the plain.
They reined in at the battle line, set foot
upon the open ground, once cattle pasture,
and walked between the Trojans and Akhaians.

Promptly Lord Agamémnon and Odysseus,
master of stratagems, arose. The criers,
noble retainers, brought the votive sheep,
prepared the bowls of wine, and rinsed the hands
of their commanders.

                    Then the son of Atreus
drew from his hip the sheath knife hanging there
beside his longsword scabbard; from the brows
of ram and ewe he cut the fleece, and criers
handed it out to officers of both armies.
With arms held wide to heaven, Agamémnon
prayed in the name of all:

                             "O Father Zeus!

Power over Ida! Greatest, most glorious!
O Hêlios, by whom all things are seen,
all overheard! O rivers! O dark earth!
O powers underground, chastisers of dead men
for breaking solemn oaths!

                          Be witness, all:

preserve this pact we swear to! If in fact
Aléxandros should kill Lord Meneláos,
let him keep Helen and keep all the gold,
while we sail home in the long ships.
But if Aléxandros be killed, the Trojans
are to surrender Helen and the treasure—
moreover they must pay a tribute, due
the Argives now, renewed to their descendants.
In the event that Priam and his sons
refuse this—though Aléxandros be killed—
then I shall stay and fight for my indemnity
until I come upon an end to war."

                             He drew

the pitiless bronze knife-edge hard across
the gullets of the sheep, and laid them
quivering on the ground, their lives ebbing,
lost to the whetted bronze.

                        Now dipping up

wine from the winebowls into golden cups,
the captains tipped their offerings and prayed

to the gods who never die. Here is the way
the Trojans and Akhaians prayed:

                                                    "O Zeus

almighty and most glorious! Gods undying!
Let any parties to this oath who first
calamitously break it have their brains
decanted like these wine-drops on the ground—
they and their children; let their wives be slaves."

The oath ran so, but Zeus would not abide
by what they swore.

                              Now Dardan Priam spoke:

"One word from me, O Trojans and Akhaians.
For my part, back I go to the windy town
of Ilion. I cannot bear to watch
my son in combat against Meneláos,
a man the wargod stands behind. No doubt
Zeus knows the end, and all the immortals know
which of the two must die his fated death."

He placed the carcasses of ram and ewe
before him in the chariot, and stepped
aboard in majesty, holding the horses
while Lord Antênor climbed the royal car.
Then circling back they drove toward Ilion.
Prince Hektor and Odysseus together
paced off the dueling ground. Next they took up
two tokens in a bronze helm, shaking it
to see which man would cast his weapon first.
Meanwhile the soldiers held their hands to heaven,
Trojans and Akhaians, in this prayer:

"Father Zeus, almighty over Ida,
may he who brought this trouble on both sides
perish! Let him waste away
into the undergloom! As for ourselves,
let us be loyal friends in peace!"

                                              They prayed

as powerful Hektor in his flashing helmet,
keeping his eyes averted, churned the tokens.

That of Paris quickly tumbled out.
And now, holding their lines, the troops sank down,
each one beside his horses and his gear.

The time had come, and Prince Aléxandros,
consort of Helen, buckled on his armor:
first the greaves, well molded to his shins,
with silver ankle circlets; then
around his chest the cuirass of his brother
Lykáôn, a good fit for him. He slung
a sword of bronze with silver-studded hilt
by a baldric on his shoulder; over this
a shield strap and the many-layered shield;
then drew a helmet with a horsetail crest
upon his head, upon his gallant brow,
the tall plume like a wave-crest grimly tossing.
He picked out, finally, a solid spear
with his own handgrip.

                              Meanwhile the great soldier,
Meneláos, put on his own equipment.
Armed now, each in his place apart, both men
walked forward in the space between the armies,
glaring at one another. Fierce excitement
ran through all who gazed—horse-breaking Trojans,
Akhaians in leg armor—as the champions
came to a stand inside the dueling ground
and hefted spears in rage. Without delay
Aléxandros opened the fight: he hurled
his long-shadowing spear and hit Atreidês
fair on the round shield.

                              Nothing brazen broke—
no, but the point of bronze at impact bent
in that hard armor.

                              Second to make his cast,
and rousing to it with his bronze-shod spear,
the son of Atreus, Meneláos, prayed
to Father Zeus:

                              "O Zeus aloft,
grant I shall make the man who wronged me first

pay for it now!
Let him be humbled, brought down at my hands,
and hearts in those born after us will shrink
from treachery to a host who offers love."

Hefting and aiming as he spoke, he hurled
his long-shadowing spear and hit his adversary
fair on the round shield. Formidably sped,
the spear went through the polished hide and through
the densely plated cuirass, where it ripped
the shirt forward along his flank and stuck—
but Paris, twisting, had eluded death.
Drawing his longsword then, Lord Meneláos
reared and struck him on the helmet ridge,
but saw his blade, broken in jagged splinters,
drop from his hand. Lifting his eyes to heaven
he groaned:

                              "O Father Zeus, of all the gods,
none is more cruel to hopeful men than you are!
I thought to make Aléxandros
pay for his crime, and what luck have I had?
My spear slipped from my grip in vain: I missed him.
And now my sword is shattered in my hand!"

But now in one bound, pouncing, he laid hold
of the horsetail crest and spun his enemy,
then yanked him backward toward the Akhaian lines,
choked by the chin strap, cutting into his throat—
a well-stitched band secured beneath his helmet.
To his own glory, Meneláos
now would in fact have pulled him all the way,
had Aphrodítê with her clear eye not
perceived him—and she snapped that band of oxhide,
cut from a clubbed ox.

                              Now, at this the helmet
came away easily in the fighter's hand.
He whirled it round his head and let it fly
amid the Akhaians, where his own men caught it.
And once again, raging to kill his man,
he lunged, aiming a lance.

But this time Aphrodítê
spirited Aléxandros away as easily
as only a god could do. She hid him in mist
and put him down in his own fragrant chamber,
while she herself went off to summon Helen.
She came upon her on the battlement, amid
a throng of Trojan ladies.

Here the goddess

plucked at a fold of her sweet-scented gown
and spoke to her. She seemed a spinning-woman
who once had spun soft wool for her, at home
in Lakedaimôn, and the princess loved her.
In this guise ravishing Aphrodítê said:

"Come home with me. Aléxandros invites you.
On the ivory-inlaid bed in your bedchamber
he lies at ease, and freshly dressed—so handsome
never could you imagine the man came
just now from combat; one would say he goes
to grace a dance, or has until this minute
danced and is resting now."

So she described him,

and Helen's heart beat faster in her breast.
Her sense being quickened so, through all disguise
she recognized the goddess' flawless throat,
her fine breasts that move the sighs of longing,
her brilliant eyes. She called her by her name
in wonder, saying:

"O immortal madness,

why do you have this craving to seduce me?
Am I to be transported even farther
eastward, into some Phrygian walled town
or into Mêioniê, if you have there
another mortal friend? Is it because
Meneláos has beaten Aléxandros
and, hateful though I am, would take me home,
is that why you are here in all your cunning?
Go take your place beside Aléxandros!
Leave the bright paths the gods take over heaven
and walk no more about Olympos! Be

unhappy for him, shield him, till at last
he marries you—or, as he will, enslaves you.

I shall not join him there! It would be base
if I should make his bed luxurious now.
There will be such whispering
among the Trojan women later—
as though I had not pain enough to bear."

To this the goddess haughtily replied:

"Better not be so difficult. You'll vex me
enough to let you go. Then I shall hate you
as I have cherished you till now. Moreover,
I can make hatred for you grow
amid both Trojans and Danäans,
and if I do, you'll come to a bad end."

Now Helen shaped by heaven was afraid.
Enfolded in her shining robe of silver
she turned to go, without a word—unseen
by all the women, for the goddess led her.

Entering Aléxandros' magnificent house,
the maids went quickly to their work, and Helen
mounted to her high chamber. Aphrodítê,
who smiles on smiling love, brought her a chair
and set it down facing Aléxandros.
Helen, daughter of Zeus beyond the stormcloud,
took her seat with downcast eyes, and greeted him:

"Home from the war? You should have perished there,
brought down by that strong soldier, once my husband.
You used to say you were the better man,
more skillful with your hands, your spear. So why not
challenge him to fight again?

                                                      I wouldn't,
if I were you. No, don't go back to war
against the tawny-headed man of war
like a rash fool. You'd crumple under his lance."

Paris replied:

                              "Love, don't be bitter with me.
These are unkind reflections.

                                                    It is true,
on this occasion he—and Athêna—won.
Next time, I may. We, too, have gods with us.
Let us drop war now, you and I,
and give ourselves to pleasure in our bed.
My soul was never so possessed by longing,
not even when I took you first aboard
off Lakedaimôn, that sweet land, and sailed
in the long ships.

                              Not at Kranaê Island
where I first went to bed with you and loved you.
Greater desire now lifts me like a tide."

He went to bed, and she went with him,
and in the inlaid ivory bed these two
made love, while Meneláos roamed the ranks
like a wild beast, hunting the godlike man,
Aléxandros.

                              But not a Trojan there,
not one of all the allies, could produce him
for the wargod's friend, Meneláos—and none
for love would ever hide him if he saw him,
the man being abhorred like death itself.
Now the Lord Marshal Agamémnon spoke
amid the armies:

                              "Give me your attention,
Trojans, Dardans, and allies;
beyond question, Meneláos is victorious.
Therefore, Helen of Argos and the treasure
are now to be surrendered; you must pay
tribute as well, the compensation due,
payable, too, in future generations."

And to this judgment of the son of Atreus
the rest of the Akhaians gave assent.

BOOK FOUR

A Bowshot Bringing War

LINES 1–10

The gods were seated near to Zeus in council,
upon a golden floor. Graciously Hêbê
served them nectar, as with cups of gold
they toasted one another, looking down
toward the stronghold of Ilion.

                          Abruptly

and with oblique intent to ruffle Hêra,
Zeus in cutting tones remarked:

                                 "Two goddesses

have Meneláos for their protégé—
Hêra, the patroness of Argos, and
Athêna, known as Guardian in Boiotia.
Still, they keep their distance here; their pleasure
comes from looking on. But Aphrodíte,

who loves all smiling lips and eyes,
cleaves to her man to ward off peril from him.
He thought he faced death, but she saved him.

                                        Clearly,

Meneláos, whom Arês backs, has won
the single combat. Let us then consider
how this affair may end; shall we again
bring on the misery and din of war,
or make a pact of amity between them?
If only all of you were pleased to see it,
life might go on in Priam's town,
while Meneláos took Helen of Argos home."

At this proposal, Hêra and Athêna
murmured rebelliously. These two together
sat making mischief for the men of Troy,
and though she held her tongue, a sullen anger
filled Athêna against her father. Hêra
could not contain her own vexation, saying:

"Your majesty, what is the drift of this?
How could you bring to nothing all my toil,
the sweat I sweated, and my winded horses,
when I called out that army to bear hard
on Priam and his sons? Act, if you must,
but not all here approve!"

                                Coldly annoyed,
the Lord Zeus, who drives the clouds of heaven,
answered:

                                "Strange one, how can Priam
and Priam's sons have hurt you so
that you are possessed to see the trim stronghold
of Ilion plundered?

                        Could you breach the gates
and the great walls yourself and feed on Priam
with all his sons, and all the other Trojans,
dished up raw, you might appease this rage!
Do as you wish to do, then. This dispute
should not leave rancor afterward between us.

I must, however, tell you one thing more:
remember it.

Whenever my turn comes

to lust for demolition of some city
whose people may be favorites of yours,
do not hamper my fury! Free my hands
as here I now free yours, my will prevailing
on my unwilling heart.

Of all the cities

men of earth inhabit under the sun,
under the starry heavens, Ilion
stood first in my esteem, first in my heart,
as Priam did, the good lance, and his people.
My altar never lacked a feast at Troy
nor spilt wine, nor the smoke of sacrifice—
perquisites of the gods."

And wide-eyed Hêra

answered:

"Dearest to me are these three cities:

Mykênê of the broad lanes, Argos, Sparta.
Let them be pulled down, if you ever find them
hateful to you. I will not interfere.
I will not grudge you these. And if I should?
Why, balking and withholding my consent
would gain me nothing, since the power you hold
so far surpasses mine.

My labor, though,

should not be thwarted; I am immortal, too,
your stock and my stock are the same. Our father,
Krónos of crooked wit, engendered me
to hold exalted rank, by birth and by
my standing as your queen—since you are lord
of all immortal gods.

Come, we'll give way

to one another in this affair: I yield
to you and you to me; the gods will follow.
Only be quick, and send Athêna down
into the hurly-burly of the armies

to make the Trojans, not the Akhaians, first
to sunder the truce they swore to."

This way Hêra

prompted him, and the father of gods and men
complied by saying briskly to Athêna:

"In all haste, down you go amid the armies
to see if Trojans, not Akhaians, first
will sunder the truce they swore to."

Given orders

to do her own will, grey-eyed Athêna left
Olympos, dropping downward from the crests—
as though the son of crooked-minded Krónos
had flung a shooting star, to be a sign
for men on the deep sea, or some broad army—
a streak of radiance and a sparkling track.
Down she flashed, to alight amid the troops,
and wonder held them all at gaze, horse-breaking
Trojans and Akhaians in leg armor.
You might have heard one, glancing at the next man,
mutter:

"What is to come? Bad days again
in the bloody lines? Or can both sides be friends?
Which will it be from Zeus, who holds the keys
and rationing of war?"

That was the question

for Trojan and Akhaian fighting men.
Athêna, meanwhile, in a soldier's guise,
that of Laódokos, Antênor's son,
a burly spearman, passed among the Trojans
looking for Pándaros, if she could find him—
Lykáôn's noble son. Find him she did,
waiting with troops, now covered by their shields,
who once had followed him from the cascades
of Aisêpos.

Near him she took her stand

and let her sharp words fly:

"Son of Lykáôn,
I have in mind an exploit that may tempt you,
tempt a fighting heart. Have you the gall
to send an arrow like a fork of lightning
home against Meneláos? Every Trojan
heart would rise, and every man would praise you,
especially Aléxandros, the prince—
you would be sure to come by glittering gifts
if he could see the warrior, Meneláos,
the son of Atreus, brought down by your bow,
then bedded on a dolorous pyre!

                                        Come, now,

brace yourself for a shot at Meneláos.
Engage to pay Apollo, the bright archer,
a perfect hekatomb of firstling lambs
when you go home to your old town, Zéleia."

That was Athêna's way, bemusing all
his wits with witless glory.

                                        He uncased

his bow of polished horn—horn of an ibex
that he had killed one day with a chest shot
upon a high crag; waiting under cover,
he shot it through the ribs and knocked it over—
horns, together, a good four feet in length.
He cut and fitted these, mortised them tight,
polished the bow, and capped the tips with gold.
This weapon, now, against the ground, Pándaros
bent hard and strung. Men of his company
at the same time held up their shields to hide him—
not to bring any Argives to their feet
before he shot at Meneláos.

                                        He bared

his quiver top and drew a feathered arrow,
never frayed, but keen with waves of pain
to darken vision.

                             Smoothly on the string
he fitted the sharp arrow. Then he prayed
to the bright archer, Lykian Apollo,
promising first-born lambs in hekatomb
on his return to his old town, Zéleia.

Pinching the grooved butt and the string, he pulled
evenly till the bent string reached his nipple,
the arrowhead of iron touched the bow,
and when the great bow under tension made
a semicircular arc, it sprang.

                                The whipping
string sang, and the arrow whizzed away,
needlesharp, vicious, flashing through the crowd.

But, Meneláos, you were not neglected
this time by the gods in bliss! Athêna,
Hope of Soldiers, helped you first of all,
deflecting by an inch the missile's flight
so that it grazed your skin—the way a mother
would keep a fly from settling on a child
when he is happily asleep. Athêna
guided the arrow down to where the golden
belt buckles and the breastplate overlapped,
and striking there, the bitter arrowhead
punctured the well-sewn belt and cut its way
into the figured cuirass, where it stuck,
although the point passed onward through the loin-guard
next his belly, plated against spearheads,
shielding him most now; yet the point entered
and gouged the warrior's mortal skin.

Then dark blood rippled in a clouding stain
down from the wound, as when a Mêionian
or a Karian woman dyes clear ivory
to be the cheekpiece of a chariot team.
Though horseman after horseman longs to carry it,
the artifact lies in a storeroom, kept
for a great lord, a splendor doubly prized—
his team's adornment and his driver's glory.
So, Meneláos, were your ivory thighs
dyed and suffused with running blood, your well-made
shins and ankles, too.

                             Now Agamémnon,
marshal of the army, looked and shuddered
to see the dark blood flowing from the wound,

and Meneláos himself went cold.
But when he saw the lashing of the iron
flange outside the wound, and barbs outside,
then life and warmth came back about his heart.
Meanwhile the troops heard Agamémnon groan,
holding his brother's hand, and heard him say,
so that they groaned as well:

                                        "The truce I made
was death for you, dear brother! When I sent you
forward alone to fight for the Akhaians,
I only gave a free shot to the Trojans.
They've ground the truce under their heels.

                                                              But not

for nothing have we sworn an oath and spilt
lamb's blood, red wine, and joined our hands and theirs—
putting our trust in ritual. No, no,
if the Olympian upon the instant
has not exacted punishment, he will
in his good time, and all the more they'll pay
for their misdeed in lives, in wives and children!
For this I know well in my heart and soul:
the day must come when holy Ilion
is given to fire and sword, and Priam perishes,
good lance though he was, with all his people.
For Zeus, the son of Krónos,
benched in the azure up there where he dwells,
will heave his shield of storm against them all
in rage at their bad faith!

                                                    So it must be.

But this for me is anguish, Menaláos,
if you have measured out your mortal time
and are to die.

                          Backward in depths of shame
I go to the drought of Argos. The Akhaians
will turn their minds again to their far lands,
and we, I have no doubt, must leave behind
the Argive woman, Helen, for the Trojans,
for Priam's glory, while your bones decay
in Trojan plowland, rotting where they lie,
your mission unachieved!

In my mind's eye

I see some arrogant Trojan on the grave
of Meneláos, the great and famous man,
leaping to say: 'Let Agamémnon's anger
in every case come out like this! Remember
he brought an army of Akhaians here
for nothing, and sailed back in the long ships
again to his own land—but had to leave
Meneláos behind!' Someone will say it,
and let the vast earth yawn for me that day!"

But red-haired Meneláos said:

"Be calm.

Courage, do not alarm the troops! The point
has hit no vital spot here where it lodged;
the faceted belt stopped it, and the loin-guard,
stiff with plate the smiths had hammered out."

Then Agamémnon said:

"God send you're right,
dear Meneláos! But the wound—
we'll have a surgeon clean the wound and dress it
with medicines to relieve the pain."

He turned

and spoke out to Talthýbios, the crier:

"Go quickly as you can and call Makháon,
son of Asklêpios, the great healer,
call him here to examine Meneláos.
A master bowman, Trojan or Lykian,
has wounded him—a feat for the enemy,
worry and pain for us."

Talthýbios

obeyed, making his way amid the army,
among the mailed Akhaians, everywhere
looking for the soldierly Makháon.
He found him standing ready, troops with shields
in rank on rank around him—companies
of his that came from grazing lands in Trikê.
Approaching him, the crier said:

"This way,
son of Asklêpios: you are called by Agamémnon
to examine Meneláos, the co-commander.
A master bowman, Trojan or Lykian,
has wounded him—a feat for the enemy,
worry and pain for us."

                                    The message stirred him,
and back the two men hastened through the army
to where the red-haired captain had been hit.
Gathered around him in a circle stood
the Akhaian peers, but through their midst Makháon
quickly gained his side, and pulled the arrow
free of the belt and clasp. As it came out,
the barbs broke off. The surgeon then unbuckled
faceted belt and, underneath, his loin-guard,
stiff with plate the smiths had hammered out,
and when he saw the arrow wound, he sucked it
clean of blood, then sprinkled it with balm,
a medicine that Kheirôn gave his father.
Now while they tended Meneláos, lord
of the warcry, Trojan ranks reformed with shields
and the Akhaians, too, put on their armor,
mindful again of battle.

                                    In that hour
no one could have perceived in Agamémnon
a moment's torpor or malingering, but fiery
ardor for the battle-test that brings
honor to men.

                                    He left aside his team,
his chariot, a-gleam with bronze: his driver,
Eurýmedôn, a son of Ptolemaios
Peiraïdês, reined in the snorting horses;
and Agamémnon gave him strict command
to bring the war-car up when weariness
should take him in the legs, after inspection
of all his many marshaled troops.

                                    On foot
he ranged around the men in their formations,
and where he saw his charioteers in units
alert for battle, he exhorted them:

"Argives, keep your courage up, for Zeus
will never back up liars! Men who are first
to sunder oaths, their flesh the kites will feed on—
tender fare; as for their wives and children,
we'll enslave them when we take the town."

On seeing any slack and unready still
for hated war, he lashed at them in anger:

"Rabbit hearts of Argos,
are you not dead with shame?

        How can you stand there
stunned as deer that have been chased all day
over a plain and are used up at last,
and droop and halt, broken in heart and wind?
That is the way you look, no fight left in you!
Will you stand by till Trojans overrun
our line of ships, beached here above the breakers,
to find out if the hand of Zeus is over you?"

So as their lord commander he reviewed them,
passing along the crowded ranks. He came
upon the Kretans, putting on their armor,
around Idómeneus. Like a wild boar,
with his great heart, this captain in the van
harangued his companies, and in the rear
Meríonês did likewise. The Lord Marshal
Agamémnon, elated at the sight,
said to Idómeneus in the warmest tones:

"Idómeneus, you are a man I prize
above all handlers of fast horses, whether
in war or any labor, or at feasts
whenever in their mixing bowls our peers
prepare the wine reserved for counselors.
Akhaian gentlemen with flowing hair
may down their portions, but your cup will be
filled up and filled again, like mine—to drink
as we are moved to!

        Now, the feast is war.
Be as you always have been up to now!"

To this Idómeneus, captain of Kretans,
answered:

"Son of Atreus, more than ever
shall I stand by you as I swore I would.
But now stir up the rest of the Akhaians
to give battle as quickly as we can!
The Trojans have dissolved the truce. Again,
death to the Trojans! Bad times are ahead
for those who overrode our pact and broke it!"

This fierceness made the son of Atreus happy
as he passed down the crowded ranks. He came
to where the two named Aías, tall and short,
were buckling on their gear. Around them armed
their cloud of infantry.

                      Like a dark cloud

a shepherd from a hilltop sees, a storm,
a gloom over the ocean, traveling shoreward
under the west wind; distant from his eyes
more black than pitch it seems, though far at sea,
with lightning squalls driven along its front.
Shivering at the sight, he drives his flock
for shelter into a cavern.

                      Grim as that

were the dense companies that armed for war
with Telamônian Aías and the other—
shields pitch-black and a spiny hedge of spears.
Lord Agamémnon, heartened at the sight,
spoke to the captains warmly:

                      "Aías and Aías,

captains of Argos in your mail of bronze,
I have no orders for you: there's no need
to put you in a mood for war: it's clear
you've passed your fighting spirit to your troops.
O Father Zeus, Athêna and Apollo,
if only every heart were strong as these!
Lord Priam's fortress would go down before us,
taken in a day, and plundered at our hands."

With this he left them there, and passing on
to others as they formed, he found Lord Nestor,
the Pylian master orator, haranguing
soldiers of Pylos, forming them for action

around the captains Pélagon, Alástôr,
Khromíos, Haimôn, and the marshal, Bías.
Charioteers with teams and cars he sent
forward, and kept his infantry behind
to be the bristling bulk and hedge of battle,
placing weak men and cowardly between
brave men on either side, so willy-nilly
all would be forced to fight.

                                        The chariot men

he first instructed in the way of battle—
charioteers to keep their teams in line,
not to be tangled, cut off in the mêlée:

"None of you should rely so far on horsemanship
or bravery as to attack alone—much less
retreat alone. That way you are most vulnerable.
Let any man in line lunge with his lance
when he can reach their chariots from his own;
you'll fight with far more power. In the old days
cities and walls were overthrown by men
who kept this plan in mind and fought with courage."

So ran the old man's exhortation, shrewd
from a long lifetime in the ways of war.
It gladdened Agamémnon, who said to him:

"I wish you had the same force in your legs
as in your fighting heart; I wish your strength
were whole again. The wrinkling years have worn you.
Better some other soldier had your age,
and you were still among the young."

                                        And Nestor,

Earl of Gerênia, charioteer, replied:

"Agamémnon, I too could wish I were
that man who killed the great Ereuthalíôn.
But the immortal gods have given men
all things in season. Once my youth, my manhood,
now my age has come.

                                        No less for that

I have my place among the charioteers

to counsel and command them. Duties fit
for elder men, these are: the young can be
good lancers, good with spears—men who were born
in a later day, and still can trust their powers."

The son of Atreus heard him out and passed
happily onward.

                    Next he found Menéstheus,
the good horse-handler, son of Péteôs, waiting,
surrounded by Athenians, good hands
in battle. Near him, too, the great tactician,
Odysseus, had his place, with Kephallênians
in ranks around him, not at all feeble; these
waited, for word of battle had not reached them,
but only a first ripple in the lines
of Trojans and Akhaians. There they stood,
as though they waited for some other troop
to move out and make contact with the Trojans.
Surveying these, Lord Agamémnon, marshal
of fighting men, in urgent speech rebuked them:

"Son of Péteôs whom the gods reared! You, too,
Odysseus, hero of battle guile and greed!
Why both so deferential, so retiring?
Waiting for other troops?

                    You two should be
among the first in action, in the blaze
of combat—as you both are first to hear
my word of feasting, every time we Akhaians
prepare a feast for our staff officers.
There is the fare you like: roast meat, and cups
of honey-hearted wine, all you desire!
But now you'd gladly see ten troops ahead of you
moving up to attack with naked bronze!"

Odysseus, the wily field commander,
scowled at him and answered:

                    "Son of Atreus,
what is this panic you permit yourself?
How can you say we'd let a fight go by,
ever, at any time when we Akhaians

against the Trojans whet the edge of war?
If you will make it your concern you'll see
the father of Telémakhos in action
hand to hand in the enemy's front ranks.
Your bluster is all wind!"

                    Lord Agamémnon,

sure of his angry man, replied,
smiling and taking back his provocation:

"Son of Laërtês and the gods of old,
Odysseus, master mariner and soldier,
I would not be unfair to you; I need not
give you orders, knowing as I do
that you are well disposed toward all I plan.
Your thought is like my own.
Come, then; in time we'll make amends for this,
if anything uncalled for has been said:
God send the seawinds blow it out of mind!"

He left them there, and going amid others
found Diomêdês, gallant son of Tydeus,
with combat cars and horses all around him,
still at a stand. Nearby stood Sthénelos,
the son of Kapanéus. And Agamémnon
at a first glimpse in scathing speech rebuked him:

"Baffling! Son of Tydeus the battle-wise
breaker of horses, why are you so shy?
So wary of the passages of war?
Your father did not lag like this, nor care to—
far from it: he would rather fight alone
ahead of all his men, or so they said
who saw him toil in battle. I myself
never met him, never laid eyes on him,
but men say that he had no peer.

                         In peace,

without a fight, as Polyneikês' ally,
he entered old Mykênê, hunting troops.
At that time they were marching to besiege
the ancient walls of Thebes, and they appealed
for first-rate men as volunteers. Our people

agreed and would have granted these, but Zeus
by inauspicious omens changed their minds.
Taking the road, and well along, the army
came to Asôpos in his grassy bed,
a river deep in rushes; there again
they ordered Tydeus forward with a message.
Forward he went, and found Kadmeíans thronging
a great feast in the manor of Eteoklês,
where, though no liege nor distant friend, and though
he came alone amid so many, Tydeus
went unafraid. He challenged them to wrestling
and easily beat them all—being seconded
so well by Athêna. Those goaders of horses,
the furious Kadmeíans, laid a trap for him
on his retreat upcountry: fifty men
deployed in a strong ambush by two leaders,
Maiôn, immortal-seeming son of Haimôn,
and Polyphontês, Autophónos' son.
But these, as well, Tydeus brought to grief:
he killed them all but one. Maiôn he spared
and sent home, bid by portents from the gods.
This, then, was Tydeus the Aitolian.
Weaker than he in war, the man he fathered,
stronger in assembly!"

                                        Diomêdês,
the rugged man, said nothing whatsoever,
accepting his commander's reprimand.
But Sthénelos, the son of Kapanéus,
made a retort:

                          "Atreidês, why distort things
when you know well how to be just? We say
we are far better men than our fathers were.
Not they, but we, took Thebes of the seven gates,
leading a smaller force
against a heavier wall—but heeding signs
the gods had shown, and helped by Zeus. Our fathers?
Their own recklessness destroyed our fathers!
Rate them less than equal to ourselves!"

Now rugged Diomêdês with a frown
turned and said:

                    "Old horse, be still. Believe me,
I do not take this ill from the Lord Marshal
Agamémnon. He must goad the Akhaians
to combat—for the glory goes to him
if his detachments cut the Trojans down
and take their powerful city—as the anguish
goes to him also, if his men are slain.
Come, both of us should put our minds on valor."

As he said this he bounded from his car
in full armor, and the bronze about his chest
rang as he hit the ground, a captain roused.
Even a stout heart would have feared him then.

As down upon a shore of echoing surf
big waves may run under a freshening west wind,
looming first on the open sea, and riding
shoreward to fall on sand in foam and roar,
around all promontories crested surges
making a briny spume inshore—so now
formations of Danääns rose and moved
relentlessly toward combat. Every captain
called to his own. The troops were mainly silent;
you could not have believed so great a host
with warcries in its heart was coming on
in silence, docile to its officers—
and round about upon the soldiers shone
the figured armor buckled on for war.

The Trojans were not silent: like the flocks
that huddle countless in a rich man's pens,
waiting to yield white milk, and bleating loud
continually as they hear their own lambs cry,
just so the warcry of the Trojans rose
through all that army—not as a single note,
not in a single tongue, but mingled voices
of men from many countries.

                           This great army
Arês urged on; the other, grey-eyed Athêna,

Terror and Rout, and Hate, insatiable
sister-in-arms of man-destroying Arês—
frail at first, but growing, till she rears
her head through heaven as she walks the earth.
Once more she sowed ferocity, traversing
the ranks of men, redoubling groans and cries.

When the long lines met at the point of contact,
there was a shock of bull's hide, battering pikes,
and weight of men in bronze.

                          Bucklers with bosses

ground into one another. A great din rose,
in one same air elation and agony
of men destroying and destroyed, and earth
astream with blood.

                          In spring, snow-water torrents

risen and flowing down the mountainsides
hurl at a confluence their mighty waters
out of the gorges, filled by tributaries,
and far away upon the hills a shepherd
hears the roar. So when these armies closed
there came a toiling clamor.

                          Antílokhos

was the first man to down a Trojan soldier,
a brave man in the front line, Ekhepôlos
Thalysíadês: he hit him on the ridge
that bore his crest, and driven in, the point
went through his forehelm and his forehead bone,
and darkness veiled his eyes. In the mêlée
he toppled like a tower. Then by the feet
the fallen man was seized by Elephênor
Khalkodóntiadês, chief of Abantês,
who tried to haul him out of range and strip him
quickly of his arms. The trial was brief.
Seeing him tugging at the corpse, his flank
exposed beside the shield as he bent over,
Agênor with his spearshaft shod in bronze
hit him, and he crumpled. As he died
a bitter combat raged over his body
between the Trojan spearmen and Akhaians,
going for one another like wolves, like wolves
whirling upon each other, man to man.

Then Aías Telamônios knocked down
the son of Anthemíon, Simoeísios,
in the full bloom of youth. On slopes of Ida
descending, by the banks of clear Simóeis,
his mother had conceived him, while she kept
a vigil with her parents over flocks;
he got his name for this. To his dear parents
he never made return for all their care,
but had his life cut short when Aías' shaft
unmanned him. In the lead, as he came on,
he took the spear-thrust squarely in the chest
beside the nipple on the right side; piercing him,
the bronze point issued by the shoulder blade,
and in the dust he reeled and fell.

                                        A poplar

growing in bottom lands, in a great meadow,
smooth-trunked, high up to its sheath of boughs,
will fall before the chariot-builder's ax
of shining iron—timber that he marked
for warping into chariot tire rims—
and, seasoning, it lies beside the river.
So vanquished by the god-reared Aías lay
Simoeísios Anthémidês.

At Aías in his turn the son of Priam,
Ántiphos, glittering in his cuirass, made
a spear-cast, but he missed and hit instead
Leukos, Odysseus' comrade, in the groin
as he bent low to pull away the corpse.
It dropped out of his grasp, and he fell over it.
Odysseus, wrought to fury at this death,
with flashing helmet shouldered through the ranks
to stand above him: glowering right and left
he kept his lance in play, and made the Trojans
facing him recoil. With no waste motion
he cast and hit a bastard son of Priam,
Demókoön, who had come down from Abýdos
where he kept racing horses. Full of rage
over his dead companion, Odysseus
speared him in the temple, and the spearhead
passed clean through his head from side to side

so darkness veiled his eyes. When he fell down
he thudded, and his armor clanged upon him.

The Trojan front gave way, Prince Hektor, too,
while Argives raised a great yell. Dragging dead men
out of the press, they made a deep advance.
Now looking down from Pergamos, Apollo
in indignation cried out to the Trojans:

"Forward! Trojans, breakers of horses, will you
bow in fury of battle to the Argives?
When hit, they are not made of iron or stone
to make the cutting bronze rebound! See, too,
Akhilleus, child of Thetis, is not fighting
but tasting wrath and wrong beside the ships!"

The terrible god cried out thus from his tower,
and on the Akhaian side Tritogeneía,
glorious daughter of Zeus, went through the ranks
to lift the hearts of those she saw dismayed.

The next on whom fate closed was Diorês
Amárungkeidês, hit by a jagged stone
low on the right leg near the ankle. Peiros threw it,
Peiros Imbrasidês, a Thracian captain,
one who had come from Ainos. With the bone
itself, the vicious stone crushed both leg tendons
utterly, and the tall man tumbled down
into the dust, flinging his arms out wide
to his companions, panting his life away;
but on the run the man who hit him, Peiros,
came with a spear to gash him by the navel.
His bowels were spilled, and darkness veiled his eyes.

Then Thoas the Aitolian lunged at Peiros,
hitting him with a spear above the nipple,
so the bronze point stuck in his lung; and Thoas
at close quarters, wrenching the heavy spear,
pulled it out of his chest, then drew his sword
and killed him with a stroke square in the belly.
His gear he could not strip, though; friends of the dead man,

topknotted Thracians, closing round with spears,
repulsed him, huge and powerful as he was,
a noble figure; staggering, he gave ground.
As for the two, they lay there in the dust
stretched out near one another: captain of Thracians
and captain of Epeians mailed in bronze,
while others, many, fell in death around them.

Thereafter no man could have scorned that fight,
no veteran of battle who might go round,
untouched amid the action—an observer
led by Athêna, with his hand in hers,
shielded by her from stones' and arrows' flight;
for that day throngs of Trojans and Akhaians,
prone in the dust, were strewn beside each other.

BOOK FIVE

A Hero Strives with Gods

Now Diomêdês' hour for great action came.
Athêna made him bold, and gave him ease
to tower amid Argives, to win glory,
and on his shield and helm she kindled fire
most like midsummer's purest flaming star
in heaven rising, bathed by the Ocean stream.
So fiery she made his head and shoulders
as she impelled him to the center where
the greatest number fought.

                              A certain Darês,
a noble man among the Trojans, rich,
and a votary of Hêphaistos, had two sons
well-trained in warfare, Phêgeus and Idaíos.
These two the Akhaian faced as they came forward
upon their car; on foot he braced to meet them.

As the range narrowed, Phêgeus aimed and cast
his long spear first: the point cleared Diomêdês'
shoulder on the left, and failed to touch him.
Then Diomêdês wheeling in his turn
let fly his bronze-shod spear. No miss,
but a clean hit midway between the nipples
knocked the man backward from his team. Idaíos
left the beautiful chariot, leaping down,
but dared not stand his ground over his brother;
nor could he have himself eluded death
unless Hêphaistos had performed the rescue,
hiding him in darkness—thus to spare
his father full bereavement, were he lost.
Yanking the horses' heads, lashing their flanks,
Diomêdês handed team and chariot over
to men of his command, to be conducted
back to the ships. Now when the Trojans saw
how Darês' two sons fared—one saved, indeed,
the other lying dead beside his car—
every man's heart misgave him.

                              Grey-eyed Athêna

took the fierce wargod, Arês, by the hand
and said to him:

                    "Arês, bane of all mankind,
crusted with blood, breacher of city walls,
why not allow the Trojans and Akhaians
to fight alone? Let them contend—why not?—
for glory Zeus may hold out to the winner,
while we keep clear of combat—and his rage."

Even as she spoke she led him from the battle
and sat him down upon Skamánder side.
Now Danääns forced back the Trojan lines,
and every captain killed his man.
First the Lord Marshal Agamémnon
struck from his car Odíos, a tall warrior,
chief of the Halizônês; he had turned,
signaling a retreat, when Agamémnon's
point went through him from the rear, between
the shoulders, driving through his chest,

and down he crashed with clang of arms upon him.
Idómeneus then killed the son of Bôros,
Phaistos, who came from good farmland at Tarnê.
As this man rose upon his car, Idómeneus
drove through his right shoulder, tumbling him
out of the chariot, and numbing darkness
shrouded him, as the Kretans took his gear.
Skamándrios, hunter son of Stróphios,
fell before Meneláos' point—Skamándrios,
expert at hunting: Artemis herself
had taught him to bring down all kinds of game
bred in the forests on wild hills. But she
who fills the air with arrows helped him not
at all this time, nor did his own good shooting.
No, as he ran before the Akhaian's lance
Meneláos caught him with a lunging thrust
between the shoulder blades, drove through his ribs,
and down he fell, head first, his armor clanging.
Meanwhile Meríonês killed Phéreklos,
son of Harmónidês, a man who knew
all manner of building art and handicraft,
for Pallas Athêna loved him well. This man
had even built Aléxandros those ships,
vessels of evil, fatal to the Trojans
and now to him, who had not guessed heaven's will.
Running behind and overtaking him,
Meríonês hit his buttock on the right
and pierced his bladder, missing the pelvic bone.
He fell, moaning, upon his hands and knees
and death shrouded him. Then Mégês killed
Pedaíos, bastard son of Lord Antênor,
a son whom Lady Theanô had cherished
equally with her own, to please her husband.
Mégês Phyléïdês, the master spearman,
closing with him, hit his nape: the point
clove through his tongue's root and against his teeth.
Biting cold bronze he fell into the dust.
Eurýpylos Euaimónidês brought down
Hypsênor, son of noble Dolopíon,
priest of Skamánder in the old time, honored
by countryfolk as though he were a god.

As this man fled, Eurýpylos leapt after him
with drawn sword, on the run, and struck his shoulder,
cutting away one heavy arm: in blood
the arm dropped, and death surging on his eyes
took him, hard destiny.

                                            So toiled the Akhaians
in that rough charge. But as for Diomêdês,
you could not tell if he were with Akhaians
or Trojans, for he coursed along the plain
most like an April torrent fed by snow,
a river in flood that sweeps away his bank;
no piled-up dyke will hold him, no revetment
shielding the bloom of orchard land, this river
suddenly at crest when heaven pours down
the rain of Zeus; many a yeoman's field
of beautiful grain is ravaged: even so
before Diomêdês were the crowded ranks
of Trojans broken, many as they were,
and none could hold him.

                                            Now when Pándaros
looked over at him, saw him sweep the field,
he bent his bow of horn at Diomêdês
and shot him as he charged, hitting his cuirass
in the right shoulder joint. The winging arrow
stuck, undeflected, spattering blood on bronze.
Pándaros gave a great shout:

                                            "Close up, Trojans!
Come on, charioteers! The Akhaian champion
is hit, hit hard; I swear my arrowshot
will bring him down soon—if indeed it was
Apollo who cheered me on my way from Lykia!"

Triumphantly he shouted; but his arrow
failed to bring Diomêdês down. Retiring
upon his chariot and team, he stood
and said to Sthénelos, the son of Kapanéus:

"Quick, Sthénelos, old friend, jump down
and pull this jabbing arrow from my shoulder!"

Sthénelos vaulted down and, pressed against him,
drew the slim arrow shaft clear of his wound

with spurts of blood that stained his knitted shirt.
And now at last Diomêdês of the warcry
prayed aloud:

                              "Oh hear me, daughter of Zeus
who bears the stormcloud, tireless one, Athêna!
If ever you stood near my father and helped him
in a hot fight, befriend me now as well.
Let me destroy that man, bring me in range of him,
who hit me by surprise, and glories in it.
He swears I shall be blind to sunlight soon."

So ran his prayer, and Pallas Athêna heard him.
Nimbleness in the legs, sure feet and hands
she gave him, standing near him, saying swiftly:

"Courage, Diomêdês. Press the fight
against the Trojans. Fury like your father's
I've put into your heart: his never quailed—
Tydeus, master shieldsman, master of horses.
I've cleared away the mist that blurred your eyes
a moment ago, so you may see before you
clearly, and distinguish god from man.
If any god should put you to the test
upon this field, be sure you are not the man
to dare immortal gods in combat—none,
that is, except the goddess Aphrodítê.
If ever she should join the fight, then wound her
with your keen bronze."

                              At this, grey-eyed Athêna
left him, and once more he made his way
into the line. If he had burned before
to fight with Trojans, now indeed blood-lust
three times as furious took hold of him.
Think of a lion that some shepherd wounds
but lightly as he leaps into a fold:
the man who roused his might cannot repel him
but dives into his shelter, while his flocks,
abandoned, are all driven wild; in heaps
huddled they are to lie, torn carcasses,
before the escaping lion at one bound

surmounts the palisade. So lion-like,
Diomêdês plunged on Trojans.

                                        First he killed

Astýnoös and a captain, Hypeirôn,
one with a spear-thrust in the upper chest,
the other by a stroke of his great sword
chopping his collarbone at the round joint
to sever his whole shoulder from his body.
These he left, and met Polýeidos
and Abas, Eurydámas' sons: the father
being an old interpreter of dreams.
He read no dreams for these two, going to war;
Diomêdês killed and stripped them.

                                        Next he met

Xánthos and Thoôn, two dear sons of Phainops,
a man worn out with misery and years
who fathered no more heirs—but these
Diomêdês overpowered; he took their lives,
leaving their father empty pain and mourning—
never to welcome them alive at home
after the war, and all their heritage
broken up among others.

                                        Next two sons

of Dardan Priam Diomêdês killed
in one war-car: Ekhémmôn and Khromíos.
Just as a lion leaps to crunch the neck
of ox or heifer, grazing near a thicket,
Diomêdês, leaping, dragged them down
convulsed out of their car, and took their armor,
sending their horses to the rear.

                                        Aineías,

observing all the havoc this man made
amid the Trojan ranks, moved up the line
of battle and along the clash of spears,
in search of Pándaros. Coming upon him,
he halted by Lykáôn's noble son
and said to him:

                        "Pándaros, where is your bow?
Where are your fledged arrows? And your fame?
No man of Troy contends with you in archery,

no man in Lykia would claim to beat you.
Here, lift your hands to Zeus, let fly at that one,
whoever he is: an overwhelming fighter,
he has already hurt the Trojans badly,
cutting down many of our best.

Let fly!

Unless it be some god who bears a grudge
against us, raging over a sacrifice.
The anger of a god is cruel anger."

To this Lykáôn's noble son replied:

"Aineías, master of battle-craft for Trojans
under arms, that spearman, as I see him,
looks very like Diomêdês: shield and helm
with his high plume-socket I recognize,
having his team in view. I cannot swear
he is no god. If it be Diomêdês,
never could he have made this crazy charge
without some god behind him. No, some god
is near him wrapped in cloud, and bent aside
that arrowhead that reached him—for I shot him
once before, I hit him, too, and squarely
on the right shoulder through his cuirass joint
over the armpit. Down to the ditch of Death
I thought I had dispatched him. Not at all:
my arrow could not bring him down.
Some angry god is in this.

Teams and chariots

I lack, or I could ride. In Father's manor
there are eleven war-cars newly built
and outfitted, with housings on them all,
and every chariot has a team nearby
that stands there champing barley meal.

God knows

how many things Lykáôn had to tell me
in the great hall before I left! He said
that I should drive a team, a chariot,
and so command the Trojan men-at-arms
in combat. How much better if I had!
But I refused: sparing the teams, I thought,

from short rations of fodder under siege.
And so I left them, made my way on foot
to Ilion, relying on my bow—
a bow destined to fail me. In this battle
I have had shots at two great fighters: one
Diomêdês and the other Meneláos;
I drew blood from both, but only roused them.
Destiny was against me on that day
I took my bow of horn down from its peg
and led my men to your sweet town of Troy,
for Hektor's sake.

                                        If ever I return,

if ever I lay eyes on land and wife
and my great hall, may someone cut my head off
unless I break this bow between my hands
and throw it into a blazing fire! It goes
everywhere with me, useless."

                                        Aineías said:

"Better not talk so. Till we act, he wins.
We two can drive my car against this man
and take him on with sword and spear.
Mount my chariot, and you'll see how fast
these horses of the line of Trôs can run:
they know our plain and how to wheel upon it
this way and that way in pursuit or flight
like wind veering. These will save us, take us
Troyward if again Zeus should confer
the upper hand and glory on Diomêdês.
Come take the whip and reins; and let me mount
to fight him from the car—or you yourself
may face the man, and let me mind the horses."

Lykáôn's noble son replied:

                                        "Aineías,

manage the reins yourself, and guide the team,
they'll draw the rounded war-car with more ease
knowing the driver, if we must give ground
to Diomêdês this time. God forbid
they panic, missing your voice,

and balk at pulling out when Diomêdês
makes his leap upon us!
God forbid he kill the two of us
and make a prize of these! No, you yourself
handle your car and team. I'll take him on
with my good spear when he attacks."

So both agreed and rode the painted car
toward Diomêdês.

                                        Sthénelos, the son

of Kapanéus, caught sight of them
and turned at once to Diomêdês, saying:

"Friend of my heart and soul,
I see two spearmen who would have your blood,
a pair of big men, bearing down on you.
One's Pándaros the bowman; by repute
his father was Lykáôn; and the other,
Aineías, claims Ankhísês as his father;
his mother is Aphrodítê.

                                        Up with you.

We'll move back somewhat in our chariot.
Now is no moment for another charge,
or you may lose your life."

                                        But Diomêdês

glanced at him scowling.

                                        "No more talk," he said,

"of turning tail. You cannot make me see it.
For me there's no style in a dodging fight
or making oneself small. I am fresh as ever.
Retire in the car? I dread it. No,
I'll meet them head on as before. Athêna
will never let me tremble. These two men
are not to get away behind their horses
after we hit them, even if one survives
to try it.

                                        Let me tell you this thing, too:

remember it. If in her craft Athêna
confers on me the honor of killing both,

you halt our horses hard upon the spot,
taking a full hitch round the chariot rail,
and jump Aineías' horses: mind you drive them
among Akhaians, out of the Trojans' range.
They are that breed that Zeus who views the wide world
gave to Trôs in fee for Ganymêdês,
under the Dawn and under Hêlios
the finest horses in the world.
Ankhísês, marshal of Troy, stole their great stock
without Laomédôn's knowledge, putting fillies
to breed with them, and from these half a dozen
foals were bred for Ankhísês at his manor,
four to be reared in his own stalls; but two
he gave Aineías as a battle team.
If we can take that team we win great honor."

This was the way these two conferred. Meanwhile
the other pair behind their team full tilt
had come in range, and Pándaros called out:

"O son of Tydeus, undaunted heart
and mind of war, my arrow
could not bring you down—a wasted shot.
This time I'll try a spear. God, let me hit you!"

Rifling it, he let the long spear fly
and struck him on the shield: his point in flight
broke through to reach the cuirass—
and Pándaros gave a great shout:

                                        "Now you're hit
square in the midriff. Can you keep your feet?
Not long, I think. This time the glory's mine!"

Unshaken by the blow, Diomêdês answered:

"A miss, no hit. I doubt you two will quit, though,
being what you are, till one of you is down
and glutting leather-covered Arês, god
of battle, with your blood!"

                                        At this he made his cast,
his weapon being guided by Athêna

to cleave Pándaros' nose beside the eye
and shatter his white teeth: his tongue
the brazen spearhead severed, tip from root,
then plowing on came out beneath his chin.
He toppled from the car, and all his armor
clanged on him, shimmering. The horses
quivered and shied away; but life and spirit
ebbed from the broken man, and he lay still.

With shield and spear Aineías, now on foot,
in dread to see the Akhaians drag the dead man,
came and bestrode him, like a lion at bay.
Keeping the spear and rounded shield before him,
thrusting to kill whoever came in range,
he raised a terrible cry. But Diomêdês
bent for a stone and picked it up—a boulder
no two men now alive could lift, though he
could heft it easily. This mass he hurled
and struck Aineías on the hip, just where
the hipbone shifts in what they call the bone-cup,
crushing this joint with two adjacent tendons
under the skin ripped off by the rough stone.
Now the great Trojan, fallen on his knees,
put all his weight on one strong hand
and leaned against the earth: night veiled his eyes.

Aineías would have perished there
but for the quickness of the daughter of Zeus,
his mother, Aphrodítê, she who bore him
to shepherding Ankhísês, and who now
pillowed him softly in her two white arms
and held a corner of her glimmering robe
to screen him, so that no Danáän spear
should stab and finish him. Then from the battle
heavenward she lifted her dear son.

Meanwhile Sthénelos, the son of Kapanéus,
remembered the command of Diomêdês.
He brought his horses to a halt, made fast
his taut reins to the chariot rail, and flung himself
upon Aineías' long-maned beautiful team.

Away, out of the Trojans' reach, he drove them
and gave them into Dèipýlos' hands—
for he esteemed this friend more than his peers
for presence of mind—to lead them to the ships.
Remounting, shaking out his polished reins,
he turned his sure-footed horses and drove hard
in Diomêdês' track—as Diomêdês
moved ahead to attack the Kyprian goddess.
He knew her to be weak, not one of those
divine mistresses of the wars of men—
Athêna, for example, or Enýô,
raider of cities—therefore he dared assail her
through a great ruck of battle. When in range
he leaped high after her and with his point
wounded her trailing hand: the brazen lancehead
slashed her heavenly robe, worked by the Graces,
and cut the tender skin upon her palm.
Now from the goddess that immortal fluid,
ichor, flowed—the blood of blissful gods
who eat no food, who drink no tawny wine,
and thereby being bloodless have the name
of being immortal.

                                    Aphrodítê screamed

and flung her child away; but Lord Apollo
caught him in his arms and bore him off
in a dark cloud, so no Danáän spear
should stab and finish him.

                                    Now Diomêdês,

lord of the battlecry, with mighty lungs
cried out to her:

                                    "Oh give up war, give up
war and killing, goddess! Is it not enough
to break soft women down with coaxing lust?
Go haunting battle, will you? I can see you
shudder after this at the name of war!"

So taunted, faint with pain, she quit the field,
being by wind-running Iris helped away
in anguish, sobbing, while her lovely skin
ran darkness. Then she came on Arês resting

far to the left, his spearshaft leaning on
a bank of mist; there stood his battle team,
and falling on one knee she begged her brother
for those gold-bangled horses.

                                              "Brother dear,
please let me take your team, do let me have them,
to go up to the gods' home on Olympos.
I am too dreadfully hurt: a mortal speared me.
Diomêdês it was; he'd even fight with Zeus!"

Then Arês gave her his gold-bangled team,
and into the car she stepped, throbbing with pain,
while Iris at her side gathered the reins
and flicked the horses into eager flight.
They came, almost at once, to steep Olympos
where the gods dwell. Iris who runs on wind
halted and unyoked the team and tossed them
heavenly fodder.

                                              In Diônê's lap
Aphrodítê sank down, and her dear mother
held and caressed her, whispering in her ear:

"Who did this to you, darling child? In heaven
who could have been so rude and wild,
as though you had committed open wrong?"

And Aphrodítê, lover of smiling eyes,
answered:

                              "Diomêdês had the insolence
to wound me, when I tried to save
my dear son from the war: Aineías, dearest
of all the sons of men to me.
It seems this horrid combat is no longer
Trojans against Akhaians—now, the Argives
are making war upon the gods themselves!"

Then said Diônê, loveliest of goddesses:

"There, child, patience, even in such distress.
Many of us who live upon Olympos
have taken hurt from men, and hurt each other.

Arês bore it, when Otos and Ephiáltês,
Alôeus' giant sons, put him in chains:
he lay for thirteen moons in a brazen jar,
until that glutton of war might well have perished
had Eëríboia, their stepmother,
not told Hermês: Hermês broke him free
more dead than alive, worn out by the iron chain.
Then think how Hêra suffered, too,
when Amphitrýôn's mighty son let fly
his triple-barbed arrow into her right breast:
unappeasable pain came over her.
And Aïdês, great lord of undergloom,
bore a shot from the same strong son of Zeus
at Pylos, amid the dead. That arrow stroke
delivered him to anguish. Then Aïdês,
pierced and stricken, went to high Olympos,
the arrow grinding still in his great shoulder,
and there Paiêôn with a poultice healed him
who was not born for death. What recklessness
in Hêraklês, champion though he was at labors,
to shrug at impious acts and bend his bow
for the discomfiture of Olympians!
But this man, he that wounded you, Athêna
put him up to it—idiot, not to know
his days are numbered who would fight the gods!
His children will not sing around his knees
'Papà! Papà!' on *his* return from war.
So let Diomêdês pause, for all his prowess,
let him remember he may meet his match,
and Aigiáleia, Adrêstos' daughter,
starting up from sleep some night in tears
may waken all the house, missing her husband,
noblest of Akhaians: Diomêdês."

Diônê soothed her, wiped away the ichor
with both her hands from Aphrodítê's palm—
already throbbing less, already healing.
But Hêra and Athêna, looking on,
had waspish things to say, to irritate Zeus.
It was the grey-eyed goddess who began:

"Oh, Father, will you be annoyed if I
make a small comment? Aphrodítê
likes to beguile the women of Akhaia
to elope with Trojans, whom she so adores:
now, fondling some Akhaian girl, I fear,
she scratched her slim white hand on a golden pin."

He smiled at this, the father of gods and men,
and said to the pale-gold goddess Aphrodítê:

"Warfare is not for you, child. Lend yourself
to sighs of longing and the marriage bed.
Let Arês and Athêna deal with war."

These were the colloquies in heaven.

                                                    Meanwhile,
Diomêdês, lord of the warcry, charged Aineías
though he knew well Apollo had sustained him.
He feared not even the great god himself,
but meant to kill Aineías and take his armor.
Three times he made his killing thrust; three times
the Lord Apollo buffeted his shield,
throwing him back. Beside himself, again
he sprang, a fourth time, but the Archer God
raised a bloodcurdling cry:

                                        "Look out! Give way!
Enough of this, this craze to vie with gods!
Our kind, immortals of the open sky,
will never be like yours, earth-faring men."

Diomêdês backed away a step or two
before Apollo's terrible anger, and
the god caught up Aineías and set him down
on Troy's high citadel of Pergamos
where his own shrine was built.
There in that noble room Lêto and Artemis
tended the man and honored him. Meanwhile
Apollo made a figure of illusion,
Aineías' double, armed as he was armed,
and round this phantom Trojans and Akhaians
cut one another's chest-protecting oxhide

shields with hanging shield-flaps. Then Apollo
said to the wargod:

                                    "Bane of all mankind,
crusted with blood, breacher of walls, why not
go in and take this man out of the combat,
this Diomêdês, who would try a cast
with Zeus himself? First he attempted Kypris
and cut her lovely hand, then like a fury
came at me."

                                       Apollo turned away

to rest in Pergamos, upon the height,
while baleful Arês through the ranks of Trojans
made his way to stiffen them. He seemed
Akámas, a good runner, chief of Thracians,
appealing to the sons of Priam:

                                             "Princes,

heirs of Priam in the line of Zeus,
how long will the Akhaians have your leave
to kill your people? Up to the city gates?
Lying in dust out there is one of us
whom we admire as we do Lord Hektor—
Aineías, noble Ankhísês' son.
Come, we can save him from the trampling rout."

He made them burn at this, and then Sarpêdon
in his turn growled at Hektor:

                                           "What of you,

Hektor, where has your courage gone?
Defend the city, will you, without troops,
without allies, you and your next of kin,
brothers-in-law and brothers? In the combat
I neither see nor hear of them—like dogs
making themselves scarce around a lion.
We do the fighting, we who are allies here
as I am—and a long journey I made of it
from Lykia and Xánthos' eddying river
far away, where I left wife and child,
with property a needy man would dream of.

Here all the same I am, sending my Lykians
forward, and going in to fight myself,
though I have no least stake in Troy:
no booty for Akhaians to carry off—
while you stand like a sheep. You have not even
called on the rest to hold their ground, to fight
for their own wives! Will you be netted, caught
like helpless game your enemies can feast on?
They will be pillaging your city soon!
Here is your duty: night and day
press every captain of your foreign troops
to keep his place in battle, and fight off
the blame and bitterness of your defeat!"

This lashing had made Hektor hot with shame,
and down he vaulted from his chariot,
hefting two spears, to pace up through the army,
flank and center, calling on all to fight,
to join battle again. The Trojans rallied
and now stood off the Akhaians, while the Akhaians
kept formation too.

                                    See in the mind's eye
wind blowing chaff on ancient threshing floors
when men with fans toss up the trodden sheaves,
and yellow-haired Dêmêtêr, puff by puff,
divides the chaff and grain: how all day long
in bleaching sun strawpiles grow white: so white
grew those Akhaian figures in the dustcloud
churned to the brazen sky by horses' hooves
as chariots intermingled, as the drivers
turned and turned—carrying their hands high
and forward gallantly despite fatigue.

Now coming to the Trojans' aid in battle,
Arês veiled them everywhere in dusk,
obeying Apollo of the golden sword
by rousing Trojan courage: he had seen
Pallas Athêna, defender of Danáäns,
depart from the other side. Apollo then
out of his sanctum, hushed and hung with gold,
sent back the marshal of Trojan troops, Aineías,

with fighting spirit restored. He stood again
amid his peers, to their relief; they saw him
whole, without a scratch, and hot for war—
but no one there could pause to question him;
Apollo brought new toil upon them now,
with Arês, bane of men, and Strife insatiable.
Amid the Akhaians those two men named Aías,
joining Diomêdês and Odysseus,
made bastion for Danáäns. See these four,
all fearless of attack or Trojan power,
patient in battle—motionless as clouds
that Zeus may station on high mountaintops
in a calm heaven, while the north wind sleeps
and so do all the winds whose gusty blowing
rifts and dispels shade-bearing cloud. So these
Danáäns held their ground against the Trojans
and never stirred, while Agamémnon passed
amid the ranks haranguing troops:

                                             "Dear friends,
be men, choose valor and pride in one another
when shock of combat comes. More men of pride
are saved than lost, and men who run for it
get no reward of praise, no safety either."

Lightning-quick, he lunged with his own spear
and hit Aineías' friend, Deïkoôn,
Pérgasos' son, spear-fighter, a man
the Trojans honored as they did their princes,
knowing him prompt to join the battle line.
His shield hit hard by Agamémnon's thrust
could not withstand the spearhead, but the point
drove through his belt low down
and crumpled him, with clang of arms upon him.
Aineías now, for his part, killed two champions
of the Danáäns: Orsílokhos and Krêthôn,
sons of Dióklês, who owned estates
in Phêrê, being descended from that river
that runs broad through the Pylian land, Alpheíos.
Alpheíos fathered Lord Ortílokhos,
powerful over many men, and he

in his turn fathered gallant Díoklês,
whose sons were twins, Orsílokhos and Krêthôn,
skillful at every kind of fight.

                                      Still fresh

in manhood they embarked in the black ships
for the wild horse country of Ilion, to gain
vengeance for the Atreidai, Agamémnon
and Meneláos. Here Death hid them both.
Imagine two young lions, reared
by a mother lioness in undergrowth
of a deep mountain forest—twins who prey
on herds and flocks, despoiling farms, till one day
they too are torn to pieces, both at once,
by sharp spears in the hands of men. So these
went down before the weapons of Aineías,
falling like lofty pines before an ax.

Pitying the two men fallen, Meneláos
came up, formidable in glittering bronze,
with menacing spear—for Arês urged him on
to see him conquered at Aineías' hands.
But Nestor's watchful son, Antílokhos,
advanced to join him, anxious for his captain,
fearing his loss, and failure of their cause.
The two champions with weapons tilted up
had faced each other, when Antílokhos
moved in, shoulder to shoulder, with Meneláos;
and agile fighter though he was, Aineías
shunned the combat, measuring this pair.
On his retreat they pulled away the dead
unlucky twins, and passed them to the rear,
then turned again to battle.

                                 First they killed

a captain of Paphlagonians, Pylaimênês,
burley as Arês; Meneláos it was
who hit him with a spear-thrust, pierced him through
just at the collarbone. Antílokhos
knocked out his driver, Atýmnios' noble son
called Mydôn. As the man wheeled his horses
a boulder smashed his elbow; in the dust
his reins, inset with ivory, curled out,

as with drawn sword Antílokhos leapt on him
and gashed his forehead. Gasping, down he went,
head first, pitching from his ornate car,
into a sandbank—so his luck would have it—
to stay embedded till his trampling horses
rolled him farther in the dust. Antílokhos
lashed at them and consigned them to the rear.

Surveying these Akhaians through the ranks
Hektor charged with a sudden cry. Beside him
strong Trojan formations moved ahead,
impelled by Arês and by cold Enyô
who brings the shameless butchery of war.
Arês wielding a gigantic spear
by turns led Hektor on or backed him up,
and as he watched this figure, Diomêdês
felt like a traveler halted on a plain,
helpless to cross, before a stream in flood
that roars and spumes down to the sea. That traveler
would look once and recoil: so Diomêdês
backed away and said to his company:

> "Friends,
all we can do is marvel at Prince Hektor.
What a spearman he is, and what a fighter!
One of the gods goes with him everywhere
to shield him from a mortal wound. Look! there,
beside him—Arês in disguise!

> Give ground
slowly; keep your faces toward the Trojans.
No good pitting ourselves against the gods."

The Trojans reached them as he spoke, and Hektor
swept into death a pair of men who knew
the joy of war—Menésthês and Ankhíalos—
both in a single car. Now, these two fallen
were pitied by great Aías Telamônios,
who moved in close, his glittering spear at play,
and overcame Selágos' son, Amphíon,
a landowner in Paísos. Destiny
had sent this man to take a stand with Priam

and Priam's sons in war. Now Aías' thrust
went through his belt, and in his lower belly
the spearpoint crunched and stuck. He fell
hard in the dust. Then Aías
came up fast to strip him, while the Trojans
cast their spears in a bright hail: his shield
took one shock after another. With one heel
braced on the corpse he pulled away his point,
but being beset by spears he could not slip
swordbelt or buckler from the dead man's shoulders.
And now, too, he began to be afraid
of Trojans coming up around the body,
brave men and many, pressing him with spears.
Big as he was, and powerful and bold,
they pushed him back, and he retired, shaken.

This way the toil of battle took its course
in that quarter. Elsewhere, all-powerful fate
moved Hêraklês' great son, Tlêpólemos,
to meet Sarpêdôn. As they neared each other,
son and grandson of cloud-massing Zeus,
Tlêpólemos began to jeer:

                                                    "Lykian,

war-counselor Sarpêdôn, why so coy
upon this field? You call yourself a fighter?
They lie who say you come of Zeus's line,
you are so far inferior to those
fathered by Zeus among the men of old.
Think what the power of Hêraklês was like,
my lion-hearted father! For Laomédôn's
chariot horses once he beached at Troy
with only six shiploads of men, a handful,
yet he sacked Ilion and left her ways
desolate. But your nerve is gone, your troops
are losing badly: it is no gain for Trojans
that you came here from Lykia, powerful
man that you are—and when you fall to me,
down through the gates of Death you go!"

                                                    Sarpêdôn

answered:

"Right enough, Tlêpólemos,
he did ruin Ilion: Laomédôn,
the greedy fool, gave him a vicious answer
after great labor well performed—refused
to make delivery of the promised horses
that Hêraklês had come for. As for you,
I promise a hard lot: a bloody death
you'll find here on this battleground,
when my spear knocks you out. You'll give up glory
to me and life to him who drives the horses
of undergloom, Aïdês."

                                    Then Tlêpólemos
raised his ashen spear, and from their hands
in unison long shafts took flight. Sarpêdôn's
hit his enemy squarely in the neck
with force enough to drive the point clear through;
unending night of death clouded his eyes.
Tlêpólemos' point, hitting the upper leg,
went jolting through between the two long bones,
but once again Sarpêdôn's father saved him.
Out of the mêlée men of his command
carried the captain in his agony, encumbered
by the long dragging spear. No one had time
to think of how the shaft might be withdrawn,
that he might use one leg at least, so hastily
they did their work, so pressed by care of battle.

Meanwhile Tlêpólemos was carried back
by the Akhaians on the other side.
Rugged Odysseus noted it with anger
and pain for him. What should he do, he thought,
track down Sarpêdôn, son of thundering Zeus,
or take the life of Lykians in throngs?
It was not given to Odysseus
to finish off Sarpêdôn, but Athêna
turned his fury upon the Lykians.
He killed Koiranos, Alastor, Khrômios,
Alkándros, Halios, Noêmon, Prýtanis,
and would have killed more Lykians, had not
great Hektor's piercing eye

under his shimmering helmet lighted on him.
Across the clashing line he came a-glitter
with burning bronze, a terror to Danáäns,
making Sarpêdôn's heart lift up to see him,
so that as Hektor passed he weakly said:

"I beg you not to leave me
lying here for Danáäns to despoil.
Defend me; afterward let me bleed away
my life within your city. Not for me
to see my home and country once again,
my dear wife in her joy, my little son."

Silent under his polished helmet, Hektor,
dazzling and impetuous, passed on
to drive the Argives back with general slaughter,
and those around Sarpêdôn
laid their commander in the royal shade
of Zeus's oak. One dear to him, Pelágôn,
worrying the spearhead, pulled it from his thigh,
at which he fainted. But his breath came back
when a cool north wind, a reprieve, blew round
and fanned him, wakened him from his black swoon.

Even though not yet routed to the ships
under attack from Arês and from Hektor,
the Argives could not gain but yielded everywhere,
knowing that Arês fought among the Trojans.
One by one, who were the fighting men
that Hektor slew, and Arês? Teuthras first;
Oréstès, breaker of horses; a spear-thrower,
Trêkhos, an Aitolian; Oinómaos;
Hélenos Oinópidês; Orésbios
whose plated breast-band glittered—in the past
he lived at Hylê on Lake Képhisos,
fond of his wealth, amid his countrymen,
Boiotians of the fertile plain.

                                        Now Hêra,
seeing these Argives perish in the fight,
appealed with indignation to Athêna:

"A dismal scene, this. O untiring goddess,
daughter of mighty Zeus who bears the stormcloud,

our word to Meneláos was a fraud—
that he should never sail for home
before he plundered Ilion! How likely,
if we allow this lunatic attack
by that sinister fool Arês? Come,
we'll put our minds on our own fighting power!"

Grey-eyed Athêna listened and agreed,
and Hêra, eldest daughter of old Krónos,
harnessed her team, all golden fringes. Hêbê
fitted upon her chariot, left and right,
the brazen wheels with eight shinbones, or spokes,
around the iron axle-tree: all gold
her felloes are, unworn, for warped upon them
are tires of bronze, a marvel; and the hubs
are silver, turning smoothly on each side.
The car itself is made of gold and silver
woven together, with a double rail,
and from the car a silver chariot pole
leans forward. Hêbê fitted to the tip
a handsome golden yoke, and added collars
all soft gold. And Hêra in her hunger
for strife of battle and the cries of war
backed her sure-footed horses in the traces.

As for Athêna, she cast off and dropped
her great brocaded robe, her handiwork,
in lapping folds across her father's doorsill,
taking his shirt, the shirt of Zeus, cloud-masser,
with breast armor, and gear of grievous war.
She hung the stormcloud shield with raveled tassels
ominous from her shoulder: all around
upon it in a garland Rout was figured,
Enmity, Force, and Chase that chills the blood,
concentered on the Gorgon's head, reptilian
seething Fear—a portent of the stormking.
Quadruple-crested, golden, double-ridged
her helmet was, enchased with men-at-arms
put by a hundred cities in the field.
She stepped aboard the glowing car of Hêra
and took the great haft of her spear in hand—

that heavy spear this child of Power can use
to break in wrath long battle lines of fighters.
Then at the crack of Hêra's whip
over the horses' backs, the gates of heaven
swung wide of themselves on rumbling hinges—
gates the Hours keep, for they have charge
of entry to wide heaven and Olympos,
by opening or closing massive cloud.
Passing through these and goading on their team,
the goddesses encountered Krónos' son,
who sat apart from all the gods
on the summit of Olympos. Reining in,
Hêra with arms as white as ivory
addressed the all-highest:

                                        "Father Zeus,
are you not thoroughly sick of Arês? All
those brutal acts of his? How great, how brave
the body of Akhaians he destroyed
so wantonly; he has made me grieve,
while Kypris and Apollo take their pleasure,
egging on that dunce who knows no decency.
Father, you cannot, can you, be annoyed
if I chastise and chase him from the field?"

Then Zeus who gathers cloud replied:

                                        "Go after him.
Athêna, Hope of Soldiers, is the one
to match with him: she has a wondrous way
of bringing him to grief."

                                        At this permission,
Hêra cracked her whip again. Her team
went racing between starry heaven and earth.
As much dim distance as a man perceives
from a high lookout over winedark sea,
these horses neighing in the upper air
can take at a bound.

                                        Upon the Trojan plain
where the two rivers run, Skamánder flowing
to confluence with Simóeis, Hêra halted

to let her horses graze. Around them both
she rained an emanation of dense cloud,
while for their pasturing Simóeis made
ambrosial grass grow soft.

                       The goddesses
gliding in a straight line like quivering doves
approached the battle to defend the Argives,
but once arrived where their best spearmen fought
at the flank of Diomêdês, giving ground
like lions or boars, like carnivores at bay,
no feeble victims—Hêra took her stand
with a loud cry. She had the look of Stentor,
whose brazen lungs could give a battle shout
as loud as fifty soldiers, trumpeting:

"Shame, shame, Argives: cowards! good on parade!
While Prince Akhilleus roamed the field the Trojans
never would show their faces in a sortie,
respecting his great spear too much—but now
they fight far from the city, near the ships!"

This shout put anger into them. Meanwhile
the grey-eyed goddess Athêna from the air
hastened to Diomêdês. By his car
she found him resting, trying to cool the wound
Pándaros' arrow gave him. Spent and drenched
with sweat beneath his broad shield strap, he felt
encumbered by his shield, being arm-weary,
and slipped the strap off, wiped his blood away.
The goddess put her hand upon the yoke
that joined his battle-team, and said:

                                    "Ah, yes,
a far cry from his father, Tydeus' son.
Tydeus was a small man, but a fighter.
Once I forbade him war or feats of arms
that time he went as messenger to Thebes
alone, detached from the Akhaian host,
amid Kadmeíans in their multitude.
Bidden to dine at ease in their great hall,
combative as he always was, he challenged
the young Kadmeíans—and he had no trouble

pinning them all, I took his part so well.
But you, now—here I stand with you, by heaven,
protect you, care for you, tell you to fight,
but you are either sluggish in the legs
from battle-weariness or hollowhearted
somehow with fear: you are not, after all,
the son of Tydeus Oineïdês."

Proud Diomêdês answered her:

                                                    "I know you,
goddess, daughter of Zeus who bears the stormcloud.
With all respect, I can explain, and will.
No fear is in me, and no weariness;
I simply bear in mind your own commands.
You did expressly say I should not face
the blissful gods in fight—that is, unless
Aphrodítê came in. One might feel free
to wound her, anyway. So you commanded,
and therefore I am giving ground myself
and ordering all the Argives to retire
shoulder to shoulder here, because I know
the master of battle over there is Arês."

The grey-eyed goddess answered:

                                                    "Diomêdês,
dear to my heart: no matter what I said,
you are excused from it; you must not shrink
from Arês or from any other god
while I am with you.

                                        Whip your team
toward Arês, hit him, hand to hand, defer
no longer to this maniacal god
by nature evil, two-faced everywhere.
Not one hour ago I heard him grunt
his word to Hêra and myself to fight
on the Argive side; now he forgets all that
and joins the Trojans."

                                        Even as she spoke,
she elbowed Sthénelos aside and threw him,

but gave him a quick hand-up from the ground,
while she herself, impetuous for war,
mounted with Diomêdês. At her step
the oaken axle groaned, having to bear
goddess and hero. Formidable Athêna
caught up the whip and reins and drove the horses
hard and straight at Arês.

                                              Brute that he was,
just at that point he had begun despoiling
a giant of a man, the Aitolians' best,
Períphas, brilliant scion of Okhêsios.
The bloodstained god had downed him. But Athêna,
making herself invisible to Arês,
put on the helm of the Lord of Undergloom.
Then Arês saw Diomêdês, whirled, and left
Períphas lying where he fell. Straight onward
for Diomêdês lunged the ruffian god.
When they arrived in range of one another,
Arês, breasting his adversary's horses,
rifled his spear over the yoke and reins
with murderous aim. Athêna, grey-eyed goddess,
with one hand caught and deflected it
and sent it bounding harmless from the car.
Now Diomêdês put his weight behind
his own bronze-headed spear. Pallas Athêna
rammed it at Arês' belted waist so hard
she put a gash in his fair flesh, and pulled
the spearhead out again. Then brazen Arês
howled to heaven, terrible to hear
as roaring from ten thousand men in battle
when long battalions clash. A pang of fear
ran through the hearts of Trojans and Akhaians,
deafened by insatiable Arês' roar.

Like a black vapor from a thunderhead
riding aloft on stormwind brewed by heat,
so brazen Arês looked to Diomêdês
as he rose heavenward amid the clouds.
High on Olympos, crag of the immortals,
he came to rest by the Lord Zeus. Aching,

mortified, he showed his bleeding wound
and querulously addressed him:

                                        "Father Zeus,
how do you take this insubordination?
What frightful things we bear from one another
doing good turns to men! And I must say
we all hold it against you. You conceived
a daughter with no prudence, a destroyer,
given to violence. We other gods
obey you, as submissive as you please,
while she goes unreproved; never a word,
a gesture of correction comes from you—
only begetter of the insolent child.
She is the one who urged Diomêdês on
to mad attempts on the immortals—first
he closed with Kypris, cut her palm, and now
he hurled himself against me like a fury.
It was my speed that got me off, or I
should still be there in pain among the dead,
the foul dead—or undone by further strokes
of cutting bronze."

                              But Zeus who masses cloud
regarded him with frowning brows and said:

"Do not come whining here, you two-faced brute,
most hateful to me of all the Olympians.
Combat and brawling are your element.
This beastly, incorrigible truculence
comes from your mother, Hêra, whom I keep
but barely in my power, say what I will.
You came to grief, I think, at her command.
Still, I will not have you suffer longer.
I fathered you, after all;
your mother bore you as a son to me.
If you had been conceived by any other
and born so insolent, then long ago
your place would have been far below the gods."

With this he told Paiêôn to attend him,
and sprinkling anodyne upon his wound

Paiêôn undertook to treat and heal him
who was not born for death.

                                              As wild fig sap

when dripped in liquid milk will curdle it
as quickly as you stir it in, so quickly
Paiêôn healed impetuous Arês' wound.
Then Hêbê bathed him, mantled him afresh,
and down he sat beside Lord Zeus,
glowing again in splendor.

And soon again to Zeus's home retired
Argive Hêra, Boiotian Athêna,
who made the bane of mankind quit the slaughter.

BOOK SIX

BOOK XIX

Interludes in Field and City

LINES I–I3

No gods, but only Trojans and Akhaians,
were left now in the great fight on the plain.
It swayed this way and that between the rivers,
with leveled spears moving on one another.

Aías Telamônios, Akhaian
bastion on defense, attacked and broke
a Trojan mass, showing his men the way,
by killing the best man of all the Thracians—
Akámas, Eüssôros' brawny son.
He hit him on the forecrest, and the spearhead
clove his frontal bone, lodged in his brain,
filling his eyes with darkness.

                                                    Diomêdês

then slew Áxylos Teuthránidês

from the walled town Arisbê. A rich man
and kindly, he befriended all who passed
his manor by the road. But none of these
could come between him and destruction now,
as the Akhaian killed him, killing with him
Kalêsios, his aide and charioteer—
leaving two dead men to be cloaked in earth.
Eurýalos killed Drêsos and Ophéltios,
then met the twins, Aisêpos and Pêdasos,
borne by Abarbareê, a sea-nymph,
to Boukolíôn, son of Laomédôn—
his first and secret child. When Boukolíôn
served as a shepherd he had loved the nymph,
and she conceived these twins. Eurýalos
now broke their valor, cut them down, and bent
to drag from their dead shoulders belted swords
and bucklers.

                              Polypoitês killed Astýalos,
Perkôsios Pidytês fell before
the spearhead of Odysseus, Aretáôn
fell before Teukros, and Antílokhos,
the son of Nestor, brought Ablêros low
with one spear-flash. Then Marshal Agamémnon
took the life of Élatos, whose home
had been in Pêdasos upon the height
near Satnióeis river. Lêïtos
killed Phýlakos as that man turned to run.
Eurýpylos dispatched Melánthios.

But great-lunged Meneláos took a prisoner,
Adrêstos. Veering wild
along the plain, this Trojan's team had caught
his hurtling car upon a tamarisk
and broken at the joint his chariot pole.
The animals then galloped on toward Troy
with all the rest who panicked; but the driver,
flung out of his car head over heels,
landed alongside face down in the dust—
and there with his long spear stood Meneláos.
Adrêstos threw his arms around his knees
and begged him:

"Son of Atreus, take me alive!
You will have all the ransom one could ask.
Plenty of precious things, gold, gold and silver
and hard-wrought iron, fill my father's house.
He would give anything, no end of ransom,
if he could only know I am alive
among the Akhaian ships."

                                        Adrêstos' plea

won his great captor to consent: he thought
of granting him safe conduct to the ships
by his own runner, when his brother
Agamémnon in grim haste came by
to bar his mercy and cried:

                                        "What now, soft heart?
Were you so kindly served at home by Trojans?
Why give a curse for them? Oh, Meneláos,
once in our hands not one should squirm away
from death's hard fall! No fugitive, not even
the manchild carried in a woman's belly!
Let them all without distinction perish,
every last man of Ilion,
without a tear, without a trace!"

                                        Implacably

thus he recalled his brother's mind to duty,
and Meneláos pushed away Adrêstos.
Then Agamémnon speared him in the flank,
and he fell backward. Stamping with one heel
hard on his chest, he disengaged the spear.
Now Nestor in a loud voice called to the Argives:

"Friends, Danáäns, fighters, companions of Arês,
no one should linger over booty now,
piling up all he can carry to the ships.
Now is the time to kill them! Later on
strip them at leisure when they lie here dead!"

Shouting, he urged them on. And once again
the Trojans, overmastered by Akhaians
and cowed, would have re-entered Ilion—

but Priam's eldest, Hélenos, an augur
better than any, halted beside Aineías
and Hektor, saying:

                              "You two bear the brunt
of Lykian and Trojan travail, always,
in every enterprise, war-plans or battle,
first among us all.

                              Take your stand here.
Here make our troops hold fast, before the gates.
Rally them everywhere, or back again
they go pell-mell into the arms of women—
a great day for our enemies.

                                        Put heart

into all our men, into every company,
and we can hold this line against Danáäns,
dead tired as we are. We have no choice.
But you go up into the city, Hektor;
speak to our mother; tell her to call together
women in age like hers, unlock the shrine
of grey-eyed Athêna on our citadel,
and choose that robe most lovely and luxurious,
most to her liking in the women's hall,
to place upon Athêna's knees.
Then heifers, twelve, are to be promised her,
unscarred and tender, if she will relent
in pity for our men, our wives and children,
and keep Diomêdès out of holy Troy.
He is so savage in pursuit and combat
I call him most formidable of Akhaians now.
We never were so afraid of Prince Akhilleus,
and he, they say, came of a goddess. No,
this fellow fights like one possessed: no man
can equal him in fury."

                                        Hektor agreed

and did his brother's bidding, first and last.
He vaulted quickly from his chariot,
waving his whetted spears high overhead,
as up and down he went, arousing war.
Then all those in retreat turned in their tracks

and stood against the Akhaians, who recoiled
before that stand and killed no more. It seemed
some one of the immortals out of heaven
had come down to put spirit in the Trojans,
they wheeled about so suddenly. And Hektor
in a great voice called out:

"Soldierly Trojans, allies famed abroad,
be men, remember courage, and defend yourselves,
while I go up to Ilion
to make our wives and elders pray the gods
with dedication of hekatombs."

                                                    Then Hektor

turned away, under his shimmering helm,
his long shield slung behind him; nape and ankle
both were brushed by the darkened oxhide rim.

Meanwhile, driving into an open space
between the armies, Hippólokhos' son, Glaukos,
and Diomêdês advanced upon each other,
hot for combat. When the range was short,
Diomêdês, face to face with him, spoke up:

"Young gallant stranger, who are you?
I have not noticed you before in battle—
never before, in the test that brings men honor—
but here you come now, far in front of everyone,
with heart enough to risk my beam of spear.
A sorrowing old age they have whose children
face me in war! If you are a god from heaven,
I would not fight with any out of heaven.
No long life remained—far from it—for
Lykourgos, Dryas' rugged son,
when he in his day strove with gods—that time
he chased the maenads on the sacred ridge
of manic Dionysos, on Mount Nysa.
Belabored by the ox-goad of Lykourgos,
killer that he was, they all flung down
their ivy-staves, while terrified Dionysos
plunged under a sea-surge. In her arms
Thetis received him, shaking from head to foot,

after that yelling man's pursuit.
And now the gods whose life is ease
turned on Lykourgos; Zeus put out his eyes;
his days were numbered, hated by them all.
I would not fight, not I, with gods in bliss,
but you, if you are man and mortal, one
who feeds on harvest of the grainland, take
one step nearer! and before you know it
you will come up against the edge of death."

Hippólokhos' distinguished son replied:

"Why ask my birth, Diomêdês? Very like leaves
upon this earth are the generations of men—
old leaves, cast on the ground by wind, young leaves
the greening forest bears when spring comes in.
So mortals pass; one generation flowers
even as another dies away.

                                                        My lineage?

If you are really bent on knowing all—
and many others know my story—listen.
Ephýra is a city on the gulf
of Argos: in Ephýra Sísyphos
Aiólidês, the craftiest of men,
lived once upon a time and fathered Glaukos,
father in turn of Prince Bellérophontês,
one to whom the gods had given beauty
with charm and bravery. But there came a day
when Proitos wished him ill—and Zeus had put him
under the power of Proitos. That strong king
now drove Bellérophontês out of Argos:
this because Ánteia, the queen,
lusted to couple with him secretly,
but he was honorable, she could not lure him,
and in the king's ear hissed a lie:

                                                        'Oh, Proitos,
I wish that you may die unless you kill
Bellérophontês: he desired to take me
in lust against my will.'

                                                        Rage filled the king
over her slander, but being scrupulous

he shrank from killing him. So into Lykia
he sent him, charged to bear a deadly cipher,
magical marks Proitos engraved and hid
in folded tablets. He commanded him
to show these to his father-in-law,
thinking in this way he should meet his end.
Guided by gods he sailed, and came to Lykia,
high country, crossed by Xánthos' running stream;
and Lykia's lord received him well.
Nine days he honored him, nine revels led
with consecrated beasts. When Dawn with rosy
fingers eastward made the tenth day bright,
he questioned him, and asked at length to see
what sign he brought him from his son-in-law.
When he had read the deadly cipher, changing,
he gave his first command: his guest should fight
and quell a foaming monster, the Khimaira,
of ghastly and inhuman origin,
her forepart lionish, her tail a snake's,
a she-goat in between. This thing exhaled
in jets a rolling fire.

                                        Well, he killed her,
by taking heed of omens from the gods.
His second test was battle with Solýmoi,
formidable aborigines. He thought
this fight the worst he ever had with men.
A third mission was to slaughter Amazons,
women virile in war. On his return,
the king devised yet one more trap for him,
laying an ambush, with picked men of Lykia.
But not a single one went home again:
Bellérophontês killed them all.

                                              His eyes
opened at last to the young man's power, godly
from godly lineage, the king detained him,
offered him his daughter, gave him, too,
a moiety of royal privileges,
and Lykians for their part set aside
their finest land for him, vineyard and plowland,
fertile for wheatfields. The king's daughter bore
three children to Bellérophontês: Ísandros,

Hippólokhos, and Laodámeia.
Zeus the Profound lay with Laodámeia,
who bore Sarpêdôn, one of our great soldiers.
But now one day Bellérophontês too
incurred the gods' wrath—and alone he moped
on Alêïon plain, eating his heart out,
shunning the beaten track of men. His son
Îsandros in a skirmish with Solýmoi
met his death at insatiable Arês' hands,
and angry Artemis killed Laodámeia.
Hippólokhos it was who fathered me,
I am proud to say. He sent me here to Troy
commanding me to act always with valor,
always to be most noble, never to shame
the line of my progenitors, great men
first in Ephýra, then in Lykia.
That is the blood and birth I claim."

                                        At this,

joy came to Diomêdês, loud in battle.
With one thrust in the field where herds had cropped
he fixed his long spear like a pole, and smiled
at the young captain, saying gently:

                                        "Why,

you are my friend! My grandfather, Oineus,
made friends of us long years ago. He welcomed
Prince Bellérophontês in his hall,
his guest for twenty days. They gave each other
beautiful tokens of amity: Grandfather's
offering was a loin-guard sewn in purple,
Bellérophontês gave a cup of gold
two-handled; it is in my house; I left it there,
coming away to Troy. I cannot remember
Tydeus, my father—I was still too young
when he departed, when the Akhaian army
came to grief at Thebes.

                        I am your friend,

sworn friend, in central Argos. You are mine
in Lykia, whenever I may come.
So let us keep away from one another's

weapons in the spear-fights of this war.
Trojans a-plenty will be left for me,
and allies, as god puts them in my path;
many Akhaians will be left for you
to bring down if you can.

                              Each take the other's
battle-gear; let those around us know
we have this bond of friendship from our fathers."

Both men jumped down then to confirm the pact,
taking each other's hands. But Zeus
had stolen Glaukos' wits away—
the young man gave up golden gear for bronze,
took nine bulls' worth for armor worth a hundred!

Now, when Hektor reached the Skaian Gates
daughters and wives of Trojans rushed to greet him
with questions about friends, sons, husbands, brothers.
"Pray to the gods!" he said to each in turn,
as grief awaited many. He walked on
and into Priam's palace, fair and still,
made all of ashlar, with bright colonnades.
Inside were fifty rooms of polished stone
one by another, where the sons of Priam
slept beside their wives; apart from these
across an inner court were twelve rooms more
all in one line, of polished stone, where slept
the sons-in-law of Priam and their wives.
Approaching these, he met his gentle mother
going in with Laódikê, most beautiful
of all her daughters. Both hands clasping his,
she looked at him and said:

                              "Why have you come
from battle, child? Those fiends, the Akhaians, fighting
around the town, have worn you out; you come
to climb our Rock and lift your palms to Zeus!
Wait, and I'll serve you honeyed wine.
First you may offer up a drop to Zeus,
to the immortal gods, then slake your thirst.

Wine will restore a man when he is weary
as you are, fighting to defend your own."

Hektor answered her, his helmet flashing:

"No, my dear mother, ladle me no wine;
You'd make my nerve go slack: I'd lose my edge.
May I tip wine to Zeus with hands unwashed?
I fear to—a bespattered man, and bloody,
may not address the lord of gloomy cloud.
No, it is you I wish would bring together
our older women, with offerings, and go visit
the temple of Athêna, Hope of Soldiers.
Pick out a robe, most lovely and luxurious,
most to your liking in the women's hall;
place it upon Athêna's knees; assure her
a sacrifice of heifers, twelve young ones
ungoaded ever in their lives, if in her mercy
relenting toward our town, our wives and children,
she keeps Diomêdês out of holy Troy.
He is a wild beast now in combat and pursuit.
Make your way to her shrine, visit Athêna,
Hope of Soldiers.

                        As for me, I go
for Paris, to arouse him, if he listens.
If only earth would swallow him here and now!
What an affliction the Olympian
brought up for us in him—a curse for Priam
and Priam's children! Could I see that man
dwindle into Death's night, I'd feel my soul
relieved of its distress!"

So Hektor spoke, and she walked slowly on
into the mégaron. She called her maids,
who then assembled women from the city.
But Hékabê went down to the low chamber
fragrant with cedar, where her robes were kept,
embroidered work by women of Sidonia
Aléxandros had brought, that time he sailed
and ravished Helen, princess, pearl of kings.
Hékabê lifted out her loveliest robe,

most ample, most luxurious in brocade,
and glittering like starlight under all.
This offering she carried to Athêna
with a long line of women in her train.
On the Akrópolis, Athêna's shrine
was opened for them by Theanô, stately
daughter of Kisseus, wife to Antênor,
and chosen priestess of Athêna. Now
all crying loud stretched out their arms in prayer,
while Theanô with grace took up the robe
to place it on fair-haired Athêna's knees.
She made petition then to Zeus's daughter:

"Lady,

excellent goddess, towering friend of Troy,
smash Diomêdês' lance-haft! Throw him hard
below the Skaian Gates, before our eyes!
Upon this altar we'll make offering
of twelve young heifers never scarred!
Only show mercy to our town,
mercy to Trojan men, their wives and children."

These were Theanô's prayers, her vain prayers.
Pallas Athêna turned away her head.

During the supplication at the shrine,
Hektor approached the beautiful house Aléxandros
himself had made, with men who in that time
were master-builders in the land of Troy.
Bedchamber, hall, and court, in the upper town,
they built for him near Priam's hall and Hektor's.
Now Hektor dear to Zeus went in, his hand
gripping a spear eleven forearms long,
whose bronze head shone before him in the air
as shone, around the neck, a golden ring.
He found his brother in the bedchamber
handling a magnificent cuirass and shield
and pulling at his bent-horn bow, while Helen
among her household women sat nearby,
directing needlecraft and splendid weaving.
At sight of him, to shame him, Hektor said:

"Unquiet soul, why be aggrieved in private?
Our troops are dying out there where they fight
around our city, under our high walls.
The hue and cry of war, because of you,
comes in like surf upon this town.
You'd be at odds with any other man
you might see quitting your accursèd war.
Up; into action, before torches thrown
make the town flare!"

                           And shining like a god

Aléxandros replied:

                                 "Ah, Hektor,

this call to order is no more than just.
So let me tell you something: hear me out.
No pettishness, resentment toward the Trojans,
kept me in this bedchamber so long,
but rather my desire, on being routed,
to taste grief to the full.

                         In her sweet way

my lady rouses me to fight again—
and I myself consider it better so.
Victory falls to one man, then another.
Wait, while I put on the wargod's gear,
or else go back; I'll follow, sure to find you."

For answer, Hektor in his shining helm
said not a word, but in low tones
enticing Helen murmured:

                                "Brother dear—

dear to a whore, a nightmare of a woman!
That day my mother gave me to the world
I wish a hurricane blast had torn me away
to wild mountains, or into tumbling sea
to be washed under by a breaking wave,
before these evil days could come!—or, granted
terrible years were in the gods' design,
I wish I had had a good man for a lover
who knew the sharp tongues and just rage of men.
This one—his heart's unsound, and always will be,

and he will win what he deserves. Come here
and rest upon this couch with me, dear brother.
You are the one afflicted most
by harlotry in me and by his madness,
our portion, all of misery, given by Zeus
that we may live in song for men to come."

Great Hektor shook his head, his helmet flashing,
and said:

                        "No, Helen, offer me no rest;
I know you are fond of me. I cannot rest.
Time presses, and I grow impatient now
to lend a hand to Trojans in the field
who feel a gap when I am gone. Your part
can be to urge him—let him feel the urgency
to join me in the city. He has time:
I must go home to visit my own people,
my own dear wife and my small son. Who knows
if I shall be reprieved again to see them,
or beaten down under Akhaian blows
as the immortals will."

                                He turned away
and quickly entered his own hall, but found
Princess Andrómakhê was not at home.
With one nursemaid and her small child, she stood
upon the tower of Ilion, in tears,
bemoaning what she saw.

                            Now Hektor halted
upon his threshold, calling to the maids:

"Tell me at once, and clearly, please,
my lady Andrómakhê, where has she gone?
To see my sisters, or my brothers' wives?
Or to Athêna's temple? Ladies of Troy
are there to make petition to the goddess."

The busy mistress of the larder answered:

"Hektor, to put it clearly as you ask,
she did not go to see your sisters, nor

your brothers' wives, nor to Athêna's shrine
where others are petitioning the goddess.
Up to the great square tower of Ilion
she took her way, because she heard our men
were spent in battle by Akhaian power.
In haste, like a madwoman, to the wall
she went, and Nurse went too, carrying the child."

At this word Hektor whirled and left his hall,
taking the same path he had come by,
along byways, walled lanes, all through the town
until he reached the Skaian Gates, whereby
before long he would issue on the field.
There his warmhearted lady
came to meet him, running: Andrómakhê,
whose father, Eëtíôn, once had ruled
the land under Mount Plakos, dark with forest,
at Thêbê under Plakos—lord and king
of the Kilikians. Hektor was her lord now,
head to foot in bronze; and now she joined him.
Behind her came her maid, who held the child
against her breast, a rosy baby still,
Hektoridês, the world's delight, as fresh
as a pure shining star. Skamándrios
his father named him; other men would say
Astýanax, "Lord of the Lower Town,"
as Hektor singlehanded guarded Troy.
How brilliantly the warrior smiled, in silence,
his eyes upon the child! Andrómakhê
rested against him, shook away a tear,
and pressed his hand in both her own, to say:

"Oh, my wild one, your bravery will be
your own undoing! No pity for our child,
poor little one, or me in my sad lot—
soon to be deprived of you! soon, soon
Akhaians as one man will set upon you
and cut you down! Better for me, without you,
to take cold earth for mantle. No more comfort,
no other warmth, after you meet your doom,
but heartbreak only. Father is dead, and Mother.

My father great Akhilleus killed when he
besieged and plundered Thêbê, our high town,
citadel of Kilikians. He killed him,
but, reverent at least in this, did not
despoil him. Body, gear, and weapons forged
so handsomely, he burned, and heaped a barrow
over the ashes. Elms were planted round
by mountain-nymphs of him who bears the stormcloud.
Then seven brothers that I had at home
in one day entered Death's dark place. Akhilleus,
prince and powerful runner, killed all seven
amid their shambling cattle and silvery sheep.
Mother, who had been queen of wooded Plakos,
he brought with other winnings home, and freed her,
taking no end of ransom. Artemis
the Huntress shot her in her father's house.
Father and mother—I have none but you,
nor brother, Hektor; lover none but you!
Be merciful! Stay here upon the tower!
Do not bereave your child and widow me!
Draw up your troops by the wild figtree; that way
the city lies most open, men most easily
could swarm the wall where it is low:
three times, at least, their best men tried it there
in company of the two called Aías, with
Idómeneus, the Atreidai, Diomêdês—
whether someone who had it from oracles
had told them, or their own hearts urged them on."

Great Hektor in his shimmering helmet answered:

"Lady, these many things beset my mind
no less than yours. But I should die of shame
before our Trojan men and noblewomen
if like a coward I avoided battle,
nor am I moved to. Long ago I learned
how to be brave, how to go forward always
and to contend for honor, Father's and mine.
Honor—for in my heart and soul I know
a day will come when ancient Ilion falls,
when Priam and the folk of Priam perish.

Not by the Trojans' anguish on that day
am I so overborne in mind—the pain
of Hékabê herself, or Priam king,
or of my brothers, many and valorous,
who will have fallen in dust before our enemies—
as by your own grief, when some armed Akhaian
takes you in tears, your free life stripped away.
Before another woman's loom in Argos
it may be you will pass, or at Messèis
or Hypereiê fountain, carrying water,
against your will—iron constraint upon you.
And seeing you in tears, a man may say:
'There is the wife of Hektor, who fought best
of Trojan horsemen when they fought at Troy.'
So he may say—and you will ache again
for one man who could keep you out of bondage.
Let me be hidden dark down in my grave
before I hear your cry or know you captive!"

As he said this, Hektor held out his arms
to take his baby. But the child squirmed round
on the nurse's bosom and began to wail,
terrified by his father's great war helm—
the flashing bronze, the crest with horsehair plume
tossed like a living thing at every nod.
His father began laughing, and his mother
laughed as well. Then from his handsome head
Hektor lifted off his helm and bent
to place it, bright with sunlight, on the ground.
When he had kissed his child and swung him high
to dandle him, he said this prayer:

                                                          "O Zeus
and all immortals, may this child, my son,
become like me a prince among the Trojans.
Let him be strong and brave and rule in power
at Ilion; then someday men will say
'This fellow is far better than his father!'
seeing him home from war, and in his arms
the bloodstained gear of some tall warrior slain—
making his mother proud."

After this prayer,
into his dear wife's arms he gave his baby,
whom on her fragrant breast
she held and cherished, laughing through her tears.
Hektor pitied her now. Caressing her,
he said:

"Unquiet soul, do not be too distressed
by thoughts of me. You know no man dispatches me
into the undergloom against my fate;
no mortal, either, can escape his fate,
coward or brave man, once he comes to be.
Go home, attend to your own handiwork
at loom and spindle, and command the maids
to busy themselves, too. As for the war,
that is for men, all who were born at Ilion,
to put their minds on—most of all for me."

He stooped now to recover his plumed helm
as she, his dear wife, drew away, her head
turned and her eyes upon him, brimming tears.
She made her way in haste then to the ordered
house of Hektor and rejoined her maids,
moving them all to weep at sight of her.
In Hektor's home they mourned him, living still
but not, they feared, again to leave the war
or be delivered from Akhaian fury.

Paris in the meantime had not lingered:
after he buckled his bright war-gear on
he ran through Troy, sure-footed with long strides.
Think how a stallion fed on clover and barley,
mettlesome, thundering in a stall, may snap
his picket rope and canter down a field
to bathe as he would daily in the river—
glorying in freedom! Head held high
with mane over his shoulders flying,
his dazzling work of finely jointed knees
takes him around the pasture haunts of horses.
That was the way the son of Priam, Paris,
ran from the height of Pergamos, his gear

ablaze like the great sun,
and laughed aloud. He sprinted on, and quickly
met his brother, who was slow to leave
the place where he had discoursed with his lady.
Aléxandros was first to speak:

                                                    "Dear fellow,"

he said, "have I delayed you, kept you waiting?
Have I not come at the right time, as you asked?"

And Hektor in his shimmering helm replied:

"My strange brother! No man with justice in him
would underrate your handiwork in battle;
you have a powerful arm. But you give way
too easily, and lose interest, lose your will.
My heart aches in me when I hear our men,
who have such toil of battle on your account,
talk of you with contempt. Well, come along.
Someday we'll make amends for that, if ever
we drive the Akhaians from the land of Troy—
if ever Zeus permit us, in our hall,
to set before the gods of heaven, undying
and ever young, our winebowl of deliverance."

BOOK SEVEN

A Combat and a Rampart

As Hektor spoke he came out through the gateway
running, with Aléxandros beside him,
both resolved on battle.

                                     Like a wind,

a sailing wind heaven may grant to oarsmen
desperate for it at the polished oars,
when they have rowed their hearts out, far at sea,
so welcome to the Trojans in their longing
these appeared.

                    And each one killed his man.

                                  Aléxandros

brought down Menésthios from Arnê, son
of a mace-wielder, Lord Arêithoös
and wide-eyed Phylomedousa.

                          Hektor speared
Eïoneus under his helmet rim
and cut his nape, so that his legs gave way.
Young Glaukos, too, leader of Lykians,
in the rough mêlée hit Iphínoös
Dexíadês just as he swung aboard
his fast war-car: he rammed him in the shoulder,
and down he tumbled from his chariot.
Seeing these Argive warriors overthrown
in the sharp fighting, grey-eyed Athêna came
in a gust downward from Olympos peaks
to the old town of Troy—and up to meet her
from Pergamos, where he surveyed the fight,
his heart set on a Trojan victory,
Apollo rose. By the great oak they met,
and the son of Zeus began:

"Down from Olympos to this field again?
What passion moves you now? To give Danáäns
power for a breakthrough? Daughter of Zeus,
you waste no pity on the Trojan dead.
If you would listen, I know a better plan.
Why not arrange an interval in battle,
a day's respite? They can fight on tomorrow
until they find the end ordained for Ilion—
as that is all you goddesses have at heart,
the plundering of this town."

                        The grey-eyed goddess
answered him:

                            "So be it, archer of heaven.
I, too, thought of a truce, on my way down
toward Trojans and Akhaians. Only tell me:
how do you plan to make them break off battle?"

Apollo said:

                            "By firing the spirit
of Hektor, breaker of wild horses. Let him
defy some champion of Danáäns
to measure spears with him in mortal combat.

When they are challenged, let them pick a man
to stand up against Hektor in his pride."

The grey-eyed one did not dissent from this,
and Priam's dear son, Hélenos, aware
of what these gods were pleased to set afoot,
moved over to Hektor and accosted him:

"Hektor, gifted as you are with foresight
worthy of Zeus himself, will you consent
to my new plan? I tell you as your brother.
Make all the others, Trojans and Akhaians,
rest on their arms, and you yourself defy
whoever may be greatest of Akhaians
to face you in a duel to the death.
Your hour, you know, has not yet come to die;
I have it from the gods who live forever."

At this, great Hektor's heart beat high. Along
the battle line he went, forcing the Trojans
back with a lance held up mid-haft. They halted
and sank down in their tracks, while Agamémnon
brought to a halt Akhaians in their armor.
Now Athêna rested, with Apollo,
god of the silver bow—both gods transformed
to hunting birds, perched on the royal oak
of Father Zeus who bears the shield of storm.
Here with delight they viewed the sea of men
in close order at rest, with shields and helms
and lances ruggedly astir.

                                    A west wind rising
will cast a rippling roughness over water,
a shivering gloom on the clear sea. Just so
the seated mass of Trojans and Akhaians
rippled along the plain.

                              Hektor addressed them:

"Hear me, Trojans and Akhaians: listen
to what I am moved to say. The peace we swore to
Lord Zeus throned on high would not confirm.
He has adversity for both in mind
until you take high Troy, or are defeated,

beaten back to your deep-sea-going ships.
Knowing the bravest of Akhaia's host
are here with you, my pride demands that I
engage some champion: let one come forward,
the best man of you all, to fight with Hektor.
And here is what I say—Zeus be my witness—
if with his whetted bronze he cuts me down,
my armor he may take away and carry
aboard the long decked ships; not so my body.
That must be given to my kin, committed
to fire by the Trojans and their women.
And if I kill this man, if Lord Apollo
grants me victory, his helm and shield
I shall unstrap and bring to Ilion
to hang before the Archer Apollo's shrine.
But his dead body I'll restore
to your encampment by the well-trimmed ships.
Akhaians there may give him funeral
and heap a mound for him by Hellê's water.
One day a man on shipboard, sailing by
on the winedark sea, will point landward and say:
'There is the death-mound of an ancient man,
a hero who fought Hektor and was slain.'
Someone will say that someday. And the honor
won by me here will never pass away."
He finished, and the Akhaians all sat hushed,
ashamed not to respond, afraid to do so,
until at length Lord Meneláos arose
groaning in disgust, and stormed at them:

"Oh god, you brave noisemakers! Women, not men!
Here is disgrace and groveling shame for us
if none of the Danääns fight with Hektor!
May you all rot away to earth and water,
sitting tight, safe in your ignominy!
I will myself tie on a breastplate with him.
Out of our hands, in the gods' hands above us,
ultimate power over victory lies."

With this he began buckling on his gear,
and now—O Meneláos!—it seemed foregone

your end of life was near at Hektor's hands,
as Hektor was far stronger; but Akhaian
officers in a rush laid hold of you,
and Agamémnon, lord of the great plains,
taking your right hand, said:

                                        "You've lost your head,
my lord; no need of recklessness like this.
Galling as it may be, hold on! Give up
this wish for emulation's sake to face
a stronger fighter. Everyone else dreads
Prince Hektor, Priam's son. Even Akhilleus
shivered when for glory he met this man
in combat—and he had more driving power
than you, by far.

                          Go back, then, take your seat
with fellow-countrymen of your command.
The Akhaians will put up another champion.
And gluttonous though he may be for carnage,
with no fear in him—still he'll be relieved
if he comes through this deadly fight, no quarter
asked or given."

                                        Greatly had he recalled
his brother's mind to a just sense of duty,
and Meneláos complied; his own retainers
happily relieved him of his gear.
Then Nestor stood up, saying to the Argives:

"Ah, what distress for our Akhaian land!
How Pêleus, the old master of horse, would grieve,
that noble counselor of Myrmidons!
One day, questioning me in his own hall,
he took delight in learning of the Argives'
lineage and birth. If he should hear
how every man here quails before Hektor now,
he'd lift his arms to the immortal gods
and pray to quit his body, to go down
into the house of Death!

                                        O Father Zeus,

Athêna and Apollo! Could I be young again
as in those days of fighting by the rapids

of Keladôn, between the mustered men
of Pylos and the pikemen of Arkadía,
near Phêra's walls and Iardanos riverside!
Ereuthalíôn was their champion,
and he stood out, foremost, magnificent,
buckled in Lord Arêithoös' arms—
Arêithoös, the mace-wielder, so called
by fighting men and by their sumptuous women
for using neither bow nor spear: he swung
an iron mace to break through ranks in battle.
Lykoörgos had killed him, but by guile
and not by force at all: in a byway
so narrow that his mace could not avail him—
there Lykoörgos, lunging first,
had run him through with his long spear
and pinned him backward to the ground. He took
the arms given to Arêithoös by Arês
and bore them afterward in grinding war.
Then Lykoörgos, when he aged, at home,
passed them on to his friend, Ereuthalíôn.
Equipped with these he challenged all our best,
but all were shaken, full of dread; no one
would take the field against him. Well, my pride
drove me to take him on with a high heart,
though I was then still youngest of us all.
I fought him, and Athêna gave me glory.
Tallest and toughest of enemies, I killed him,
that huge man, and far and wide he sprawled.
Would god I had my youth again, my strength
intact: Lord Hektor would be soon engaged!
But you that are the best men of Akhaia
will not go forward cheerfully to meet him."

So chided by the old man, volunteers
arose then, nine in all—first on his feet
being Lord Marshal Agamémnon, second
Diomêdês, powerful son of Tydeus,
and, joining these, those two who were called Aías,
rugged impetuous men, and joining these
Idómeneus and that lord's right-hand man,
Meríonês, the peer of the battle-god

in butchery of war; along with these
Eurýpylos, Euaimôn's handsome son,
Thoas Andraimónidês, and Odysseus.
These were all willing to encounter Hektor
in single combat. Then again they heard
from Nestor of Gerênia, charioteer:

"By lot now: whirl for the one who comes out first.
He is the one to make Akhaians proud,
and make himself, too, proud, if he survives
this bitter fight, no quarter asked or given."

At this each put his mark upon a stone
and dropped it in the helmet of Agamémnon.
Meanwhile the troops addressed the gods in prayer
with hands held up. You might have heard one say,
his eyes on heaven:

                                    "Father Zeus, let Aías'
pebble jump! Or make it Diomêdês!
Make it the king himself of rich Mykênê!"

So they murmured. Then Lord Nestor gave
the helm a rolling shake and made that stone
which they desired leap out: Aías' token.
A herald took it round amid the nine,
showing the fortunate mark, this way and that,
to all the Akhaian champions; but none
could recognize it or acknowledge it.
Only when he had come at length to him
who made the sign and dropped it in the helmet,
Aías, the giant, putting out his hand
for what the pausing herald placed upon it,
knew his mark. A thrill of joy ran through him.
Down at his feet he tossed the stone, and said:

"Oh, friends, the token's mine! And glad I am,
as I believe I can put Hektor down.
Come, everyone, while I prepare to fight,
pray to Lord Zeus the son of Krónos! Keep it
under your breath so Trojans will not hear—
or else be open about it; after all,

we have no fear of any. No man here
will drive me from the field against my will,
not by main force, not by a ruse. I hope
I was not born and bred on Sálamis
to be a dunce in battle."

                                        At this the soldiers
prayed to Zeus. You might have heard one say,
his eyes on heaven:

                                        "Father Zeus, from Ida
looking out for us all: greatest, most glorious:
let Aías win the honor of victory!
Or if you care for Hektor and are inclined
to favor him, then let both men be even
in staying power and honor!"

                                        So they prayed,
while Aías made his brazen helmet snug,
fitted his shield and sword strap. He stepped out
as formidable as gigantic Arês,
wading into the ranks of men, when Zeus
drives them to battle in bloodletting fury.
Huge as that, the bastion of Akhaians
loomed and grinned, his face a cruel mask,
his legs moving in great strides. He shook
his long spear doubled by its pointing shadow,
and the Argives exulted. Now the Trojans
felt a painful trembling in the knees,
and even Hektor's heart thumped in his chest—
but there could be no turning back; he could not
slip again into his throng of troops;
he was the challenger. Aías came nearer,
carrying like a tower his body shield
of seven oxhides sheathed in bronze—a work
done for him by the leather-master Tykhios
in Hylê: Tykhios made the glittering shield
with seven skins of oxhide and an eighth
of plated bronze. Holding this bulk before him,
Aías Telamônios came on
toward Hektor and stood before him. Now he spoke,
threatening him:

"Before long, man to man,
Hektor, you'll realize that we Danäans,
have our champions, too—I mean besides
the lionhearted breaker of men, Akhilleus.
He lies now by the beaked seagoing ships
in anger at Lord Marshal Agamémnon.
But here are those among us who can face you—
plenty of us. Fight then, if you will!"

To this, great Hektor in his shimmering helmet
answered:

"Son of the ancient line of Télamôn,
Aías, lordly over fighting men,
when you try me you try no callow boy
or woman innocent of war. I know
and know well how to fight and how to kill,
how to take blows upon the right or left
shifting my guard of tough oxhide in battle,
how to charge in a din of chariots,
or hand to hand with sword or pike to use
timing and footwork in the dance of war.
Seeing the man you are, I would not trick you
but let you have it with a straight shot,
if luck is with me."

Rifling his spear,
he hurled it and hit Aías' wondrous shield
square on the outer and eighth plate of bronze.
The spearhead punched its way through this and through
six layers, but the seventh oxhide stopped it.
Now in his turn great Aías made his cast
and hit the round shield braced on Hektor's arm.
Piercing the bright shield, the whetted spearhead
cut its way into his figured cuirass,
ripping his shirt along his flank; but he
had twisted and escaped the night of death.
Now both men disengaged their spears and fell
on one another like man-eating lions
or wild boars—no tame household creatures. Hektor's
lancehead scored the tower shield—but failed
to pierce it, as the point was bent aside.

Then Aías, plunging forward, rammed his spear
into the round shield, and the point went through
to nick his furious adversary, making
a cut that welled dark blood below his ear.
But Hektor did not slacken, even so.
He drew away and in one powerful hand
picked from the plain a boulder lying there,
black, rough and huge, and threw it,
hitting Aías' gigantic sevenfold shield
square on the boss with a great clang of bronze.
Then Aías lifted up a huger stone
and whirled, and put immeasurable force
behind it when he let it fly—as though
he flung a millstone—crushing Hektor's shield.
The impact caught his knees, so that he tumbled
backward behind the bashed-in shield. At once
Apollo pulled him to his feet again,
and now with drawn swords toe to toe
they would have doubled strokes on one another,
had not those messengers of Zeus and men,
the heralds, intervened—one from the Trojans,
one from the Akhaian side—for both
Idaíos and Talthýbios kept their heads.
They held their staves out, parting the contenders,
and that experienced man, Idaíos, said:

"Enough, lads. No more fighting. The Lord Zeus,
assembler of bright cloud, cares for you both.
Both are great spearmen, and we all know it.
But now already night is coming on,
and we do well to heed the fall of night."

Said Aías Telamônios in reply:

"Idaíos, call on Hektor to say as much.
He was the one who dared our champions
to duel with him. Let him take the lead.
Whatever he likes, I am at his disposition."

Hektor in his shimmering helmet answered:

"Aías, a powerful great frame you had
as a gift from god, and a clear head; of all

Akhaians you are toughest with a spear.
And this being shown, let us break off our duel,
our bloodletting, for today. We'll meet again
another time—and fight until the unseen
power decides between these hosts of ours,
awarding one or the other victory.
But now already night is coming on,
and we do well to heed the fall of night.
This way you'll give them festive pleasure there
beside the ships, above all to your friends,
companions at your table. As for me,
as I go through Priam's town tonight
my presence will give joy to Trojan men
and to our women, as in their trailing gowns
they throng the place of god with prayers for me.
Let us make one another memorable gifts,
and afterward they'll say, among Akhaians
and Trojans: 'These two fought and gave no quarter
in close combat, yet they parted friends.'"

This he said, and lifting off his broadsword,
silver-hilted, in its sheath, upon
the well-cut baldric, made a gift of it,
and Aías gave his loin-guard, sewn in purple.
Each then turned away. One went to join
the Akhaian troops; the other joined his Trojans,
and all were full of joy to see him come
alive, unhurt, delivered from the fury
of Aías whose great hands no man withstood.
Almost despairing of him still, they led him
into the town.
                          On their side, the Akhaians
conducted Aías in his pride of victory
to Agamémnon. In the commander's hut
Lord Marshal Agamémnon sacrificed
a five-year ox to the overlord of heaven.
Skinned and quartered and cut up in bits
the meat was carefully spitted, roasted well,
and taken from the fire. When all the food
lay ready, when the soldiers turned from work,
they feasted to their hearts' content, and Lord

Agamémnon, ruler of the great plains,
gave Aías the long marrowy cuts of chine.
Then, hunger and thirst being dispelled, they heard
Lord Nestor first in discourse. The old man
had new proposals to elaborate—
he whose counsel had been best before.
Concerned for them, he said:

                                        "Lord Agamémnon,
princes of Akhaia, think of our losses.
Many are dead, their dark blood poured by Arês
around Skamánder river, and their souls
gone down to undergloom. Therefore at dawn
you should suspend all action by Akhaians.
Gathering here, we'll bring the dead men back
in wagons drawn by oxen or by mules.
These corpses we must fire abaft the ships
a short way from the sterns, that each may bear
his charred bones to the children of the dead
whenever we sail home again. We'll bring
earth for a single mound about the fire,
common earth from landward; based on this,
a line of ramparts to defend our ships
and troops—with gates well fitted in the walls
to leave a way out for our chariots.
Outside, beyond the walls, we'll dig a moat
around the perimeter, to hold at bay
their teams and men, and break the impetus
of Trojans in assault."

                                        To this proposal
all the great captains gave assent. And now
at that same hour, high in the upper city
of Ilion, a Trojan assembly met
in tumult at the gates of Priam. First
to speak before them all, clear-eyed Antênor
cried out:

                                "Trojans, Dardans, and allies,
listen to me, to what I am moved to say!
Bring Argive Helen and the treasure with her,
and let us give her back to the Atreidai

to take home in the ships! We fight as men
proven untrustworthy, truce-breakers. I see
no outcome favorable to ourselves unless
we act as I propose."

                                        With this short speech,
he took his seat. But Prince Aléxandros,
husband of the fair-haired beauty, Helen,
rose and in a sharp tone answered him:

"What you propose, Antênor, I do not like.
You can conceive of better things to say.
Or if you take it seriously, this plan,
the gods themselves have made you lose your wits.
To all you Trojan handlers of fast horses
here is my speech: I say 'No' to your face:
I will not give the woman up! The treasure,
all that I once brought home from Argos, though,
I offer willingly, and with increment."

After this declaration he took his seat.
Then Priam, son of Dárdanos, arose,
sage as a god in counsel, and spoke out
in his concern amid them all:

                                        "Now hear me,
Trojans, Dardans, and allies,
listen to what I feel I must propose.
At this hour take your evening meal as always
everywhere in the city. Bear in mind
that sentries must be posted, every man
alert. Then let Idaíos go at dawn
among the decked ships, bearing the Atreidai,
Agamémnon and Meneláos, report
of what was said here by Aléxandros
because of whom this quarrel began. Then too
let him make inquiry to this effect:
will they accept a truce in the hard fighting,
allowing us to burn our dead? Next day
again we'll fight, until inscrutable power
decides between us, giving one side victory."

They listened and abided by his words.
In companies the soldiers took their meal,
and then at dawn Idaíos made his way
amid the decked ships. Finding the Danáäns,
companions of Arês, gathered in assembly
before the bow of Agamémnon's ship,
he took his stand among them, calling out:

"Agamémnon and all princes of Akhaia,
Priam and the noble men of Troy
direct me to report, and may it please you,
the offer of Aléxandros
because of whom this quarrel began. The treasure,
all that he brought to Troy in his long ships—
would god he had foundered on the way!—he now
desires to give back, with increment.
Meneláos' wife, on the other hand,
he has affirmed that he will not restore,
let Trojans urge it as they will.

                          I am directed
further to make this inquiry:
will you accept a truce in the hard fighting,
allowing us to burn our dead? Next day
again we'll fight, until inscrutable power
decides between us, giving one side victory."

He finished, and they all sat hushed and still.
At last Diomêdês of the great warcry
burst out:

                        "Let no man here accept
treasure from Aléxandros—nor Helen
either. Even a child can see the Trojans
live already on the edge of doom!"

The Akhaian soldiers all roared "Aye!" to this,
aroused by Diomêdês' words, and Lord
Agamémnon responded to Idaíos:

"Idaíos, there by heaven you yourself
have heard the Akhaians' answer! For my part
I am content with it. As to the dead,
I would withhold no decency of burning;

a man should spare no pains to see cadavers
given as soon as may be after death
to purifying flame. Let thundering Zeus,
consort of Hêra, witness I give my word."

And as he spoke he gestured with his staff
upward toward all the gods.

                                  Turning around,
Idaíos made his way again to Ilion.
Upon the assembly ground Trojans and Dardans
were waiting all together for him to come.
Soon he arrived and standing in their midst
delivered his report.

                            Then all equipped themselves
at once, dividing into two working parties,
one for timber, one to bring in the dead,
as on the other side, leaving their ships,
the Argives labored, gathering firewood
and bringing in the dead.

                                 Bright Hêlios
had just begun to strike across the plowlands,
rising heavenward out of the deep
smooth-flowing Ocean stream, when these two groups
met on the battlefield, with difficulty
distinguishing the dead men, one by one.
With pails they washed the bloody filth away,
then hot tears fell, as into waiting carts
they lifted up their dead. All cries of mourning
Priam forbade them; sick at heart therefore
in silence they piled corpses on the pyre
and burned it down. Then back they went to Ilion.
Just so on their side the Akhaians piled
dead bodies on their pyre, sick at heart,
and burned it down. Then back to the ships they went.
Next day before dawn, in the dim of night,
around the pyre, chosen Akhaian men
assembled to make one mound for all, with common
earth brought in from landward. Based on this
they built a wall, a rampart with high towers,
to be protection for their ships and men.
And well-framed gateways in the wall they made

to leave a way out for the chariots.
Outside, beyond the wall, they dug a moat
and planted it with stakes driven in and pointed.
These were the labors of the long-haired carls
of Akhaia.

         And the gods arrayed with Zeus,
lord of the lightning flash, looked down
on this great work of the Akhaian army.
Then he who shakes the mainland and the islands,
Poseidon, made his comment:

                         "Father Zeus,
will any man on boundless earth again
make known his thought, his plan, to the immortals?
Do you not see? The long-haired carls of Akhaia
put up a rampart, inshore from the ships,
and ran a moat around; but they would not
propitiate us with glory of hekatombs!
The fame of this will be diffused as far
as Dawn sends light. Men will forget the wall
I drudged at with Apollo for Laomédôn."

Hot with irritation, Zeus replied:

"By thunder! Lord of the wide sea's power, shaking
islands and mainland, sulking, you? Another
god, a hundred times feebler than you are
in force of hand and spirit, might be worried
over this stratagem, this wall. Your own
renown is widespread as the light of Dawn!
Come, look ahead! When the Akhaians take
again to their ships and sail for their own land,
break up the wall and wash it out to sea,
envelop the whole shore with sand! That way
the Akhaian wall may vanish from the earth."

So ran their colloquy. The sun went down
and now the Akhaian labor was accomplished.
Amid their huts they slaughtered beasts and made
their evening meal. Wine-ships had come ashore
from Lemnos, a whole fleet loaded with wine.
These ships were sent by Eunêos, Iêson's son,

born to that hero by Hypsipylê.
To Agamémnon, as to Meneláos,
he gave a thousand measures of the wine
for trading, so the troops could barter for it,
some with bronze and some with shining iron,
others with hides and others still with oxen,
some with slaves. They made a copious feast,
and all night long Akhaians with flowing hair
feasted, while the Trojans and their allies
likewise made a feast.

                                        But all night long

Zeus the Profound made thunder overhead
while pondering calamities to come,
and men turned pale with fear. Tilting their cups
they poured out wine upon the ground; no man
would drink again till he had spilt his cup
to heaven's overlord. But at long last
they turned to rest and took the gift of sleep.

BOOK EIGHT

The Battle Swayed by Zeus

Dawn in her saffron robe came spreading light
on all the world, and Zeus who plays in thunder
gathered the gods on peaked Olympos' height,
then said to that assembly:

                                        "Listen to me,
immortals, every one,
and let me make my mood and purpose clear.
Let no one, god or goddess, contravene
my present edict; all assent to it
that I may get this business done, and quickly.
If I catch sight of anyone slipping away
with a mind to assist the Danáäns or the Trojans,
he comes back blasted without ceremony,
or else he will be flung out of Olympos

into the murk of Tartaros that lies
deep down in underworld. Iron the gates are,
brazen the doorslab, and the depth from hell
as great as heaven's utmost height from earth.
You may learn then how far my power
puts all gods to shame.

                              Or prove it this way:
out of the zenith hang a golden line
and put your weight on it, all gods and goddesses.
You will not budge me earthward out of heaven,
cannot budge the all-highest, mighty Zeus,
no matter how you try.

                              But let my hand

once close to pull that cable—up you come,
and with you earth itself comes, and the sea.
By one end tied around Olympos' top
I could let all the world swing in mid-heaven!
That is how far I overwhelm you all,
both gods and men."

                              They were all awed and silent,
he put it with such power. After a pause,
the grey-eyed goddess Athêna said:

                                        "O Zeus,

highest and mightiest, father of us all,
we are well aware of your omnipotence,
but all the same we mourn the Akhaian spearmen
if they are now to meet hard fate and die.
As you command, we shall indeed
abstain from battle—merely, now and again,
dropping a word of counsel to the Argives,
that all may not be lost through your displeasure."

The driver of cloud smiled and replied:

                                        "Take heart,
dear child, third born of heaven. I do not speak
my full intent. With you, I would be gentle."

Up to his car he backed his bronze-shod team
of aerial runners, long manes blowing gold.

He adorned himself in panoply of gold,
then mounted, taking up his golden whip,
and lashed his horses onward. At full stretch
midway between the earth and starry heaven
they ran toward Ida, sparkling with cool streams,
mother of wild things, and the peak of Gárgaron
where are his holy plot and fragrant altar.
There Zeus, father of gods and men, reined in
and freed his team, diffusing cloud about them,
while glorying upon the crest he sat
to view the far-off scene below—Akhaian
ships and Trojan city.

                                                        At that hour

Akhaian fighting men with flowing hair
took a meal by their huts and armed themselves.
The Trojans, too, on their side, in the city,
mustered under arms—though fewer, still
resolved by dire need to fight the battle
for wives' and children's sake.

                                                    Now all the gates

were flung wide and the Trojan army sortied,
charioteers and foot, in a rising roar.

When the two masses met on the battle line
they ground their shields together, crossing spears,
with might of men in armor. Round shield-bosses
rang on each other in the clashing din,
and groans mingled with shouts of triumph rose
from those who died and those who killed: the field
ran rivulets of blood. While the fair day
waxed in heat through all the morning hours
missiles from both sank home and men went down,
until when Hêlios bestrode mid-heaven
the Father cleared his golden scales. Therein
two destinies of death's long pain he set
for Trojan horsemen and Akhaian soldiers
and held the scales up by the midpoint. Slowly
one pan sank with death's day for Akhaians.

Zeus erupted in thunder from Ida, with burning
flashes of lightning against the Akhaian army,

dazing them all: now white-faced terror seized them.
Neither Idómeneus nor Agamémnon
held his ground, and neither Aías held,
the Tall One nor the Short One, peers of war;
only the old lord of the western approaches,
Nestor, stayed in place—
not that in fact he willed to. No, one horse
had been disabled by Aléxandros,
whose arrow hit him high, just at the spot
most vulnerable, where the springing mane begins.
The beast reared in agony, for the point
entered his brain, and round and round
he floundered, fixed by the bronze point, making havoc
among the horses. While the old man hacked
to cut away the trace horse with his sword,
amid the rout Lord Hektor's team appeared
and the car that bore the fierce man. Soon enough,
old Nestor would have perished in that place,
had not Diomêdês of the great warcry
seen Hektor coming. With a tremendous shout
he tried to rouse Odysseus, and called to him:

"Where are you off to, turning tail like a dog?
Son of Laërtês and the gods of old,
Odysseus, master mariner and soldier,
someone's lance might nail you from behind
between the shoulders, god forfend. Hold on with me
to fight this wild man off the old man's back!"
Odysseus did not hear him, as he ran
far wide of him and seaward toward the ships.
Then, singlehanded, Diomêdês joined
the mêlée forward of the old man's horses
and called to him, in a piercing voice:

                                          "Old man,

they have you in a bad way, these young Trojans.
Age bears hard on you, your strength is going,
your groom is wobbly and your beasts are spent.
Here, mount my chariot, and see how fast
the horses are in the line of Trôs: they know
this Trojan plain and how to wheel upon it
this way and that way in pursuit or flight.

I had this team as booty from Aineías,
and they are masters at stampeding troops.
Let the men take over yours, while we two
drive these on the Trojans! Hektor will find
my spear is mad for battle, like his own."

Lord Nestor of Gerênia, master of chariots,
did not refuse; his team was taken in hand
by Sthénelos and noble Eurýmedôn.
Boarding the car alongside Diomêdês,
Lord Nestor took the reins and whipped the horses
forward until they came in range of Hektor,
as Hektor drove upon them at full speed;
then Diomêdês made his throw.
He missed his man but hit the charioteer,
Êniopeus, a son of Thêbaios—
hit him squarely just beside the nipple
so that he tumbled backward, and his horses
shied away as the man died where he fell.
Now a cold gloom of grief passed over Hektor
and anger for the driver. Still, he left him
and wheeled to spot a replacement—but his team
would not be driverless more than an instant,
for soon he came on Arkheptólemos,
Íphitos' son, and took him on,
giving him reins and horses.

                                        Now at the hands
of Diomêdês there might soon have been
a ruin of Trojans, irreversible rout,
and Ilion crowded like a shepherd's pen,
had not the father of gods and men perceived it.
Thundering he let fly a white-hot bolt
that lit in front of Diomêdês' horses
and blazed up terribly with a sulphur fume.
The team quailed, cowering against the chariot,
and the flashing reins ran out of Nestor's hands. His heart
failed him, and he said to Diomêdês:

"Give way, now; get the team to pull us out!
Do you not realize that power from Zeus
is being denied you? Glory goes today

to Hektor, by favor of the son of Krónos.
Another day he may bestow it on us
if he only will. No man defends himself
against the mind of Zeus—even the ruggedest
of champions. His power is beyond us."

Diomêdês, lord of the warcry, answered:

"All that you say is right enough, old man.
But here's atrocious pain low in my chest
about my heart, when I imagine Hektor
among the Trojans telling them one day:
'Diomêdês made for the ships with me behind him!'
That's the way he'll put it. May broad earth
yawn for me then and hide me!"

                                                      Nestor said:

"Ai, Diomêdês, keep your head, what talk!
Even if Hektor calls you a coward
he cannot make them think so, Trojans or Dardans,
no, nor the Trojan soldiers' wives who saw
their fine men in the dust, dead at your hands!"

Then Nestor whipped the horses into a turn
and joined the rout.

                                    With a wild yell
behind them Hektor and his men let fly
their spears and grievous arrows in a shower,
and Hektor towering in his bright helmet
shouted out:

                                    "O Diomêdês, once
Akhaian skirmishers gave you the place of honor!
Heart of the roast, cups brimming full! But they'll
despise you now—turned woman, after all!
You empty doll, ride on!
Never will I give way to you, and never
will you climb hand over hand upon our ramparts
or load our women in your ships: you face
your doom from me!"

Hearing this, Diomêdês

hesitated and had half a mind
to wheel his horses, face around, and fight.
Three times he put it to himself; three times
from Ida's mountaintop great Zeus who views
the wide world thundered, as a sign to Trojans
that now the tide of battle swung to them.
And Hektor could be heard among them shouting:

"Trojans, Lykians, Dardans! Fighters all!
Be men, friends, keep up your driving power.
I know now that Zeus has accorded me
victory and glory—and the Danáäns
bloody defeat. What fools, to build that wall,
soft earth, no barrier: it will not stop me.
Our horses in one jump can take the ditch,
but when I reach the decked ships, one of you
remember to bring incendiary torches
burning, so I can set the ships afire
and kill the Argives round them, blind with smoke."

Then he spoke to his team:

"Tawny and Whitefoot,
Dusky and Dapple, now is the time to pay
for all that delicate feeding by Andrómakhê:
the honeyhearted grain she served, the wine
she mixed for you to drink when you desired—
before me, though I am her own true husband.
Press the Akhaians hard, give all you have,
and we may capture Nestor's shield whose fame
has gone abroad to the sky's rim: all in gold
they say it's plated, crossbars too. Then too
remember the enameled cuirass worn
by Diomêdês, crafted by Hêphaistos.
If we can take these arms, I have a chance
to drive the Akhaians aboard ship tonight!"
While he appealed to them, Queen Hêra tossed
with rancor and indignation in her chair,
making mighty Olympos quake, and said
into Poseidon's ear:

"Oh, what a pity!

God of the wide sea, shaker of the islands,
are you not moved to see Danáäns perish
who send so many and lovely gifts to you
at Hélikê and Aigai? You had wished them
victory.

                              If only we who take
the Akhaian side would have the will to fight,
to repel the Trojans and keep Zeus away,
there he might sit and fret alone on Ida!"

But the Earthshaker growled at her in anger:

"Hêra, mistress of babble that you are,
what empty-headed talk is this? I would not
dream of pitting all the rest of us
against Lord Zeus. He overmasters all."

That ended their exchange. Meanwhile, below,
and inland from the ships, the strip of shore
enclosed by moat and rampart now was thronged
with chariots and men, rolled back
by whirlwind Arês' peer, the son of Priam,
as glory shone on him from Zeus. And soon
he would have set the ships ablaze—had not
a thought from Hêra come to Agamémnon,
to rouse himself and rally his Akhaians.
Along the line of huts and ships he came,
holding a purple cloak in his great hand,
and stood beside the black wide-bellied ship
of Lord Odysseus. Midway in the line
this ship was placed; one there could send his voice
as far as Telamônian Aías' camp
at one end, or Akhilleus' at the other—
for these had drawn their ships up on the flanks,
relying on their valor and force of arms.
Agamémnon's harangue reached all his troops:

"Shame, shame, you pack of dogs, you only *looked* well.
What has become of all our fighting words,
all that brave talk I heard from you in Lemnos,
when you were feasting on thick beef and drinking

bowls a-brim with wine? Then every man
could take on Trojans by the hundred! Now
we are no match for one of them, for Hektor.
He will set our black ships afire, and soon.
O Father Zeus, what great prince before this
have you so blinded in disastrous folly,
taking his glory and his pride away? And yet
no altar of yours did I pass by, not one,
in my mad voyage this way in the ships.
On every one I burned thigh flesh and fat,
in hope to take walled Troy by storm. Ah, Zeus!
Grant me this boon: let us at least
escape the worst: do not allow the Trojans
to crush the Akhaians as it seems they will!"

The father on Ida pitied the weeping man
and nodded; his main army should be saved.
And Zeus that instant launched above the field
the most portentous of all birds, an eagle,
pinning in his talons a tender fawn.
He dropped it near the beautiful altar of Zeus
where the Akhaians made their offerings
to Zeus of Omens: and beholding this,
knowing the eagle had come down from Zeus,
they flung themselves again upon the Trojans,
with joy renewed in battle. Of all Danääns
as many as were crowded there, not one
could say he drove his team across the moat
and faced the enemy before Diomêdês.
Far out ahead of all, he killed his man—
Ageláos, Phradmon's son. As this man wheeled
his chariot in retreat, the spear went into him
between the shoulder blades and through his chest.
He toppled, and his armor clanged upon him.
After Diomêdês came the Atreidai,
Agamémnon and Meneláos, and then
the two named Aías, jacketed with brawn;
then came Idómeneus and his lieutenant
Meríonês, peer of Enyálios,
the god of slaughter. After these Eurýpylos
Euaimôn's son, and ninth in order, Teukros,

his bow bent hard and strung. He took his stand
behind the shield of Telamônian Aías,
and Aías would put up his shield a bit: beneath it
the archer could take aim—and when his shot
went home, his enemy perished on the spot,
while he ducked back to Aías' flank the way
a boy does to his mother, and with his shield
Aías concealed him. Whom did he hit first?
Orsílokhos and Órmenos, Opheléstês,
Daítor and Khromíos and Lykophóntês,
Amopáon Polyaimónidês, Melaníppos—
one after another he brought them down
upon the cattle-pasturing earth. And Marshal
Agamémnon exulted to see him slash
the Trojan ranks with shots from his tough bow.
He moved over nearby and said to him:

"Teukros, good soldier and leader that you are,
that is the way to shoot. Your marksmanship
will be a gleam of pride for the Danääns
and for your father, too, for Télamôn.
He reared you at home despite your bastard birth;
now distant as he is, lift him to glory.
And I can tell you how the case will be,
if Zeus beyond the stormcloud, and Athêna,
allow me ever to storm and pillage Troy:
I pledge a gift to you, next after mine,
a tripod or a team with car, or else
a woman who will sleep with you."

                                              To this
the noble Teukros answered:

                                              "Agamémnon,
excellency, I am doing all I can; no point
in promising things to cheer me on. As long
as I have it in me I will never quit.
No, from the time we held and pushed them back
on Ilion, I have watched here with my bow
for openings to kill them: eight good shots
I've had by now with my barbed shafts—

and all on target in the flesh of men.
But that mad dog I cannot hit!"

                                                         So saying,
he let one arrow more leap from the string
in passionate hope to knock Lord Hektor down.
He missed once more, but did hit in the chest
a noble son of Priam, Gorgythíon,
whom Kastianeira of Aisýmê bore,
a woman tall in beauty as a goddess.
Fallen on one side, as on the stalk
a poppy falls, weighed down by showering spring,
beneath his helmet's weight his head sank down.
Then Teukros, aiming hard at Hektor, let
an arrow leap from the string, and yet again
he missed; this time Apollo nudged its flight
toward Arkheptólemos, driver to Hektor,
as he came on. It struck him near the nipple.
Down he tumbled from the car, his horses
shying back as the man died where he fell.
A gloom passed over Hektor for his driver,
but angered as he was he left him there
and called out to his brother, Kebríonês,
to take the reins. As he did so, Lord Hektor
sprang out of the glittering chariot
with a savage cry, picked up a stone, and ran
for Teukros in a fury to strike him down.
Out of his quiver the cool archer drew
one more keen arrow, fitting it to the string,
but even as he pulled it back Lord Hektor
cast the rough stone and caught him on the shoulder
just at the collarbone, that frail crossbeam
that separates the chest and throat. A tendon
snapped; the archer's arm went numb; he dropped
on one knee, and his bow fell.

                                         Now great Aías,
seeing his brother fallen, threw himself
forward to give him cover with his shield,
and Mêkisteus and brave Alástôr, two
of Aías' men, reached under him and bore him
groaning toward the ships.

The Olympian
again at this put heart into the Trojans,
and straight into the moat they drove the Akhaians,
Hektor, elated, leading the attack.
You know the way a hunting dog will harry
a wild boar or a lion after a chase,
and try to nip him from behind, to fasten
on flank or rump, alert for an opening
as the quarry turns and turns: darting like that,
Hektor harried the long-haired men of Akhaia,
killing off stragglers one by one, and when
the main mass had got through the stakes and ditch,
many had perished at the Trojans' hands.
Now at the ships they tried to stand and fight,
and shouted to each other, calling out
with hands held high to all the gods as well,
as Hektor drove his beautiful team around them,
blazing-eyed as a Gorgon, or as Arês,
bane of men.

But Hêra, looking down,
was touched by the sight and said to Athêna:

"Daughter
of Zeus who bears the stormcloud, can it be
that we'll no longer care for the Danáäns
in their extremity? All is fulfilled
to the bitter end, they are being cut to pieces
under one man's attack. No one can hold him,
the son of Priam, in his battle fury,
adding slaughter to slaughter."

Grey-eyed Athêna
answered:

"Death twice over to this Trojan!
Let him be broken at the Argives' hands,
give up his breath in his own land and perish!
My father, now, is full of a black madness,
evil and perverse. All that I strive for
he brings to nothing; he will not remember
how many times I intervened to save

his son, worn out in trials set by Eurýstheus.
How Hêraklês would cry to heaven! And Zeus
would send me out of heaven to be his shield.
Had I foreseen this day
that time he went down, bidden by Eurýstheus,
between Death's narrow gates to bring from Érebos
the watchdog of the Lord of Undergloom,
he never would have left the gorge of Styx!
Now Zeus not only scorns me, he performs
what Thetis wills: she kissed his knees, she begged him
to give back honor to that stormer of towns,
Akhilleus!
                                    But in time to come he'll call me
dear Grey Eyes again. Harness the team for us,
while I go in to get my battle-gear
in Zeus's hall. Then let me see
if Hektor in his flashing helm exults
when we appear on the precarious field,
or if a certain Trojan, fallen by the shipways,
gluts the dogs and birds with flesh and fat!"

Hêra whose arms are white as ivory
attended to her horses, their heads nodding
in frontlets of pure gold: the eldest goddess,
Hêra, daughter of Krónos, harnessed them.
Meanwhile Athêna at her father's door
let fall the robe her own hands had embroidered
and pulled over her head a shirt of Zeus.
Armor of grievous war she buckled on,
stepped in the fiery car, caught up her spear—
that massive spear with which this child of Power
can break in rage long battle lines of fighters.
Hêra flicked at the horses with her whip,
and moving of themselves the gates of heaven
grated a rumbling tone. Their keepers are
the Hours by whom great heaven and Olympos
may be disclosed or shut with looming cloud.
Between these gates the goddesses drove on.

Zeus, looking out from Ida, terribly angered,
roused his messenger, Iris of Golden Wings,
and said:

                    "Away with you, turn them around,
allow them no way through. It is not well
that we should come together in this battle!
But if we do, I swear
I shall hamstring their horses' legs and toss
the riders from their car; the chariot
I'll break to pieces: not in ten long years
will their concussions from that lightning stroke
be healed.

                              Let Grey Eyes realize the peril
of going into battle with her father.
I cannot be so furious with Hêra—
she balks me from sheer habit, say what I will."

At his command his emissary, Iris,
who runs on the rainy wind, from Ida's range
went up to grand Olympos. At the gate
of that snow-craggy mountain, where she met them,
she held them back and spoke the word of Zeus:

"Where are you going? Have you lost your minds?
The son of Krónos does not countenance
aid to the Argives: here is the penalty
he threatens to impose, and will impose:
your horses he will cripple, first of all,
then toss you both out of the chariot
and break it into pieces: not in ten years
can what you suffer from that lightning stroke
be healed. So, Grey Eyes, you may learn
the peril of doing battle with your father.
With Hêra he cannot be so furious:
her habit is to balk him, say what he will;
but as for you, you are a brazen bitch
if you dare lift your towering spear against him!"

When she had finished, Iris departed swiftly,
and Hêra said to Athêna:

                              "Very upsetting.
I cannot now consent, I am afraid,
that we make war with Zeus over mankind.

No, let them live or die as it befalls them!
Let him be arbiter, as he desires,
between Danáäns and Trojans. It is due
his majesty."

                                    And she turned the horses back.
Then acting for the goddesses the Hours
unharnessed those fine horses with long manes
and tied them up at their ambrosial troughs.
Against the glittering wall they stood the car,
its tilted pole upended, and the goddesses
rested on golden chairs amid the gods,
with hearts still beating high.

                                    Now Father Zeus
from Ida to Olympos drove his chariot
back to the resting place of gods. For him
the illustrious one who makes the islands tremble
freed the team, spread out a chariot-housing,
and drew the car up on a central stand.
The Zeus who views the wide world took his chair,
his golden chair, as underfoot
the mighty mountain of Olympos quaked.
Alone, apart, sat Hêra and Athêna
speaking never a word to him. He knew
their mood and said:

                                    "Athêna, why so gloomy?
And Hêra, why? In war, where men win glory,
you have not had to toil to bring down Trojans
for whom both hold an everlasting grudge.
Such is my animus and so inexorable
my hands that all the gods upon Olympos
could not in any case deflect or turn them.
Fear shook your gracious knees before you saw
the nightmare acts of warfare. I can tell you
why, and what defeat was sure to come of it:
no riding in your chariot back to Olympos,
back to your seats here, after my lightning bolt."

Zeus fell silent, and they murmured low,
Athêna and Hêra, putting their heads together,

meditating the Trojans' fall. Athêna
held her peace toward Zeus, though a fierce rancor
pervaded her; Hêra could not contain it,
and burst out to him:

                              "Fearsome as you are,
why take that tone with goddesses, my lord?
We are well aware how far from weak you are;
but we mourn still for the Akhaian spearmen
if they are now to meet hard fate and die.
As you command, we shall indeed
abstain from battle—merely, now and again,
dropping a word of counsel to the Argives,
that all may not be lost through your displeasure."

Then Zeus who gathers cloud replied to her:

"At dawn tomorrow you will see still more,
my wide-eyed lady, if you care to see
the Lord Zeus in high rage scything that army
of Argive spearmen down—for Hektor shall not
give his prowess respite from the war
until the marvelous runner, son of Pêleus,
rouses beside his ship—when near at hand,
around the sterns, in a desperate narrow place,
they fight over Patróklos dead. That way
the will of heaven lies. You and your anger
do not affect me, you may betake yourself
to the uttermost margin of earth and sea,
where Iápetos and Krónos rest and never
bask in the rays of Hêlios who moves
all day in heaven, nor rejoice in winds,
but lie submerged in Tartaros. You, too,
may roam that far, you bitch unparalleled,
I'll be indifferent still to your bad temper!"

Hêra whose arms are white as ivory
made no reply.

                              Now in the western Ocean
the shining sun dipped, drawing dark night on
over the kind grainbearing earth—a sundown
far from desired by Trojans; but the night

came thrice besought and blest by the Akhaians.
Hektor at once called Trojans to assembly,
leading the way by night back from the ships
to an empty field beside the eddying river—
a space that seemed free of the dead. The living
halted and dismounted there to listen
to a speech by Hektor, dear to Zeus. He held
his lance erect—eleven forearms long
with bronze point shining in the air before him
as shone, around the shank, a golden ring.
Leaning on this, he spoke amid the Trojans:

"Hear me, Trojans, Dardans, and allies!
By this time I had thought we might retire
to windy Ilion, after we had destroyed
Akhaians and their ships; but the night's gloom
came before we finished. That has saved them,
Argives and ships, at the sea's edge near the surf.
All right, then, let us bow to the black night,
and make an evening feast! From the chariot poles
unyoke the teams, toss fodder out before them;
bring down beeves and fat sheep from the city,
and lose no time about it—amber wine
and wheaten bread, too, from our halls. Go, gather
piles of firewood, so that all night long,
until the first-born dawn, our many fires
shall burn and send to heaven their leaping light,
that not by night shall the unshorn Akhaians
get away on the broad back of the sea.
Not by night—and not without combat, either,
taking ship easily, but let there be
those who take homeward missiles to digest,
hit hard by arrows or by spears as they
shove off and leap aboard. And let the next man
hate the thought of waging painful war
on Trojan master-horsemen.

                                         Honored criers
throughout our town shall publish this command:
old men with hoary brows, and striplings, all
camp out tonight upon the ancient towers;
women in every mégaron kindle fires,
and every sentry keep a steady watch

against a night raid on the city, while
my troops are in the field. These dispositions,
Trojans, are to be taken as I command. And may
what I have said tonight be salutary;
likewise what I shall say at Dawn. I hope
with prayer to Zeus and other immortal gods
we shall repulse the dogs of war and death
brought on us in the black ships. Aye, this night
we'll guard ourselves, toward morning arm again
and whet against the ships the edge of war!
I'll see if Diomêdês has the power
to force me from the ships, back on the rampart,
or if I kill him and take home his gear,
wet with his blood. He will show bravery
tomorrow if he face my spear advancing!
In the first rank, I think, wounded he'll lie
with plenty of his friends lying around him
at sunup in the morning.

> > > > > > > > Would I were sure

of being immortal, ageless all my days,
and reverenced like Athêna and Apollo,
as it is sure this day will bring defeat
on those of Argos!"

> > > > > > > This was the speech of Hektor,
and cheers rang out from the Trojans after it.
They led from under the yokes their sweating teams,
tethering each beside his chariot,
then brought down from the city beeves and sheep
in all haste—brought down wine and bread as well
out of their halls. They piled up firewood
and carried out full-tally hekatombs
to the immortals. Off the plain, the wind
bore smoke and savor of roasts into the sky.
Then on the perilous open ground of war,
in brave expectancy, they lay all night
while many campfires burned. As when in heaven
principal stars shine out around the moon
when the night sky is limpid, with no wind,
and all the lookout points, headlands, and mountain
clearings are distinctly seen, as though

pure space had broken through, downward from heaven,
and all the stars are out, and in his heart
the shepherd sings: just so from ships to river
shone before Ilion the Trojan fires.
There were a thousand burning in the plain,
and round each one lay fifty men in firelight.
Horses champed white barley, near the chariots,
waiting for Dawn to mount her lovely chair.

BOOK NINE

A Visit of Emissaries

So Trojans kept their watch that night.

To seaward

Panic that attends blood-chilling Rout
now ruled the Akhaians. All their finest men
were shaken by this fear, in bitter throes,
as when a shifting gale
blows up over the cold fish-breeding sea,
north wind and west wind wailing out of Thrace
in squall on squall, and dark waves crest, and shoreward
masses of weed are cast up by the surf:
so were Akhaian hearts torn in their breasts.

By that great gloom hard hit, the son of Atreus
made his way amid his criers and told them
to bid each man in person to assembly

but not to raise a general cry. He led them,
making the rounds himself, and soon the soldiers
grimly took their places. Then he rose,
with slow tears trickling, as from a hidden spring
dark water runs down, staining a rock wall;
and groaning heavily he addressed the Argives:

"Friends, leaders of Argives, all my captains,
Zeus Kronidês entangled me in folly
to my undoing. Wayward god, he promised
solemnly that I should not sail away
before I stormed the inner town of Troy.
Crookedness and duplicity, I see now!
He calls me to return to Argos beaten
after these many losses. That must be
his will and his good pleasure, who knows why?
Many a great town's height has he destroyed
and will destroy, being supreme in power.
Enough. Now let us act on what I say:
Board ship for our own fatherland! Retreat!
We cannot hope any longer to take Troy!"

At this a stillness overcame them all,
the Akhaian soldiers. Long they sat in silence,
hearing their own hearts beat. Then Diomêdês
rose at last to speak. He said:

                                        "My lord,

I must contend with you for letting go,
for losing balance. I may do so here
in assembly lawfully. Spare me your anger.
Before this you have held me up to scorn
for lack of fighting spirit; old and young,
everyone knows the truth of that. In your case,
the son of crooked-minded Krónos gave you
one gift and not both: a staff of kingship
honored by all men, but no staying power—
the greatest gift of all.
What has come over you, to make you think
the Akhaians weak and craven as you say?
If you are in a passion to sail home,
sail on: the way is clear, the many ships

that made the voyage from Mykênê with you
stand near the sea's edge. Others here will stay
until we plunder Troy! Or if they, too,
would like to, let them sail for their own country!
Sthénelos and I will fight alone
until we see the destined end of Ilion.
We came here under god."

When Diomêdês
finished, a cry went up from all Akhaians
in wonder at his words. Then Nestor stood
and spoke among them:

"Son of Tydeus, formidable
above the rest in war, in council, too,
you have more weight than others of your age.
No one will cry down what you say, no true
Akhaian will, or contradict you. Still,
you did not push on to the end.
I know you are young; in years you might well be
my last-born son, and yet for all of that
you kept your head and said what needed saying
before the Argive captains. My own part,
as I am older, is to drive it home.
No one will show contempt for what I say,
surely not Agamémnon, our commander.
Alien to clan and custom and hearth fire
is he who longs for war—heartbreaking war—
with his own people.

Let us yield to darkness
and make our evening meal. But let the sentries
take their rest on watch outside the rampart
near the moat; those are my orders for them.
Afterward, you direct us, Agamémnon,
by right of royal power. Provide a feast
for older men, your counselors. That is duty
and no difficulty: your huts are full of wine
brought over daily in our ships from Thrace
across the wide sea, and all provender
for guests is yours, as you are high commander.
Your counselors being met, pay heed to him

who counsels best. The army of Akhaia
bitterly needs a well-found plan of action.
The enemy is upon us, near the ships,
burning his thousand fires. What Akhaian
could be highhearted in that glare? This night
will see the army saved or brought to ruin."

They heeded him and did his will. Well-armed,
the sentries left to take their posts, one company
formed around Thrasymêdês, Nestor's son,
another mustered by Askálaphos
and Iálmenos, others commanded by
Meríonês, Aphareus, Dêípyros,
and Kreion's son, the princely Lykomêdês.
Seven lieutenants, each with a hundred men,
carrying long spears, issued from the camp
for outposts chosen between ditch and rampart.
Campfires were kindled, and they took their meal.

The son of Atreus led the elder men
together to his hut, where he served dinner,
and each man's hand went out upon the meal.
When they had driven hunger and thirst away,
Old Nestor opened their deliberations—
Nestor, whose counsel had seemed best before,
point by point weaving his argument:

"Lord Marshal of the army, Agamémnon,
as I shall end with you, so I begin,
since you hold power over a great army
and are responsible for it: the Lord Zeus
put in your keeping staff and precedent
that you might gather counsel for your men.
You should be first in discourse, but attentive
to what another may propose, to act on it
if he speak out for the good of all. Whatever
he may initiate, action is yours.
On this rule, let me speak as I think best.
A better view than mine no man can have,
the same view that I've held these many days
since that occasion when, my lord, for all

Akhilleus' rage, you took the girl Brisêis
out of his lodge—but not with our consent.
Far from it; I for one had begged you not to.
Just the same, you gave way to your pride,
and you dishonored a great prince,
a hero to whom the gods themselves do honor.
Taking his prize, you kept her and still do.
But even so, and even now, we may
contrive some way of making peace with him
by friendly gifts, and by affectionate words."

Then Agamémnon, the Lord Marshal, answered:

"Sir, there is nothing false in your account
of my blind errors. I committed them;
I will not now deny it. Troops of soldiers
are worth no more than one man cherished by Zeus
as he has cherished this man and avenged him,
overpowering the army of Akhaians.
I lost my head, I yielded to black anger,
but now I would retract it and appease him
with all munificence. Here before everyone
I may enumerate the gifts I'll give.
Seven new tripods and ten bars of gold,
then twenty shining caldrons, and twelve horses,
thoroughbreds, who by their wind and legs
have won me prizes: any man who owned
what these have brought me could not lack resources,
could not be pinched for precious gold—so many
prizes have these horses carried home.
Then I shall give him seven women, deft
in household handicraft—women of Lesbos
I chose when he himself took Lesbos town,
as they outshone all womankind in beauty.
These I shall give him, and one more, whom I
took away from him then: Briseus' daughter.
Concerning her, I add my solemn oath
I never went to bed or coupled with her,
as custom is with men and women.
These will be his at once. If the immortals
grant us the plundering of Priam's town,

let him come forward when the spoils are shared
and load his ship with bars of gold and bronze.
Then he may choose among the Trojan women
twenty that are most lovely, after Helen.
If we return to Argos of Akhaia,
flowing with good things of the earth, he'll be
my own adopted son, dear as Orestês,
born long ago and reared in bounteous peace.
I have three daughters now at home, Khrysóthemis,
Laódikê, and Iphiánassa.
He may take whom he will to be his bride
and pay no bridal gift, leading her home
to Pêleus' hall. But I shall add a dowry
such as no man has given to his daughter.
Seven flourishing strongholds I'll give him:
Kardamylê and Enopê and Hirê
in the wild grassland; holy Phêrai too,
and the deep meadowland of Ántheia,
Aipeia and the vineyard slope of Pêdasos,
all lying near the sea in the far west
of sandy Pylos. In these lands are men
who own great flocks and herds; now as his liegemen,
they will pay tithes and sumptuous honor to him,
prospering as they carry out his plans.
These are the gifts I shall arrange if he
desists from anger. Let him be subdued!
Lord Death indeed is deaf to appeal, implacable;
of all gods therefore he is most abhorrent
to mortal men. So let Akhilleus bow to me,
considering that I hold higher rank
and claim the precedence of age."

                                                              To this

Lord Nestor of Gerênia replied:

"Lord Marshal of the army, Agamémnon,
this time the gifts you offer Lord Akhilleus
are not to be despised. Come, we'll dispatch
our chosen emissaries to his quarters
as quickly as possible. Those men whom I
may designate, let them perform the mission.

Phoinix, dear to Zeus, may lead the way.
Let Aías follow him, and Prince Odysseus.
The criers, Hódios and Eurýbatês,
may go as escorts. Bowls for their hands here!
Tell them to keep silence, while we pray
that Zeus the son of Krónos will be merciful."

Nestor's proposal fell on willing ears,
and criers came at once to tip out water
over their hands, while young men filled the winebowls
and dipped a measure into every cup.
They spilt their offerings and drank their fill,
then briskly left the hut of Agamémnon.
Nestor accompanied them with final words
and sage looks, especially for Odysseus,
as to the effort they should make to bring
the son of Pêleus round.

                                        Following Phoinix,

Aías and Odysseus walked together
beside the tumbling clamorous whispering sea,
praying hard to the girdler of the islands
that they might easily sway their great friend's heart.
Amid the ships and huts of the Myrmidons
they found him, taking joy in a sweet harp
of rich and delicate make—the crossbar set
to hold the strings being silver. He had won it
when he destroyed the city of Eëtíôn,
and plucking it he took his joy: he sang
old tales of heroes, while across the room
alone and silent sat Patróklos, waiting
until Akhilleus should be done with song.
Phoinix had come in unremarked, but when
the two new visitors, Odysseus leading,
entered and stood before him, then Akhilleus
rose in wonderment, and left his chair,
his harp still in his hand. So did Patróklos
rise at sight of the two men. Akhilleus
made both welcome with a gesture, saying:

"Peace! My two great friends, I greet your coming.
How I have needed it! Even in my anger,
of all Akhaians, you are closest to me."

And Prince Akhilleus led them in. He seated them
on easy chairs with purple coverlets,
and to Patróklos who stood near he said:

"Put out an ampler winebowl, use more wine
for stronger drink, and place a cup for each.
Here are my dearest friends beneath my roof."

Patróklos did as his companion bade him.
Meanwhile the host set down a carving block
within the fire's rays; a chine of mutton
and a fat chine of goat he placed upon it,
as well as savory pork chine. Automédôn
steadied the meat for him, Akhilleus carved,
then sliced it well and forked it on the spits.
Meanwhile Patróklos, like a god in firelight,
made the hearth blaze up. When the leaping flame
had ebbed and died away, he raked the coals
and in the glow extended spits of meat,
lifting these at times from the firestones
to season with pure salt. When all was done
and the roast meat apportioned into platters,
loaves of bread were passed round by Patróklos
in fine baskets. Akhilleus served the meat.
He took his place then opposite Odysseus,
back to the other wall, and told
Patróklos to make offering to the gods.
This he did with meat tossed in the fire,
then each man's hand went out upon the meal.
When they had put their hunger and thirst away,
Aías nodded silently to Phoinix,
but Prince Odysseus caught the nod. He filled
a cup of wine and lifted it to Akhilleus,
saying:

                                   "Health, Akhilleus. We've no lack
of generous feasts this evening—in the lodge
of Agamémnon first, and now with you,
good fare and plentiful each time.
It is not feasting that concerns us now,
however, but a ruinous defeat.
Before our very eyes we see it coming

and are afraid. By a blade's turn, our good ships
are saved or lost, unless you arm your valor.
Trojans and allies are encamped tonight
in pride before our ramparts, at our sterns,
and through their army burn a thousand fires.
These men are sure they cannot now be stopped
but will get through to our good ships. Lord Zeus
flashes and thunders for them on the right,
and Hektor in his ecstasy of power
is mad for battle, confident in Zeus,
deferring to neither men nor gods. Pure frenzy
fills him, and he prays for the bright dawn
when he will shear our stern-post beaks away
and fire all our ships, while in the shipways
amid that holocaust he carries death
among our men, driven out by smoke. All this
I gravely fear; I fear the gods will make
good his threatenings, and our fate will be
to die here, far from the pastureland of Argos.
Rouse yourself, if even at this hour
you'll pitch in for the Akhaians and deliver them
from Trojan havoc. In the years to come
this day will be remembered pain for you
if you do not. No remedy, no remedy
will come to hand, once the great ill is done.
While there is time, think how to keep this evil
day from the Danáäns!

                                        My dear lad,

how rightly in your case your father, Pêleus,
put it in his farewell, sending you out
from Phthía to take ship with Agamémnon!
'Now as to fighting power, child,' he said,
'if Hêra and Athêna wish, they'll give it.
Control your passion, though, and your proud heart,
for gentle courtesy is a better thing.
Break off insidious quarrels, and young and old,
the Argives will respect you for it more.'
That was your old father's admonition:
you have forgotten. Still, even now, abandon
heart-wounding anger. If you will relent,
Agamémnon will match this change of heart

with gifts. Now listen and let me list for you
what just now in his quarters he proposed:
seven new tripods, and ten bars of gold,
then twenty shining caldrons, and twelve horses,
thoroughbreds, that by their wind and legs
have won him prizes: any man who owned
what these have brought him would not lack resources,
could not be pinched for precious gold—so many
prizes have these horses carried home.
Then he will give you seven women, deft
in household handicraft: women of Lesbos
chosen when you yourself took Lesbos town,
as they outshone all womankind in beauty.
These he will give you, and one more, whom he
took away from you then: Briseus' daughter,
concerning whom he adds a solemn oath
never to have gone to bed or coupled with her,
as custom is, my lord, with men and women.
These are all yours at once. If the immortals
grant us the pillaging of Priam's town,
you may come forward when the spoils are shared
and load your ship with bars of gold and bronze.
Then you may choose among the Trojan women
twenty that are most lovely, after Helen.
And then, if we reach Argos of Akhaia,
flowing with good things of the earth, you'll be
his own adopted son, dear as Orestês,
born long ago and reared in bounteous peace.
He has three daughters now at home, Khrysóthemis,
Laódikê, and Iphiánassa.
You may take whom you will to be your bride
and pay no gift when you conduct her home
to your ancestral hall. He'll add a dowry
such as no man has given to his daughter.
Seven flourishing strongholds he'll give to you:
Kardamylê and Enopê and Hirê
in the wild grassland; holy Phêrai too,
and the deep meadowland of Antheia,
Aipeia and the vineyard slope of Pêdasos,
all lying near the sea in the far west
of sandy Pylos. In these lands are men

who own great flocks and herds; now as your liegemen,
they will pay tithes and sumptuous honor to you,
prospering as they carry out your plans.
These are the gifts he will arrange if you
desist from anger.

                                              Even if you abhor
the son of Atreus all the more bitterly,
with all his gifts, take pity on the rest,
all the old army, worn to rags in battle.
These will honor you as gods are honored!
And ah, for these, what glory you may win!
Think: Hektor is your man this time: being crazed
with ruinous pride, believing there's no fighter
equal to him among those that our ships
brought here by sea, he'll put himself in range!"

Akhilleus the great runner answered him:

"Son of Laërtês and the gods of old,
Odysseus, master soldier and mariner,
I owe you a straight answer, as to how
I see this thing, and how it is to end.
No need to sit with me like mourning doves
making your gentle noise by turns. I hate
as I hate Hell's own gate that man who hides
one thought within him while he speaks another.
What I shall say is what I see and think.
Give in to Agamémnon? I think not,
neither to him nor to the rest. I had
small thanks for fighting, fighting without truce
against hard enemies here. The portion's equal
whether a man hangs back or fights his best;
the same respect, or lack of it, is given
brave man and coward. One who's active dies
like the do-nothing. What least thing have I
to show for it, for harsh days undergone
and my life gambled, all these years of war?
A bird will give her fledglings every scrap
she comes by, and go hungry, foraging.
That is the case with me.
Many a sleepless night I've spent afield

and many a day in bloodshed, hand to hand
in battle for the wives of other men.
In sea raids I plundered a dozen towns,
eleven in expeditions overland
through Trojan country, and the treasure taken
out of them all, great heaps of handsome things,
I carried back each time to Agamémnon.
He sat tight on the beachhead, and shared out
a little treasure; most of it he kept.
He gave prizes of war to his officers;
the rest have theirs, not I; from me alone
of all Akhaians, he pre-empted her.
He holds my bride, dear to my heart. Aye, let him
sleep with her and enjoy her!

                                                    Why must Argives
fight the Trojans? Why did he raise an army
and lead it here? For Helen, was it not?
Are the Atreidai of all mortal men
the only ones who love their wives? I think not.
Every sane decent fellow loves his own
and cares for her, as in my heart I loved
Brisêis, though I won her by the spear.
Now, as he took my prize out of my hands,
tricked and defrauded me, he need not tempt me;
I know him, and he cannot change my mind.
Let him take thought, Odysseus, with you
and others how the ships may be defended
against incendiary attack. By god,
he has achieved imposing work without me,
a rampart piled up overnight, a ditch
running beyond it, broad and deep,
with stakes implanted in it! All no use!
He cannot hold against the killer's charge.
As long as I was in the battle, Hektor
never cared for a fight far from the walls;
his limit was the oak tree by the gate.
When I was alone one day he waited there,
but barely got away when I went after him.
Now it is I who do not care to fight.
Tomorrow at dawn when I have made offering
to Zeus and all the gods, and hauled my ships

for loading in the shallows, if you like
and if it interests you, look out and see
my ships on Hellê's waters in the offing,
oarsmen in line making the sea-foam scud!
And if the great Earthshaker gives a breeze,
the third day out I'll make it home to Phthía.
Rich possessions are there I left behind
when I was mad enough to come here; now
I take home gold and ruddy bronze, and women
belted luxuriously, and hoary iron,
all that came to me here. As for my prize,
he who gave her took her outrageously back.
Well, you can tell him all this to his face,
and let the other Akhaians burn
if he in his thick hide of shamelessness
picks out another man to cheat. He would not
look me in the eye, dog that he is!
I will not share one word of counsel with him,
nor will I act with him; he robbed me blind,
broke faith with me: he gets no second chance
to play me for a fool. Once is enough.
To hell with him, Zeus took his brains away!
His gifts I abominate, and I would give
not one dry shuck for him. I would not change,
not if he multiplied his gifts by ten,
by twenty times what he has now, and more,
no matter where they came from: if he gave
what enters through Orkhómenos' town gate
or Thebes of Egypt, where the treasures lie—
that city where through each of a hundred gates
two hundred men drive out in chariots.
Not if his gifts outnumbered the sea sands
or all the dust grains in the world could Agamémnon
ever appease me—not till he pays me back
full measure, pain for pain, dishonor for dishonor.
The daughter of Agamémnon, son of Atreus,
I will not take in marriage. Let her be
as beautiful as pale-gold Aphrodítê,
skilled as Athêna of the sea-grey eyes,
I will not have her, at any price. No, let him

find someone else, an eligible Akhaian,
kinglier than I.

                                        Now if the gods
preserve me and I make it home, my father
Pêleus will select a bride for me.
In Hellas and in Phthía there are many
daughters of strong men who defend the towns.
I'll take the one I wish to be my wife.
There in my manhood I have longed, indeed,
to marry someone of congenial mind
and take my ease, enjoying the great estate
my father had acquired.

                                        Now I think
no riches can compare with being alive,
not even those they say this well-built Ilion
stored up in peace before the Akhaians came.
Neither could all the Archer's shrine contains
at rocky Pytho, in the crypt of stone.
A man may come by cattle and sheep in raids;
tripods he buys, and tawny-headed horses;
but his life's breath cannot be hunted back
or be recaptured once it pass his lips.
My mother, Thetis of the silvery feet,
tells me of two possible destinies
carrying me toward death: two ways:
if on the one hand I remain to fight
around Troy town, I lose all hope of home
but gain unfading glory; on the other,
if I sail back to my own land my glory
fails—but a long life lies ahead for me.
To all the rest of you I say: 'Sail home:
you will not now see Ilion's last hour,'
for Zeus who views the wide world held his sheltering
hand over that city, and her troops
have taken heart.

                                        Return, then, emissaries,
deliver my answer to the Akhaian peers—
it is the senior officer's privilege—
and let them plan some other way, and better,
to save their ships and save the Akhaian army.
This one cannot be put into effect—

their scheme this evening—while my anger holds.
Phoinix may stay and lodge the night with us,
then take ship and sail homeward at my side
tomorrow, if he wills. I'll not constrain him."

After Akhilleus finished, all were silent,
awed, for he spoke with power.
Then the old master-charioteer, Lord Phoinix,
answered at last, and let his tears come shining,
fearing for the Akhaian ships:

                                              'Akhilleus,

if it is true you set your heart on home
and will not stir a finger to save the ships
from being engulfed by fire—all for this rage
that has swept over you—how, child, could I
be sundered from you, left behind alone?
For your sake the old master-charioteer,
Pêleus, made provision that I should come,
that day he gave you godspeed out of Phthía
to go with Agamémnon. Still a boy,
you knew nothing of war that levels men
to the same testing, nothing of assembly
where men become illustrious. That is why
he sent me, to instruct you in these matters,
to be a man of eloquence and action.
After all that, dear child, I should not wish
to be left here apart from you—not even
if god himself should undertake to smooth
my wrinkled age and make me fresh and young,
as when for the first time I left the land
of lovely women, Hellas. I went north
to avoid a feud with Father, Amyntor
Orménidês. His anger against me rose
over a fair-haired slave girl whom he fancied,
without respect for his own wife, my mother.
Mother embraced my knees and begged that I
make love to this girl, so that afterward
she might be cold to the aging man. I did it.
My father guessed the truth at once, and cursed me,
praying the ghostly Furies that no son

of mine should ever rest upon his knees:
a curse fulfilled by the immortals—Lord
Zeus of undergloom and cold Perséphonê.
I planned to put a sword in him, and would have,
had not some god unstrung my rage, reminding me
of country gossip and the frowns of men;
I shrank from being called a parricide
among the Akhaians. But from that time on
I felt no tie with home, no love for lingering
under the rooftree of a raging father.
Our household and our neighbors, it is true,
urged me to stay. They made a handsome feast
of shambling cattle butchered, and fat sheep;
young porkers by the litter, crisp with fat,
were singed and spitted in Hêphaistos' fire,
rivers of wine drunk from the old man's store.
Nine times they spent the night and slept beside me,
taking the watch by turns, leaving a fire
to flicker under the entrance colonnade,
and one more in the court outside my room.
But when the tenth night came, starless and black,
I cracked the tight bolt on my chamber door,
pushed out, and scaled the courtyard wall, unseen
by household men on watch or women slaves.
Then I escaped from that place, made my way
through Hellas where the dancing floors are wide,
until I came to Phthía's fertile plain,
mother of flocks, and Pêleus the king.
He gave me welcome, treated me with love,
as a father would an only son, his heir
to rich possessions. And he made me rich,
appointing me great numbers of retainers
on the frontier of Phthía, where I lived
as lord of Dolopês. Now, it was I
who formed your manhood, handsome as a god's,
Akhilleus: I who loved you from the heart;
for never in another's company
would you attend a feast or dine in hall—
never, unless I took you on my knees
and cut your meat, and held your cup of wine.
Many a time you wet my shirt, hiccuping

wine-bubbles in distress, when you were small.
Patient and laborious as a nurse
I had to be for you, bearing in mind
that never would the gods bring into being
any son of mine. Godlike Akhilleus,
you were the manchild that I made my own
to save me someday, so I thought, from misery.
Quell your anger, Akhilleus! You must not
be pitiless! The gods themselves relent,
and are they not still greater in bravery,
in honor and in strength? Burnt offerings,
courteous prayer, libation, smoke of sacrifice,
with all of these, men can placate the gods
when someone oversteps and errs. The truth is,
prayers are daughters of almighty Zeus—
one may imagine them lame, wrinkled things
with eyes cast down, that toil to follow after
passionate Folly. Folly is strong and swift,
outrunning all the prayers, and everywhere
arriving first to injure mortal men;
still they come healing after. If a man
reveres the daughters of Zeus when they come near,
he is rewarded, and his prayers are heard;
but if he spurns them and dismisses them,
they make their way to Zeus again and ask
that Folly dog that man till suffering
has taken arrogance out of him.

                                              Relent,

be courteous to the daughters of Zeus, you too,
as courtesy sways others, and the best.
If Agamémnon had no gifts for you,
named none to follow, but inveighed against you
still in fury, then I could never say,
'Discard your anger and defend the Argives—'
never, no matter how they craved your help.
But this is not so: he will give many things
at once; he promised others; he has sent
his noblest men to intercede with you,
the flower of the army, and your friends,
dearest among the Argives. Will you turn
their words, their coming, into humiliation?

Until this moment, no one took it ill
that you should suffer anger; we learned this
from the old stories of how towering wrath
could overcome great men; but they were still
amenable to gifts and to persuasion.
Here is an instance I myself remember
not from our own time but in ancient days:
I'll tell it to you all, for all are friends.
The Kourêtês were fighting a warlike race,
Aitolians, around the walls of Kálydôn,
with slaughter on both sides: Aitolians
defending their beloved Kálydôn
while the Kourêtês longed to sack the town.
The truth is, Artemis of the Golden Chair
had brought the scourge of war on the Aitolians;
she had been angered because Oineus made
no harvest offering from his vineyard slope.
While other gods enjoyed his hekatombs
he made her none, either forgetful of it
or careless—a great error, either way.
In her anger, the Mistress of Long Arrows
roused against him a boar with gleaming tusks
out of his wild grass bed, a monstrous thing
that ravaged the man's vineyard many times
and felled entire orchards, roots,
blooms, apples and all. Now this great boar
Meléagros, the son of Oineus, killed
by gathering men and hounds from far and near.
So huge the boar was, no small band could master him,
and he brought many to the dolorous pyre.
Around the dead beast Artemis set on
a clash with battlecries between Kourêtês
and proud Aitolians over the boar's head
and shaggy hide. As long, then, as Meléagros,
backed by the wargod, fought, the Kourêtês
had the worst of it for all their numbers
and could not hold a line outside the walls.
But then a day came when Meléagros
was stung by venomous anger that infects
the coolest thinker's heart: swollen with rage
at his own mother, Althaiê, he languished

in idleness at home beside his lady,
Kleopátrê.

                               This lovely girl was born
to Marpessê of ravishing pale ankles,
Euênos' child, and Idês, who had been
most powerful of men on earth. He drew
the bow against the Lord Phoibos Apollo
over his love, Marpessê, whom her father
and gentle mother called Alkýonê,
since for her sake her mother gave that seabird's
forlorn cry when Apollo ravished her.
With Kleopátrê lay Meléagros,
nursing the bitterness his mother stirred,
when in her anguish over a brother slain
she cursed her son. She called upon the gods,
beating the grassy earth with both her hands
as she pitched forward on her knees, with cries
to the Lord of Undergloom and cold Perséphonê,
while tears wetted her veils—in her entreaty
that death come to her son. Inexorable
in Érebos a vampire Fury listened.
Soon, then, about the gates of the Aitolians
tumult and din of war grew loud; their towers
rang with blows. And now the elder men
implored Meléagros to leave his room,
and sent the high priests of the gods, imploring him
to help defend the town. They promised him
a large reward: in the green countryside
of Kálydôn, wherever it was richest,
there he might choose a beautiful garden plot
of fifty acres, half in vineyard, half
in virgin prairie for the plow to cut.
Oineus, master of horsemen, came with prayers
upon the doorsill of the chamber, often
rattling the locked doors, pleading with his son.
His sisters, too, and then his gentle mother
pleaded with him. Only the more fiercely
he turned away. His oldest friends, his dearest,
not even they could move him—not until
his room was shaken by a hail of stones

as Kourêtês began to scale the walls
and fire the city.

                                        Then at last his lady
in her soft-belted gown besought him weeping,
speaking of all the ills that come to men
whose town is taken: soldiers put to the sword;
the city razed by fire; alien hands
carrying off the children and the women.
Hearing these fearful things, his heart was stirred
to action: he put on his shining gear
and fought off ruin from the Aitolians.
Mercy prevailed in him. His folk no longer
cared to award him gifts and luxuries,
yet even so he saved that terrible day.
Oh, do not let your mind go so astray!
Let no malignant spirit
turn you that way, dear son! It will be worse
to fight for ships already set afire!
Value the gifts; rejoin the war; Akhaians
afterward will give you a god's honor.
If you reject the gifts and then, later,
enter the deadly fight, you will not be
accorded the same honor, even though
you turn the tide of war!"

                                        But the great runner
Akhilleus answered:

                                "Old uncle Phoinix, bless you,
that is an honor I can live without.
Honored I think I am by Zeus's justice,
justice that will sustain me by the ships
as long as breath is in me and I can stand.
Here is another point: ponder it well:
best not confuse my heart with lamentation
for Agamémnon, whom you must not honor;
you would be hateful to me, dear as you are.
Loyalty should array you at my side
in giving pain to him who gives me pain.
Rule with me equally, share half my honor,
but do not ask my help for Agamémnon.

My answer will be reported by these two.
Lodge here in a soft bed, and at first light
we can decide whether to sail or stay."

He knit his brows and nodded to Patróklos
to pile up rugs for Phoinix' bed—a sign
for the others to be quick about departing.
Aías, however, noble son of Télamôn
made the last appeal. He said:

                                                    "Odysseus,
master soldier and mariner, let us go.
I do not see the end of this affair
achieved by this night's visit. Nothing for it
but to report our talk for what it's worth
to the Danääns, who sit waiting there.
Akhilleus hardened his great heart against us,
wayward and savage as he is, unmoved
by the affections of his friends who made him
honored above all others on the beachhead.
There is no pity in him. A normal man
will take the penalty for a brother slain
or a dead son. By paying much, the one
who did the deed may stay unharmed at home.
Fury and pride in the bereaved are curbed
when he accepts the penalty. Not you.
Cruel and unappeasable rage the gods
put in you for one girl alone. We offer
seven beauties, and much more besides!
Be gentler, and respect your own rooftree
whereunder we are guests who speak for all
Danääns as a body. Our desire
is to be closest to you of them all."

Akhilleus the great runner answered him:

"Scion of Télamôn and gods of old,
Aías, lord of fighting men, you seemed
to echo my own mind in what you said!
And yet my heart grows large and hot with fury
remembering that affair: as though I were

some riffraff or camp follower, he taunted me
before them all!

                            Go back, report the news:
I will not think of carnage or of war
until Prince Hektor, son of Priam, reaches
Myrmidon huts and ships in his attack,
slashing through Argives, burning down their ships.
Around my hut, my black ship, I foresee
for all his fury, Hektor will break off combat."
That was his answer. Each of the emissaries
took up a double-handed cup and poured
libation by the shipways. Then Odysseus
led the way on their return. Patróklos
commanded his retainers and the maids
to make at once a deep-piled bed for Phoinix.
Obediently they did so, spreading out
fleeces and coverlet and a linen sheet,
and down the old man lay, awaiting Dawn.
Akhilleus slept in the well-built hut's recess,
and with him lay a woman he had brought
from Lesbos, Phorbas' daughter, Diomêdê.
Patróklos went to bed at the other end,
and with him, too, a woman lay—soft-belted
Iphis, who had been given to him by Akhilleus
when he took Skyros, ringed by cliff, the mountain
fastness of Enyéus.

                                Now the emissaries
arrived at Agamémnon's ledge. With cups
of gold held up, and rising to their feet
on every side, the Akhaians greeted them,
curious for the news. Lord Agamémnon
put the question first:

                                "Come, tell me, sir,
Odysseus, glory of Akhaia—will Akhilleus
fight off ravenous fire from the ships
or does he still refuse, does anger still
hold sway in his great heart?"

                                That patient man,
the Prince Odysseus, made reply:

"Excellency,

Lord Marshal of the army, son of Atreus,
the man has no desire to quench his rage.
On the contrary, he is more than ever
full of anger, spurns you and your gifts,
calls on you to work out your own defense
to save the ships and the Akhaian army.
As for himself, he threatens at daybreak
to drag his well-found ships into the surf,
and says he would advise the rest as well
to sail for home. 'You shall not see,' he says,
'the last hour that awaits tall Ilion,
for Zeus who views the wide world held his sheltering
hand over the city, and her troops
have taken heart.' That was Akhilleus' answer.
Those who were with me can confirm all this,
Aías can, and the two clearheaded criers.
As to old Phoinix, he is sleeping there
by invitation, so that he may sail
to his own country, homeward with Akhilleus,
tomorrow, if he wills, without constraint."

When he had finished everyone was still,
sitting in silence and in perturbation
for a long time. At last brave Diomêdês,
lord of the warcry, said:

"Excellency,

Lord Marshal of the army, Agamémnon,
you never should have pled with him, or given
so many gifts to him. At the best of times
he is a proud man; now you have pushed him far
deeper into his vanity and pride.
By god, let us have done with him—
whether he goes or stays! He'll fight again
when the time comes, whenever his blood is up
or the god rouses him. As for ourselves,
let everyone now do as I advise
and go to rest. Your hearts have been refreshed
with bread and wine, the pith and nerve of men.
When the fair Dawn with finger tips of rose

makes heaven bright, deploy your men and horses
before the ships at once, and cheer them on,
and take your place, yourself, in the front line
to join the battle."

                                    All gave their assent
in admiration of Diomêdês,
breaker of horses. When they had spilt their wine
they all dispersed, each man to his own hut,
and lying down they took the gift of sleep.

BOOK TEN

Night in the Camp: A Foray

They slept then, all the rest, along the shipways,
captains of Akhaia, overcome
nightlong by slumber; but their high commander,
Agamémnon, lay beyond sweet sleep
and cast about in tumult of the mind.
As when the lord of fair-haired Hêra flashes,
bringing on giant storms of rain or hail
or wintry blizzard, sifting on grey fields—
or the wide jaws of drear and bitter war—
so thick and fast the groans of Agamémnon
came from his heart's core, and his very entrails
shook with groaning. Ai! When he looked out
in wonder and dismay upon the plain
where fires burned, a myriad, before Troy,
and heard flute sounds and pipes, nocturnal hum

of men encamped there; when he looked again
at his Akhaians and their ships, before
high Zeus he tore his hair out by the roots
and groaned, groaned from the well of his great heart.
But this expedient came into his mind:
to visit Nestor, first of all, and see
what plan if any could be formed with him—
some well-wrought plan that might avoid the worst
for the Danääns. And, rising,
he pulled his tunic on over his ribs
and tied his smooth feet into good rawhide sandals,
took a great tawny lionskin for mantle,
dangling to his heels, and gripped a spear.

Now Meneláos, like his brother, shaken,
lay unsleeping, open-eyed, foreboding
anguish for the Argives, who had come
for his sake many a long sea mile to Troy
to wage the daring war. He rose and cloaked
his broad back with a spotted leopardskin,
picked up a bronze-rimmed helmet for his head,
and took a long spear in his fist, to go
arouse his brother, lord of all the Argives,
whom as a god the common folk revered.
He found him buckling on his handsome baldric
close to the ship stern, and he turned in joy
to see Meneláos come. Then Meneláos,
lord of the warcry, said:

                                          "Why under arms,
dear brother? Will you call for a volunteer
to look the Trojans over? Hardly one
will take that duty on, I fear: alone
to circle and scout the dangerous enemy
in the starry night. It will take nerve to do it."

Agamémnon answered:

                                          "You and I
must have some plan of action, Meneláos,
and a good one, too—some plan to keep the troops
and ships from ruin. Zeus's mood has changed;

he cares for Hektor's offerings more than ours.
In my lifetime I have not seen or heard
of one man doing in a day's action
what Hektor did to the Akhaian army—
one man, son of neither god nor goddess,
in one day's action—but for years to come
that havoc will be felt among the Argives.
Go now, wake Idómeneus and Aías.
Go on the run along the ships, and I
will turn out Nestor, if he'll come to join us
at the first sentry post and give commands.
He is the one they should most willingly
obey: his own son heads a company
with Idómeneus' lieutenant, Meríonês.
We put the sentries mainly in their charge."

Said Meneláos in reply:

                                                    "But how
do you intend this order? Am I to stay
with those two, waiting till you come,
or track you on the run, after I tell them?"

The Lord Marshal Agamémnon answered:

"Stay in their company. We might not meet,
coming and going: there are many paths
through the encampment. When you go, speak out,
tell them to rouse themselves, but courteously,
giving each man his patronymic and
his rank; and do not feel it is beneath you.
We must do service, too. That is the way
the Lord Zeus burdened us when we were born."

With these words, making clear what he commanded,
he sent his brother off, while he himself
went on toward Nestor. Close to his hut and ship
he found him in a bed of fleece. Nearby
his glinting arms were lying: a round shield,
two lances, and a helmet burnished bright.
There lay his many-faceted kilt or loin-guard,
girded on when the old man armed for war

to take his soldiers forward, undeterred
by doleful age.

                    He heaved up on his elbow,
lifting his head, and peering in the dark,
he asked: "Who are you, going about alone
amid the host by night when others sleep?
Looking for some stray mule or some companion?
Speak: don't stand there silent; what do you want?"

Then the Lord Marshal Agamémnon answered:

"Nestor, son of Nêleus, pride of Akhaians,
know me for Agamémnon, son of Atreus,
plunged by Zeus into the worst trouble
a man could know, for as long as I draw breath,
as long as my own legs will carry me.
I roam this way because no sleep will come
to settle on my eyes; the war stays with me
and what the army suffers. How I fear
for our Akhaians! Quietude of heart
I have none: fever of dread is in my brain,
my heart leaps from my ribs, my knees give way.
If you will act—and even you are sleepless—
let us inspect the sentries and make sure
they are not drugged by weariness,
not lying asleep, their duty all forgotten.
Hard enemies are encamped nearby. We cannot
say for sure they'll not attack by night."

Earl Nestor of Gerênia answered:

                              "Lord
Marshal of the army, Agamémnon,
Zeus the Profound will not achieve for Hektor
all that the man imagines now, or hopes for.
I think he, too, will have his difficulties,
and more, if ever Akhilleus drops his anger.
But I will come with you, and gladly. Why not
awaken others to join us—Diomêdês,
who is a wonder with a spear, Odysseus, and
Aías, the fast one, and the son of Phyleus?
Someone might go as well and waken Aías,
the tall one, and Idómeneus—their ships

are not so near, any of them. Moreover,
dear and respected as your brother is,
I have hard words for him. You may resent it;
I will not hide it: see the way he sleeps
and leaves the toil and worry to you alone!
He should be up and asking help of all
our noblest, now the inexorable need
has come upon us."

                                    The Lord Marshal said:

"Sir, I should say, accuse him another time.
He often does go easy and holds off,
not out of laziness or lightness of mind
but following my lead, deferring to me.
This time, though, he was the first to rise,
and came to me. I sent him off to summon
the very men you name. Let us go on,
we'll come across them at the sentry post
outside the gates. All were to gather there."

Earl Nestor of Gerênia replied:

"No Argive then can take it ill; no one
will disregard him when he calls to action."

With this he pulled his tunic to his waist,
tied his smooth feet into good rawhide sandals,
and gathered round him with a brooch
his great red double mantle, lined with fleece.
He picked a tough spear capped with whetted bronze
and made his way along the Akhaian ships.
Coming first on Odysseus, peer of Zeus
in stratagems, he gave a call to wake him.
Clear in the sleeper's shrouded mind it rang
and he burst startled from his hut to ask:

"Why are you out wandering through the army,
you alone, in the starry night? What brings you?"

Earl Nestor of Gerênia replied:

"Son of Laërtês and the gods of old,
Odysseus, master mariner and soldier,

do not be vexed at this. The Akhaians' peril
warrants it. Now, come along with us,
and we shall find another man to waken—
someone fit to advise retreat or war."

The great tactician stepped inside and picked
a painted shield to hang from his broad shoulders,
then he went after them. The next in line
was Diomêdês, and outside his hut
they found him with his gear of war. Around him
his men were sleeping, pillowed on their shields,
with spears driven upright, butt-spikes in the ground:
point after point of bronze reflecting light
into the distance, like a glare of lightning
flung by Father Zeus. But the hero slept,
a bull's hide spread beneath him, and a bright
unfolded rug beneath his head. Beside him
Nestor of Gerênia took his stand
and jogged him with his foot, then lectured him:

"Up; get up, Diomêdês! Will you snore
the whole night through? Do you not know the Trojans
have taken up positions near the ships
where the beach rises—only a stone's throw off?"

At this the hero, starting up from sleep,
gave back a rough reply:

                                    "Hard as a knife
is what you are, old man. By night and day
you never rest. Are there no younger men
who might go round about to wake the captains
one by one? Can no one hold you down?"

Then Nestor said:

                                    "No doubt of it, dear lad,
there's reason in what you say. I have indeed
able young sons and soldiers, many of them,
any of whom could go and bear the summons.
Terrible pressure is upon us, though;
the issue teeters on a razor's edge
for all Akhaians—whether we live or perish.

Go and rouse Mégês, rouse Aías the runner,
if as a younger man you'd spare my age."

Diomêdês took for full-length cape the skin
of a great tawny lion, picked a spear,
and ran to rouse the others and conduct them.
Filing out among the sentries, then,
they found that not one captain was asleep;
each man sat up, all wakeful, under arms.
As shepherd dogs keep bristling watch, their ears
pricked up at the approach of a wild beast
roaming down hills through woodland, toward the fold;
they hear an outcry, far away, of men
and watchdogs, and their rest is at an end:
so for these sentries rest had been dispelled
as they kept watch on that bad night, forever
facing the plain, peering when they could catch
a sound of Trojans moving. And old Nestor,
in his relief at seeing them, said heartily:

"That is the way to keep your watch, dear lads,
sleep must not capture one of you, or all
may well give cause for gloating to the enemy."

He crossed the moat then, and the peers who came
to attend the council followed him,
as did Meríonês and Nestor's son,
whom they had asked to join them. Once across,
they sat down in the clear, an open space
not littered with dead bodies—the same place
where Hektor in his power had turned back
from slaughtering Argives, when the night came down
and shrouded all. Here, then, they sat and talked,
and first to speak was Nestor.

                              "Friends," he said,
"is there no man who trusts his own brave heart
enough to make a foray on the Trojans,
killing some isolated guard, perhaps,
or picking up information—overhearing
plans they exchange among themselves? Have they

a mind to stay afield, here by the ships,
or to re-enter Troy, since they defeated us?
A man might learn these things and get away
unhurt to join us; and his feat would be
renowned among all people under heaven.
A handsome prize will be awarded him:
every commander of a ship division
gives him a black ewe, with a suckling lamb—
no token of honor like it. Afterward
he can attend all feasts and drinking parties."

Now at this challenge everyone grew still,
but Diomêdês in their midst spoke out:

"Nestor, pride and excitement urge me on
to make a foray into the enemy camp
so close at hand here. If some other soldier
goes along, it will be better, though—
more warmth to it. Two men can make a team:
one will catch on quicker than the other
when there's a chance of bringing something off,
while one man's eyes and wit may move more slowly."

Volunteers aplenty desired to go
with Diomêdês: Aías the Tall; Short Aías;
Meríonês the eager son of Nestor;
the spearman, Meneláos. Then Odysseus,
that rugged man, wished, too, to pierce the lines,
bold for adventure, as he always was.
Now the Lord Marshal Agamémnon said:

"Diomêdês, my own right arm, you name
your own companion; take the one you want,
the best of those whose hands are up. You have
plenty to choose from. No damned bashfulness
that might incline you to pass by the strongest
and take a lesser man, through deference
to birth or to rank higher than your own."
He said this, fearing for his red-haired brother,
Meneláos. But Diomêdês said:

"If this is a command, and I may choose,
could I pass by that kingly man, Odysseus?

Shrewd as he is, and cool and brave, beyond
all others in rough work. Pallas Athêna
loves that man. If he were at my side
we'd go through fire and come back,
the two of us. No man knows war as he does."

Rejoined the Lord Odysseus:

                                        "Diomêdês,
no good flattering me, or carping, either—
not before men who know me through and through.
We should be on our way. How the night passes!
Dawn is near: high stars have all gone down.
Two thirds of night are gone; one third is left us."

Then both men buckled on grim gear of war.
Diomêdês was given by Thrasymêdês
a two-edged sword—for his own was at the ship—
and a shield, too. Upon his head he pulled
a bull's-hide helmet with no ridge or plume,
a so-called "cut down" made to guard the skulls
of rugged men-at-arms. Meríonês
handed Odysseus his bow and quiver,
gave him a two-edged sword, and fitted on
a helmet that was first a cap of hide
with bands of leather crisscrossed, and on these
a boar's white teeth were thickly set, disposed
with cunning on all sides. A felt lining
padded the cap. This helm Autólykos
brought in the old days out of Eleôn,
where he had made a breach in the palace wall
of Amyntor, the son of Órmenos.
He gave it to Amphídamas the Kýthêran,
Skandeia-bound; Amphídamas in return
for hospitality gave it to Mólos,
and Mólos handed it on to his own son,
Meríonês, to wear in battle. Now
it capped Odysseus' head.

                                        Grimly accoutered,
the two moved out into the darkness, leaving
all their peers behind. Off to the right

along their path, Pallas Athêna sent
a heron gliding down the night. They could not
see it passing, but they heard its cry;
and heartened by that fisher bird, Odysseus
prayed:

> "O child of Zeus who bears the stormcloud,
> hear me. In hard hours ever at my side
> you follow every move I make: tonight
> befriend me most, Athêna.
> Before we two retire on the ships
> let us bring off some feat to gall the Trojans."

In his turn Diomêdês, lord of the warcry,
prayed:

> "O tireless one, hear me as well:
> be with me, as with Tydeus once, my father,
> when he advanced as messenger to Thebes
> ahead of all Akhaians—left the Akhaians
> on the Asôpos river under arms.
> His words to the Kadmeians were like honey,
> but terrible were the actions he devised
> as he withdrew, bright goddess, with your blessing.
> Now in the same way bless me, guard me now.
> For my part I shall offer at your altar
> a virgin heifer, a yearling, never yoked,
> her horns all sheathed in gold."

> These were their prayers,
and Pallas Athêna, Zeus's daughter, heard them.

Falling silent after invoking her,
they made their way like lions through black night
toward kills and carnage, braving spears and blood.

Neither were Trojan leaders permitted sleep
by Hektor, but he called them all together,
all who were lords and captains of the Trojans,
to put his plan before them:

> "Who volunteers
to undertake this mission and see it through

for a great prize? He will have satisfaction!
A chariot and two mettlesome fine horses,
best of those beside the Akhaian ships,
for the man who dares to win fame for himself
by a night patrol along the ships, to learn
if they are guarded as before. It may be
the Akhaians were so battered by our charge
that now they talk of sailing, and are so weary
that now they have no will for a night watch."

The listening Trojans all grew mute and still.
Among them there was one by the name of Dolôn;
rich in gold, and rich in bronze, this man
was heir to the great herald, Eumêdês,
and a good runner, puny though he seemed,
an only son, with five sisters. He spoke
before the Trojans in response to Hektor:

"Hektor, pride and excitement urge me on
to make this night patrol close to the ships
for information. Only, lift up your staff
and swear that my reward will be that team
and brazen car that bear the son of Pêleus.
For my part, I take oath not to be blind
on this patrol, or let you down. I'll make it
straight through all the camp until I reach the ship
of Agamémnon. There the Akhaian captains
must be debating battle or retreat."

Hektor complied, held up his staff, and swore:

"May Zeus in thunder, consort of Hêra, witness
this: no other Trojan rides that car
behind that team. I say that you will do so.
It is to be your glory."

                                                    So he swore

an oath to incite the man—and swore in vain.
At once the runner slung his curving bow
over his shoulders, and for cloak the skin
of a grey wolf. He took a cap of weasel,
picked up a javelin, and headed down

for the line of ships, leaving the Trojan camp—
but he would not return with news for Hektor.
When he had left the troops and tethered horses,
trotting eagerly on the seaward path,
Odysseus caught sight of the man coming
and whispered to Diomêdês:

                                        "Who is this,
now headed toward us from the camp? A scout,
on night patrol along the ships, or bent
on rifling some dead body—I can't say.
Let him just pass into open ground a little
and we can catch him from behind. If he outruns us,
once we are in between him and his base,
attack with a spear-throw, force him on the ships:
not to let him cut back to the town."

The two conversed in whispers, then lay still,
flattened among dead bodies off the path,
while the unwary man came running by.
But when he had passed them fifty yards or so—
a field's width, say, a team of mules could plow,
being faster at this work than oxen, dragging
a bolted plowshare in a furrow—both
ran after him. And at the sound of feet
he stood stock-still, for in his heart he hoped
that at a nod from Hektor fellow Trojans
were on their way to fetch him back. Now only
a spear-throw distant from him, maybe less,
he recognized the Akhaian enemies
and took to his heels. The two veered after him.
As when two hounds, well-trained in tricks of game,
hang on behind a young buck or a hare
through wooded land, and the quarry races on
emitting shrieks of dread—so Diomêdês
and Odysseus, raider of cities, chased their man
after they cut him off from his own army.
Seaward he fled, and now when he seemed headed
straight into the sentries' arms, Athêna
set Diomêdês raging not to give
some other lucky Akhaian the first shot

by being slow to catch up. Poising his lance,
Diomêdês managed a great burst of speed
and called out:

                    "Halt!—or else my spear goes through you!
Plunging death is coming at my hands!
You cannot get away!"

                                        In fact, he threw,
but missed deliberately: the spearhead passed
above the man's right shoulder and stuck fast
before him in the ground. In panic fear
the runner tripped and stopped, a chattering noise
came from his mouth, and he turned faint and pale.
The two men, panting, soon came up with him
to pin his arms. But now in tears he begged them:

"Take me alive! I can arrange a ransom!
Iron and bronze and gold I have at home,
and Father will not count the cost if only
he knows me safe amid the Akhaian ships!"

The shrewd captain, Odysseus, answered him:

"Courage, you need not feel your death so near.
Tell me this, though, and plainly: what has brought you
out of your camp and this way toward the ships
alone by night, when others take their rest?
Would you despoil some corpse among the dead,
or were you sent by Hektor to find out
our dispositions at the ships?—or did you
wish to find out, yourself?"

                                        Dolôn replied,
his legs shaking under him:

                                        "Carried away,
I was, against my own good sense, by Hektor.
He said Akhilleus' team would be my prize,
his chariot, too, all trimmed with bronze. He told me
to go through the black night, now swiftly passing,
and to approach our enemies—to learn
if guards are posted at the ships as usual
or if the Akhaians, punished at our hands,

are in accord to sail and, being far gone
in weariness, have no will for a night watch."

At this the great tactician smiled. He said:

"By heaven, quite a reward was in your grasp—
the car and horses owned by the great fighter,
Aíakos' grandson. That is a fractious team
for mortal men to master! Not for Akhilleus,
but he was born of an immortal mother.
Tell me this now, give me a plain answer:
Where is Hektor?
Where did you leave him when you took this path?
His arms, where are they lying? Where are his horses?
How have the other Trojans planned their watches
and hours for sleep?"

                                 Dolôn again made answer:

"Hektor is with his staff, holding a council
beside the funeral mound of the patriarch
Ilos, far from the battlefield. No watches
in your sense, sir, are being stood, no sentries
chosen to guard the camp. At every fire
the necessary number are awake
and keep one another vigilant. Detachments
of allies, though, are everywhere asleep
and leave the sentry duty to the Trojans.
Allies have no families near at hand."

The great tactician, Odysseus, said to him:

"And how are they encamped? Mixed in with Trojans
or separately? Tell me about each one;
I must know this."

                                         Dolôn replied:

                                         "I'll tell you.

Nearest the sea are Karians and Paiônês
with Lelegês, Kaukônês, and Pelasgians.
Up the Skamánder are the Lykians, Mysians,
Phrygian horsemen, and Mêionians—

but why do you question me on these details?
If you are bent on raiding a Trojan company,
yonder are Thracians just arrived, far out
on the left wing, apart from everyone.
Their king is Rhêsos Eïónidês,
his horses the most royal I have seen,
whiter than snow and swift as the seawind.
His chariot is a masterwork in gold
and silver, and the armor, huge and golden,
brought by him here is marvelous to see,
like no war-gear of men but of immortals . . .
You'll take me to the ships now, will you not?
Or will you leave me here, bound hand and foot,
while you go forward, testing what I told you
for accuracy and advantage to yourselves?"

Diomêdês frowned and looked at him and said:

"As I see it, you need not hold this thought
of slipping through our hands, now you are in them,
accurate though your facts may be. Suppose
we let you go, or let you go for ransom?
Later, by god, you'll come down on the ships
to spy again, or to make open war!
Resign your life now at my hands.
You make no further trouble for the Argives."

Even as he spoke, the man leaned forward, reaching
to touch his chin, beseeching; but he brought
his sword-blade in a flash down on the nape
and severed the two tendons. In the dust
the head of the still crying man was muffled.
Now they pulled off his cap of weasel skin,
his grey wolf jacket, javelin, and bow,
and Lord Odysseus held these trophies high
to Athêna, Hope of Soldiers. He appealed to her:

"Joy in this armor, goddess, first on Olympos,
first of immortals in our invocation!
Give us more luck, send us against that Thracian
bivouac and horses!"

                                          And at this
he rid himself of Dolôn's gear by lifting it
into a tamarisk tree. He bundled it
and made it easier to see by breaking
tamarisk shoots and twigs from underneath,
so he and Diomêdês could not miss it
on their way back in the night now swiftly passing.
Onward they pressed now, braving spears and blood,
and came soon to the bivouac of Thracians
at the camp's edge. Here weary troops were sleeping,
armor beside them canted on the ground
in three well-ordered rows. The chariot teams
were tethered, each one, near their charioteer,
and in the center Rhêsos slept. Beside him
snowy horses were tethered by the reins
that ran from the chariot rail. Odysseus first
distinguished him and whispered, pointing him out
to Diomêdês:

                          "There is the man; there are
the horses Dolôn whom we killed described.
Come put your back in it, your heart: why stand here
in arms for nothing? Go untie the horses,
or let me do it, while you kill the men."

Grey-eyed Athêna filled Diomêdês' heart
with fury. Whirling left and right he struck,
and pitiable sounds came from the bodies
cleft by the sword's edge. Earth ran red with blood.
As on a flock of goats or sheep, unshepherded
and undefended, a baleful lion falls,
the son of Tydeus fell upon those Thracians
until he had killed twelve. And at his shoulder
Odysseus, adept at war, moved up
to drag out by the heels each man he killed,
thinking by this to save the beautiful horses
from shying at the bodies when they passed—
being unused to dead men yet.

                                          At last

when Diomêdês reached the Thracian king,
he took a thirteenth precious life away

as the man gasped in sleep, nightmare upon him.
Meanwhile patient Odysseus freed the horses,
hitching them together by the reins,
and drove them off. He used his bow to whack them,
missing the whip fixed in the painted chariot
ready to his hand. With a low whistle
he made Diomêdês look—but Diomêdês
waited, pondering what next to try
in the way of outrage. Would he lift the pole
and pilfer the king's chariot with his weapons,
or take the life of still more Thracian men?
His heart distended at the thought, when near him
out of the night air turning, Athêna stood
and said:

                  "No, put your mind on getting back
to your own camp, son of great-hearted Tydeus,
unless you choose to run for it, supposing
some other god may wake the Trojans now."

Diomêdês respected the goddess' voice
and turned to mount the chariot. Odysseus
used his bow for whip, and off they went
to the ships of the Akhaians.

                           No blind watch

was kept by Apollo of the silver bow,
who saw Athêna following Diomêdês.
Irritated by her, he joined a company
of Trojans, and aroused Hippokoôn,
a noble cousin of Rhêsos. Out of sleep
the man awoke and saw the empty ground
where once fast teams had stood; he saw the soldiers
massacred and soaking in their blood,
and cried aloud at this, calling his friends.
Soon there were other cries, and a wild din
of troops who ran up, staring at the horrors
done in that sortie from the ships.

                               Now those

who did that work had reached, on their return,
the spot where they had killed Hektor's observer.
Noble Odysseus here reined in the team

while Diomêdês vaulted down to sweep
the bloody trophies into Odysseus' hands
and then remounted—and he whipped the horses
into a willing run.

Of all Akhaians
Nestor first heard the beat of distant hooves
and said:

"Friends, lords, and captains of the Argives,
do I imagine it or is it real?
A drumming of distant hooves is in my ears.
May it turn out, already, to be Odysseus
and rugged Diomêdês—back again,
with no time lost and driving Trojan horses!
I have been fearful that they might be hurt
in the Trojan outcry!"

He had not yet finished
all he was going to say, when up they came
and set foot on the quiet ground. Their friends
with warm handgrips and greeting gave them welcome;
Nestor, lord of Gerênia, put the question:

"Tell me, Odysseus, great in all men's eyes,
how did you take these horses? How slip by
into the Trojan camp? Or did some god
come down to meet you and bestow them on you,
horses like the white flames of the sun!
I join the fighting every day with Trojans,
never, I think, malingering at the ships,
old soldier that I am; but teams like these
I never saw or heard of. Well, some god
who crossed your path bestowed them, I suppose.
I know both men are dear to the cloud-herder
Zeus, and to his daughter, grey-eyed Athêna."

Odysseus, the resourceful man, replied:

"O Nestor, son of Nêleus, light of Akhaians,
a god might easily give still better horses,
gods being so much stronger than ourselves.
But these you ask about were new arrivals,

Thracians, excellency. Diomêdês killed
their master and a dozen fellow officers.
A thirteenth man, a scout, abaft the ships
we executed: Hektor and his peers
had sent him forward to observe the army."

Down through the moat he drove the horses now
and laughed a rumbling laugh. Along with him
the others crossed, exulting. When they reached
Diomêdês' quarters, they tied up the horses
by their own well-cut reins before the trough
where the master's chariot horses fed on grain.
Astern upon his ship, Odysseus hung
the bloodstained gear of Dolôn—
pending a proper offering to Athêna.
Wading into the sea, the men themselves
splashed at their coats of sweat—shins, nape, and thighs—
until the surf had washed it from their skin
and they were cool again. Then out they came
to take warm baths in polished tubs. Being bathed
and rubbed with olive oil, the two sat down
to take refreshment. From a full winebowl
they dipped sweet wine and poured it to Athêna.

BOOK ELEVEN

Prowess and Wounds
of Akhaians

Dawn came up from the couch of her reclining,
leaving her lord Tithonos' brilliant side
with fresh light in her arms for gods and men,
and Zeus commanded Strife down to the beachhead—
hard-bitten goddess, bearing in her hands
the stormcloud sign of war.

                            At the dead center
upon Odysseus' black-tarred ship she paused—
in earshot of both wings, if a man shouted,
as far as Aías' quarters and Akhilleus'.
Confident of their powers, these had beached
their ships at the far right and the far left.
Now from Odysseus' lugger Strife gave tongue
to a shivering cry. It stirred Akhaian hearts
to battle without rest; now warfare seemed

lovelier than return, lovelier than sailing
in the decked ships to their own native land.

The son of Atreus cried out, "Troops in arms!"
and clothed himself in armor of bright bronze.
Upon his legs he fitted beautiful greaves
with silver ankle straps. Around his chest
he buckled on a cuirass, long ago
a pledge of friendship from the Lord Kinyrês,
who heard his fame at Kypros, on the eve
of the Akhaian sailings against Troy.
To please the Akhaian king he made this gift,
a cuirass with ten bands of dark enamel,
twelve of gold, twenty of tin. Dark blue
enamel serpents, three on either side,
arched toward the neck, like rainbows that Lord Zeus
will pose on cloud as presages to men.
Across his shoulder and chest he hung a sword
whose hilt bore shining golden studs, and bands
of silver glinted on the scabbard, hooked
to a gilt baldric. Next he took his shield,
a broad one and a work of art for battle,
circled ten times with bronze; the twenty studs
were pale tin round the rim, the central boss
dark blue enamel that a fire-eyed Gorgon's
horrifying maw enclosed, with Rout
and Terror flanking her. Silver the shield strap
whereon a dark blue serpent twined—three heads,
put forth by one trunk, flexing every way.
Then Agamémnon fitted on his brow
a helmet double-ridged, with four white crests
of horsehair nodding savagely above it.
Last, two tough spears he took, with brazen spearheads
whetted sharp, and that clear bronze reflected
gleams of sunlight far into heaven. Athêna
thundered overhead, and Hêra thundered
honor in heaven to golden Mykênê's lord.

Now every captain told his charioteer,

"Dress on the moat, hold hard here!"

and on foot
in battle-gear, with weapons, all these fighters
moved ahead. Into the sky of dawn
an irrepressible cry went up, as lines
of men preceded war-cars at the moat
and war-cars in support came just behind.
Now Zeus the son of Krónos roused an uproar
along this host, and sprinkled bloody dew
from highest heaven, being resolved that day
to crowd great warriors into the undergloom.

Across the moat, on rising ground, the Trojans
mustered around tall Hektor, noble Poulýdamas,
Aineías, whom they honored as a god,
Antênor's three sons, Pólybos, Agênor,
and young Akámas—godlike prince.
Hektor moved forward with his round-faced shield.
As from night clouds a baleful summer star
will blaze into the clear, then fade in cloud,
so Hektor shone in front or became hidden
when he harangued the rear ranks—his whole form
in bronze aflash like lightning of Father Zeus.

Imagine at each end of a rich man's field
a line of reapers formed, who cut a swath
in barley or wheat, and spiky clumps of grain
are brought low by the scything: even so
those armies moved to cut each other down,
and neither Trojans nor Akhaians thought
of ruinous retreat. The line of battle
held them face to face, lunging like wolves,
and Strife who thrives on groaning
looked on that field in joy, for she alone
of goddesses or gods mixed in the fighting.

The rest were absent now and were at ease
in great halls of their own, beautiful chambers
built for immortals on Olympos' ridges,
all being bitter against the dark stormking
for decreeing this day's battle to the Trojans.
But their father ignored them. In his chair

withdrawn from all, he gloried, looking down
on wall and ship and metal flash of battle,
men slaying others, and the quiet slain.

While the sun rose and morning grew in splendor,
javelins were launched and soldiers fell
on both sides equally. But at the hour
a woodsman takes his lunch in a cool grove
of mountain pines, when he has grown arm-weary
chopping tall timber down, and, sick of labor,
longs for refreshment—at that height of noon
Danáäns calling fiercely back and forth
broke the Trojan line. First Agamémnon
charged and killed a Trojan chief, Biênor,
and Oïleus, his charioteer: this man
dismounted to face him, aye! but only met
a spear-thrust square between the eyes, unchecked
by his bronze helmet rim. Through bronze and bone
the spearhead broke into the brain within
and left it spattered. Down he went. And Marshal
Agamémnon abandoned Biênor and Oïleus
with glistening bare chests when he had stripped them.
Onward he went to kill two sons of Priam,
Isos and Ántiphos, one bastard stripling,
one in the royal line—both brothers riding
a single chariot. Isos held the reins
with Ántiphos, the gently bred, beside him.
These two one day, while they were tending flocks
in Ida's vales, Akhilleus took and bound
with willow shoots, but later freed for ransom.
Now the Lord of the Great Plains, Agamémnon,
hit one with a spear-cast in the chest
above the nipple; the other, Ántiphos,
he struck with his long sword beside the ear,
toppling him from his car. He bent to take
their arms and knew them: he had seen them once
in the encampment by the ships, that day
Akhilleus brought them down the mountainside.
A lion, discovering a forest bed,
and picking up in his great fangs the fawns
of a swift doe, will shake and break their backs

and rend their tender lives away with ease,
while she is powerless to help, though near,
but feels a dreadful trembling come upon her;
bolting the spot, she leaps through underbrush
at full stretch, drenched in sweat, before the onset
of the strong beast of prey. Just so, not one
among the Trojans could prevent those two
from being destroyed: the rest, too, turned and ran.
Next came Peisándros and Hippólokhos,
sons of Antímakhos. Expecting gold
and gifts of luxury from Aléxandros,
Antímakhos had harangued against returning
Helen to Meneláos. Now his sons
were caught by Agamémnon. Both were driving
a single chariot, when the shining reins
ran out of their limp hands, and panic shook them:
Agamémnon, bounding like a lion,
faced them. But they begged him from the car:

"O son of Atreus, take us alive! Be sure
you shall have fitting ransom! Treasures lie
by hundreds in Antímakhos' great hall,
things made of bronze and gold and hard-wrought iron.
Our father would not count the cost in these,
if he could know we are still alive
amid the Akhaian ships!"

                              So they appealed to him
in tears, and begged for mercy from the king,
but heard a voice beyond appeal:

                                        "Ah, you are
Antímakhos' sons? On Troy's assembly ground
when Meneláos went there with Odysseus
to make our argument, Antímakhos
held out for killing both men then and there
and no safe conduct back to the Akhaians.
That is the infamy you'll pay for now!"

With this he hit Peisándros in the chest
with a spear-thrust that threw him from the chariot
and smashed him on his back. Hippólokhos leapt,

but Agamémnon caught him on the ground
with one sword-cut, then slashed his arms away
and sent him rolling out amid the mêlée
like a round mortar stone. He left them there.
And now, wherever Trojans in the mass
were thrown most into confusion, there he charged,
and soldiers of Akhaia ran along
behind him. Infantry killed infantry
in forced retreat, and chariot fighters killed
chariot fighters. Dust rose underfoot
as thudding hooves of horses shook the plain
and men plied deadly bronze. King Agamémnon,
calling the Argives in the chariots' wake,
pressed on, slaughtering. As a fire catches
in parching brushwood without trees, and wind
this way and that in a whirl carries the blaze
to burn off crackling thickets to the root,
so under Agamémnon's whirling charge
the routed Trojans fell. Mettlesome teams
drew empty clattering cars down lanes of war,
bereft of drivers. These lay on the field,
more lovable to kites than to their wives.
But Zeus mysteriously guided Hektor
out of the spears and dust, out of the slaughter,
out of the blood and tumult—while Atreidês
led the chase and cheered the Danáäns on.
Past the old tomb of Ilos in mid-plain
the Trojans streamed, and past the wild figtree,
fighting to reach the city; and Agamémnon
followed with battlecries, attacking ever,
bloodying his inexorable hands.
At last they reached the West Gate and the oak
and halted there, awaiting one another,
as those behind in mid-plain struggled on
like cows a lion terrifies at dusk
into a stampede. One cow at a time
will see breathtaking death: clamped on her neck
with powerful fangs, the lion crunches her
to make his kill, then gulps her blood and guts.
Even so in pursuit was Agamémnon,
forever killing laggards as they fled.

Dozens fell, thrown headfirst from the chariots,
or on their backs, as with his spear he ran
around them and ahead.

                                        Now, in the end,
when he was near the city and the wall,
to earth from heaven the father of gods and men
descended and sat down on Ida's crests
amid her springs, bearing his jaggèd lightning.
He made Iris of golden wings his herald,
saying:

                        "Away with you who walk the wind,
tell this to Hektor: while he still can see
Lord Marshal Agamémnon in the forefront,
devastating the ranks, let him retire
and call on other troops to fight, to bear
the brunt of battle with his enemies.
But when spear-cast or bowshot hits the man
so that he mounts his chariot again,
at that point I give Hektor power of massacre
down to the deepsea ships of the Akhaians,
till the sun dips and starry darkness comes."

Iris who walks on the swift wind obeyed him,
running down Ida's hills to Ilion.
There godlike Hektor, son of Priam, stood
amid the horses and the welded cars,
and swooping down like wind Iris addressed him:

"Son of Priam, Hektor, great in craft
of battle, Zeus commissioned me to tell you:
while you can see Lord Marshal Agamémnon
in the forefront, devastating the ranks,
you must retire, and call on other troops
to bear the brunt of battle with your enemies.
But when the man is hit, by spear or bowshot,
so that he takes to his chariot again,
at that point Zeus will give you power of massacre
as far as the deepsea ships of the Akhaians,
till the sun dips and starry darkness comes."

When she had said this, Iris veered away,
and from his chariot Hektor vaulted down,

shaking his whetted spears, making the rounds
to put fight into Trojans everywhere
and rouse a bloody combat. Now they turned
and held a line again against Akhaians,
whom on their side new companies reinforced.
They closed up ranks for action hand to hand
and Agamémnon strove to outstrip them all.

Heaven-dwelling Muses of Olympos,
tell me who first, among allies or Trojans,
braved Agamémnon?

                                   It was young Iphídamas,
Antênor's brawny and athletic son,
who had been reared in Thrace, that fertile country,
billowy grassland, nourisher of flocks.
Kissês, father of Theanô, his mother,
brought up the child, and when he reached the stage
of promising manhood tried to hold him there,
betrothing to him a daughter. But he left
his bridal chamber for the Akhaian war
when the word came. Twelve ships put out with him,
and these he duly beached at Perkôtê,
making his way to Ilion on foot.
Now it was he who tackled Agamémnon.
When they came near each other, Agamémnon
thrust but missed as the haft turned in his hand.
Iphídamas' point went home below the cuirass
hard on the belt. He put his weight on it
with heavy thews, leaning after the blow,
but could not pierce the armored loin-guard. Rather,
his point was turned, like lead on silver bent.
The Lord of the Great Plains now took hold and drew
the weapon toward him, raging, lionlike,
wrenching it from the Trojan's hands; then struck him
with a sword-cut across the neck and killed him.
Down he dropped into the sleep of bronze.
Sad that he fought for the townsmen of his bride
and died abroad before he could enjoy her,
lavish though he had been for her: he gave
one hundred beeves, and promised a thousand head
of sheep and goats, for myriads grazed his land.

Now Agamémnon stripped his corpse and bore
amid the Akhaian host his beautiful armor.

Koôn saw him: Koôn, a notable fighter,
eldest son of Antênor; and cruel grief
clouded his eyes at the downfall of his brother.
Taking Agamémnon on the flank
he hit his arm below the elbow: straight
through skin and tendon passed the bright spearpoint.
Now the Lord Marshal Agamémnon shuddered—
not that he quit the battle, not at all,
but swung on Koôn with gale-hardened spear—
the man by now furiously pulling his brother,
Iphídamas, by the foot, calling his peers.
But as he pulled the corpse to the Trojan side
Agamémnon sent home his polished spear
and mortally wounded him under his shield.
He moved in to behead him, and the head
rolled on Iphídamas. Thus Antênor's sons
had met their destiny at Atreidês' hands,
entering the gloom of Death.

                                        And still the victor
roamed back and forth along the living ranks
with spear and sword attacking, or with stones,
as long as hot blood gushed from his wound. But when
his blood no longer flowed, and the gash dried,
then rays of pain lacerated Agamémnon.
Comparable to the throes
a writhing woman suffers in hard labor
sent by the goddesses of Travail, Hêra's
daughters, Twisters, mistresses of pangs,
the anguish throbbed in Agamémnon now.
Mounting his chariot, he told the driver:

"Make for the ships!"

                                        and sore at heart he was,
but raised a piercing cry to the Danáäns:

"Friends, nobles, captains of Argives, now
the fight is yours, to beat the tide of battle
back from our ships—for Zeus

who views the wide world would not give me leave
to battle against Trojans all this day."

His driver whipped the beautiful chariot horses
back to the ships, and willingly they ran
with foaming chests, and dust coating their bellies,
to bear the wounded king out of the battle.
Hektor had kept his eyes on this departure
and gave a shout to Trojans and Lykians:

"Trojans, Lykians, and Dardan spears,
remember valor, friends, and fight like men.
Their champion has left the field! Oh, here,
here is my great chance, granted me by Zeus!
Now forward with your teams into the center
and win the highest prize of all!"

                                        He stirred them,
rallying each man's courage. As a hunter
would send his hounds against a lion or boar
so Hektor sent his Trojans headlong in
against the Akhaians: Hektor, Priam's son,
hard as the wargod—now in pride and zeal
this hunter led his fighters on. He fell
on the battle line like a high screaming squall
that blows down on the purple open sea!
And who were the adversaries that he killed
when Zeus accorded him this rush of glory?
Asaios first, Autónoös and Opítês,
Dolops Klytídês, Opheltios, Agélaos,
Aisymnos, Ôros, rugged Hipponoös—
these leaders of Danääns he destroyed,
then turned on the rank and file. A lashing gale
out of the west will rift high snowy clouds
the south wind piled, as big seas rise and roll
with foam and spindrift from the whistling wind:
so were Akhaian masses rent by Hektor.
Ruin was near, irreparable defeat,
Akhaians all but driven on the ships,
had not Odysseus called to Diomêdês:

"Son of great Tydeus, what has come over us?
Have we lost all our power of attack?

Come here and stand with me, old horse. Dishonor
lies ahead if Hektor fires the ships."

Diomêdês answered him:

> "I'll stand with you
and take what comes, by heaven! Only small
good it will do us! Lord Zeus, master of cloud,
wills them the upper hand, and not ourselves."

At this he knocked Thymbraios from his chariot
with a direct hit on the left breast. Odysseus
killed Moliôn, the squire to that lord.
From these who were out of action, they turned round
against the pursuing pack—you would have said
two boars that turned on hounds—and charging back
did slaughter among Trojans. Thus the Akhaians
had some relief, a respite, as they yielded
before magnificent Hektor. Next, the two
destroyed a Trojan pair in their war-car—
sons of Mérops Perkôsios, clairvoyant
beyond all men, who had denied his sons
permission to join man-wasting war. But they
paid him no heed: dark death-spirits led them on;
and now the incomparable spearman Diomêdês
ripped them out of life and took their gear.
Hippódamas besides Hypeírokhos
went down before Odysseus, who stripped them.
For a short time, downgazing out of Ida,
Zeus kept the battle doubtful, tense and even,
as each side made its kills.

> Now Diomêdês

fighting Agástrophos, a son of Paiôn,
gave him a hip wound, but the warrior's chariot
was not at hand to save him—a bad error;
his driver held it far away. On foot
Agástrophos went limping through the fight
until he perished.

> Looking across at this,

Hektor attacked the Akhaians with a yell
while Trojan companies fell in behind.
Diomêdês shivered as he watched him come
and turning said to Odysseus beside him:

"We are the ones this wave is heading for—
a black wave, too; here is Hektor in his power.
Come, let's brace for it and defend ourselves."

He whirled and cast, and the long spear trailed swift shadow
straight to the mark he aimed for, the helm crest;
but it rebounded, clanging, bronze from bronze,
and never reached or broke his handsome skin:
the ridged and triple-welded helm
Apollo gave him was impervious.
But Hektor swerved in shock and, running wide,
rejoined his men. Then fallen on his knees
he leaned on his great hand, and a black swoon
veiled his eyes. While Diomêdês went
a long way down the line, tracking his weapon
to where it lay, Hektor got back his breath
and, once more mounted on his chariot,
he rode among the other cars and shunned
the shadow of death. Diomêdês shook his spear
and called:

                    "You dodged away from death again,
you dog, and a close thing, too; Phoibos Apollo
pulled you through. He it must be you pray to
whenever you go near the jolt of spears!
One more throw, by heaven, will finish you,
if there is any god on my side, too.
Now I'll face any others I can find."

He leaned over to strip the son of Paiôn,
and then the lord of Helen, Aléxandros,
resting against the gravestone on the mound
of Ilos, patriarch son of Dárdanos,
bent his bow at the Lord Marshal Diomêdês.
Imagine Diomêdês taking the dead man's
cuirass from his ribs, and from his shoulders
the shield all glimmering, and his heavy helm,
even as the adversary drew his bow
to the grip and shot—and not in vain the arrow
sprang from his fist, but through the right foot bonework
of Diomêdês into the earth it punched.

Aléxandros jumped out of ambush laughing
and called to him vaunting:

                                        "Hit you are, and hard!
No wasted shot, that! But I should have hit you
under the ribs and brought you down.
That would relieve the Trojans from their ordeal.
You spook them as a lion does bleating goats."

Undaunted, Diomêdês answered:

"You bow-and-arrow boy, you curly-head,
all eyes for little girls, I wish you'd try me
face to face with pike and shield: your archery
would do you no good then. You brag this way
for having scratched my instep. It is nothing,
a woman's shot, or a silly little boy's.
A weak-kneed half-wit's arrow has no point!
By heaven, arrows of mine are whetted differently.
One that grazes a man will stretch him dead.
His woman's cheeks are torn with grief,
his children orphaned. He must soak the earth
and rot, with kites for company, not women!"

As he said this, Odysseus moved over
and stood in front of him. Then, sitting back,
Diomêdês pulled the arrow from his foot
and dragged agony with it through his flesh.
He climbed his chariot and told his driver,
"Make for the ships!" And he was grieved at heart.
Odysseus now, the good spear, stood alone;
no Argive held that ground with him, as fear
had gripped them all. And grimly vexed,
he spoke to his own valor:

                                        "Here is trouble.
What will become of me? A black day, this,
if I show fear and run before this crowd;
but worse if I am captured, being alone.
Zeus routed all the rest of the Danäans.
But why this bandying inward words, my friend?
Cowards are men who leave the front in war.

The man who will be worth respect in battle
holds on, whether he's hit or hits another."

During these meditations, on they came,
the lines of Trojan infantry, and broke
around and hemmed him in—hemmed in their peril.
As when around a wild boar lusty hunters
and hounds deploy, until the beast trots out
from heavy thicket, whetting his white tusks
against his lower jaws; the hounds go circling
in to attack, and under the hue and cry
a gnashing sound of tusks and teeth is heard;
even so now, around rugged Odysseus,
the Trojans ran. Dêiopitês was the first
Odysseus wounded, on the slope of shoulder,
making a spring with his sharp spear; and next
he hit Thoôn and Ennomos and killed them;
then Khersídamas, who had vaulted down
out of his car, he caught square in the navel
under his bulging shield; the man fell hard
in dust and with his hand spread gripped the earth.
Leaving them there, he hit Hippásidês
Kharops, a brother of the rich man, Sôkos—
and Sôkos gallantly ran up to shield him,
taking a stand before the attacker, saying:

"Odysseus, great in all men's eyes, unwearied
master of guile and toil, today the sons
of Híppasos will be your claim to glory:
either you kill and strip such men as these
or die, hit by my spear."

                                    Even as he spoke,
he let fly at the round shield, and his weapon
pierced the shining surface, pierced the bright
elaborate cuirass with his weight behind it,
flaying Odysseus' ribs. Athêna barred
all access to her hero's heart and lungs.
Odysseus knew the wound had not been mortal,
and yielding ground he said to Sôkos:

                                                "Ah,
poor soldier, your own death-plunge into the dark

lies before you now: you crippled me
for any further fight today with Trojans,
but as for you, I say a bloody death,
a black nightmare of death, is close upon you;
my spear kills you. You'll give up the fight
to me, your soul to that strong driver, Death."

This made the other turn as if to run,
but as he turned the spear crashed in his back
between the shoulders, driving through his chest,
and down he went with clanging gear. Odysseus
made his boast over the fallen:

                                                        "Son

of Híppasos, that fighting man and horseman,
death ran ahead to meet you: no escape.
Poor soldier, father and mother will not bend
to close your eyes in death, but carrion birds
will tear them out and clap their wings around you.
My own corpse will be fired by the Akhaians
if in fact I die."

                                        On this he drew

Sôkos' hard weapon from his flesh and through
his convex shield. After the extracted spearhead
blood welled up in streams and grieved his heart.
Elated when they saw Odysseus' blood
flow out, the Trojans yelled, converging on him.
Now he gave ground, backing away, and called
his own companions. Three tremendous shouts
he gave, as loud as a man's head could hold,
and each time he was heard by Meneláos,
who turned and said to Aías at his side:

"Son of Télamôn and the gods of old,
Lord Aías of the army, a faint shout
has reached my ears—Odysseus' voice it is,
as though the man were in trouble, and great trouble,
with Trojans who had cut him off alone.
We must get through the mêlée; better save him.
I am afraid some hurt will come to him,
and loss irreparable to the Akhaians."

At this he led the way, and Aías followed,
godlike, formidable, and before long
they found Odysseus: Trojans had closed round him
as tawny jackals from the hills will ring
an antlered deer, gone heavy with his wound.
After the hunter's arrow strikes, the deer
goes running clean away: he runs as long
as warm blood flows and knees can drive him on.
Then when at last the feathered arrow downs him,
carrion jackals in a shady grove
devour him. But now some power brings down
a ravenous lion, and the shrinking jackals
go off cowering: he must have their prey.
Just so around Odysseus, man of war
with versatile wits, the Trojans closed. But he
by stabbing out and feinting with his spear
averted death's hard hour for that day.
And now came Aías with his tower of shield
to stand beside him. This way and that the Trojans
shrank away, and soldierly Meneláos led
their quarry by the hand out of the fight
to where his driver brought his chariot up.
Now Aías, charging, brought down Dóryklos,
a bastard son of Priam; then he wounded
Pándokos, Lýsandros, and Pýrasos,
Pylártês, too. As when a river in flood
from mountain snowfields reaches the flat land
whipped by a storm of rain, it sweeps away
hundreds of withered oaks, hundreds of pines,
and casts black tons of driftwood in the sea,
so Aías in his glory swept the field,
wrecking both chariots and men. But Hektor
had no report of it, being in a fight
along Skamánder bank on the left wing
amid great slaughter, where a battlecry
indomitable had risen around Nestor
and soldierly Idómeneus. These Hektor
faced in battle; he performed prodigies
in spearmanship and chariot-handling, making
havoc in the young men's ranks. And yet
the Akhaians might not yet have given him passage

had not Aléxandros, husband of Helen,
put a stop to Makháon's gallantry
with one bowshot, an arrow triple-barbed,
in the right shoulder. And the grimmest Akhaians
feared for him, feared the enemy might take him
now that the tide of war had turned. Idómeneus
called over at once to Nestor:

                          "Son of Nêleus,
glory of Akhaians, quick! Remount
your car and let Makháon came aboard,
and make your team race to the ships. A surgeon
is worth an army full of other men
at cutting shafts out, dressing arrow wounds."

Nestor, Gerênian lord of horse, complied,
regaining his own chariot as Makháon, son
of the healer Lord Asklêpios, came aboard.
Nestor flicked his team, and willingly
they ran for their safe haven at the ships.
At Hektor's side Kebríonês made out
the mêlée's pattern:

                          "You and I," he said,
"are fighting, Hektor, on the outer edge
of a great deafening battle. Other Trojans
are in confusion, chariots and men.
Telamônian Aías flurries them.
I know him well: he is the one who bears
the wide shield round his shoulders. Why not guide
our horses toward him where the charioteers
and infantry are locked in deadly combat,
putting each other in the dust; their cries
are never still."

                              At this, he shook out reins
to his glossy team with blowing manes, and used
the cracking whip. And when they felt the lash,
they drew the nimble chariot briskly on
through Trojans and Akhaians, trampling shields
and bodies of the dead. The axle-tree
beneath was blood-bespattered; round the car

the rails were spattered; from the horses' hooves
and from the wheel-rims blood flew up in spray.
Into the man-eating moil Hektor now longed
to plunge and make a breach; he pressed the Akhaians,
never gave way an inch to any spear,
but ranged among the ranks of other fighters,
using his javelin, longsword, and big stones,
and shunning only Aías in the combat:
Zeus took it ill when he engaged his betters.
Now Father Zeus, benched high on Ida, moved
great Aías to retreat. He stood stock-still
and tossed his sevenfold shield over his shoulder,
dazed with dread. With half-closed eyes
he glared at the crowd, a wild thing brought to bay,
turning a little, shifting knee past knee.
So formidable in his fear he was—
like a dun lion from a stable yard
driven by hounds and farmhands: all night long
they watch and will not let him take his prey,
his chosen fat one. Prowling, craving meat,
he cannot make a breakthrough. Volleying javelins
are launched against him by strong arms, firebrands
bring him to heel, for all his great élan,
and heartsick he retreats at dawn. So Aías,
heartsick before the Trojans, foot by foot
retreated grudgingly for the ships' sake.
An ass that plods along a field will be
too much for attacking boys; on his dumb back
stick after stick may break; still he will enter
standing grain and crop it, even as boys
are beating him—so puny is their strength,
and barely will they drive him from the field
when he is gorged on grain. In the same way
the confident Trojans and their best allies
continuously made the son of Télamôn
their target, with direct hits on his shield.
Remembering his power in attack,
sometimes he turned at bay and held the advance
of Trojan squadrons, then resumed retreat,
but kept them from the straight path to the ships
while he himself, between Akhaians and Trojans,

forged his way. Spears thrown by brawny hands
at times would stick in his great shield; the rest
stood fixed midway in earth before they reached
the white flesh they were famished for.

                                              Eurýpylos,

Euaimôn's great son, realized his danger,
seeing him hard pressed by the missile hail,
and moved over beside him. Stabbing out
with his bright spear he hit Phausios' son,
Apisáôn, a marshal, in the liver
under his midriff and unstrung his knees,
then bent to take the armor from his shoulders.
Godlike Aléxandros had seen him come,
now saw him strip Apisáôn: in all haste
he drew his bow upon Eurýpylos
and hit him in the right thigh with an arrow,
splintering the shaft, weighting the leg.
Retiring now to bleed among his men
and shun black death, Eurýpylos cried sharply:

"Friends, lords and nobles of the Argives, halt!
turn round and try to keep off death's hard hour
from Aías; he is driven back by spears.
I would not say for sure he will survive
the grinding war! Go form a wedge for Aías,
the son of Télamôn!"

                                        So, with his leg wound,
Eurýpylos begged them. And they formed the wedge
for Aías, moving near, shoulder to shoulder,
leaning shield on shield, with spears held high,
while Aías gave way toward them. When he joined them
he turned and took his stand.

                                        That way they fought
as the very body of fire strives and bends,
while out of battle Nêlean horses foaming
carried Nestor, carried Makháon.

                                                            And

Akhilleus the great runner saw Makháon!

He had been standing on his ship's high stern
to view the moil of war, over the rampart,

heart-rending struggle and pursuit. But now
he called to Patróklos from the after-deck,
and hearing in the hut, the other came,
rugged, it seemed, as Arês—though his doom
was fixed that instant. He it was spoke first:

"Why call me out, Akhilleus? How can I help you?"

And the great runner answered:

                    "Son of Menoitios,
dear to my heart, the Akhaians now will come
to beg and pray, I think, around my knees!
Inexorable need presses upon them.
Only go now, Patróklos, and ask Nestor
who is this wounded man he ferries back
out of the battle. All his gear behind
looks like the gear of Makháon—
but I could not get a good look at the man;
the chariot shot beyond me at full gallop."

Doing as his companion willed, Patróklos
ran off along the Akhaian huts and ships.
Now Nestor and the wounded man, arriving
at Nestor's hut, dismounted on the turf,
and Eurýmedôn, the squire, unhitched the team.
Standing against the sea breeze on the beach
they cooled off, letting sweat-soaked khitons dry,
then entering Nestor's hut they took their seats
in armchairs. Mulled drink was prepared for them
by softly braided Hékamêdê, Nestor's
prize from Akhilleus' plundering of Ténedos—
Arsínoös' daughter. The Akhaians
had chosen her for Nestor, honoring excellence
in council. First the girl pushed up before them
a beautiful table with enameled legs,
then she set out a basket all of bronze,
an onion to give relish to their wine,
pale yellow honey, sacred barley meal,
beside a cup of wondrous beauty, brought
from Pylos by the old king: golden nails
it had for studding, and four handles on it,

each adorned by a pair of golden doves
who perched to drink, with double stems beneath.
Another man would strain to budge this cup
once full, clear of the table. But not Nestor:
old though he was, he lifted it with ease.
Now mixing Pramnian wine for them in this,
the servant like a goddess in demeanor
grated a goat's milk cheese over the wine
upon a brazen grater, and sifted in
white barley meal. Her potion thus prepared,
she called on both to drink.

                                        Now the two men
drank long to rid themselves of burning thirst.
In their relief they were exchanging talk
when at the door Patróklos, like a god,
appeared and stood. Old Nestor left his chair
to take his hand, to lead him in and seat him.
But from the door Patróklos shook his head
and said:

                        "No time to take a chair, your grace:
I will not be persuaded: he that sent me
is worthy of respect and quick to anger,
and sent me here to learn who that man was
you brought in wounded. But I see myself
it is Makháon, marshal of troops. I'll bear
this word back to Akhilleus. Well you know
how dangerous the man can be, your grace!
In a flash he could accuse me without cause."

Lord Nestor of Gerênia replied:

"How is this, that Akhilleus cares for any
Akhaians who are hit? He has no notion
of what distress has come upon the army.
Wounded and out of action, our best men
are lying by the ships: Lord Diomêdês;
Odysseus, the great spearman; Agamémnon;
Eurýpylos, hit by an arrow in the thigh;
and this man whom I brought just now from war,
disabled by an arrow from a bowstring.
Splendid Akhilleus pities no Danáäns,

waiting—is he not?—until the ships
on the sea verge are fanned by billowing fire,
whether we Argives will or not, and we
ourselves are killed off one by one.

My strength is
not what it was, in my bent leg or arm.
If I were only young and had my powers
intact, as when the quarrel rose between
the Elians and ourselves for cattle-raiding!
I killed Itýmoneus, Hypeirókhos' son,
a champion then in Elis, and drove home
his rustled cattle. Trying to protect them,
he met a javelin from my hand and fell,
his bumpkin herdsmen panicking around him.
Prizes out of the plain we drove together
in a great host: of cows there were fifty herds,
as many flocks of sheep and droves of swine
and roaming herds of goats: and chestnut horses—
one hundred and fifty tawny horses,
mares every one, many with suckling foals.
We drove them into Pylos, Nêleus' land,
up to the town, at night. And Nêleus' pride
was pleased that spoil so great had fallen to me,
a green hand at war. Loud in the dawnlight,
heralds announced that all men who had claims
on ancient Elis should present themselves,
and on their assembling, leading men of Pylos
made the apportionment—for there were many
to whom the Epeioi were in debt. We suffered
wrongs in Pylos, being a scanty people.
Hêraklês in the years before had come
with depredation, and death upon our best.
Twelve, for example, were the sons of Nêleus,
and I alone was left, the rest were killed.
These exploits puffed the Epeioi up; they showed
their insolence devising crimes against us.
Now our old king sequestered for himself
a herd of oxen and a flock of sheep,
three hundred beasts with herdsmen—for in Elis
a great debt was his due: a four-horse team
of racing horses and their chariot

that once would have contended in the games
and raced to win the tripod, but Augeías,
lord of Elians, kept them, and sent home
the empty-handed, grieving charioteer.
In his long anger for these words and deeds
the old king now made choice
of plenty for himself, and to the people
gave all the rest to be distributed,
seeing to it that no man lacked his share.
We were proceeding with all this, and making
sacrifice around the town
when on the third day the Epeioi came
in multitudes, with horses driven hard,
Molionê's two boys among them armed,
though still untrained in warfare.

                                              There's a city,

Thryoessa, on a beetling hill
above the Alpheíos at the verge of Pylos.
This they besieged, in fury to pull it down,
and scoured the whole plain, but Athêna bore
a warning for us, running from Olympos
by night, to take up arms, and she assembled
troops of Pylos keen to fight. Now Nêleus
would not hear of my arming, hid my horses,
denied I had ever learned the arts of war!
Yet even so I made my mark among
our charioteers, foot soldier though I was,
Athêna so conducted that affray.
A stream called Minyêios joins the sea
near Arênê. Horsemen of Pylos there
awaited the unearthly dawn, while infantry
flowed up to join us. Arming with all speed,
by noon we reached Alpheíos' ancient waters,
making our offerings there, to Zeus all-powerful,
to Alpheíos and to Poseidon, bulls,
a heifer to Athêna, Hope of Soldiers.
Afterward we took our evening meal
along the column by companies, and slept
each man in his own gear beside the river.
Meanwhile the bold invading Epeioi kept
the town besieged. They burned to pull it down,

but first had sight of Arês' handiwork!
For as the flaming sun rose on the land
we met them in battle, calling on Lord Zeus
and on Athêna. Pylians and Epeioi
contended. I was the first to kill a man
and take his horses—the spearman Moulios.
He was Augeías' son-in-law, his sister
russet-haired Agamêdê, she who knew
all medicinal herbs the wide world bears.
This man I hit with my bronze-bladed spear
as he came on, and he tumbled into the dust.
Then I mounted his war-car, and I stood
amid our forward fighters. The Epeioi
shrank away, this way and that: they saw
their captain charioteer, splendid in battle,
fallen. And my hour had come: I drove
into them like a black stormcloud and captured
fifty chariots. Two men bit the dust
alongside each, overpowered by my spear.
Then, too, I would have pillaged the two 'sons
of Aktor' and Molionês—but their true sire
who rules the wide sea and sets earth a-tremble
hid them in cloud and saved them from the war.
After that, Zeus gave power into the hands
of Pylians, and we pursued our enemy
through all the great plain, taking many lives,
amassing their fine armor, till we brought
our horses to the grainland, Bouprasíon,
Olênie Rock, and the hill called Aleisíos.
There, as Athêna made our troops turn back,
I killed and left my last foe.

The Akhaians

withdrew briskly and turned their horses' heads
toward Pylos. Among gods, they prayed to Zeus,
to Nestor among men.

So was I then,

if that was I and not a dream. Not so
Akhilleus, who alone gains by his valor.
Ah, but I can prophesy his weeping
after his people perish!

My dear fellow,
Menoitios made your duty doubly clear
when he sent you from Phthía to Agamémnon!
Standing inside, Odysseus and I
overheard him, every word, so clearly!
We had arrived at Pêleus' great house
on our recruiting journey through Akhaia,
and found the old soldier, Menoitios, there with you
at Akhilleus' side. Then Pêleus, master of horses,
burned thighbones to Zeus, lord of the lightning,
in the enclosure of his court, and held
a cup of smooth gold, pouring dusky wine
on the burnt offerings. You two were carving,
right and left, the carcass of the ox,
when we two reached the entranceway. Akhilleus
rose in surprise, and taking both our hands
required us to rest, then placed before us
all that a guest should have. We were refreshed
by food and drink, and thereupon I spoke,
inviting both to go with us. Most heartily
you wished to go. And now your fathers both
repeatedly enjoined your duties on you.
The old man, Pêleus, urged his child, Akhilleus,
to do none but great feats, to be distinguished
above the rest. As for Menoitios,
the son of Aktor, these were his words to you:

'My child, Akhilleus is a higher being
by his immortal blood; but you are older.
He is more powerful, but your part should be
to let him hear close reasoning and counsel,
even commands. He will be swayed by you
for his own good.'

                                These were your father's words,
although you now forget them. Ah, but now,
late though it is, tell all this to Akhilleus,
hoping he may come round. Who knows what power
may help a plea from you to stir his heart!
There's sweetness in persuasion by a friend.
If in his own mind he is keeping clear

of an oracle: if her ladyship, his mother,
declared to him some prophecy from Zeus,
all right: then let him send *you* into battle!
Let the battalion of Myrmidons follow *you!*
Victory light for Danáäns you may be!
And let him give you all his beautiful armor
to wear in battle. Taking you for him
the Trojans may retire from the field
and let the young Akhaians have a respite
exhausted as they are. War gives brief rest!
You and your soldiers, fresh against tired men,
might easily throw them back upon the town
away from our encampment and our ships."

At this, Patróklos' heart bounded within him
and he went running back along the shipways
toward Akhilleus. Just as he passed the ship
of great Odysseus, where the assembly ground
and place of justice were, and gods' altars,
there came Eurýpylos, the wounded man,
Euaimôn's noble son, struck by the arrow,
limping out of combat. Sultry sweat
ran down his shoulders and his face, dark blood
still trickled from his wound, but he limped on,
unshaken spirit.

                         Seeing him, Patróklos,
moved to compassion, said:

                                  "Poor soldiers!
Captains, lords of Danáäns, how you all
were fated here, across the sea from home,
to glut wild dogs in this rich realm of Troy!
But tell me this, Eurýpylos, your grace,
are the Akhaians holding Hektor still
or will they perish, downed by his spear?"

                                 Eurýpylos
replied:

                          "Noble Patróklos, there will be
no longer any defensive line of Akhaians.
They will fall back on the black ships soon. Our best

in other combats lie now in the camp
with missile wounds or gashes made by spears
in Trojan hands. Enemy power grows.
As for myself, give me a hand here, take me
down to your ship and cut this shaft away
from my leg wound; then wash the black blood out
with warm water, and sift into the wound
that anodyne you learned of from Akhilleus—
a drug that, people say, the very best
of centaurs, Kheirôn, taught him. We have surgeons,
Podaleírios and Makháon, but the one
I think is lying wounded in his hut,
himself in need of a healer, and the other
faces the Trojan charge, still in the plain."

The staunch son of Menoitios replied:

"How can this be? What action can we take,
Eurýpylos? I am on my way to give
Akhilleus, the great mind of war, a word
of counsel from Lord Nestor of Gerênia,
lord of the western approaches to Akhaia.
But not for that will I neglect or fail you,
badly hurt as you are."

                                        Supporting him
with one arm round him, under his chest, he led him
into the hut. A squire put oxhides out
on which he laid the wounded man, then took
his sheath knife and laid open the man's thigh
to excise the biting arrow. With warm water
he washed the black blood flowing from the wound,
then rubbed between his hands into a powder
over the wound a bitter yarrow root,
that dulled all pangs of pain. Now the gash dried
as the blood and powder clotted.

BOOK TWELVE

The Rampart Breached

After this fashion
in his own hut Menoitios' gallant son
tended Eurýpylos, the wounded man,
while Argives fought the Trojan mass attack
their moat no longer could contain—nor could
the rampart they had built to save the ships,
carrying the moat around it. To the gods
they gave no hekatombs that might have won them
to guard the wall as shield for the deepsea craft
and plunder that it ringed. The immortal gods
had never willed it, and its time was brief.
While Hektor lived and while Akhilleus raged,
and while Lord Priam's town lived on, unsacked,
so long the Akhaians' rampart stood. But after
the flower of Troy went down, with many Argives

fallen or bereft, when Priam's Troy
was plundered in the tenth year, and the Argives
shipped again for their dear homeland—then
Poseidon and Apollo joined to work
erosion of the wall by fury of rivers
borne in flood against it, all that flow
seaward from Ida: Rhêsos, Heptáporos,
Karêsos, Rhodíos, Grênikos, Aisêpos,
Skamánder's ancient stream, and Simóeis
round which so many shields and crested helms
had crashed in dust with men who were half gods.
These rivers were diverted at their mouths
and blent into one river by Apollo,
who sent that flood nine days against the rampart.
Zeus let his rain fall without pause, to bring
the wall more quickly under inshore water;
as for the god who shakes the islands, he
in person with his trident in his hands
led on the assault. Foundation logs and stones
the Akhaians toiled to lay he shunted seaward,
leveling all by the blue running sea.
In sand again he hid the long seashore
when he had washed the wall down, and he turned
the rivers to their old, fair watercourses.
Thus before long Poseidon and Apollo
settled this earthwork. Now, though, on both sides
tumult and combat raged around the wall
whose tower-beams rang from battering. The Argives
under Zeus's lash were beaten back
upon the long ships, all in fear of Hektor,
master of rout that day. Aye, as before,
furious as a high wind when it strikes,
he wheeled and fought—boarlike, or like a lion
that rounds in mighty joy on dogs and men:
the hunters close ranks in a wall and face him
to make a broadside volley of javelins,
but his high heart will neither quail nor flee;
his own courage kills him; everywhere
he turns to test the ranks, and when he charges
all give way.

                                    So forward into the mêlée
Hektor charged and turned and called his men
to cross the moat. But his own chariot team
dared not, but on the very brink arrested,
whinnied and reared away in panic, seeing
the ditch could not be taken in a leap
or passed through easily. On either side
banks overhung it with stakes pointing inward,
sharp and long and close together, set
by the Akhaians as a ground defense
against their dire attackers. No beast drawing
a nimble car could easily descend there,
and men on foot thought hard if they could pass.
At this, Poulýdamas at Hektor's elbow
said:

                         "Hektor, and the rest of you, our captains,
captains of auxiliaries: we are fools
to drive our teams into the moat, so rough
it is to get across—the stakes inside
like fangs against us—and then comes the wall.
There is no chance at all with chariots
to get down in the place and fight—no room;
impaled there, I can see us now.

                                                    If Zeus

in thunder will make havoc of Akhaians,
if he is hot in the Trojans' cause,
by heaven, I wish this fight were over soon—
the Akhaians wiped out, distant far from Argos,
winning no glory!

                                        If they once reform,
braced on the ships, and counterattack, while we
are trapped here in the ditch, then I foresee
not even a messenger will reach the town;
no one escapes the Akhaians, once they rally.
Well, then, everyone do as I propose:
charioteers pull up at the moat's edge
while we ourselves in harness and on foot
follow Hektor in closed ranks. The Akhaians
cannot hold, if now their ultimate
destruction is at hand."
Poulýdamas' counsel to avoid the risk

won Hektor over, and he vaulted down
with weapons from his chariot. Other Trojans
stayed no longer huddled behind their teams
but, seeing that Hektor had dismounted, each
commanded his charioteer to keep in line
outside the ditch, with a tight rein on his horses,
while fighting men moved out ahead. They formed
five companies under leaders, each in column.
Those who deployed with Hektor and Poulýdamas
were bravest and most numerous, grimly bent
on carrying battle to the long ships
when they had breached the wall. Kebríonês
joined them, third in command, and in his place
as driver Hektor left a weaker man.
Paris headed a second company
whose officers were Alkáthoös and Agênor.
A third was under Hélenos and Dêíphobos,
two of Priam's sons, and Ásïos
Hyrtákidês, whose great roan horses brought him
from Arísbê and the Sellêeis river.
Over the fourth Aineías held command,
Ankhísês' powerful son, whom Lord Antênor's
two sons joined: Arkhélokhos and Akámas,
trained in every fighting skill. Sarpêdôn
held command of the allies; he chose
for officers Glaukos and Asteropaíos,
far and away the best men, he thought,
of the auxiliaries, after himself, who stood
high in the whole army.

                              Bull's-hide shields
being dressed in line, they rushed at the Danáäns,
certain that these could not resist the charge
that swept now on the black ships. And all Trojans,
all allies, obeyed the battle plan
of cool Poulýdamas: all except Ásïos
Hyrtákidês. He did not care to leave
his team and driver but, still mounted, rode
to attack the Akhaian ships—the idiot,
he would not give his own hard fate the slip
or ride in glory from the beachhead back
to windy Ilion in his war-car.

Miserable death would shroud him, by the spear
of Idómeneus, Deukálión's noble son.
Ásïos drove to the left around the ships
to a place where the Akhaians were withdrawing
chariots and horses from the plain.
Here he swerved for the wall, and found the gates
of planking with great bolts as yet unshut;
men held them open to admit and save
stray fugitives from battle. Straight ahead
he drove his team, while after him his men
ran yelling—for, they thought the Akhaians could not
hold, but had to fall back on the ships.
All a delusion: at the entranceway
they met two Lapith spearmen, champions,
Polypoitês, the son of Peiríthoös,
and Leonteus, tough as the wargod. These
outside the tall gates held their ground like oaks
that tower on high hills, enduring wind
and rain through all their days, with roots deep down,
tenacious of the earth. Like oaks indeed
the two stood fast and trusted their right arms,
their fighting power, against great Ásïos.
On came the Trojans toward the wall with shields
uplifted, with a long-drawn battlecry
around Lord Ásïos, Iámenos, Orestês
Adámas Asíadês, Thoôn, and Oinómaos.

Until just now the Lapiths, the defenders,
had been inside the wall issuing orders
to Akhaian troops to form around the ships,
but when they saw the Trojans charge, and when
a cry came from the Danáäns in retreat,
they bounded through the gateway to give battle.
Think of two savage boars in a mountain place
awaiting a loud rabble of dogs and men:
they swing their heads from side to side and rip
through underbrush, snapping the twigs off short,
with a sharp noise of gnashing tusks
until some hunter makes the kill.

                                                      Just so,

the bright bronze breastplates clanged

as these two took their blows. Prodigiously
they fought, putting their trust in their own power
and in the marksmen on the wall above.
In fact, now from high places, in defense
of camp and ships and their own lives, the men
were pitching stones: and the stones showered to earth
like snow driven by a stormwind thick and fast
in a murky veil swept over pastureland.
So missiles came in torrents, from Akhaian
hands as well as Trojan. Helmets rang
and bossed shields rang with hits.

                               But Ásïos

Hyrtákidês pummeled his thighs and groaned
and bit his lip and said:

                                    "O Father Zeus,

you, even you, turn out to be a liar.
I thought destiny was against the Akhaians
holding before our drive and our spear-arms
unleashed. Now see, like agile-waisted hornets
or bees who build their hives on a stony road—
hornets that will not leave their homes but wait
for hunters, and in fury defend their young—
those two men, two men only, at the gate
will not give way. For them, kill or be killed!"

But Ásïos' complaint left Zeus unmoved:
it pleased him to award the day to Hektor.

Now there was fighting at the various gates—
a difficult thing for me to tell it all
as though I were a god! Around the rampart
at every point, blaze upon blaze of war
leapt upward. Out of savage need the Argives
fought on bitterly to save the ships,
and all the gods who took their part were grieved;
still the two Lapiths dealt terrific blows.
Polypoitês, Peiríthoös' son,
hit Damásos' helm hard on a cheekplate,
bronze too frail to take the blow. Straight through
into the skull the spearhead crunched its way,

demolishing the brain. Down went the man.
Then Polypoitês killed Pylon and Ormenas.
War-bred Leonteus killed Hippónakhos
with a spear-thrust at the loin-guard, drew his sword,
and at close quarters, leaping through the press,
ran through Antíphatês, who went down backward;
next at Menôn and Iámenos he lunged
and at Orestês, taking their lives away.
Now while the Lapiths made these kills and took
the dead men's flashing armor, those who followed
Poulýdamas and Hektor—their young troops
in number and valor greatest, sworn to breach
the Akhaian wall and set the ships afire—
halted hesitant at the moat. Just then
as they desired to cross, a bird flew by them,
heading to the left across the army,
an eagle beating upward, in its claws
a huge snake, red as blood, alive and jerking,
full of fight: it doubled on itself
and struck the captor's chest and throat. At this
the eagle in its agony let go
and veered away screaming downwind. The snake
fell in the mass of troops, and Trojans shuddered
to see the rippling thing lie in their midst,
a portent from Lord Zeus who bears the stormcloud.
Poulýdamas at Hektor's elbow said:

"Hektor, you always manage to rebuke me
when I talk well to assemblies: it won't do
at all to cross you, peace or war, in council;
only to confirm you. Well, once more,
I intend to speak as I think best.
Let us not carry the fighting to the ships!
The end, I think, is what the bird portended—
if a true portent—when we wished to cross,
the eagle bearing left across the army,
beating upward, grappling this great snake,
alive. She dropped it here, she never gained
her own nest with it, never had her will
to give it to her nestlings. Ah, we too
are grappling danger! Granted we break the gates

and force a breach in the Akhaian wall,
granted they fall back, we shall never make it
intact to the ships by these same paths,
but many a Trojan must we leave behind
lacerated with bronze by the defenders.
That is what you'd hear from a diviner
learnèd in signs and heeded by the troops!"

Hektor in the bright helm frowned and said:

"This time I have no liking for your counsel.
You must have other and braver things to say.
If this comes from the heart, why, then the gods
themselves have wrecked your wits! You try to tell me
I should forget what Zeus of the long thunder
planned and promised with his nod to me!
You—you would have me put my faith in birds
whose spreading wings I neither track nor care for,
whether to the right hand sunward they fly
or to the left hand, westward into darkness.
No, no, I say, rely on the will of Zeus
who rules all mortals and immortals. One
and only one portent is best: defend
our fatherland! And why should you turn pale
at war and combat? Even if the rest of us
are killed to a man beside the Argive ships,
no fear that you will be: you lack ability
for warfare, and you lack the nerve to face it!
I tell you, though, that if you hold off now
or make one soldier falter in this battle,
you are a dead man on the spot
with my own spearblade in you!"

                                        So he finished,

turning to go forward, as the others
followed him with a bloodcurdling cry,
and from the slopes of Ida Zeus who plays
in thunder roused a gale against the ships,
blowing a dustcloud to bewilder spent
Akhaians, while to Trojans and to Hektor
he made his gift of glory. Trustful now

of Zeus's omens and their own right arms,
they made trial of the wall to break it down.
Layers of earth and stone they undermined,
and the revetments of the fighting wall
they tore away by prying loose the posts
the Akhaians drove to hold the earthwork in.
They pulled these up, thinking when they were gone
to breach the wall. But even now the Danáäns
would not yield free passage: jamming oxhide
bags of earth into the gaping dyke,
they cast stones from above on the attackers.

Everywhere along the parapet
one Aías and the other, acting marshals,
roamed and cheered the Akhaians on: at times
with pleading and at other times with iron
words of rebuke, if they caught sight of anyone
hanging back from the fight.

                                        "Friends," one would say,
"whether you are among the best, or fair,
or a poor fighter—all men cannot be
equal in war—this challenge is for everyone;
you see it for yourselves. Now not one man
may let himself be turned back on the ships
by any baying enemy he hears.
Keep your shots going forward, cheer each other,
so Zeus who is Olympian lord of lightning
may let us throw them back upon the town."

With words like these, and urgent battlecries,
both men cheered the Akhaians on.

                                                        Imagine

flakes of snow that come down thick and fast
on a winter day when Zeus who views the wide world
brings on a fall of snow, showing mankind
his means of making war. He lulls the winds
and sifts white flakes in stillness hour by hour
until hilltop and foreland are all hid
as are the farmers' meadowlands and fields,
while snow comes down over the hoary sea,

on harbors and on shores. Though running surf
repel it, all things else are muffled white,
weighed down by snow from heaven, a storm of Zeus.
So thick and fast the stones flew. Here they fell
on Trojans, there from Trojans on Akhaians,
by all hands thrown and thudding along the wall.

But even so, and even now, the Trojans
led by great Hektor could not yet have breached
the wall and gate with massive bar, had not
Lord Zeus impelled Sarpêdôn, his own son,
against the Argives like a lion on cattle.
Circular was the shield he held before him,
hammered out of pure bronze: aye, the smith
had hammered it, and riveted the plates
to thick bull's hide on golden rods rigged out
to the full circumference. Now gripping this,
hefting a pair of spears, he joined the battle,
formidable as some hill-bred lion, ravenous
for meat after long abstinence. His valor
summons him to attempt homesteads and flocks—
and though he find herdsmen on hand with dogs
and spears to guard the sheep, he will not turn
without a fling at the stockade. One thing
or the other: a mighty leap and a fresh kill,
or he will fall at the spearmen's feet, brought down
by a javelin thrown hard.

So valor drove

Sarpêdôn to the wall to make a breakthrough.
Turning to Glaukos, Hippólokhos' son, he said:

"What is the point of being honored so
with precedence at table, choice of meat,
and brimming cups, at home in Lykia,
like gods at ease in everyone's regard?
And why have lands been granted you and me
on Xánthos bank: to each his own demesne,
with vines and fields of grain?

So that we two

at times like this in the Lykian front line
may face the blaze of battle and fight well,
that Lykian men-at-arms may say:

'They are no common men, our lords who rule
in Lykia. They eat fat lamb at feasts
and drink rare vintages, but the main thing is
their fighting power, when they lead in combat!'

Ah, cousin, could we but survive this war
to live forever deathless, without age,
I would not ever go again to battle,
nor would I send you there for honor's sake!
But now a thousand shapes of death surround us,
and no man can escape them, or be safe.
Let us attack—whether to give some fellow
glory or to win it from him."

                                                            Glaukos

listened and moved only to obey,
and leading the great Lykian tribe the two men
charged. Now Menéstheus shivered, seeing them come
with menace for him against the wall. He glanced
around him at the battlements of Akhaians,
looking for some chief who might repel
destruction from his men. Aías the Tall
and Aías the Short he saw, avid for war,
both standing there, and Teukros, from his hut
this moment come to join them: all were near,
and yet he could not reach them with a shout,
so loud the clangor that went up to heaven,
clash of shields and helms that rang with blows
and blows upon the gates, now all were shut,
besieged by Trojans trying to break them down.
In haste he sent Thoötês off to Aías,
telling him:

                                "Run to Aías; call him here;
or call both, rather: that is best by far,
since sure destruction is upon me here.
The Lykian captains bring such weight to bear
in battle, as in the past; they are formidable.
If our two on the wall there are hard pressed,
get Aías Telamônios alone
and with him Teukros, who knows bowmanship."

When he had heard him out, the messenger
darted along the wall manned by Akhaians
to halt by those named Aías. He said at once:

"Aías and Aías, marshals of the Argives,
the son of Péteôs, reared under heaven, begs
your presence for a time at least, to share
the danger—both of you, if possible;
that would be best by far, as sure destruction
comes upon him there. But you can see
the Lykian captains bring such weight to bear
in battle, as in the past; they are formidable.
But if the fight is hot here, too, then Aías
Telamônios alone can go,
and the good bowman, Teukros, with him."

                                          Tall

Aías, son of Télamôn, complied,
first saying swiftly to the son of Oïleus:

"Aías, you and Lykomêdês hold
your ground here, and keep shouting at Danáäns
to put their hearts into the fight. Meanwhile
I will go lend a hand there in the battle.
But I should soon be back, when I have given
our men support."

                                 So off he went,

and Teukros, too, his brother, went along.
Passing inside the wall, they found Menéstheus'
tower and those who manned it hard beset,
as now the Lykian chiefs like a thundersquall
loomed at the rampart. These two hurled themselves
into the fight against the attacking line,
and a great shout went up.

                               Telamônian Aías

made the first kill—Sarpêdôn's brave companion,
Epiklês—by heaving a jagged block,
the topmost of a pile that lay inside
against one of the battlements. Not easily
could any mortal now alive
hold it in both hands, even in his prime;

but Aías raised it high and hurled it down,
shattering helmet, skull, and brains
at one blow. Down the Lykian dropped
headlong from the wall's height like a diver,
as warm life ebbed from his bones.

                                         Then Teukros shot
Glaukos, powerful son of Hippólokhos,
with an arrow as he rushed the wall—a bowshot
just where he saw his arm bared. Joy in battle
left the young fighter; off the wall he leapt,
not to be seen and taunted by Akhaians.
Glaukos' withdrawal made Sarpêdôn grieve
the instant he perceived it; still the battle
gave him joy. He pierced Alkmáôn, son
of Thestôr, and drew the spearblade out, as doubling
forward after the spear the man fell hard,
his brazen gear clanging. Then Sarpêdôn,
grasping a battlement with massive hands,
wrenched—and the parapet came toppling down,
so men could mount by it to the stripped wall.
Aías and Teukros met him now together.
Teukros put a shaft in the bright belt
on which his shield hung, but Zeus brushed away
death's shadow from his child: his fate was not
to die abaft the ships. Though Aías lunged
and hit the shield, his point would not pass through;
it only stopped Sarpêdôn. He fell back
a little from the crumbled battlement—
not in retreat, though, but still craving honor—
and whirled and called his godlike countrymen:

"Lykians, why are you lagging, slackening off
your driving power? It is hard for me
alone, strong as I am, to make a breakthrough,
clear a way to the ships. Come up alongside!
More hands here will do a better job!"

Inwardly shrinking from their lord's rebuke,
they bunched around him and attacked in force.
The Argives, for their part, inside the wall,
reinforced their companies. Both found it

heavy work, for neither could the Lykians
breach the wall and clear a way to the ships,
nor could Danáän spears dislodge
the Lykians from the wall once they had reached it.
Think of two men contending over boundary stones,
each with his measuring rod, in the common field,
in a narrow place, disputing what is fair:
so here the parapet divided these,
and for the parapet they tore each other's
chest-protecting, oxhide-aproned shields.
Many were gashed by the coldhearted bronze—
every man who left his back uncovered,
turning, and some men through the shield itself,
and everywhere, towers and battlements
were blood-bespattered from both sides. But still
the attacking Trojans could not rout the Akhaians.
They held. Think of an honest cottage spinner
balancing weight in one pan of the scales
and wool yarn on the other, trying to earn
a pittance for her children: evenly poised
as that were these great powers making war,
until at last Lord Zeus conferred on Hektor,
Priam's son, the glory of bursting through
the Akhaian wall. In a piercing voice he called:

"On, on, Trojans, horse-breakers, breach
the Argive wall and pitch a hell of fire
into the ships!"

                              The listening troops obeyed
and surged in a great throng against the wall
to clamber between towers, carrying spears.
Now Hektor picked a boulder that had stood,
broad-bottomed, sharp on top, before the gate.
The strongest pair of men in the whole realm,
as men are now, could not with ease heave up
this boulder from the ground into a wagon.
Lightly Hektor handled it alone,
for Zeus, the son of crooked-minded Krónos,
made it a trifling weight for him. A shepherd
will carry easily, in either hand,

a new-shorn ram's fleece—no great weight for him;
so Hektor, lifting up the stone, went forward
to the high double doors of heavy timber
closing the gateway. Two crossbars inside
were rammed in place and one pin fastened them.
He took a stance before the doors and braced,
with feet apart, for full force in the blow,
then smashed down at the center. Hinges cracked
on both sides as the great mass tumbled through,
the doors groaned inward, bars gave way, the planks
were splintered by the impact right and left,
and through the breach in glory Hektor leapt,
his visage dark as nightfall, though he shone
terribly from the bronze that he was dressed in,
carrying a brace of spears.

                                        No one could stop him,
none but the gods, as he leapt through the gate,
his eyes burning. Then he wheeled and called
the mass of Trojans to come charging on
across the wall. And they obeyed him, some
by swarming over, others pouring through
the very gateway.

                                        And the Danáäns broke
for their long ships in an uproar always rising.

BOOK THIRTEEN

Assault on the Ships

LINES 1–12

When Zeus had brought great Hektor and his Trojans
into the beachhead by the ships, he left them
to cruel toil of battle, and to grief,
while he himself with shining eyes turned north,
gazing on the far lands of Thracian horsemen,
Mysoi, hand-to-hand fighters, Hippêmolgoi,
who live on mare's milk, nomads, Ábioi,
most peaceable and just of men. And Zeus
now kept his shining eyes away from Troy,
confident that no other god would come
to take a hand for Trojans or Danáäns.
But the strong god who makes the mainland shake
had not been blind.

                              Enthralled, watching the battle,
he sat on woody Samos' highest ridge

off Thrace, whence Ida could be seen entire
and Priam's town and the Akhaian ships.
He had climbed up from the salt sea, and now
he pitied Akhaians beaten down by Trojans.
Rancor within him deepened against Zeus.
Then from the stony mountain down he went
with mighty strides; a tremor shook the crags
and forest under Poseidon's immortal feet.
Three giant steps, then four, and he was home
at Aigai, where his golden chambers glimmer
in the green depth and never wash away.
Here he entered; into his chariot shafts
he backed his racing team with golden manes,
put on his golden mantle, took his whip
of pliant gold, stepped up into his car,
and rolled out on the waves. Great fish beneath him
gamboled from every quarter of the deep,
aware their lord rode overhead; in laughter
whitecaps parted, and the team full tilt
airily drew unwetted the axle-tree;
with leap on leap they bore him toward the beachhead.
There is a cavern deep in the deep sea
midway between the rocky isle of Imbros
and Ténedos: here he who shakes the islands
drove his horses down, unharnessed them,
tossed them heavenly fodder, looped their hocks
with golden hobbles none could break or slip—
that they should abide here their lord's return;
and off he went to the Akhaian army.

Now like a storm or prairie fire, swarming
steadily after Hektor son of Priam,
the Trojans roared as one man—on the verge,
they thought, of capturing the Akhaian ships
and dealing death to the best men around them.
But now from the deep water,
girdler of earth and shaker of earth, Poseidon
came to arouse new spirit in the Argives.
Kalkhas he seemed, with his unwearied voice,
addressing first those two, fiery as he,
the men named Aías:

                                        "Aías and Aías, fight
to save the Akhaian army! Joy of action
is what you must remember, and have done
with clammy dread. Elsewhere I do not fear
the free spear-arms of Trojans, though they've crossed
our big rampart in force. They can be held,
all of them, by Akhaians! Only here,
in this one place, I am most afraid
it will go badly for us. Here this madman,
Hektor, like a conflagration leads them,
bragging he is a child of almighty Zeus.
I wish you were inspired by some god
to hold the line hard, clamped hard here, you two,
rallying others: you could block and turn
his whirlwind rush away from the long ships,
even if the Olympian sets him on."

The god who girdles earth, even as he spoke,
struck both men with his staff, instilling fury,
making them springy, light of foot and hand.
Then upward like a hawk he soared—a hawk
that, wafted from a rockpoint sheer and towering
shoots to strike a bird over the plain:
so arrowy in flight Poseidon left them.
The son of Oïleus knew his nature first
and turned to say to the son of Télamôn:

"That was one of the gods who hold Olympos,
here in the seer's shape telling us to fight
abaft the ships. It was not Kalkhas, not
the reader of birdflight; from his stride, his legs
as he went off, I knew him for a god.
The gods are easily spotted! As for me,
I feel more passion to do battle now;
I tingle from the very soles of my feet
to my finger tips!"

                                        And Telamônian Aías
answered:

                                        "So it is with me:
my hands itch to let the spearshaft fly!

Power is rising in me; I can feel
a springing freshness in my legs. I long
to meet this implacable Hektor face to face!"

So they assured each other, in that joy
of battle which the god inspired; and he
meanwhile put heart in the Akhaian soldiers
rearward, taking a respite among the ships.
Dead on their feet from toil of war, these men
were losing heart; now they could see the Trojans
massing as they crossed the rampart. Watching,
in silence the Akhaians' eyes grew wet;
they saw no way to escape the evil hour.
But he who makes the islands tremble, passing
lightly among them, stiffened the backbone
of all those rugged companies. Teukros first
and Lêïtos he commanded as he came,
then Pênéleos and Thoas, Dêípyros,
and last Meríonês and Antílokhos,
clarion in battle. Urgently and swiftly
he cried to them:

                              "Shame, Argives, shame, young men!
By fighting you can save our ships,
but if you shirk the battle, then we face
defeat this day at the Trojans' hands.
By heaven, what a thing to see! I never
dreamed the war would come to this: our beachhead
raided by Trojans! Until now those men
were timorous as greenwood deer, light fare
for jackals, leopards, wolves—wandering deer
with no fight in them and no joy in battle.
Trojans in other days would never meet
Akhaian power on the attack—not they!
Far from the city now, they press the combat
to the very ships—by our commander's fault
and by our soldiers' fault in giving in.
At odds with him, our men will not hold fast
beyond the ships, but die around them!

                                                  Call it

proved and true beyond a doubt
that Agamémnon, Lord of the Great Plains,

caused this by contempt shown to Akhilleus.
Are we to break off battle, then? How can we?
Rather, find a remedy; good men's hearts
respond to remedies! You must no longer
hang back, but attack, for honor's sake,
as every one of you is a first-rate soldier.
Would I now quarrel with one who shunned the war
if he were a man unfit for it? No. With you,
I am full of anger. Soldiers, you'll bring on
worse things yet by your halfheartedness.
Let each man get a fresh grip on his pride
and look to his standing. The great contest begins,
Hektor begins his drive along the ships
in force: he has broken the gate-bar and the gate."

In terms like these Poseidon stirred the Akhaians,
and round the two named Aías they made stand,
hard companies the wargod would not scorn,
nor would Athêna, Hope of Soldiers. Gathering,
picked men faced the Trojan charge, faced Hektor,
spear by spear and shield by shield in line
with shield rims overlapping, serried helms,
and men in ranks packed hard—their horsehair plumes
brushed one another when the shining crests
would dip or turn: so dense they stood together,
as from bold hands the spearshafts, closing up,
were pointed, quivering. And the men looked ahead,
braced for battle.

                       Trojans massed and running
charged them now, with Hektor in the lead
in furious impetus, like a rolling boulder
a river high with storm has torn away
from a jutting bank by washing out what held it;
then the brute stone upon the flood
goes tossed and tumbling, and the brush gives way,
crashing before it. It must roll unchecked
as far as level ground, then roll no more,
however great its force had been. So Hektor
threatened at first to sweep clear to the sea
through huts and ships of the Akhaians, killing
along the way—but when he reached the line

of packed defenders he stopped dead in his tracks.
His adversaries lunging out with swords
and double-bladed spears beat him away,
so that he stepped back, shaken. Then he cried:

"Trojans, Lykians, Dardans, fight hard here!
They cannot hold me, not for long,
by making bastion, closed in line together!
No, I can see them break before the spear,
if it is sure I have the first of gods
behind me, Hêra's consort, lord of thunder!"

Shouting, he cheered them on to the attack,
and Priam's son, Dêíphobos, inflamed
by a great hope, moved out ahead, his round shield
forward as he trod, catlike, compact
behind it. Then Meríonês took aim
and cast his shining spear. A direct hit
on the round shield of bull's hide—but no breakthrough;
the long haft snapped off at the blade. Dêíphobos
had held his shield before him at arm's length
to counter that hard blow. And now Meríonês
retired amid his company, full of rage
to see spearhead and victory broken off.
Rearward he went, along the huts and ships,
to get a long spear left inside his hut.

The rest fought on, with long-drawn battlecries,
and Telamônian Teukros drew first blood
by killing a son of Mentor, herder of horses,
Imbrios the pikeman. He had lived
at Pêdaios before the Akhaians came
and had a young wife, Mêdesikástê, born
of a slave to Priam. When the rolling ships
of the Danääns beached, he journeyed back
to Ilion, stood high, and lived near Priam,
who ranked him with his own sons. Teukros gashed
Imbrios under the ear with his long weapon,
then withdrew it. Down the Trojan went,
as on a hilltop, visible far and wide,
an ash hewn by an ax puts down its verdure

shimmering on the ground. So he went down,
and round him clanged his harness wrought in bronze.
Teukros rushed in to strip him; as he did so,
Hektor aimed a thrust with his bright spear,
but the alert man swerved before the point,
escaping by a hair's breadth. Hektor hit
a son of Ktéatos Aktoridês,
Amphímakhos, with a spear-thrust in the chest
just as he joined the fight. He thudded down
and his armor clanged upon him. Hektor lunged
to pull away the brave man's fitted helm,
and Aías reached for Hektor with his spear—
but nowhere shone his bare flesh, all concealed
by his grim armor. Aías hit his shield-boss
hard and forced him backward, making Hektor
yield the dead. Akhaians drew them off.
Stikhíos and Menéstheus, in command
of the Athenians, bore Amphímakhos
amid the Akhaians. As for Imbrios,
one Aías and the other, fast and bold,
took him as lions carry off a goat
under the noses of a biting pack
into a forest undergrowth: aloft,
clear of the ground, they lug him in their jaws.
Just so, with tossing plumes like manes, these two
lugged Imbrios, and stripped him of his gear.
Then from his tender neck Aías Oïliadês,
in anger for Amphímakhos, lopped his head
and bowled it through the mêlée till it tumbled
in dust at Hektor's feet.

                                                           Poseidon, too,

grew hot over Amphímakhos, his grandson.
Passing amid the huts and ships, he kindled
fire in Danääns and devised Trojans' woe.
Idómeneus now crossed his path, just come
from a fellow-captain slashed behind the knee,
who had been helped by others from the battle.
Idómeneus had commended him to the surgeons
and made his way now to his hut; he longed
once more to join the fighting. The Earthshaker
addressed him in the form and voice of Thoas,

Andraimôn's son, who ruled all Pleurôn, all
that steep land, Kálydôn of Aitolians,
where country folk revered him as a god.
As Thoas, now Poseidon said:

"Idómeneus,
marshal and mind of Kretans, what has become
of those Akhaian threats against the Trojans?"

The Kretan captain in reply said:

"Thoas,
the blame cannot be pinned on any man,
so far as I know, up to now. Our people
understand war, none is unmanned by fear,
not one has lagged or slipped away from carnage.
Only it must be somehow to the pleasure
of arrogant Zeus, that here ingloriously
far from Argos the Akhaians perish!
Ah, Thoas!
before this you have shown courage in danger,
and when you see a man go slack, you brace him.
No quitting now! Let every soldier hear it!"

Poseidon answered him:

"Idómeneus,
let that man never voyage home from Troy
but be a carcass for the dogs to play with
who would give up the fight this day! Come on,
and bring your gear; no time to lose; we must
hit hard and hit together, both of us,
if we are going to make our presence felt.
When feeble men join forces, then their courage
counts for something. Ours should count for more,
since we can fight with any."

So the god
took part with men once more in toil of combat.
When he had reached his hut, Idómeneus
bound on his handsome armor, took two spears,
and ran out like a lightning bolt, picked up

by Zeus to handle flickering on Olympos
when he would make a sign to men—the jagged
dance of it blinding bright. So as he ran
bronze flashed about his breast.

                                        Meriônês,

his valiant aide, came up, still near the hut,
on his way to get a bladed spear to carry,
and mighty Idómeneus said:

                                        "Meriônês,

Mólos' dear son, good runner, best of friends,
how is it that you left the battle?
Have you been hit? Some arrow grinding in you?
Or were you bringing word to me? No sitting
still in huts for me: I long to fight!"

The cool man said:

                            "Idómeneus, counselor

of battle-craft to Kretans under arms,
I came to see if any spear is left here
I can use. I shattered mine just now
against Déíphobos' shield."

Idómeneus answered:

                            "Spears? All you desire,

twenty-one spears, you'll find inside, arrayed
against the bright wall of the entranceway—
all Trojan; I win weapons from the dead.
I do not hold with fighting at long range,
therefore I have the spears, and shields as well,
and helms as well, and bright-faced cuirasses."

Meriônês the cool man in reply
said:

                            "In my quarters, at my ship, I too
have plenty of Trojan gear; not near at hand, though.
I say I am not—*not*, I say—a man
to pass up any attack. I take my place
in the front rank for action and for honor
whenever battle's joined. There may be others

who have not seen me fight, but I believe
you know me."

                    And the captain of Kretans answered:

"Know you, and how you stand. Why need you say it?
Suppose amid the ships we picked our best
for a surprise attack: that is the place
where fighting qualities in truth come out,
and you can tell a brave man from a coward.
This one's face goes greener by the minute;
he is so shaky he cannot control himself
but fidgets first on one foot, then the other,
his teeth chattering, his heart inside him pounding
against his ribs at shapes of death foreseen.
As for the brave man, his face never changes,
and no great fear is in him, when he moves
into position for an ambuscade;
his prayer is all for combat, hand to hand,
and sharp, and soon. Well, no man then
would look down on your heart and fighting skill!
And were you hit by a missile or a thrust
in the toil of war, the blow would never come
from behind on nape or back, but in the chest
or belly as you waded in
to give and take at the battle line.
But no more talk or dawdling here like children!
Someone might sneer and make an issue of it.
Go to my hut and choose a battle spear."

Meríonês, peer of Arês, in a flash
picked from the hut a bladed spear and ran
after Idómeneus, athirst for battle.
Imagine Arês, bane of men, when he
goes into combat with Rout close behind,
his cold and powerful son,
who turns the toughest warrior in his tracks.
From Thrace these two take arms against Ephyroi
or gallant Phlegyai; but not for them
to heed both sides: they honor one with glory.
Just so, Meríonês and Idómeneus,

helmed in fiery bronze, captains of men,
made their way to battle. But Meríonês
asked his friend:

                                    "Son of Deukálion, where
do you say we join the combat? On the right,
or in the center, or on the left? I find
the Akhaians there, if anywhere, shorthanded
in this attack."

                              And the Kretan captain said:

"The middle ships have their defenders:
Aías Telamônios, Aías Oïliadês,
Teukros, our best hand with a bow—and brave
at close quarters. They will give Hektor
more than he can handle in this battle,
hot as he is for war. He's powerful, yes,
but he will find it uphill work to conquer
these sharp fighters, formidable hands,
and set our ships aflame—unless Lord Zeus
should toss a firebrand aboard himself.
No mortal nourished on Dêmêtêr's meal,
none vulnerable to bronze or stones will make
great Telamônian Aías yield. He would not
in a stand-up fight give ground to dire Akhilleus—
whom in a running fight no man can touch.
This way for us, then, to the army's left:
to see how soon we'll give some fellow glory
or win it from him."

                                    Swift as the god of war,
Meríonês was off, and led the way
to that part of the line his friend required.
When the Akhaians saw Idómeneus
in fresh strength, like a flame, with his companion,
richly armed, all gave a shout and grouped
about him: and a great fight, hand to hand,
arose at the ship sterns. Gusts of crying wind
on days when dust lies thickest on the lanes
will wrestle and raise a dustcloud high: so spread
this mêlée as men came together, sworn
with whetted bronze to kill and strip each other.

Bristling spines of long flesh-tearing spears
went home in the deadly press; and a man's eyes
failed before the flash of brazen helmets,
cuirasses like mirrors, and bright shields
in sunlight clashing. Only a man of iron
could have looked on lighthearted at that fight
and suffered nothing.

                                        At cross-purposes,
the sons of Krónos in their power brought on
bitter losses and death for brave men. Zeus
on the one hand willed for Hektor and the Trojans
victory, to vindicate Akhilleus;
at the same time, he willed no annihilation
of the Akhaians before Troy, but only
honor to Thetis and her lion-like son.
Poseidon for his part now roused the Argives,
moving among them, after he emerged
in secret from the grey sea; being grieved
by Argive losses at the Trojans' hands,
he felt bitter indignation against Zeus.
Both gods were of the same stock, had one father,
but Zeus had been first-born and knew far more.
In giving aid, Poseidon therefore would not
give it openly: always under cover,
in a man's likeness, he inspired the ranks.
These gods had interlocked and drawn
an ultimate hard line of strife and war
between the armies; none
could loosen or break that line
that had undone the knees of many men.

Idómeneus belied his grizzled head
and, calling on Danáäns, with a bound
scattered the Trojans, for he killed Othrýoneus
of Kabêsos, a guest of Troy. This man
had come, on hearing lately of the war,
and bid for Kassandra, the most beautiful
of Priam's daughters. Though he had brought no gifts,
he promised a great feat: to drive from Troy
the army of Akhaians, willy-nilly.
Then old Priam had agreed to give her,

nodding his head on it; so the man fought
confident in these promises. Idómeneus
aimed at him with long spear flashing bright
and caught him in mid-stride. His plate of bronze
could not deflect the point driven in his belly,
and down he crashed. The other taunted him:

"Othrýoneus, I'll sing your praise
above all others, if you do your part
for Priam! He had promised you his daughter.
Well, we could promise, and fulfill it, too,
to give you Agamémnon's loveliest daughter
brought out of Argos for you as your bride—
if you would join to plunder Troy.
Come, and we'll make the marriage bond
aboard the long ships. There's no parsimony
in us when it comes to bridal gifts."

                                                    With this,
he dragged him by one foot out of the combat.
Asïos, now dismounted, moved up fast
to fight over the body, while his driver
held the horses panting at his shoulders.
Putting his heart into the cast, he tried
to hit Idómeneus; but the Akhaian whipped
his missile in ahead and struck his throat
under the chin, running him through with bronze.
Tall Asïos fell the way an oak or poplar
falls, or a towering pine, that shipbuilders
in mountain places with fresh-whetted axes
fell to make ship's timber. So, full length,
he lay before his team and chariot,
wheezing, clutching at the bloody dust.
His stunned driver had lost what wits he had
and did not dare to break from his enemies
by wheeling his team around. Antílokhos
put a spear into him. The bronze he wore
could not deflect the point driven in his belly,
and with a gasp he pitched down from the car.
His team was taken by Antílokhos,
greathearted Nestor's son, amid the Akhaians.

Enraged at Ásïos' fall, Dêíphobos
went for Idómeneus with a hard spear-cast,
but he foresaw the blow and dodged the point
by disappearing under his round shield
of bull's hide, fitted on two struts or bars,
and plated with concentric rings of bonze.
Under this he packed himself, as over it
the bronze-shod spear passed; and his shield rang out
under the glancing blow. But not for nothing
thrown by Dêíphobos' brawny hand,
the spear hit a commander, Hypsênor
son of Híppasos, in the liver under
the diaphragm, and brought him tumbling down.
Dêíphobos gave a great shout and exulted:

"Ásïos is down, but there's revenge!
On his journey to Death's iron gate
he will be glad I gave him company."

This went home to the Argives, most of all
Antílokhos, whose heart was stirred,
but in his grief he still bethought himself
for his companion. On the run he reached him,
straddled him and held his shield above him.
Two other friends, Mêkisteus, Ekhios' son,
and brave Alástôr, bent to lift and carry him
groaning deeply to the sheltering ships.

Idómeneus' passion for battle never waned:
he strove to shroud some Trojan in hell's night
or else himself to fall, as he fought off
the black hour for Akhaians.

                                             Now he met

Alkáthoös, Aisyêtês' noble son,
Ankhísês' son-in-law. This man had married
Hippodameia, eldest of the daughters,
dearest to her father and gentle mother
in their great hall. In beauty, skill, and wit,
she had excelled all girls of her own age.
For this reason, too, the man who won her
had been the noblest suitor in all Troy.

Now it was he that by Idómeneus' hand
Poseidon overcame. The god entranced
his shining eyes and hobbled his fine legs,
so that he could not turn back or maneuver,
but like a pillar or a full-grown tree
he stood without a tremor. Square in the chest
Idómeneus caught him, sundering the cuirass
that until now had saved his flesh from harm.
And now at last he cried aloud, the rending
spear between his ribs, and down he crashed,
his heart, being driven through, in its last throes
making the spearbutt quake. The mighty wargod
then extinguished all his force.
Idómeneus yelled and exulted savagely:

"Ah, then, Dêíphobos, shall we call it quits
when three are downed for one? You counted first!
Bright soul, come forward now, yourself, and face me!
Learn what I am! I come in the line of Zeus,
who fathered Mínos, lord of the Kretan seas,
and he in turn fathered Deukálion
who fathered me, commander of many fighters
in the wide land of Krete. Then here to Troy
my ships brought me to plague you and your father
and all the Trojans."

                                    Challenged so, Dêíphobos
weighed the choice before him: should he pair
with some brave Trojan—going back to get him—
or take Idómeneus on alone? It seemed
more promising to him to join Aineías,
whom he discovered in the battle's rear,
standing apart, resentful against Priam,
as Priam slighted him among his peers.
Dêíphobos reached his side and said to him swiftly:

"Counselor of Trojans, you must come
defend your kinsman, if his death affects you.
Follow me, to protect Alkáthoös,
your sister's husband, who made you his ward
when you were still a small child in his house.
The great spearman, Idómeneus, brought him down."

The appeal aroused Aineías. Craving battle,
he charged Idómeneus; and he, no child
to be overtaken by a qualm of fear,
steadily waited, like a mountain boar
who knows his power, facing a noisy hunt
in a lonely place: his backbone bristles rise;
both eyes are fiery; gnashing his tusks
he waits in fury to drive back dogs and men.
Idómeneus, great spearman, so awaited
without a backward step Aineías' onset.
But to his friends he called out, looking back
at Aphareus, Askálaphos, Dêípyros,
and those two masters of the battlecry,
Meríonês and Antílokhos; he sent
an urgent cry to alert them:

                                        "This way, friends!
Give me a hand here, I am alone!
I have a nasty fear of the great runner,
Aineías, now upon me: he has power
to kill, and has the bloom
of youth that is the greatest strength of all.
If we were matched in age as in our spirit
in single fight, then quickly he or I
should bear away the glory."

                                        As he spoke,
with one mind all the others closed around him,
taking position, shields hard on their shoulders.
Aineías, too, on his side turned and called
Dêíphobos and Paris and Agênor,
fellow-captains of Trojans. Troops moved up
behind him now, as a flock out of a pasture
follows a ram to drink—and the shepherd's heart
rejoices: so did Aineías' heart rejoice
to see the men-at-arms follow his lead.
Both masses came together, hand to hand,
around Alkáthoös, long polished spearshafts
crossing, and the bronze on the men's ribs
rang like anvils from the blows they aimed
at one another. Most of all, those peers
of Arês, Aineías and Idómeneus,

strove with heartless bronze to rend each other.
Aineías made the first throw, but his adversary
saw the aim and twisted to elude it,
so that Aineías' point went home in earth
and stuck with quivering shaft, the force he gave it
with his great arm spent on the air. Idómeneus
for his part thrust and hit Oinómaos
mid-belly, breaking through his cuirass-joint,
and the bronze lancehead spilt his guts like water.
Dropping in dust, the Trojan clawed the ground.
Idómeneus pulled his long spear out, but could not
strip the Trojan's shoulders of his gear,
being driven back by spear-throws. And then, too,
he was no longer certain of his footwork
in lunging or recovery, but fought
defensively against the evil hour,
his legs no longer nimble in retreat.
Now as he gave way step by step, Dêíphobos,
implacable against him, made a throw
but missed again; he hit Askálaphos,
a son of the god Arês, running him through
the shoulder with his heavy spear. He fell
in dust and clawed the ground. And roaring Arês
heard no news as yet that his own son
died in that mêlée—no, for he was sitting
on high Olympos under golden clouds,
restrained by the will of Zeus, as were the other
immortal gods, all shut away from war.
But hand to hand around Askálaphos
the fight went on: Dêíphobos took the dead man's
helm, but Meríonês, fast as the wargod,
leaped and speared the Trojan's outstretched arm.
The crested helm fell with a hollow clang,
and with a falcon's pounce Meríonês
regained his spear and jerked it from Dêíphobos'
upper arm at the shoulder joint, then back
he turned to merge into his company.
A brother of the wounded man, Polítês,
putting an arm around his waist, withdrew him
out of the battle-din to where his team
stood waiting in the rear, with car and driver.

Away to Troy they bore Déíphobos,
who groaned in his distress, while blood ran down
his arm from the open wound.

                                        And still the others
fought as the long-drawn battlecry arose.
Lunging at Aphareus, son of Kalêtôr,
Aineías hit his throat as he turned toward him
and cut it with his sharp spearpoint: the head
fell to one side as shield and helm sank down
and death, destroyer of ardor, flooded him.
Antílokhos' sharp eye on Thoôn saw him
turn away, and in one leap he slashed
the vein that running up the back comes out
along the neck; he sheared it from the body,
so that the man fell backward in the dust
with arms out to his friends. Antílokhos
closed to take the harness from his shoulders
watchfully, as the Trojans from all sides
moved up and struck at his broad glittering shield.
But none with his coldhearted bronze could scratch
Antílokhos' tender skin—because Poseidon
protected him amid those many blows.
And never out of range of them he turned
and turned upon his enemies: the spearshaft
swerving, never still, with his intent
to throw it and bring someone down
or to close in and kill.

                                        Now Ásios' son
Adámas caught him as he aimed and struck him,
stepping in close, driving his point mid-shield,
but felt the spearshaft broken by Poseidon,
who grudged him this man's life. One half the spear
hung like a fire-hardened stake impaled
in the shield of Antílokhos, while on the ground
the other half lay. Then Adámas backed
into his throng of friends, away from death,
but as he drew away, Meríonês
went after him and hit him with a spear-throw
low between genitals and navel, there
where pain of war grieves mortal wretches most.
The spear transfixed him. Doubled up on it,

as a wild bullock in the hills will writhe
and twitch when herdsmen fetter and drag him down,
so did the stricken man—but not for long
before Meríonês bent near and pulled out
spearhead from flesh. Then night closed on his eyes.

Now with his Thracian broadsword Hélenos
cut at Dêípyros' head and broke his helm off:
buffeted to the ground and underfoot
it rolled till an Akhaian fighter caught it,
but black night closed on Dêípyros' eyes.
Grief at his death took great-lunged Meneláos,
and menacing with hefted spear he bore
down on Lord Hélenos, while Hélenos
drew arrowhead to handgrip. All at once
one made his cast, the other man let fly,
and Priam's son hit Meneláos' breast
upon his armor's rondure—but the barbed
shaft went skittering.

                                        On a threshing floor
one sees how dark-skinned beans or chickpeas leap
from a broad shovel under a sharp wind
at the toss of the winnower: just so
from shining Meneláos' cuirass now
the bitter arrow bounced up and away.
Meanwhile the son of Atreus, clarion
in battle, struck the hand that held the bow:
he drove his brazen spearhead through the knuckles
into the bowstave. Hélenos recoiled
amid his countrymen, eluding death,
his dangling left hand dragging the ashwood spear.
Greathearted Agênor drew the spearhead out
and bound his hand in sheepswool from a sling
an aide supplied him. Then came Peísandros
in a rush at the great figure of Meneláos—
impelled by fatal destiny to fall
before you in the mêlée, Meneláos—
and when the range narrowed between these two
Meneláos missed: the spear was turned aside:
but Peísandros got home his stroke upon
Meneláos' shield. Only, he could not

drive his metal in and through: the shield
held fast; the shaft below the spearhead broke,
yet even so in joy he hoped for victory.
By the silver-studded hilt Meneláos drew
his longsword as he leapt on Peísandros—
who now brought out from underneath his shield
a double ax on a long polished helve.
In one great shock both men attacked at once,
axhead on helmet ridge below the crest
came hewing down, but the sword stroke
above the nose on the oncoming brow
went home; it cracked the bone, and both his eyes
were spilt in blood into the dust at his feet
as he bent over and fell. Meneláos followed
to spurn the man's chest with his foot and strip
his gear away. And glorying over him
he said:

                              "Here is the way back from the ships!
This way you'll leave our beachhead,
Trojans who have not yet enough of war.
You don't lack vileness otherwise, or crime
committed against me, you yellow dogs;
you knew no fear of Zeus in his high thunder,
lord of guests—no forethought of his anger
harshly rising! He will yet destroy
your craggy city for you. My true queen
you carried off by sea with loads of treasure
after a friendly welcome at her hands.
This time you lust to pitch devouring fire
into our deepsea ships, and kill Akhaians.
You will be stopped somehow, though savage war
is what you crave!"

                                        Then in a lower tone
he said:

                              "O Father Zeus, imcomparable
they say you are among all gods and men
for wisdom; yet this battle comes from you.
How strange that you should favor the offenders—
favor the Trojans in their insolence
ever insatiable for war! All things

have surfeit—even sleep, and love, and song,
and noble dancing—things a man may wish
to take his fill of, and far more than war.
But Trojans will not get their fill of fighting."

Meneláos as he spoke had ripped away
and given his men the dead man's bloodstained arms.
Now once more, yet again, he entered combat.
Here in a surge against him came
Harpálion, King Pylaiménês' son,
who journeyed with his father to make war
at Troy—never thereafter to come home.
At close quarters this fighter hit the shield
of Meneláos, but he could not drive the bronze
onward and through it. Backward in recoil
he shrank amid his people, shunning death,
with wary glances all around
for anyone whose weapon might have nicked him.
After him, though, Meríonês
let fly a bronze-shod arrow, and it punched
through his right buttock, past the pelvic bone,
into his bladder. On the spot he sank
down on his haunches, panting out his life
amid the hands of fellow-soldiers: then
he lengthened out like an earthworm
as dark blood flowing from him stained the ground.
Falling to work around him, Paphlagonians
lifted him in a car and drove him back
to Troy in sorrow. And his father, weeping,
walked behind; there was no retribution
for the dead son. But the death angered Paris,
because among the Paphlagonians
the man had been his guest and his great friend.
In anger now he let an arrow fly.

There was a young Akhaian named Eukhênor,
noble and rich, having his house at Korinth,
a son of the visionary, Polyïdos.
When he took ship he knew his destiny,
for Polyïdos had foretold it often:
he was to die of illness in his mégaron

or else go down to death at Trojan hands
amid the Akhaian ships. Two things at once
he had therefore avoided: the heavy fine
men paid who stayed at home, and the long pain
of biding mortal illness. Paris' arrow
pierced him below jaw and ear, and quickly
life ebbed from his body, the cold night
enwrapped him.

                  And the rest fought on like fire's
body leaping. Hektor had not learned
that Trojans on their left flank near the ships
were being cut to pieces; victory there
was almost in Akhaian hands, Poseidon
urged them on so, and so lent them strength.
But Hektor held that ground where first he broke
through gate and wall and deep ranks of Danääns—
there where the ships of Aías and Prôtesílaos
were drawn up on the grey sea beach, and landward
the parapet had been constructed lowest.
Here in chariots or on foot
the Akhaians fought most bitterly: Boiotians,
Ionians in long khitons, men of Lokris,
men of Phthía, illustrious Epeioi
fought off Hektor from the ships, but could not
throw him back as he came on like flame.
Athenians, picked men, were here, their chief
Péteôs' son, Menéstheus, and his aides,
Pheidas and Strikhíos, rugged Bías. Next
the Epeian leaders, Mégês, son of Phyleus,
Amphíon and Drakíos; of Phthía then,
Medôn and staunch Podárkês. Aye, this Medôn,
noble Oïleus' bastard son and Aías'
brother, lived in Phýlakê
far from his fatherland, as he had killed
a kinsman of Oïleus' second lady,
Eriôpis. As for the Lord Podárkês,
he was a son of Íphiklos Phylákidês.
These, then, in arms before the men of Phthía,
fought for the ships at the Boiotians' side.
But Aías, Oïleus' quick son, would never,
not for a moment, leave Telamônian Aías.

These two men worked together, like dark oxen
pulling with equal heart a bolted plow
in fallow land. You know how, round the base
of each curved horn, the sweat pours out, and how
one smooth-worn yoke will hold the oxen close,
cutting a furrow to the field's edge? So
these toiling heroes clove to one another.
Surely the Telamônian had retainers—
many and courageous countrymen—
who took his shield when weariness came on him
and sweat ran down his knees. No Lokrians
backed up the other Aías, Oïleus' son:
they could not have sustained close-order combat,
having no helms of bronze with horsehair crests,
no round shields and no spears of ash. In fact,
when they took ship together for Ilion,
they put their faith in bows and braided sheepswool
slings, with which they broke the Trojan lines
by pelting volleys.

                        Now the men in armor
fought with Trojans in the front lines, fought
with Hektor, hand to hand, but in the rear
the bowmen shot, being safely out of range—
and Trojans lost their appetite for battle
as arrows drove them in retreat.

                                  At this,
they might have left the ships and the encampment
wretchedly to return to windy Troy,
had not Poulýdamas moved close to Hektor,
saying:

                       "You are a hard man to persuade.
Zeus gave you mastery in arms; therefore
you think to excel in strategy as well.
And yet you cannot have all gifts at once.
Heaven gives one man skill in arms, another
skill in dancing, and a third man skill
at gittern harp and song; but the Lord Zeus
who views the wide world has instilled clear thought
in yet another. By his aid men flourish,
and there are many he can save; he knows

better than any what his gift is worth.
Let me tell you the best thing as I see it,
now everywhere around you in a ring
the battle rages.

                              Ever since the Trojans
crossed the wall, some have hung back, though armed,
while others do the fighting—and these few,
outnumbered, are dispersed along the ships.
Give way, call all our captains back, we'll test
their plans of action, every one. Shall we
attack the deepsea ships, can we assume
god wills to grant the day to us? And could we
retire from the ships without a slaughter?
As for me, I fear
the Akhaians may still pay the debt they owe
for yesterday, as long as the man we know,
famished for battle, lingers on the beachhead:
I doubt he'll keep from fighting any longer."
This wariness won Hektor's nod. At once
down from his chariot he swung to earth,
with all his weapons, and commanded swiftly:

"Poulýdamas—
it is up to you to call and hold our captains
while I take on the battle over there.
I will come back as soon
as I have made my orders clear to them."

And towering like a snowpeak off he went
with a raucous cry, traversing on the run
Trojans and allied troops. Their officers
collected near Poulýdamas on hearing
new commands from Hektor.

                                         Dêíphobos,
Lord Hélenos, Adámas, son of Ásïos,
and Ásïos, Hyratakos' son, were those
he looked for down the front. Safe and unhurt
he scarcely found them. Those who lost their lives
at Argive hands were lying near the sterns;
others were thrown back on the wall with wounds.
But one man he soon found, on the left flank
of grievous battle: Prince Aléxandros,

husband of Helen of the shining hair.
He stood there cheering on his company,
and stepping near him Hektor spoke to him
in bitterness:

                              "Paris, you bad-luck charm,
so brave to look at, woman-crazed, seducer,
where is Dêíphobos? And Hélenos?
Ásïos, Hyrtakos' son? Adámas, *his* son?
Where is Othrýoneus? If these are gone,
tall Ilion is crumbling, sure disaster
lies ahead."

                                          Aléxandros replied:

"Hektor, since you are moved to blame the blameless,
there may be times when I break off the fighting,
but I will not now. My mother
bore me to be no milksop.

                                          From the hour
you roused our men to battle for the ships
we have been here engaging the Danääns
without respite. As for the friends you look for,
some are dead. Dêíphobos and Hélenos
went off, I think, with spear wounds in the hand,
but the Lord Zeus has guarded them from slaughter.
Lead us now, wherever your high heart
requires. We are behind you, we are fresh
and lack no spirit in attack, I promise,
up to the limit of our strength.
Beyond that no man fights, though he may wish to."

With these mild words he won his brother over.
Into the thick of battle both men went,
round Kebríonês, Poulýdamas, and Phálkês,
Orthaíos, godlike Polyphêtês, Palmys,
and the sons of Hippotíôn, Askánios
and Mórys. These had come the day before
at dawn, replacements from Askaniê's plowland.

Zeus now intensified the fight. Men charged
like rough winds in a storm launched on the earth

in thunder of Father Zeus, when roaring high
the wind and ocean rise together; swell
on swell of clamorous foaming sea goes forward,
snowy-crested, curling, ranked ahead
and ranked behind: so line by compact line
advanced the Trojans glittering in bronze
behind their captains.

                                    Hektor in the lead,
peer of the man-destroying god of war,
held out his round shield, thick in bull's hide, nailed
with many studs of bronze, and round his temples
his bright helmet nodded. Feinting attack
now here, now there, along the front, he tried
the enemy to see if they would yield
before his shielded rush—but could not yet
bewilder the tough hearts of the Akhaians.
Aías with a giant stride moved out
to challenge him:

                                    "Come closer, clever one!
Is this your way to terrify the Argives?
No, we are not so innocent of battle,
only worsted by the scourge of Zeus.
And now your heart's desire's to storm our ships,
but we have strong arms, too, arms to defend them.
Sooner your well-built town shall fall
to our assault, taken by storm and plundered.
As for yourself, the time is near, I say,
when in retreat you'll pray to Father Zeus
that your fine team be faster than paired falcons,
pulling you Troyward, making a dustcloud boil
along the plain!"

                                    At these words, on the right
an eagle soared across the sky. "Iakhê!"
the Akhaian army cried at this. In splendor
Hektor shouted:

                                    "Aías, how you blubber;
clumsy ox, what rot you talk! I wish
I were as surely all my days
a son of Zeus who bears the stormcloud, born
to Lady Hêra, honored like Athêna

or like Apollo—as this day will surely
bring the Argives woe, to every man.
You will be killed among them! Only dare
stand up to my long spear! That fair white flesh
my spear will cut to pieces: then you'll glut
with fat and lean the dogs and carrion birds
of the Trojan land! You'll die there by your ships!"

He finished and led onward. The front rank
moved out after him with a wild cry,
and from the rear the troops cheered. Facing them,
the Argives raised a shout; they had not lost
their grip on valor but now braced to meet
the Trojan onslaught. Clamor from both sides
went up to the pure rays of Zeus in heaven.

BOOK FOURTEEN

BOOK FOURTEEN

Beguilement on Mount Ida

LINES I–II

Now Nestor heard that tumult while he drank,
but finished drinking. Then he turned and said
to Asklêpios' son:

                      "Consider now, Makháon,
what had best be done here. Battlecries
of young fighters are louder, near the ships.
As for yourself, be easy, drink my wine,
till Hékamêdê has a caldron warmed
and bathes your clotted blood away. For my part,
I'll go outside and find a lookout point."

He picked up in the hut a shield that lay there
all aglow with bronze—one that belonged
to a son of his, the horseman Thrasymêdês,

who bore that day his father's shield. Then Nestor
chose a burly newly whetted spear,
and stepping out he saw that grim day's work:
Akhaians driven back, at bay; elated
Trojans pressing on; the wall torn down.

As when the open ocean
rises in a leaden smooth ground swell,
forerunner of high winds; a rocking swell,
directionless, that neither rolls nor breaks
until the blow comes on from Zeus: just so
the old man pondered, with divided mind,
whether to turn toward the Danáän mass
or find and join Lord Marshal Agamémnon.
Then he decided; it seemed best to him
to join the son of Atreus.

                                        In the line,

soldiers meanwhile fought on to strip each other,
metal upon their bodies clanging loud
with sword blows and the double-bladed spears.

But now to Nestor's side the princes came
along the shipways, those who had been hit:
Diomêdês, Odysseus, Agamémnon,
leaving the rear where, distant from the fighting,
ships were beached along the wash of surf—
higher inland were those first dragged ashore
around whose sterns the wall was built.

                                        In rows

they kept the ships drawn up; even that wide shore
could not contain the fleet in one long line;
they hauled them up, therefore, wave after wave,
and filled the beach between two promontories.
Now headed inland, eyes upon the mêlée,
the princes came that way, leaning on spears,
with aching hearts; and the advent of Nestor
gave their hearts a new twinge. Agamémnon
hailed him, saying:

                        "Nestor, son of Nêleus,
pride of Akhaians! Why turn this way, seaward,

away from the battle-danger? Now I fear
their champion, Hektor, will make good his word,
the threat he made in his harangue to Trojans,
not to return to Ilion from the beachhead
until he fired our ships and killed our men.
So he proclaimed; now it is coming true.
My god, it seems the rest of the Akhaians,
like Akhilleus, hold a grudge against me!
They have no will to fight, to save the ships."

Lord Nestor of Gerênia replied:

"What you describe is all too clear. High-thundering
Zeus himself could not now otherwise
dispose the fight: those walls are overthrown
we put our trust in as impregnable,
a bulwark for the ships and for ourselves.
The enemy have brought the battle down
hard on the ships; you could not if you tried
make out whether from left or right our troops
are harried most and thrown into confusion.
Men go down on every hand; their death-cries
rise in air.

                 We must think what to do,
if any good can be achieved by thinking.
I do not say that we should enter combat;
hurt men cannot fight."

                       And the Lord Marshal
Agamémnon said:

                   "Since now they press the fight
around the ships' sterns, neither wall nor moat
made any difference, though painful labor
built them, and Danáäns dearly hoped
they'd make a shield to save our ships and men—
this must be somehow satisfactory
to the high mind of Zeus, that far from Argos
Akhaians perish here without a name.
I knew it when he favored us and saved us,
I know it now, when he glorifies our enemies,

treating them like gods! He tied our hands,
he took the heart out of us.

                                        Come, everyone

do as I say: haul down the line of ships
nearest the sea to launch on the bright breakers,
moor them afloat till starry night comes on
and Trojans break off battle. Under cover
of darkness we may launch the rest.
There's no disgrace in getting away from ruin,
not by a night retirement. Better a man
should leave the worst behind him than be caught."

Odysseus, the great tactician, frowned
and looked at him and answered:

                                        "Son of Atreus,

what kind of talk is this?
Hell's misery! I'd put you in command
of some disordered rabble, not an army
strong as our own. Our lot from youth to age
was given us by Zeus: danger and war
to wind upon the spindle of our years
until we die to the last man.

                                        Would you, then,

quit and abandon forever the fine town
of Troy that we have fought for all these years,
taking our losses? Quiet! or some other
Akhaians may get wind of this. No man
who knew what judgment is in speech could ever
allow that thought to pass his lips—no man
who bore a staff, whom army corps obeyed,
as Argives owe obedience to you.
Contempt, no less, is what I feel for you
after the sneaking thing that you propose.
While the two armies are in desperate combat,
haul our ships into the sea? You'd give
the Trojans one more thing to glory over—
and they are winning out, god knows, already!
As for ourselves, sheer ruin is what it means.
While our long ships are hauled down, will the soldiers
hold the line? Will they not look seaward

and lose their appetite for battle? There,
commander, is your way to wreck us all."

Lord Marshal Agamémnon answered him:

"You hit hard, and the blow comes home, Odysseus.
Let it be clear I would not urge the troops
to launch, against their will and yours, not I.
Whoever has a better plan should speak,
young man or old; I would be glad to hear it."

Now Diomêdês of the great warcry
spoke up:

             "Here's one. No need to go afield for it.
If you are willing to be swayed, and are not
irritated with me, the youngest here.

                     I, too,
can claim a brave and noble father, Tydeus,
whom funeral earth at Thebes has mounded over.
To Portheus three excellent sons were born,
who lived in Pleurôn and in Kálydôn—
Ágrios, Mélas, and the horseman Oineus,
bravest of all and father of my father.
Oineus remained there, while my wandering father
settled in Argos. It was the will of Zeus
and of the other gods.

                  He took Adrêstos'
daughter as bride and founded a great house:
grainlands enough he owned, and he owned orchards
thick with trees, and herds and flocks aplenty.
Beyond that, he was best of all Akhaians
in handling a spear: you must have heard this
and know the truth of it. My lineage
therefore is noble. If what I say's well said
you may not disregard it.

                    Let us go
this way to battle, wounded as we are;
we have no choice. There in the field we may
keep clear of missiles, not to be hit again,
but put heart in the rest. Just as before,
they save themselves, and shirk the fight."

                                    To this
the others listening hard gave their assent.
They turned, and Agamémnon led them forward.

This was not lost on the god who shakes the earth,
who now appeared as an old man and walked
beside them, taking Agamémnon's hand,
saying to him in a clear voice rapidly:

"Son of Atreus, think how the fierce heart
must sing now in Akhilleus' breast,
to see the slaughter and rout of the Akhaians!
Compassion is not in him. Let him rot, then!
Some god crush him! But the gods in bliss
are not unalterably enraged with you.
Somehow the hour will come when Trojan captains
make the wide plain smoke with dust, in chariots
racing from camp and ships back to the city!"

Launching himself upon the field of war,
he broke into a shout nine or ten thousand
men who yelled in battle might have made,
meeting in shock of combat: from his lungs
the powerful Earthshaker sent aloft
a cry like that. In every Akhaian heart
he put the nerve to fight and not be broken.

Now Lady Hêra of the Golden Chair
had turned her eyes upon the war. She stood
apart upon a snowcrest of Olympos
and recognized her brother-in-law, her brother,
striving in battle, breathing hard—a sight
that pleased her. Then she looked at Zeus, who rested
high on the ridge of Ida bright with springs,
and found him odious.

                                Her ladyship
of the wide eyes took thought how to distract
her lord who bears the stormcloud. Her best plan,
she thought, was this: to scent and adorn herself
and visit Ida, hoping hot desire
might rise in him—desire to lie with her

and make love to her nakedness—that so
she might infuse warm slumber on his eyes
and over his shrewd heart.

She entered then

the chamber built for her by her own son,
Hêphaistos, who had fitted door to doorpost
using a secret bolt no god could force.
These shining doors the goddess closed behind her,
and with ambrosia cleansed all stain away
from her delectable skin. Then with fine oil,
she smoothed herself, and this, her scented oil,
unstoppered in the bronze-floored house of Zeus,
cast fragrance over earth and heaven. Hêra,
having anointed all her graceful body,
and having combed her hair, plaited it shining
in braids from her immortal head. That done,
she chose a wondrous gown, worked by Athêna
in downy linen with embroideries.
She caught this at her breast with golden pins
and girt it with a waistband, sewn all around
with a hundred tassels.

Then she hung

mulberry-colored pendants in her earlobes,
and loveliness shone round her. A new headdress
white as the sun she took to veil her glory,
and on her smooth feet tied her beautiful sandals.
Exquisite and adorned from head to foot
she left her chamber. Beckoning Aphrodítê,
she spoke to her apart from all the rest:

"Will you give heed to me, and do as I say,
and not be difficult? Even though you are vexed
that I give aid and comfort to Danáäns
as you do to the Trojans."

Aphrodítê,

daughter of Zeus, replied:

"Hêra, most honored

of goddesses, being Krónos' own daughter,
say what you have in mind!

I am disposed to do it if I can,
and if it is a thing that one may do."

And Lady Hêra, deep in her beguilement,
answered:

                              "Lend me longing, lend me desire,
by which you bring immortals low
as you do mortal men!

                              I am on my way
to kind Earth's bourne to see Okéanos,
from whom the gods arose, and Mother Tethys.
In their great hall they nurtured me, their gift
from Rhea, when Lord Zeus of the wide gaze
put Krónos down, deep under earth and sea.
I go to see them and compose their quarrel:
estranged so long, they have not once made love
since anger came between them. Could I coax them
into their bed to give and take delight,
I should be prized and dear to them forever."

Aphrodítê, lover of smiling eyes,
replied to her:

                              "It is not possible
and not expedient, either, to deny you,
who go to lie in the great arms of Zeus."
Now she unfastened from around her breast
a pieced brocaded girdle. Her enchantments
came from this: allurement of the eyes,
hunger of longing, and the touch of lips
that steals all wisdom from the coolest men.
This she bestowed in Hêra's hands and murmured:

"Take this girdle, keep it in your breast.
Here are all suavities and charms of love.
I do not think you will be ineffective
in what you plan."

                              Then wide-eyed Hêra smiled
and smiling put the talisman in her breast.
Aphrodítê entered her father's house,

but Hêra glided from Olympos, passing
Piéria and cherished Emathía,
flashing above the snowy-crested hills
of Thracian horsemen. Never touching down,
she turned from Athos over the sea waves
to Lemnos, to the stronghold of old Thoas.
Here she fell in with Sleep, brother of Death,
and took his hand and held it, saying warmly:

"Sleep, sovereign of gods and all mankind,
if ever you gave heed to me before,
comply again this time, and all my days
I shall know well I am beholden. Lull
to sleep for me the shining eyes of Zeus
as soon as I lie down with him in love.
Then I shall make a gift to you, a noble,
golden, eternal chair: my bandy-legged
son Hêphaistos by his craft will make it
and fit it with a low footrest
where you may place your feet while taking wine."

But mild sweet Sleep replied:

                                        "Most venerable

goddess, daughter of Krónos, great of old,
among the gods who never die, I might
easily lull another to sleep—yes, even
the ebb and flow of cold Okéanos,
the primal source of all that lives.
But Zeus, the son of Krónos? No, not I.
I could not venture near him, much less lull him,
unless by his command.

                                        One other time

you taught me something, giving me a mission,
when Hêraklês, the prodigious son of Zeus,
had plundered Ilion and come away.
That day indeed I cast my spell
on the Father's heart; I drifted dim about him,
while you prepared rough sailing for the hero.
In the open sea you stirred a gale that drove
Hêraklês on Kos Island, far from friends.
Then Zeus woke up and fell into a fury

and hurled the gods about his hall, in quest
of me above all. Out of heaven's air
into deep sea to be invisible forever
he would have plunged me, had not Night preserved me,
all-subduing Night,
mistress of gods and men. I fled to her,
and he for all his rage drew back, for fear
of doing a displeasure to swift Night.
A second time you ask me to perform
something I may not."

                              But to this she answered:

"Why must you dwell on that unhappy day?
Can you believe that Zeus who views the wide world
will be as furious in defense of Trojans
as for his own son, Hêraklês?

                                        No, no.

Come. I should add, my gift to you will be
one of the younger Graces for a mistress,
ever to be called yours."

                              In eager pleasure,

Sleep said:

              "Swear by Styx' corroding water!
Place one hand on earth, grassland of herds,
and dip your other hand in dazzling sea:
all gods with Krónos in the abyss, attest
that I shall marry one of the younger Graces,
Pásithea, the one I have desired
all my living days."

                              Without demur,

Hêra whose arms shone white as ivory
took oath as he demanded. Each by name
she called on all the powers of the abyss,
on all the Titans. Then, when she had sworn,
these two departed in the air from Lemnos,
putting on veils of cloudrack, lightly running
toward Ida, mother of beasts and bright with springs.
At Lekton promontory, from the sea

they veered inland and upland. At their passage
treetops were in commotion underfoot.
But Sleep soon halted and remained behind
before he came in range of Zeus's eyes.
He mounted a tall pine, the tallest one
on Ida, grown through mist to pierce the sky.
Amid the evergreen boughs he hid and clung
and seemed that mountain thrush of the clear tone,
called "khalkis" by the gods, by men "kymindis."

Hêra swept on to Gárgaron, Ida's crest,
and there Zeus, lord of cloud, saw her arrive.
He gazed at her, and as he gazed desire
veiled his mind like mist, as in those days
when they had first slipped from their parents' eyes
to bed, to mingle by the hour in love.

He stood before her now and said:

                                        "What brings you
down from Olympos to this place?
The chariot you ride is not in sight."

The Lady Hêra answered him in guile:

"I go my way to the bourne of Earth, to see
Okéanos, from whom the gods arose,
and Mother Tethys. In their distant hall
they nourished me and cared for me in childhood.
Now I must see them and compose their strife.
They live apart from one another's bed,
estranged so long, since anger came between them.
As for my team, it stands at Ida's base
ready to take me over earth and sea.
On your account I came to see you first,
so that you will not rage at me for going
in secret where Okéanos runs deep."

The lord of cloud replied:

                                        "But you may go there
later, Hêra. Come, lie down. We two
must give ourselves to love-making. Desire

for girl or goddess in so wild a flood
never came over me! Not for Ixion's bride
who bore that peerless man, Peiríthoös;
or Dánaë with her delicious legs,
illustrious Perseus' mother; or Eurôpa,
daughter of Phoinix, world-renowned, who bore me
Mínos and magnificent Rhadamánthys;
Sêmêlê or Alkmênê, Theban ladies—
one bore the rugged hero Hêraklês,
the other Dionysos, joy of men—
or Dêmêtêr, the queen, in her blond braids;
or splendid Lêto; or yourself! No lust
as sweet as this for you has ever taken me!"

To this the Lady Hêra in her guile
replied:

                    "Most formidable son of Krónos,
how impetuous! Would you lie down here
on Ida's crest for all the world to see?
Suppose one of the gods who never die
perceived us here asleep and took the story
to all the rest? I could not bear to walk
directly from this love-bed to your hall,
it would be so embarrassing.

                                But if you must,
if this is what you wish, and near your heart,
there is my own bedchamber. Your dear son,
Hêphaistos, built it, and he fitted well
the solid door and doorjamb. We should go
to lie down there, since bed is now your pleasure."

But the lord marshal of stormcloud said:

                                          "No fear
this act will be observed by god or man,
I shall enshroud us in such golden cloud.
Not even Hêlios could glimpse us through it,
and his hot ray is finest at discerning."

At this he took his wife in his embrace,
and under them earth flowered delicate grass

and clover wet with dew; then crocuses
and solid beds of tender hyacinth
came crowding upward from the ground. On these
the two lay down and drew around them purest
vapor of golden cloud; the droplets fell
away in sunlight sparkling. Soon the Father,
subjugated by love and sleep, lay still.
Still as a stone on Gárgaron height he lay
and slumbered with his lady in his arms.

The god of sleep went gliding to the beachhead
bearing word to the god who shakes the earth.
He halted at his side and swiftly said:

"Warm to your work now, comfort the Danáäns,
even award them glory in the fight—
for a while at any rate—while Zeus is sleeping,
now that I've wrapped him in a night of sleep.
Hêra beguiled him into making love."

And he was gone into far lands of fame
when he had stirred Poseidon to fight harder.
The god now gained the line in a single bound
and called out:

                "Argives, shall we yield to Hektor
once again? And let him take the ships,
let him win glory? He would have it so
because Akhilleus lingers by his ships,
anger in his heart.

                Well, that great man
need not be missed too badly, if the rest of us
rally each other to defend ourselves.
Come, every man, and act on what I say:
the army's best and biggest body shields
are those that we should wear, our heads encased
in helms that flash on every side, our hands
upon the longest spears! And then attack!
I will myself go first. My life upon it,
Hektor for all his valor cannot hold us!

Any fresh man who bears against his shoulder
a light shield, give it now to a tired fighter,

and slip his own arm in a heavier one."
The attentive soldiers acted on his words,
while Diomêdês, Odysseus, and Agamémnon,
wounded as they were, kept all in order.

Down the ranks they made exchange of gear,
good gear to good men, poor to the inferior,
and when hard bronze was fitted to their bodies
all moved out. Poseidon took the lead,
in his right fist a blade fine-edged as lightning
that mortals may not parry in grievous war—
for blinding fear makes men stand back from it.
Hektor drew up the Trojan lines opposing,
and now the blue-maned god of sea and Hektor
brought to a dreadful pitch the clash of war,
one giving heart to Trojans, one to Argives.
Waves of the sea ran berserk toward the Argive
huts and ships as the two armies closed
with a great cry. No surge from open sea,
whipped by a norther, buffets down on land
with such a roar, nor does a forest fire
in mountain valleys blazing up through woods,
nor stormwind in the towering boughs of oaks
when at its height it rages, make a roar
as great as this, when Trojans and Akhaians
hurled themselves at one another.

                                                        Hektor

drove at Aías first with his great spear,
as Aías had swung round at him. He hit him
at that point where two belts crossed on his chest,
one for his shield, one for his studded sword,
and both together saved his skin. In rage
because the missile left his hand in vain,
Hektor fell back in ranks away from danger,
but as he drew away Telamônian Aías
picked up one of the wedging stones for ships
rolled out there, many, at the fighters' feet,
and smote him in the chest, above his shield-rim,
near his throat. The impact spun him round
reeling like a spent top. As an oak tree
under the stroke of Father Zeus goes down,

root and branch, and deadly fumes of brimstone
rise from it, and no man's courage keeps him
facing it if he sees it—Zeus's bolt
being rough indeed—so all Hektor's élan
now dropped in dust. He flung his spear, his shield
and helm sank down with him, his blazoned armor
clanged about him.

                    Yelling Akhaian soldiers
ran toward him, hoping to drag him off,
and they made play with clumps of spears. But none
could wound or hit the marshal of the Trojans,
being forestalled by the Trojan peers,
Aineías, Poulýdamas, and Agênor,
Sarpêdôn, chief of Lykians, and Glaukos.
None of the rest neglected him, but over him
all held up their round shields. Fellow-soldiers
lifted him in their arms to bear him off
out of the grind of battle to his horses.
These were waiting in the battle's rear
with painted chariot and driver. Now
toward Troy they carried Hektor, hoarsely groaning.
Reaching the ford of Xánthos, the clear stream
of eddying water that immortal Zeus
had fathered, from the car they laid him down
on the riverbank and splashed cool water on him.
Taking a deep breath, opening his eyes wide,
he got to his knees and spat dark blood, then backward
sank again as black night hooded him,
stunned still by the hurled stone.

                    But the Argives,
seeing Hektor leave the field, were swift
to step up their attacks upon the Trojans,
taking new joy in battle. Out in front,
the runner, Aías, son of Oïleus, lunged
and wounded Sátnios Enópidês,
whom by the banks of Satnióeis river
a flawless naiad bore the herdsman, Enops.
This Sátnios the famous son of Oïleus,
coming in fast, speared in the flank. He tumbled,
and then around him Trojans and Danáäns
clashed in bitter combat. Poulýdamas

took the lead, shaking his spear to guard him,
and struck Arëilýkos' son,
Prothoênor, square on the right shoulder,
his big spear passing through. Into the dust
he fell and clutched at earth with his spread hand.
Then Poulýdamas gloried, shouting high:

"By god, this time the spearshaft from the hand
of Pánthoös' son leapt out to some effect.
One of the Argives caught it in his flesh;
I can see him now, using it for a crutch,
as he stumps to the house of Death!"

                                        His boasting brought
anguish to Argives, most of all to Aías,
veteran son of Télamôn: beside him
the dying man fell. Now with his shining spear
he thrust at the withdrawing enemy,
but he, Poulýdamas, with a sidewise leap
avoided that dark fate. Another got it—
Arkhélokhos, for the gods had planned his ruin.
Just at the juncture of his neck and skull
the blow fell on his topmost vertebra
and cut both tendons through. Head, mouth, and nostrils
hit the earth before his shins and knees.
Now Aías in his turn to Poulýdamas
shouted:

                    "Think now, Poulýdamas, tell me truly
if this man was not worthy to be killed
for Prothoênor? as he seemed to me
no coward nor of cowards' kind, but brother
to Lord Antênor, master of horse, or else
his son, for he was very nearly like him."

He said this knowing the answer well. And pain
seized Trojan hearts. Standing above his brother,
Akámas brought down Prómakhos, a Boiotian,
as he was tugging at the dead man's feet.
Then gloating over him with a wild cry
Akámas said:

                        "You Argive arrow boys,
greedy for the sound of your own voices,

hardship and grief will not be ours alone!
You'll be cut down as he was! Only think,
the way your Prómakhos has gone to sleep
after my spear downed him—and no delay
in the penalty for my brother's death. See why
a soldier prays that a kinsman left at home
will fight for him?"

                              And this taunt hurt the Argives.
Most of all, it angered Pênéleos
and he attacked Akámas, who retired
before his charge. Pênéleos, instead,
brought down Ilioneus, a son of Phórbas,
the sheepherder, whom of all Trojans Hermês
favored most and honored with possessions,
although Ilioneus' mother bore the man
that son alone.

                              Pênéleos drove his spearhead
into the eye-socket underneath the brow,
thrusting the eyeball out. The spearhead ran
straight through the socket and the skull behind,
and throwing out both hands he sat down backward.
Pênéleos, drawing his long sword, chopped through
the nape and set the severed helmeted head
and trunk apart upon the field. The spear
remained in the eye-socket. Lifting up
the head by it as one would lift a poppy,
he cried out to the Trojans, gloating grimly:

"Go tell Ilioneus' father and his mother
for me, Trojans, to mourn him in their hall.
The wife of Prómakhos, Alegênor's son,
will not be gladdened by her husband's step,
that day when we Akhaians make home port
in the ships from Troy."

                              And the knees of all the Trojans
were shaken by a trembling as each one
looked for a way to escape breath-taking death.

Muses in your bright Olympian halls,
tell me now what Akhaian most excelled

in winning bloodstained spoils of war
when the Earthshaker bent the battle line.
Aías Telamônios cut down
the Mysian leader, Hýrtios Gyrtíadês;
Antílokhos killed Mérmeros and Phálkês;
Meríonês, Mórys and Hippotíôn;
Teukros, Prothoön and Períphêtês.
After that, Meneláos hit Hyperênor's
flank, and the spearhead spilt his guts like water.
By the wound-slit, as by a doorway, life
left him in haste, and darkness closed his eyes.
But Aías the swift runner, son of Oïleus,
killed more than any: none could chase as he could
a soldier panicked in that god-sent rout.

BOOK FIFTEEN

The Lord of Storm

Running among the stakes, crossing the moat,
many of them were cut down by Danääns;
the remnant reached the chariots and stood there,
pale with fear, beaten.

                                        And now Zeus

on Ida's top by Hêra's queenly side
awoke and rose in a single bound. He saw
the Trojans and Akhaians—Trojans routed,
pressed by Akhaians whom Poseidon joined;
saw Hektor stretched out on the battlefield,
brothers-in-arms around him, squatting down
where he lay, faint and fighting hard for breath,
vomiting blood. The man who knocked him out
was not the weakest of Akhaians.

Watching,

the father of gods and men was moved to pity.
He turned with a dark scowl and said to Hêra:

"Fine underhanded work, eternal bitch!
putting Lord Hektor out of action,
breaking his fighting men! I should not wonder
if this time you will be the first to catch it,
a whip across your shoulders for your pains!
Do you forget swinging so high that day?
I weighted both your feet with anvils,
lashed both arms with golden cord
you couldn't break, and there you dangled
under open heaven amid white cloud.
Some gods resented this,
but none could reach your side or set you free.
Any I caught I pitched headfirst
over our rampart, half-dead, down to earth!
Yet even so my heartache for the hero,
Hêraklês, would not be shaken off.
You and the north wind had connived, sent gales
against that man, brewed up sea-perils for him,
driven him over the salt waste to Kos Island.
I set him free, I brought him back
from all that toil to the bluegrass land of Argos.

These things I call to mind once more
to see to it that you mend your crooked ways.
Learn what you gain by lechery with me,
tricking me into it! That's why you came,
apart from all the gods!"

Now Hêra shuddered

answering in a clear low tone, protesting:

"Earth be my witness, and the open sky,
and oozing water of Styx—the gods can take
no oath more solemn or more terrifying—
and by your august person, too, I swear
as by our sacred bed—how could I lightly
swear by that?—no prompting word of mine
induced the god who makes the mainland shake

to do harm to the Trojans and to Hektor,
backing their enemies. It cannot be
anything but his own heart that impels him.
Seeing the tired Akhaians in retreat
upon their own ships' sterns, he pitied them.
But I—I too—should counsel him to go
where you command him, lord of darkening cloud."

At this he smiled, the father of gods and men,
and lightly came his words upon the air:

"Then in the time to come, my wide-eyed lady,
supposing you should care to sit with me
in harmony among the immortal gods,
for all Poseidon's will to the contrary,
he must come round to meet your wish and mine.
If what you say is honest, then rejoin
the gods' company now, and call for Iris,
call for Apollo with his wondrous bow.
Iris will go amid the mailed Akhaians
with my word to Poseidon: *Quit the war,
return to your own element.* Apollo
must then brace Hektor for the fight and breathe
new valor in him, blot from his memory
the pangs that now wear out his spirit. Let him
shatter the Akhaians into retreat,
helpless, in panic, till they reach the ships
of Pêleus' son, Akhilleus. Then that prince
will send Patróklos, his great friend, to war,
and Hektor in glory before Ilion
by a spear-cast will bring Patróklos down,
though he destroy a host of men, my son,
Sarpêdôn, being among them. Aye, for this
the Prince Akhilleus in high rage
will kill heroic Hektor. From that moment
I'll turn the tide of battle on the beach
decisively, once and for all,
until the Akhaians capture Ilion,
as Athêna planned and willed it. But until
that killing I shall not remit my wrath.
Nor shall I let another god take part

on the Danááns' side—no, not before
the heart's desire of the son of Pêleus
shall have been consummated. So I promised,
so with a nod I swore, that day when Thetis
touched my knees and begged me to give honor
to Akhilleus, raider of cities."

                                        When he finished,
Hêra took pains to follow his command:
from Ida's crests she flashed to high Olympos
quick as a thought in a man's mind.
Far and wide a journeying man may know
the earth and with his many desires may dream,
"Now let me be in that place or that other!"
Even so instantaneously Queen Hêra
passed to steep Olympos. She appeared
in the long hall of Zeus amid the immortals,
who rose, lifting their cups to her.

                                        She passed,
ignoring all the rest, but took a cup
from rose-cheeked Themis, who came running out
to meet her, crying:

                                                "Hêra,
why have you come back? Oh, how dazed you look!
Your husband must have given you a fright!"

To this the beautiful goddess with white arms
replied:

                        "No need to ask, my lovely Themis.
You know how harsh and arrogant he is.
Preside now at our feast,
here in the hall of the gods, and with the rest
you'll hear what cruelty he shows.
Among mortals or gods, I rather think
not everyone will share his satisfaction,
although one still may feast and be at ease."

The Lady Hêra finished and sat down,
and all turned sullen in the hall of Zeus.
Her lips were smiling, but the frown remained

unsmoothed upon her brow. Then she broke out
in her bad temper:

                                        "Oh, what mindless fools
to lay plans against Zeus! And yet we do,
we think we can be near him, and restrain him,
by pleading or by force. But there he sits
apart from us, careless of us, forever
telling us he is quite beyond us all
in power and might, supreme among the gods!
So each must take what trouble he may send.
And this time grief's at hand
for Arês; yes, his son died in the fighting,
dearest of men to him: Askálaphos.
The strong god Arês claimed that man for son."

Now Arês smote his thighs with open hands
and groaned:

                                        "You must not take it ill, Olympians,
if I go down amid the Akhaian ships
to avenge my son—and so I will, though fate
will have me blasted by the bolt of Zeus
to lie in bloody dust among the dead!"

He called to Terror and Rout to yoke his horses
while he put on his shining gear. Now soon
another greater and more bitter fury
would have been roused in Zeus against the gods,
had not Athêna, gravely fearing for them,
left the chair she sat on, and come forward
out of the forecourt. She removed the helm
from Arês' head, the great shield from his shoulder,
and laid his spear down, lifted from his hand.
Then she spoke to rebuke the angry god:

"You've lost your mind, mad one, this is your ruin!
No use your having ears to listen with—
your self-possession and your wits are gone.
Have you not taken in what Hêra says,
who just now came from Zeus? Do you desire
to have your bellyful of trouble first

and find yourself again upon Olympos,
rage as you will, brought back by force, moreover
bringing a nightmare on the rest of us?
In a flash he'll turn from Trojans and Akhaians
and create pandemonium on Olympos,
laying hands on everyone alike,
guilty or not. Therefore I call on you
to drop your anger for your son. By now
some better man than he in strength and skill
has met his death in battle, or soon will.
There is no saving the sons of all mankind."

Then in his chair she seated burly Arês.
Hêra now called Apollo from the hall
with Iris, messenger of the immortals.
Lifting her voice, addressing both, she said:

"Zeus commands you with all speed to Ida.
Once you are there and face him, you'll perform
whatever mission he may set for you."

With this the Lady Hêra turned away
and took her chair again, as off they soared
toward Ida, bright with springs, mother of beasts.
On Gárgaron height they found him at his ease,
the broad-browed son of Krónos, garlanded
by fragrant cloud. The two gods took their stand
before him who is master of the storm—
and he regarded them, unstirred by anger,
seeing their prompt obedience to his lady.
Then to Iris he said:

                                        "Away with you,
light foot, take my message to Poseidon,
all of it; do not misreport it; say
he must give up his part in war and battle,
consort with gods or else go back to sea.
But if he disobeys or disregards me,
let him remember: for all his might,
he does not have it in him to oppose me.
I am more powerful by far than he,
and senior to him. He has forgotten this,

claiming equality with me. All others
shrink from that."

                                        Then running on the wind
swift Iris carried out his order. Down
from Ida's hills she went to Ilion,
as snow or hail flies cold from winter cloud,
driven by north wind born in heights of air.
So Iris flew in swiftness of desire,
halting beside the Earthshaker to say:

"O girdler of the earth, sea-god, blue-maned,
I bear a message from the lord of storm.
You must give up the battle, must retire
amid the gods, or else go back to sea.
But if you disobey or disregard him,
he warns you he will take a hand in war
against you, coming here himself. You would
do well to avoid that meeting, he advises,
seeing he's far more powerful than you
and senior to you. You have overlooked this,
claiming equality with him. All others
shrink from that."

                                   His face grown dark with rage,
the great Earthshaker said:

                                        "The gall of him!
Noble no doubt he is, but insolent, too,
to threaten me with forcible restraint
who am his peer in honor.

                                        Sons of Krónos
all of us are, all three whom Rhea bore,
Zeus and I and the lord of those below.
All things were split three ways, to each his honor,
when we cast lots. Indeed it fell to me
to abide forever in the grey sea water;
Hadês received the dark mist at the world's-end,
and Zeus the open heaven of air and cloud.
But Earth is common to all, so is Olympos.
No one should think that I shall live one instant
as he thinks best! No, let him hold his peace

and power in his heaven, in his portion,
not try intimidating me—
I will not have it—as though I were a coward.
Better to roar and thunder at his own,
the sons and daughters he himself has fathered!
They are the ones who have to listen to him."

Wind-swift Iris answered:

                                        "Shall I put it
just that way, god of the dark blue tresses,
bearing this hostile message back to Zeus?
Or will you make some change? All princely hearts
are capable of changing. And, you know,
the Furies take the part of elder brothers!"

Poseidon made reply:

                                        "Excellent Iris,
very well said; that is a point well taken;
it is a fine thing when a messenger
knows what is fitting.

                                        But it irks me
his being so quarrelsome, railing at me
who am his peer in destiny and rank.
I yield, though—but I take it ill, by heaven.
And there is more to say: with all my power
I warn him, if without me and Athêna,
Hêra and Hermês and the Lord Hêphaistos,
he should make up his mind alone
to spare steep Ilion, and will not sack it,
will not give the Argives the upper hand,
then he incurs our unappeasable anger."

When he had said this, turning from the Akhaians,
into the deep he plunged, and the soldiers missed him.
Then, to Apollo, Zeus who gathers cloud
said:

                        "Go, dear Phoibos, to the side of Hektor,
now that the god who shakes the earth has gone
into the salt immortal sea. He shunned
our towering anger. Had he not, some others

might have had lessons in the art of war—
even the gods below, round fallen Krónos.
But it is better far for both
that even though he hates it he give way
before my almighty hands. Not without sweat
would that affair have been concluded.

                                                                    Well,

take for yourself my tasseled shield of stormcloud,
and shake it hard with lightning overhead
to rout the Akhaian soldiers. God of archery,
make Hektor your own special charge.
Arouse his utmost valor till, in rout,
the Akhaians reach the ships and Hellè's waters.
There I myself shall conjure word and act
to give once more a respite to Akhaians."

Without demurring at his father's words
Apollo glided from the heights of Ida,
like that swiftest of birds, the peregrine.
He found Prince Hektor, Priam's son,
no longer supine but just now recovered,
sitting up, able to see and know
his friends' faces around him; his hard panting
and sweating had been eased. The mind of Zeus,
master of cloud, reanimated him.
And standing near the man, Apollo said:

"Hektor, why do you sit here, weak and sick,
far from the rest? What has come over you?"

And Hektor of the shining helmet answered,
whispering hoarsely:

                                        "Excellency, who are you?
A god? What god, to face and question me?
Do you not know that near the Akhaian sterns
where I had killed his friends, formidable
Aías hit my chest with a great stone
and knocked the fighting spirit out of me?
In fact I thought this day I'd see the dead
in the underworld—I thought I had breathed my last!"

Apollo, lord of archery, replied:

"Be of good heart. The god you see, from Ida,
the Lord Zeus sent to fight with you in battle.
I am Apollo of the golden sword;
I rescued you before, you and your city.
Up, then; tell your host of charioteers
to charge the deepsea ships. I shall go first
and cut a passage clean for chariot horses,
putting Akhaian soldiery to rout."

This inspired a surge of fighting spirit
in the commander's heart.

                                      As when a stallion,
long in the stall and full-fed at his trough,
snaps his halter and goes cantering off
across a field to splash in a clear stream,
rearing his head aloft triumphantly
with mane tossed on his shoulders, glorying
in his own splendor, and with driving knees
seeking familiar meadowland and pasture:
just so Hektor, sure-footed and swift,
sped on the chariots at the god's command.

And the Akhaians? Think of hunting dogs
and hunters tracking a wild goat or a stag
to whom steep rock and dusky wood
give cover, so the hunters are at a loss
and by their cries arouse a whiskered lion
full in their path, at which they all fall back,
eager as they have been for prey: just so,
Danääns thronging in pursuit, and drawing
blood with swords and double-bladed spears,
when they caught sight of Hektor coming on
toward their front rank, turned round in sudden terror,
courage ebbing to their very feet.

But now they heard from Thoas, son of Andraimôn,
bravest of the Aitolians, a tough man
at spear-throwing and in close combat, too;
and few Akhaians bested him in assembly
when the young vied in argument:

"Bad luck,"

he cried, "this marvel that I see ahead:
Hektor escaped from death, he's on his feet.
God knows, each one of us had hoped and prayed
he died from Aías' blow! But no, some god
protected him and saved him. This same Hektor
broke the strength of many a Danáän,
and now he will again. Without some help
from Zeus who thunders in high heaven
he could not lead this charge so furiously.
Come, then, everyone do as I advise:
the rank and file we'll order to the rear,
back to the ships. But we who count ourselves
as champions in the army will stand fast.
We may contain him if we face him first
with ranked spears. Wild as he is, I think
that in his heart he fears to mix with us."

Assenting to this speech they acted on it.
Those with Aías and Idómeneus,
Teukros, Meríonês, the veteran Mégês,
formed for close-order combat, calling first-rate
spearmen to face Hektor and the Trojans.
Meanwhile the rank and file fell back
upon the Akhaian ships.

                                                    All in a mass

with jutting spears the Trojans came, as Hektor
strode in command. Apollo, leading him,
was cloaked in a white cloud, and held the shield
of ominous stormcloud, with its trailing fringe.
The smith Hêphaistos gave this shield to Zeus
to carry and strike fear in men. Apollo
handled it now as he led on the Trojans.
All in a mass the Argive captains stood,
and a sharp cry rose from both sides; then arrows
bounded from bowstrings; then from bold men's hands
a rain of spears came. Some stuck fast in agile
fighters' bodies; many between the ranks
fell short of the white flesh and stood a-quiver,
fixed in earth, still craving to be sated.
As long as Phoibos held the shield of stormcloud

motionless, from both sides missiles flew,
men fell on both. But when he made it quake
with lightning, staring Danáäns in the face,
and gave, himself, a deafening battlecry,
he stunned them all and they forgot their valor.
As when a pair of wild beasts in the dusk
stampedes a herd of cows or a flock of sheep,
by a sudden rush, and no herdsman is near,
so the Akhaians lost their nerve and panicked.
Apollo sent the soul of rout among them,
but glory to the Trojans and to Hektor.

Each man slew his man in the broken field:
Hektor killed Stikhíos and Arkesílaös,
one a Boiotian captain, and the other
comrade of brave Menéstheus; then Aineías
dispatched Medôn and Iasos: the first-named
a bastard son of Oïleus, and half-brother
of Aías: he had lived in Phýlakè
in exile from his own land, having murdered
a kinsman of his stepmother, Eriôpis.
Iasos was a captain of Athenians
and son, so called, of Sphêlos Boukólidès.
Poulýdamas killed Mêkisteus—Ekhíos,
his father, fell in the early battle line
before Polítès—and heroic Agênor
killed Kloníos. As Dêïokhos ran,
Paris hit his shoulder from behind
and drove the brazen spearhead through his chest.

While Trojans stripped these dead, Akhaians
crowding into the ditch among the stakes
were forced in a wild scramble across the wall.
So Hektor with a great shout called his men:

"Sweep on the ships! Let bloodstained gear alone!
The man I see on the wrong side of the wall,
away from the ships, will die there by my hand.
They won't be lucky enough to burn his corpse—
his women and his kin; wild dogs will drag him
before our city."

                                    Swinging from the shoulder
he whipped his horses on, and called the Trojans
after him into the enemy's ragged ranks,
and all together, guiding the chariot horses,
gave a savage cry. Far in the lead
Apollo kicked the embankment of the ditch
into the middle and so made a causeway,
wide as a spear-throw when a powerful man
puts his back into throwing. Over this
they poured in column, led on by Apollo
holding the dusky splendid shield of cloud.
As for the Akhaian rampart, in one sweep
he leveled it, as a boy on the seashore
wipes out a wall of sand he built
in a child's game: with feet and hands, for fun,
he scatters it again. Just so,
bright Phoibos, you threw down the Argive wall,
so long and hard to build, and terrified
the Argives. Backed up on the ships, they waited,
crying out to each other, lifting prayerful
hands to all the gods.

                                    Gerênian Nestor,
lord of the western approaches to Akhaia,
stretching his hands out to the sky of stars,
prayed:

                                    "Father Zeus, if someone long ago
in Argos of the grainfields offered up
fat haunches of a cow or sheep in fire
and begged you for a safe return from Troy,
winning your promise and your nod, remember
now, Olympian! Defend us
against this pitiless day! Do not allow
Akhaians to be crushed this way by Trojans!"

Fervently he prayed, and the lord of wisdom,
thundered a great peal, hearing the old man's prayer.
And at that peal of Zeus's thunder, Trojans
thrilled with joy of battle, running harder
after the Argives.

                                    Like a surging wave
that comes inboard a ship when a gale blows—

wind giving impetus to sea—the Trojans
crossed the rampart with a mighty cry
and whipped their chariots toward the sterns. Once there,
they fought close-up with double-bladed spears,
attackers from the chariots, defenders
high on the black hulls, thrusting down long pikes
that lay aboard for sea-fights, double-length
in fitted sections, shod with biting bronze.

As long as both sides fought around the rampart
still remote from the ships, Patróklos stayed
inside the shelter with Eurýpylos
to give him pleasure, talking, and to treat
his aching wound with salve against the pain;
but when he knew the Trojans had crossed over,
knew by their cry the Danáäns were in rout,
he groaned and smote his thighs with open hands,
and miserably he said:

                                                              "Eurýpylos,
I cannot linger with you here,
much as you need me. The big fight begins.
One of your men can keep you company,
but I must go to Akhilleus in a hurry
to make him join the battle. Who can say
if with god's help I may convince and move him?
A friend's persuasion is an excellent thing."
Even as he spoke, he strode out. The Akhaians
meanwhile held position at the ships
against the Trojan rush, but they could not
repel the Trojans, even outnumbering them,
nor could the Trojans break the Danáän line
to penetrate amid the huts and ships.
But as a chalkline in a builder's hands—
a man who learned his whole craft from Athêna—
makes a deck-beam come out straight, just so
the line of battle had been sharply drawn.

Fighting went on around the various ships.
Hektor headed for Aías, and these two
fought hard for a single ship; neither could Hektor
dislodge his enemy and fire the ship,

nor could the other force his attacker back—
for Hektor had Apollo on his side.
But Aías downed Kalêtôr, Klytíos' son,
as he bore fire against the ships. He hit him
full in the chest, and down with clanging arms
he tumbled, as the torch fell from his hand.
When Hektor saw his cousin fall
before the black ship in the dust, he cried
in a loud voice to Trojans and Lykians:

"Trojans, Lykians, Dardanoi, all soldiers,
now is no time to yield even an inch
here in the narrow ways! Defend Kalêtôr,
or they will take his arms! He died fighting
to win the ships!"

                                   With this he aimed a cast
of shining spear at Aías, but he missed him,
aimed then a second cast at Lykophrôn,
a son of Mastôr, and a squire to Aías,
native of Kýthêra, but Aías' guest
on Sálamis, for he had killed a Kýthêran.
Now Hektor cleft this man above the ear
with his sharp spearhead as he stood by Aías.
Down in the dust upon his back he fell,
down from the ship's stern, flopping, all undone.
Then Aías shivered and called out to his brother:

"Teukros, old soul, our friend Mastoridês,
our faithful friend, is dead. When he left Kýthêra
and lived with us, we loved and honored him
as much as our own parents. And now Hektor
has killed the man. Where are your deadly arrows?
Where is the tough bow that Apollo gave you?"

Teukros took it all in, and on the run
he came to join his brother. In his hand
he held the strung bow and a quiver of arrows.
Shooting, he made them flash upon the Trojans,
and hit Kleitos, Peisênor's brilliant son,
companion of Poulýdamas Panthoïdês,
as he held hard his reins

in trouble with his horses, trying to hold them
close in where the wheeling lines were packed,
to do his best for Hektor and the Trojans.
Now in a flash his evil moment came,
and no one by his strength of will could stop it:
a quill of groaning pierced his neck behind.
He dropped out of the car. The horses reared,
then jerked the empty chariot backward rattling.
Lord Poulýdamas noticed it at once
and ran to catch the horses. These he gave
to Astynóös, Protiáon's son,
commanding him to hold the chariot near
and keep his eyes open. He himself
went back to join the mêlée.

One more arrow

Teukros drew for Hektor helmed in bronze,
and would have stopped the battle for the ships
if that shot had dispatched him in his triumph.
But Zeus perceived it, and he guarded Hektor—
wrested that boon from Telamônian Teukros,
who as he pulled the smooth bow snapped the string.
The heavy-headed shaft went wide, the bow
dropped from his hands, and with a shiver Teukros
said to his brother:

"Damn the luck. Some god

is cutting off our prospects in this fight.
He forced the bow out of my hand and broke
the new gut I had whipped on it this morning
to stand the spring of many shafts."

To this

Telamônian Aías answered:

"Well, old friend,

just let the bow and sheaf of arrows lie,
since a god wrecked them, spiting the Danáäns.
Take up a long pike, get a shield, and fight
the Trojans that way, make the soldiers fight.
If the enemy is to take the ships,
they'll know they are in a battle. Let us hold on
to joy of combat!"

                                      Teukros put his bow
inside his hut. He took his four-ply shield
hard on his shoulder, pulled on a well-made helm,
picked out a strong shaft shod with cutting bronze,
and ran out, taking his stand at Aías' side.

Hektor had seen that weaponry undone,
and now he shouted to Trojans and Lykians:

"Trojans, Lykians, Dardanoi, all soldiers,
friends, be men, take a fresh grip on courage
here by the decked ships. I have just seen
how Zeus crippled their champion's archery!
Easy to see how men get strength from Zeus:
on the one hand, when he gives them glory,
on the other, when he saps their enemies.
Taking the heart out of the Argives now,
he reinforces us. Fight for the ships
as one man, all of you! And if one finds
his death, his end, in some spear-thrust or cast,
then that is that, and no ignoble death
for a man defending his own land. He wins
a peaceful hearth for wife and children later,
his home and patrimony kept entire,
if only the Akhaians sail for home."

He put fresh heart in every man by this.
But from the opposing line Aías called out
to his companions:

                              "Argives, where is your pride?
Isn't it clear enough? Either we perish
or else fight off this peril and are saved.
If Hektor burns our ships, will you get home
on foot, do you think? Maybe you cannot hear him
calling his whole army on, already
mad to fire the ships? No invitation
to dance, that shouting, but to a fight.

                                        No plan,
no cleverness can serve us now but this:
to close with them and fight with all we have.
Better to win life or to lose it fighting

now, once and for all, than to be bled
to death by slow degrees in grinding war
against these ships, by lesser men than we."

This aroused and stiffened them. Then Hektor
slaughtered Skhedíos, son of Perimêdês,
chief of Phôkians, but Aías slaughtered
Laódamas, a captain of infantry,
Antênor's brilliant son. And Poulýdamas
killed the Kyllênian, Ótar, comrade-in-arms
of Mégês and a captain of Epeians.
Seeing this, Mégês rushed, but Poulýdamas
dodged aside and the spear-thrust missed. Apollo
would not allow the son of Pánthoös
to perish in that mêlée. Mégês wounded
Kroismos instead, full in the chest, and down
he tumbled, thudding. Mégês stripped his gear.
Against him then came Dólops, a good spearman,
skilled in warfare, valorous,
fathered by Lampós, best of men, a son
of Laomédôn. Dólops at close quarters
broke through the center of Mégês' shield,
but his close-woven battle jacket saved him,
one that he wore all fitted with bronze plates,
a cuirass Phyleus, his father, brought
out of Ephyra, from the Sellêeis river.
Marshal Euphêtês, host and friend, had given it
to wear as a defense against attackers
in war; this time it saved from mortal hurt
the body of his son. Now that son, Mégês,
thrust at the crown of Dólops' helm. He broke
the horsehair plume away, and down it fell,
resplendent with fresh purple, in the dust.
While Dólops kept his feet and went on fighting,
hoping for victory, the formidable
Meneláos came to Mégês' aid,
obliquely and unseen, and hit the Trojan's
shoulder from behind. The famished spearhead,
driven hard, passed through his chest, and down
headfirst he sprawled. The two Akhaians bent
to strip his shoulders of his gear. Then Hektor

called to Dólops' kinsmen, first of all
to Melánippos, Hiketáôn's son,
who pastured shambling cattle in the old days
in Perkôtê, Troy's foes being far away,
but when the ships of the Danääns came
he went again to Ilion, and grew
distinguished among Trojans, lived with Priam
on equal terms with Priam's sons.

                                   Now Hektor
called to him, called him by name, rebuked him,
saying:

                        "Melánippos, are we slackening?
Are you not moved at all by your cousin's death?
See how they make for Dólops' armor! Go in
after them! No fighting at a distance
now, until we kill them—or they'll storm
Troy's height and lay her waste with all her sons."

With this he plunged ahead, and the godlike man,
Melánippos, kept at his side.

                                   Great Aías
tried to put fighting spirit in the Argives:

"Friends," he cried, "respect yourselves as men,
respect each other in the moil of battle!
Men with a sense of shame survive
more often than they perish. Those who run
have neither fighting power nor any honor."

The men themselves wished to put up a fight
and took his words to heart. Around the ships
they formed a barrier of bronze. But Zeus
rallied the Trojans. Then Lord Meneláos,
clarion in war, said to Antílokhos:

"Antílokhos, of all the young Akhaians
no one is faster on his feet than you,
or tough as you in combat: you could make
a sortie and take out some Trojan soldier."

He himself hastened on, but roused the man,
who ran out with his shining javelin poised

and scanned the battle line. Trojans gave way
before the javelin-thrower, but his throw
was not wasted. He hit proud Melánippos,
Hiketáôn's son, beside the nipple
as he moved up to battle. Down he went
slumping to earth, and darkness hid his eyes.
Antílokhos broke forward like a hound
on a stricken deer that a hunter met and shot
on its way out of a thicket: even so,
Antílokhos threw himself upon you
to take your gear, Melánippos. But Hektor
made for him on the run along the line,
and fighter though he was, and fast, Antílokhos
would not resist but fled him—as a beast
that has done some depredation, killed a dog
or cowherd near the cattle, slinks away
before a crowd can gather. Nestor's son
ran off like that, while Hektor and the Trojans,
shouting high, rained javelins after him.
Once in the mass again, he turned and stood.

And now like lions, carnivores, the Trojans
hurled themselves at the ships. They brought to pass
what Zeus commanded, and he kept their valor
steadily awake. He dazed the Argives,
wresting glory away from them. That day
the purpose of his heart was to confer
the glory on Hektor, Priam's son, enabling him
to cast bright tireless fire on the ships
and so fulfill the special prayer of Thetis.
Zeus the lord of wisdom awaited that,
to see before his eyes the lightning glare
of a ship ablaze: for from that moment on
he had in mind reversal for the Trojans
and glory for Danáäns. Knowing all this,
he sent against the deepsea ships a man
who longed to burn them: Priam's son,
Hektor, furious in arms as Arês
raging, his spear flashing, or as fire
that rages, devastating wooded hills.
His mouth foamed with slaver, and his eyes

were flaming under dreadful brows, the helm
upon his temples nodded terribly
as he gave battle. From the upper air
Lord Zeus himself defended him and gave him
honor and power alone amid the host—
for he would be diminished soon: a day
of wrath for him at Lord Akhilleus' hands
was being wrought even then by Pallas Athêna.

Hektor, attacking, tried to break the lines
at that point where the Akhaian soldiery
was thickest, and their gear the best.
But not with all his ardor could he break them.
They held hard, locked solid, man to man,
like a sheer cliff of granite near the sea,
abiding gale winds on their shrieking ways
and surf that climbs the shingle with a roar:
so the Danäans bore the Trojan rush
and kept their feet and would not flee. But Hektor
ran with a flashing torch and tried them, first
from one side, then the other, and he plunged
the way a billow whipped up by a gale
beneath dark scud descends upon a ship,
and she is hidden stem to stern in foam,
as a great gust of wind howls in the sail
and sailors shake in dread; by a hair's breadth
are they delivered from their death at sea:
just so Akhaian hearts were rent. And Hektor
was like a pitiless lion coming down
on cattle, gone to graze in a great meadow,
hundreds of them, tended by a herdsman
not yet skilled at fighting a wild beast
to prevent the slaughter of a cow: poor fellow,
either at the forefront of the herd
or at the rear he keeps pace with his cattle,
but into their midst the lion leaps to take one
as all the rest stampede. Now the Akhaians,
under attack by Hektor and Father Zeus,
broke and ran like cattle. One man only
Hektor killed: Períphêtês, a Mykênaian,
son of Kopreus, who went back and forth

announcing labors that Eurýstheus set
for brawny Hêraklês. A poorer man
by far was Kopreus, and the son superior
in every gift, as athlete and as soldier,
noted for brains among Mykênaians.
Now he afforded Hektor glory: twisting
back, he tripped upon the body shield
he bore full-length, shoulder to foot, a tower
against all weapons. On the rim he tripped
and, hindered, fell down backward, and his helm
rang out around his temples as he fell.
Hektor's sharp eye perceived this. On the run
he reached Períphêtês, halted at his side,
and speared him through the chest, killing him there
with all his friends nearby. They could not help him,
bitterly as they grieved for him, their dread
of Hektor being so great.

                      The Akhaians now
were driven back within the line of ships,
those that were first drawn inland: prow and stern
enclosed them. Trojans poured into the shipways,
forcing the Argives back from the first ships.
Then by the huts they made a stand, massed there,
and would not scatter through the camp, constrained
by pride and fear, but ceaselessly called out
to one another. Nestor of Gerênia,
lord of the western approaches to Akhaia,
implored the soldiers for their children's sake:

"Be men, dear friends, respect yourselves as men
before the others! All of you, remember
children and wives, possessions, and your parents,
whether they be alive or dead! I beg you,
on their account, although they are not here,
to hold your ground: no panic and no rout!"

So Nestor rallied them. Athêna now
dispelled the nebulous haze before their eyes,
and light burst shining on them, front and rear,
from ships and from the battle. They saw clearly
Hektor of the warcry and his soldiery,

those in reserve who had not joined the fight
and those in combat, storming the long ships.

Now the stout heart of Aías cared no longer
to stay where others had withdrawn; he moved
with long strides on the ships' decks, making play
with his long polished pike, the sections joined
by rivets, long as twenty-two forearms.
Think of an expert horseman, who has harnessed
a double team together from his string
and rides them from the plain to a big town
along the public road, where many see him,
men and women both; with perfect ease,
he changes horses, leaping, at a gallop.
That was Aías, going from deck to deck
of many ships with his long stride, his shout
rising to heaven, as in raging tones
he ordered the Danääns to defend them.
Neither would Hektor stay amid the ruck
of battle-jacketed Trojans. Like an eagle
flashing down on a flock of long-winged birds
who feed at a riverside—white geese or cranes
or long-necked swans—so Hektor struck ahead
and charged a ship with its black prow, for Zeus
behind him drove him on with his great hand
and cheered on soldiers with him.

                                              Now again

there was a sharp fight near the ships: you'd say
that iron men, untiring, clashed in battle,
so fiercely they fought on. And to what end?
There was no way to escape, the Akhaians thought,
sure they would be destroyed. But every Trojan's
heart beat fast against his ribs with hope
of firing ships and killing Akhaian soldiers.
These were their secret thoughts as they gave battle.

Hektor gripped the stern of a deepsea ship,
a fast sailer, a beauty, which had brought
Prôtesílaos to Troy but would not bring him
back to his own land. Around this ship
they slaughtered one another in close combat,

Trojans and Akhaians. Neither side
could stand a hail of arrows or javelins,
but for like reasons moved toward one another,
hewing with battle-ax and hatchet, wielding
longsword and double-bladed spear. The swords
were many and beautiful, black-sheathed and hilted,
that fell to earth out of the hands of men
or off their shoulders. Earth ran dark with blood.
Once Hektor had the stern-post in his hands,
he kept a deathgrip on the knob and gave
command to the Trojans:

                                    "Fire now! Bring it up,
and all together raise a battle shout!
Zeus gave this day to us as recompense
for everything: now we may burn the ships
that came against the gods' will to our shore
and caused us years of siege—through cowardice
of our old counselors who held me back
when I said 'Battle at the ships' sterns!'
They held back soldiers, too.

                                    In those days, ah,
if Zeus who views the wide world blocked our hearts,
now it is he who cheers and sends us forward!"

At this they all attacked more furiously,
and Aías could no longer hold. The missiles
forced him back, he yielded a few paces,
thinking his time had come, and left the deck
of the trim ship for the seven-foot bench amidships.
There he stood fast, alert, with his long pike
to fend off any Trojan with a torch,
and kept on shouting fiercely to Danáäns:

"Friends, Danáän soldiers, hands of Arês,
take a fresh grip on courage! Fight like men!
Can we rely on fresh reserves behind us?
A compact wall, to shield our men from death?
Not that, nor any town with towers where
we might defend ourselves and find allies
enough to turn the tide. No, here we are,
on the coastal plain of Trojans under arms,

nothing but open sea for our support,
and far from our own country. Safety lies
in our own hands, not going soft in battle."

Saying this, he made a vicious lunge
with his sharp-bladed pike. And any Trojan
bound for the decked ships with a blazing torch
for Hektor's satisfaction would be hit
by Aías, waiting there with his long pike.
He knocked down twelve, close in, before the ships.

BOOK SIXTEEN

A Ship Fired, a Tide Turned

LINES 1-12

That was the way the fighting went
for one seagoing ship. Meanwhile Patróklos
approached Akhilleus his commander, streaming
warm tears—like a shaded mountain spring
that makes a rockledge run with dusky water.
Akhilleus watched him come, and felt a pang for him.
Then the great prince and runner said:

                                        "Patróklos,
why all the weeping? Like a small girlchild
who runs beside her mother and cries and cries
to be taken up, and catches at her gown,
and will not let her go, looking up in tears
until she has her wish: that's how you seem,
Patróklos, winking out your glimmering tears.
Have you something to tell the Myrmidons

or me? Some message you alone have heard
from Phthía? But they say that Aktor's son,
Menoitios, is living still, and Pêleus,
the son of Aíakos, lives on
amid his Myrmidons. If one of these
were dead, we should be grieved.

                             Or is this weeping
over the Argives, seeing how they perish
at the long ships by their own bloody fault!
Speak out now, don't conceal it, let us share it."

And groaning, Patróklos, you replied:

"Akhilleus, prince and greatest of Akhaians,
be forbearing. They are badly hurt.
All who were the best fighters are now lying
among the ships with spear or arrow wounds.
Diomêdês, Tydeus' rugged son, was shot;
Odysseus and Agamémnon, the great spearman,
have spear wounds; Eurýpylos
took an arrow shot deep in his thigh.
Surgeons with medicines are attending them
to ease their wounds.

                           But you are a hard case,
Akhilleus! God forbid this rage you nurse
should master me. You and your fearsome pride!
What good will come of it to anyone, later,
unless you keep disaster from the Argives?
Have you no pity?
Pêleus, master of horse, was not your father,
Thetis was not your mother! Cold grey sea
and sea-cliffs bore you, making a mind so harsh.
If in your heart you fear some oracle,
some word of Zeus, told by your gentle mother,
then send me out at least, and send me quickly,
give me a company of Myrmidons,
and I may be a beacon to Danáäns!
Lend me your gear to strap over my shoulders;
Trojans then may take me for yourself
and break off battle, giving our worn-out men
a chance to breathe. Respites are brief in war.

We fresh troops with one battlecry might easily
push their tired men back on the town,
away from ships and huts."

                                    So he petitioned,
witless as a child that what he begged for
was his own death, hard death and doom.

                                                Akhilleus
out of his deep anger made reply:

"Hard words, dear prince. There is no oracle
I know of that I must respect, no word
from Zeus reported by my gentle mother.
Only this bitterness eats at my heart
when one man would deprive and shame his equal,
taking back his prize by abuse of power.
The girl whom the Akhaians chose for me
I won by my own spear. A town with walls
I stormed and sacked for her. Then Agamémnon
stole her back, out of my hands, as though
I were some vagabond held cheap.

                                                All that
we can let pass as being over and done with;
I could not rage forever. And yet, by heaven, I swore
I would not rest from anger till the cries
and clangor of battle reached my very ships!
But you, now, you can strap my famous gear
on your own shoulders, and then take command
of Myrmidons on edge and ripe for combat,
now that like a dark stormcloud the Trojans
have poured round the first ships, and Argive troops
have almost no room for maneuver left,
with nothing to their rear but sea. The whole
townful of Trojans joins in, sure of winning,
because they cannot see my helmet's brow
aflash in range of them. They'd fill the gullies
with dead men soon, in flight up through the plain,
if Agamémnon were on good terms with me.
As things are, they've outflanked the camp. A mercy
for them that in the hands of Diomêdês
no great spear goes berserk, warding death

from the Danääns! Not yet have I heard
the voice of Agamémnon, either, shouting
out of his hateful skull. The shout of Hektor,
the killer, calling Trojans, makes a roar
like breaking surf, and with long answering cries
they hold the whole plain where they drove the Akhaians.
Even so, defend the ships, Patróklos.
Attack the enemy in force, or they
will set the ships ablaze with whirling fire
and rob Akhaians of their dear return.
Now carry out the purpose I confide,
so that you'll win great honor for me, and glory
among Danääns; then they'll send me back
my lovely girl, with bright new gifts as well.
Once you expel the enemy from the ships,
rejoin me here. If Hêra's lord,
the lord of thunder, grants you the day's honor,
covet no further combat far from me
with Trojan soldiers. That way you'd deny me
recompense of honor. You must not,
for joy of battle, joy of killing Trojans,
carry the fight to Ilion! Some power
out of Olympos, one of the immortal gods,
might intervene for them. The Lord Apollo
loves the Trojans. Turn back, then, as soon
as you restore the safety of the ships,
and let the rest contend, out on the plain.
Ah, Father Zeus, Athêna, and Apollo!
If not one Trojan of them all
should get away from death, and not one Argive
save ourselves were spared, we two alone
could pull down Troy's old coronet of towers!"

These were the speeches they exchanged. Now Aías
could no longer hold: he was dislodged
by spear-throws, beaten by the mind of Zeus
and Trojan shots. His shining helm rang out
around his temples dangerously with hits
as his helmplates were struck and struck again;
he felt his shoulder galled on the left side
hugging the glittering shield—and yet they could not

shake it, putting all their weight in throws.
In painful gasps his breath came, sweat ran down
in rivers off his body everywhere;
no rest for him, but trouble upon trouble.

Now tell me, Muses, dwellers on Olympos,
how fire first fell on the Akhaian ships!
Hektor moved in to slash with his long blade
at Aías' ashwood shaft, and near the spearhead
lopped it off. Then Telamônian Aías
wielded a pointless shaft, while far away
the flying bronze head rang upon the ground,
and Aías shivered knowing in his heart
the work of gods: how Zeus, the lord of thunder,
cut off his war-craft in that fight, and willed
victory to the Trojans. He gave way
before their missiles as they rushed in throwing
untiring fire into the ship. It caught
at once, a-gush with flame, and fire lapped
about the stern.

                      Akhilleus smote his thighs
and said to Patróklos:

                           "Now go into action,

prince and horseman! I see roaring fire
burst at the ships. Action, or they'll destroy them,
leaving no means of getting home. Be quick,
strap on my gear, while I alert the troops!"

Patróklos now put on the flashing bronze.
Greaves were the first thing, beautifully fitted
to calf and shin with silver ankle chains;
and next he buckled round his ribs the cuirass,
blazoned with stars, of swift Aiákidês;
then slung the silver-studded blade of bronze
about his shoulders, and the vast solid shield;
then on his noble head he placed the helm,
its plume of terror nodding high above,
and took two burly spears with his own handgrip.
He did not take the great spear of Akhilleus,
weighty, long, and tough. No other Akhaian

had the strength to wield it, only Akhilleus.
It was a Pêlian ash, cut on the crest
of Pêlion, given to Akhilleus' father
by Kheirôn to deal death to soldiery.
He then ordered his war-team put in harness
by Automédôn, whom he most admired
after Prince Akhilleus, breaker of men,
for waiting steadfast at his call in battle.
Automédôn yoked the fast horses for him—
Xánthos and Balíos, racers of wind.
The stormgust Podargê, who once had grazed
green meadowland by the Ocean stream, conceived
and bore them to the west wind, Zephyros.
In the side-traces Pêdasos, a thoroughbred,
was added to the team; Akhilleus took him
when he destroyed the city of Eëtíôn.
Mortal, he ran beside immortal horses.
Akhilleus put the Myrmidons in arms,
the whole detachment near the huts. Like wolves,
carnivorous and fierce and tireless,
who rend a great stag on a mountainside
and feed on him, their jaws reddened with blood,
loping in a pack to drink springwater,
lapping the dark rim up with slender tongues,
their chops a-drip with fresh blood, their hearts
unshaken ever, and their bellies glutted:
such were the Myrmidons and their officers,
running to form up round Akhilleus' brave
companion-in-arms.

                                    And like the god of war
among them was Akhilleus: he stood tall
and sped the chariots and shieldmen onward.

Fifty ships there were that Lord Akhilleus,
favored of heaven, led to Troy. In each
were fifty soldiers, shipmates at the rowlocks.
Five he entrusted with command and made
lieutenants, while he ruled them all as king.
One company was headed by Menésthios
in his glittering breastplate, son of Spérkheios,
a river fed by heaven. Pêleus' daughter,

beautiful Polydôrê, had conceived him
lying with Spérkheios, untiring stream,
a woman with a god; but the world thought
she bore her child to Periêrês' son,
Bôros, who married her in the eyes of men
and offered countless bridal gifts. A second
company was commanded by Eudôros,
whose mother was unmarried: Polymêlê,
Phylas' daughter, a beautiful dancer
with whom the strong god Hermês fell in love,
seeing her among singing girls who moved
in measure for the lady of belling hounds,
Artemis of the golden shaft. And Hermês,
pure Deliverer, ascending soon
to an upper room, lay secretly with her
who was to bear his brilliant son, Eudôros,
a first-rate man at running and in war.
When Eileithyía, sending pangs of labor,
brought him forth to see the sun-rays, then
strong-minded Ekheklêos, Aktor's son,
led the girl home with countless bridal gifts;
but Phylas in his age brought up the boy
with all kind care, as though he were a son.
Company three was led by Peísandros
Maimálidês, the best man with a spear,
of all Myrmidons after Patróklos.
Company four the old man, master of horse,
Phoinix, commanded. Alkimédôn, son
of Laërkês, commanded company five.
When all were mustered under their officers,
Akhilleus had strict orders to impart:

"Myrmidons, let not one man forget
how menacing you were against the Trojans
during my anger and seclusion: how
each one reproached me, saying, 'Ironhearted
son of Pêleus, now we see: your mother
brought you up on rage, merciless man,
the way you keep your men confined to camp
against their will! We might as well sail home
in our seagoing ships, now this infernal

anger has come over you!' That way
you often talked, in groups around our fires.
Now the great task of battle is at hand
that you were longing for! Now every soldier
keep a fighting heart and face the Trojans!"

He stirred and braced their spirit; every rank
fell in more sharply when it heard its king.
As when a builder fitting stone on stone
lays well a high house wall to buffet back
the might of winds, just so
they fitted helms and studded shields together:
shield-rim on shield-rim, helmet on helmet, men
all pressed on one another, horsehair plumes
brushed on the bright crests as the soldiers nodded,
densely packed as they were.

                         Before them all
two captains stood in gear of war: Patróklos
and Automédôn, of one mind, resolved
to open combat in the lead.

                                Akhilleus
went to his hut. He lifted up the lid
of a seachest, all intricately wrought,
that Thetis of the silver feet had stowed
aboard his ship for him to take to Ilion,
filled to the brim with shirts, wind-breaking cloaks,
and fleecy rugs. His hammered cup was there,
from which no other man drank the bright wine,
and he made offering to no god but Zeus.
Lifting it from the chest, he purified it
first with brimstone, washed it with clear water,
and washed his hands, then dipped it full of wine.
Now standing in the forecourt, looking up
toward heaven, he prayed and poured his offering out,
and Zeus who plays in thunder heard his prayer:

"Zeus of Dôdôna, god of Pelasgians,
O god whose home lies far! Ruler of wintry
harsh Dôdôna! Your interpreters,
the Selloi, live with feet like roots, unwashed,
and sleep on the hard ground. My lord, you heard me
praying before this, and honored me

by punishing the Akhaian army. Now,
again, accomplish what I most desire.
I shall stay on the beach, behind the ships,
but send my dear friend with a mass of soldiers,
Myrmidons, into combat. Let your glory,
Zeus who view the wide world, go beside him.
Sir, exalt his heart,
so Hektor too may see whether my friend
can only fight when I am in the field,
or whether singlehanded he can scatter them
before his fury! When he has thrown back
their shouting onslaught from the ships, then let him
return unhurt to the shipways and to me,
his gear intact, with all his fighting men."

That was his prayer, and Zeus who views the wide world
heard him. Part he granted, part denied:
he let Patróklos push the heavy fighting
back from the ships, but would not let him come
unscathed from battle.

                                        Now, after Akhilleus
had made his prayer and offering to Zeus,
he entered his hut again, restored the cup
to his seachest, and took his place outside—
desiring still to watch the savage combat
of Trojans and Akhaians. Brave Patróklos'
men moved forward with high hearts until
they charged the Trojans—Myrmidons in waves,
like hornets that small boys, as boys will do,
the idiots, poke up with constant teasing
in their daub chambers on the road,
to give everyone trouble. If some traveler
who passes unaware should then excite them,
all the swarm comes raging out
to defend their young. So hot, so angrily
the Myrmidons came pouring from the ships
in a quenchless din of shouting. And Patróklos
cried above them all:

                                        "O Myrmidons,
brothers-in-arms of Pêleus' son, Akhilleus,
fight like men, dear friends, remember courage,

let us win honor for the son of Pêleus!
He is the greatest captain on the beach,
his officers and soldiers are the bravest!
Let King Agamémnon learn his folly
in holding cheap the best of the Akhaians!"

Shouting so, he stirred their hearts. They fell
as one man on the Trojans, and the ships
around them echoed the onrush and the cries.
On seeing Menoitios' powerful son, and with him
Automédôn, aflash with brazen gear,
the Trojan ranks broke, and they caught their breath,
imagining that Akhilleus the swift fighter
had put aside his wrath for friendship's sake.
Now each man kept an eye out for retreat
from sudden death. Patróklos drove ahead
against their center with his shining spear,
into the huddling mass, around the stern
of Prôtesílaos' burning ship. He hit
Pyraikhmês, who had led the Paiônês
from Amydôn, from Áxios' wide river—
hit him in the right shoulder. Backward in dust
he tumbled groaning, and his men-at-arms,
the Paiônês, fell back around him. Dealing
death to a chief and champion, Patróklos
drove them in confusion from the ship,
and doused the tigerish fire. The hull half-burnt
lay smoking on the shipway. Now the Trojans
with a great outcry streamed away; Danáäns
poured along the curved ships, and the din
of war kept on. As when the lightning master,
Zeus, removes a dense cloud from the peak
of some great mountain, and the lookout points
and spurs and clearings are distinctly seen
as though pure space had broken through from heaven:
so when the dangerous fire had been repelled
Danáäns took breath for a space. The battle
had not ended, though; not yet were Trojans
put to rout by the Akhaian charge
or out of range of the black ships. They withdrew
but by regrouping tried to make a stand.

                                                                        In broken
ranks the captains sought and killed each other,
Menoitios' son making the first kill.
As Arêilykos wheeled around to fight,
he caught him with his spearhead in the hip,
and drove the bronze through, shattering the bone.
He sprawled face downward on the ground.

                                                                        Now veteran
Meneláos thrusting past the shield
of Thoas to the bare chest brought him down.
Rushed by Ámphiklos, the alert Mégês
got his thrust in first, hitting his thigh
where a man's muscles bunch. Around the spearhead
tendons were split, and darkness veiled his eyes.
Nestor's sons were in action: Antílokhos
with his good spear brought down Atýmnios,
laying open his flank; he fell headfirst.
Now Maris moved in, raging for his brother,
lunging over the dead man with his spear,
but Thrasymêdês had already lunged
and did not miss, but smashed his shoulder squarely,
tearing his upper arm out of the socket,
severing muscles, breaking through the bone.
He thudded down and darkness veiled his eyes.
So these two, overcome by the two brothers,
dropped to the underworld of Érebos.
They were Sarpêdôn's true brothers-in-arms
and sons of Amisôdaros, who reared
the fierce Khimaira, nightmare to many men.
Aías, Oïleus' son, drove at Kleóboulos
and took him alive, encumbered in the press,
but killed him on the spot with a sword stroke
across his nape—the whole blade running hot
with blood, as welling death and his harsh destiny
possessed him. Now Pênéleos
and Lykón clashed; as both had cast and missed
and lunged and missed with spears,
they fought again with swords. The stroke of Lykôn
came down on the other's helmet ridge
but his blade broke at the hilt. Pênéleos
thrust at his neck below the ear and drove

the blade clear in and through; his head toppled,
held only by skin, and his knees gave way.
Meríonês on the run overtook Akámas
mounting behind his horses and hit his shoulder,
knocking him from the car. Mist swathed his eyes.
Idómeneus thrust hard at Erýmas' mouth
with his hard bronze. The spearhead passed on through
beneath his brain and split the white brain-pan.
His teeth were dashed out, blood filled both his eyes,
and from his mouth and nostrils as he gaped
he spurted blood. Death's cloud enveloped him.
There each Danáän captain killed his man.
As ravenous wolves come down on lambs and kids
astray from some flock that in hilly country
splits in two by a shepherd's negligence,
and quickly wolves bear off the defenseless things,
so when Danáäns fell on Trojans, shrieking
flight was all they thought of, not of combat.
Aías the Tall kept after bronze-helmed Hektor,
casting his lance, but Hektor, skilled in war,
would fit his shoulders under the bull's-hide shield,
and watch for whizzing arrows, thudding spears.
Aye, though he knew the tide of battle turned,
he kept his discipline and saved his friends.
As when Lord Zeus would hang the sky with storm,
a cloud may enter heaven from Olympos
out of crystalline space, so terror and cries
increased about the shipways. In disorder
men withdrew. Then Hektor's chariot team
cantering bore him off with all his gear,
leaving the Trojans whom the moat confined;
and many chariot horses in that ditch,
breaking their poles off at the tip, abandoned
war-cars and masters. Hard on their heels
Patróklos kept on calling all Danáäns
onward with slaughter in his heart. The Trojans,
yelling and clattering, filled all the ways,
their companies cut in pieces. High in air
a blast of wind swept on, under the clouds,
as chariot horses raced back toward the town
away from the encampment. And Patróklos

rode shouting where he saw the enemy mass
in uproar: men fell from their chariots
under the wheels and cars jounced over them,
and running horses leapt over the ditch—
immortal horses, whom the gods gave Pêleus,
galloping as their mettle called them onward
after Hektor, target of Patróklos.
But Hektor's battle-team bore him away.

As under a great storm black earth is drenched
on an autumn day, when Zeus pours down the rain
in scudding gusts to punish men, annoyed
because they will enforce their crooked judgments
and banish justice from the market place,
thoughtless of the gods' vengeance; all their streams
run high and full, and torrents cut their way
down dry declivities into the swollen sea
with a hoarse clamor, headlong out of hills,
while cultivated fields erode away—
such was the gasping flight of the Trojan horses.

When he had cut their first wave off, Patróklos
forced it back again upon the ships
as the men fought toward the city. In between
the ships and river and the parapet
he swept among them killing, taking toll
for many dead Akhaians. First,
thrusting past Prónoös' shield, he hit him
on the bare chest, and made him crumple: down
he tumbled with a crash. Then he rushed Thestôr,
Enop's son, who sat all doubled up
in a polished war-car, shocked out of his wits,
the reins flown from his hands—and the Akhaian
got home his thrust on the right jawbone, driving
through his teeth. He hooked him by the spearhead
over the chariot rail, as a fisherman
on a point of rock will hook a splendid fish
with line and dazzling bronze out of the ocean:
so from his chariot on the shining spear
he hooked him gaping and face downward threw him,
life going out of him as he fell.

                                                    Patróklos

now met Erýlaos' rush and hit him square
mid-skull with a big stone. Within his helm
the skull was cleft asunder, and down he went
headfirst to earth; heartbreaking death engulfed him.
Next Erýmas, Amphóteros, Epaltês,
Tlêpolemos Damastoridês, Ekhíos,
Pyris, Ipheus, Euíppos, Polymêlos,
all in quick succession he brought down
to the once peaceful pastureland.

                                          Sarpêdôn,

seeing his brothers-in-arms in their unbelted
battle jackets downed at Patróklos' hands,
called in bitterness to the Lykians:

"Shame, O Lykians, where are you running?
Now you show your speed!

                              I'll take on this one,
and learn what man he is that has the power
to do such havoc as he has done among us,
cutting down so many, and such good men."

He vaulted from his car with all his gear,
and on his side Patróklos, when he saw him,
leapt from his car. Like two great birds of prey
with hooked talons and angled beaks, who screech
and clash on a high ridge of rock, these two
rushed one another with hoarse cries. But Zeus,
the son of crooked-minded Krónos, watched,
and pitied them. He said to Hêra:

                                              "Ai!

Sorrow for me, that in the scheme of things
the dearest of men to me must lie in dust
before the son of Menoitios, Patróklos.
My heart goes two ways as I ponder this:
shall I catch up Sarpêdôn
out of the mortal fight with all its woe
and put him down alive in Lykia,
in that rich land? Or shall I make him fall
beneath Patróklos' hard-thrown spear?"

                                              Then Hêra
of the wide eyes answered him:

                                        "O fearsome power,
my Lord Zeus, what a curious thing to say.
A man who is born to die, long destined for it,
would you set free from that unspeakable end?
Do so; but not all of us will praise you.
And this, too, I may tell you: ponder this:
should you dispatch Sarpêdôn home alive,
anticipate some other god's desire
to pluck a man he loves out of the battle.
Many who fight around the town of Priam
sprang from immortals; you'll infuriate these.
No, dear to you though he is, and though you mourn him,
let him fall, even so, in the rough battle,
killed by the son of Menoitios, Patróklos.
Afterward, when his soul is gone, his lifetime
ended, Death and sweetest Sleep can bear him
homeward to the broad domain of Lykia.
There friends and kin may give him funeral
with tomb and stone, the trophies of the dead."

To this the father of gods and men agreed,
but showered bloody drops upon the earth
for the dear son Patróklos would destroy
in fertile Ilion, far from his home.
When the two men had come in range, Patróklos
turned like lightning against Thrasydêmos,
a tough man ever at Sarpêdôn's side,
and gave him a death-wound in the underbelly.
Sarpêdôn's counterthrust went wide, but hit
the trace horse, Pêdasos, in the right shoulder.
Screaming harshly, panting his life away,
he crashed and whinnied in the dust; the spirit
left him with a wingbeat. The team shied
and strained apart with a great creak of the yoke
as reins were tangled over the dead weight
of their outrider fallen. Automédôn,
the good soldier, found a way to end it:
pulling his long blade from his hip

he jumped in fast and cut the trace horse free.
The team then ranged themselves beside the pole,
drawing the reins taut, and once more,
devoured by fighting madness, the two men clashed.
Sarpêdôn missed again. He drove his spearhead
over the left shoulder of Patróklos,
not even grazing him. Patróklos then
made his last throw, and the weapon left his hand
with flawless aim. He hit his enemy
just where the muscles of the diaphragm
encased his throbbing heart. Sarpêdôn fell
the way an oak or poplar or tall pine
goes down, when shipwrights in the wooded hills
with whetted axes chop it down for timber.
So, full length, before his war-car lay
Sarpêdôn raging, clutching the bloody dust.
Imagine a greathearted sultry bull
a lion kills amid a shambling herd:
with choking groans he dies under the claws.
So, mortally wounded by Patróklos
the chief of Lykian shieldsmen lay in agony
and called his friend by name:

                                        "Glaukos, old man,
old war-dog, now's the time to be a spearman!
Put your heart in combat! Let grim war
be all your longing! Quickly, if you can,
arouse the Lykian captains, round them up
to fight over Sarpêdôn. You, too, fight
to keep my body, else in later days
this day will be your shame. You'll hang your head
all your life long, if these Akhaians take
my armor here, where I have gone down fighting
before the ships. Hold hard; cheer on the troops!"

The end of life came on him as he spoke,
closing his eyes and nostrils. And Patróklos
with one foot on his chest drew from his belly
spearhead and spear; the diaphragm came out,
so he extracted life and blade together.
Myrmidons clung to the panting Lykian horses,
rearing to turn the car left by their lords.

But bitter anguish at Sarpêdôn's voice
had come to Glaukos, and his heart despaired
because he had not helped his friend. He gripped
his own right arm and squeezed it, being numb
where Teukros with a bowshot from the rampart
had hit him while he fought for his own men,
and he spoke out in prayer to Lord Apollo:

"Hear me, O lord, somewhere in Lykian farmland
or else in Troy: for you have power to listen
the whole world round to a man hard pressed as I!
I have my sore wound, all my length of arm
a-throb with lancing pain; the flow of blood
cannot be stanched; my shoulder's heavy with it.
I cannot hold my spear right or do battle,
cannot attack them. Here's a great man destroyed,
Sarpêdôn, son of Zeus. Zeus let his own son
die undefended. O my lord, heal this wound,
lull me my pains, put vigor in me! Let me
shout to my Lykians, move them into combat!
Let me give battle for the dead man here!"

This way he prayed, and Phoibos Apollo heard him,
cutting his pain and making the dark blood dry
on his deep wound, then filled his heart with valor.
Glaukos felt the change, and knew with joy
how swiftly the great god had heard his prayer.
First he appealed to the Lykian captains, going
right and left, to defend Sarpêdôn's body,
then on the run he followed other Trojans,
Poulýdamas, Pánthoös' son, Agênor,
and caught up with Aineías and with Hektor,
shoulder to shoulder, urgently appealing:

"Hektor, you've put your allies out of mind,
those men who give their lives here for your sake
so distant from their friends and lands: you will not
come to their aid! Sarpêdôn lies there dead,
commander of the Lykians, who kept
his country safe by his firm hand, in justice!
Arês in bronze has brought him down: the spear
belonged to Patróklos. Come, stand with me, friends,

and count it shame if they strip off his gear
or bring dishonor on his body—these
fresh Myrmidons enraged for the Danáäns
cut down at the shipways by our spears!"

At this, grief and remorse possessed the Trojans,
grief not to be borne, because Sarpêdôn
had been a bastion of the town of Troy,
foreigner though he was. A host came with him,
but he had fought most gallantly of all.
They made straight for the Danáäns, and Hektor
led them, hot with anger for Sarpêdôn.
Patróklos in his savagery cheered on
the Akhaians, first the two named Aías, both
already aflame for war:

                                              "Aías and Aías,
let it be sweet to you to stand and fight!
You always do; be lionhearted, now.
The man who crossed the rampart of Akhaians
first of all lies dead: Sarpêdôn. May we
take him, dishonor him, and strip his arms,
and hurl any friend who would defend him
into the dust with our hard bronze!"

At this they burned to throw the Trojans back.
And both sides reinforced their battle lines,
Trojans and Lykians, Myrmidons and Akhaians,
moving up to fight around the dead
with fierce cries and clanging of men's armor.
Zeus unfurled a deathly gloom of night
over the combat, making battle toil
about his dear son's body a fearsome thing.
At first, the Trojans drove back the Akhaians,
fiery-eyed as they were; one Myrmidon,
and not the least, was killed: noble Epeigeus,
a son of Agaklês. In Boudeion,
a flourishing town, he ruled before the war,
but slew a kinsman. So he came as suppliant
to Pêleus and to Thetis, who enlisted him
along with Lord Akhilleus, breaker of men,

to make war in the wild-horse country of Ilion
against the Trojans. Even as he touched the dead man,
Hektor hit him square upon the crest
with a great stone: his skull split in the helmet,
and he fell prone upon the corpse. Death's cloud
poured round him, heart-corroding. Grief and pain
for this friend dying came to Lord Patróklos,
who pounced through spear-play like a diving hawk
that puts jackdaws and starlings wildly to flight:
straight through Lykians, through Trojans, too,
you drove, Patróklos, master of horse,
in fury for your friend. Sthenélaos
the son of Ithaiménês was the victim:
Patróklos with a great stone broke his nape-cord.

Backward the line bent, Hektor too gave way,
as far as a hunting spear may hurtle, thrown
by a man in practice or in competition
or matched with deadly foes in war. So far
the Trojans ebbed, as the Akhaians drove them.
Glaukos, commander of Lykians, turned first,
to bring down valorous Báthyklês, the son
of Khalkôn, one who had his home in Hellas,
fortunate and rich among the Myrmidons.
Whirling as this man caught him, Glaukos hit him
full in the breastbone with his spear, and down
he thudded on his face. The Akhaians grieved
to see their champion fallen, but great joy
came to the Trojans, and they thronged about him.
Not that Akhaians now forgot their courage,
no, for their momentum carried them on.
Meríonês brought down a Trojan soldier,
Laógonos, Onêtor's rugged son,
a priest of Zeus on Ida, honored there
as gods are. Gashed now under jaw and ear
his life ran out, and hateful darkness took him.
Then at Meríonês Aineías cast
his bronze-shod spear, thinking to reach his body
under the shield as he came on. But he
looked out for it and swerved, slipping the spear-throw,
bowing forward, so the long shaft stuck

in earth behind him and the butt quivered;
the god Arês deprived it of its power.
Aineías raged and sneered:

"Meríonês,

fast dodger that you are, if I had hit you
my spearhead would have stopped your dance for good!"
Meríonês, good spearman, answered him:

"For all your power, Aineías, you could hardly
quench the fighting spirit of every man
defending himself against you. You are made
of mortal stuff like me. I, too, can say,
if I could hit you square, then tough and sure
as you may be, you would concede the game
and give your soul to the lord of nightmare, Death."

Patróklos said to him sharply:

"Meríonês,

you have your skill, why make a speech about it?
No, old friend, rough words will make no Trojans
back away from the body. Many a one
will be embraced by earth before they do.
War is the use of arms, words are for council.
More talk's pointless now; we need more fighting!"

He pushed on, and godlike Meríonês
fought at his side. Think of the sound of strokes
woodcutters make in mountain glens, the echoes
ringing for listeners far away: just so
the battering din of these in combat rose
from earth where the living go their ways—the clang
of bronze, hard blows on leather, on bull's hide,
as longsword blades and spearheads met their marks.
And an observer could not by now have seen
the Prince Sarpêdôn, since from head to foot
he lay enwrapped in weapons, dust, and blood.
Men kept crowding around the corpse. Like flies
that swarm and drone in farmyards round the milkpails
on spring days, when the pails are splashed with milk:
just so they thronged around the corpse. And Zeus

would never turn his shining eyes away
from this mêlée, but watched them all and pondered
long over the slaughter of Patróklos—
whether in that place, on Sarpêdôn's body,
Hektor should kill the man and take his gear,
or whether he, Zeus, should augment the moil
of battle for still other men. He weighed it
and thought this best: that for a while Akhilleus'
shining brother-in-arms should drive his foes
and Hektor in the bronze helm toward the city,
taking the lives of many. First of all
he weakened Hektor, made him mount his car
and turn away, retreating, crying out
to others to retreat: for he perceived
the dipping scales of Zeus. At this the Lykians
themselves could not stand fast, but all turned back,
once they had seen their king struck to the heart,
lying amid swales of dead—for many
fell to earth beside him when Lord Zeus
had drawn the savage battle line. So now
Akhaians lifted from Sarpêdôn's shoulders
gleaming arms of bronze, and these Patróklos
gave to his soldiers to be carried back
to the decked ships. At this point, to Apollo
Zeus who gathers cloud said:

wipe away the blood mantling Sarpêdôn;
take him up, out of the play of spears,
a long way off, and wash him in the river,
anoint him with ambrosia, put ambrosial
clothing on him. Then have him conveyed
by those escorting spirits quick as wind,
sweet Sleep and Death, who are twin brothers. These
will set him down in the rich broad land of Lykia,
and there his kin and friends may bury him
with tomb and stone, the trophies of the dead."

Attentive to his father, Lord Apollo
went down the foothills of Ida to the field
and lifted Prince Sarpêdôn clear of it.
He bore him far and bathed him in the river,

scented him with ambrosia, put ambrosial
clothing on him, then had him conveyed
by those escorting spirits quick as wind,
sweet Sleep and Death, who are twin brothers. These
returned him to the rich broad land of Lykia.

Patróklos, calling to his team, commanding
Automédôn, rode on after the Trojans
and Lykians—all this to his undoing,
the blunderer. By keeping Akhilleus' mandate,
he might have fled black fate and cruel death.
But overpowering is the mind of Zeus
forever, matched with man's. He turns in fright
the powerful man and robs him of his victory
easily, though he drove him on himself.
So now he stirred Patróklos' heart to fury.

Whom first, whom later did you kill in battle,
Patróklos, when the gods were calling deathward?
First it was Adrêstos, Autônoös,
and Ekheklos; then Périmos Megadês,
Eristôr, Melánippos; afterward,
Elasos, Moulios, Pylartês. These
he cut down, while the rest looked to their flight.
Troy of the towering gates was on the verge
of being taken by the Akhaians, under
Patróklos' drive: he raced with blooded spear
ahead and around it. On the massive tower
Phoibos Apollo stood as Troy's defender,
deadly toward him. Now three times Patróklos
assaulted the high wall at the tower joint,
and three times Lord Apollo threw him back
with counterblows of his immortal hands
against the resplendent shield. The Akhaian then
a fourth time flung himself against the wall,
more than human in fury. But Apollo
thundered:

                              "Back, Patróklos, lordly man!
Destiny will not let this fortress town
of Trojans fall to you! Not to Akhilleus,
either, greater far though he is in war!"

Patróklos now retired, a long way off
and out of range of Lord Apollo's anger.
Hektor had held his team at the Skaian Gates,
being of two minds: should he re-engage,
or call his troops to shelter behind the wall?
While he debated this, Phoibos Apollo
stood at his shoulder in a strong man's guise:
Ásïos, his maternal uncle, brother
of Hékabê and son of Dymas, dweller
in Phrygia on Sangaríos river.
Taking his semblance now, Apollo said:

"Why break off battle, Hektor? You need not.
Were I superior to you in the measure
that I am now inferior, you'd suffer
from turning back so wretchedly from battle.
Action! Lash your team against Patróklos,
and see if you can take him. May Apollo
grant you the glory!"

                              And at this, once more
he joined the mêlée, entering it as a god.
Hektor in splendor called Kebríonês
to whip the horses toward the fight. Apollo,
disappearing into the ranks, aroused
confusion in the Argives, but on Hektor
and on the Trojans he conferred his glory.
Letting the rest go, Hektor drove his team
straight at Patróklos; and Patróklos faced him
vaulting from his war-car, with his spear
gripped in his left hand; in his right
he held enfolded a sparkling jagged stone.
Not for long in awe of the other man,
he aimed and braced himself and threw the stone
and scored a direct hit on Hektor's driver,
Kebríonês, a bastard son of Priam,
smashing his forehead with the jagged stone.
Both brows were hit at once, the frontal bone
gave way, and both his eyes burst from their sockets
dropping into the dust before his feet,
as like a diver from the handsome car

he plummeted, and life ebbed from his bones.
You jeered at him then, master of horse, Patróklos:

"God, what a nimble fellow, somersaulting!
If he were out at sea in the fishing grounds
this man could feed a crew, diving for oysters,
going overboard even in rough water,
the way he took that earth-dive from his car.
The Trojans have their acrobats, I see."

With this, he went for the dead man with a spring
like a lion, one that has taken a chest wound
while ravaging a cattle pen—his valor
his undoing. So you sprang, Patróklos,
on Kebríonês. Then Hektor, too, leapt down
out of his chariot, and the two men fought
over the body like two mountain lions
over the carcass of a buck, both famished,
both in pride of combat. So these two
fought now for Kebríonês, two champions,
Patróklos, son of Menoitios, and Hektor,
hurling their bronze to tear each other's flesh.
Hektor caught hold of the dead man's head and held,
while his antagonist clung to a single foot,
as Trojans and Danääns pressed the fight.
As south wind and the southeast wind, contending
in mountain groves, make all the forest thrash,
beech trees and ash trees and the slender cornel
swaying their pointed boughs toward one another
in roaring wind, and snapping branches crack:
so Trojans and Akhaians made a din
as lunging they destroyed each other. Neither
considered ruinous flight. Many sharp spears
and arrows trued by feathers from the strings
were fixed in flesh around Kebríonês,
and boulders crashed on shields, as they fought on
around him. And a dustcloud wrought
by a whirlwind hid the greatness of him slain,
minding no more the mastery of horses.
Until the sun stood at high noon in heaven,
spears bit on both sides, and the soldiers fell;

but when the sun passed toward unyoking time,
the Akhaians outfought destiny to prevail.
Now they dragged off gallant Kebríonês
out of range, away from the shouting Trojans,
to strip his shoulders of his gear. And fierce
Patróklos hurled himself upon the Trojans
in onslaughts fast as Arês, three times, wild
yells in his throat. Each time he killed nine men.
But on the fourth demonic foray, then
the end of life loomed up for you, Patróklos.
Into the combat dangerous Phoibos came
against him, but Patróklos could not see
the god, enwrapped in cloud as he came near.
He stood behind and struck with open hand
the man's back and broad shoulders, and the eyes
of the fighting man were dizzied by the blow.
Then Phoibos sent the captain's helmet rolling
under the horses' hooves, making the ridge
ring out, and dirtying all the horsehair plume
with blood and dust. Never in time before
had this plumed helmet been befouled with dust,
the helmet that had kept a hero's brow
unmarred, shielding Akhilleus' head. Now Zeus
bestowed it upon Hektor, let him wear it,
though his destruction waited. For Patróklos
felt his great spearshaft shattered in his hands,
long, tough, well-shod, and seasoned though it was;
his shield and strap fell to the ground; the Lord
Apollo, son of Zeus, broke off his cuirass.
Shock ran through him, and his good legs failed,
so that he stood agape. Then from behind
at close quarters, between the shoulder blades,
a Dardan fighter speared him: Pánthoös' son,
Euphórbos, the best Trojan of his age
at handling spears, in horsemanship and running:
he had brought twenty chariot fighters down
since entering combat in his chariot,
already skilled in the craft of war. This man
was first to wound you with a spear, Patróklos,
but did not bring you down. Instead, he ran back
into the mêlée, pulling from the flesh

his ashen spear, and would not face his enemy,
even disarmed, in battle. Then Patróklos,
disabled by the god's blow and the spear wound,
moved back to save himself amid his men.
But Hektor, seeing that his brave adversary
tried to retire, hurt by the spear wound, charged
straight at him through the ranks and lunged for him
low in the flank, driving the spearhead through.
He crashed, and all Akhaian troops turned pale.
Think how a lion in his pride brings down
a tireless boar; magnificently they fight
on a mountain crest for a small gushing spring—
both in desire to drink—and by sheer power
the lion conquers the great panting boar:
that was the way the son of Priam, Hektor,
closed with Patróklos, son of Menoitios,
killer of many, and took his life away.
Then glorying above him he addressed him:

"Easy to guess, Patróklos, how you swore
to ravage Troy, to take the sweet daylight
of liberty from our women, and to drag them
off in ships to your own land—you fool!
Between you and those women there is Hektor's
war-team, thundering out to fight! My spear
has pride of place among the Trojan warriors,
keeping their evil hour at bay.
The kites will feed on you, here on this field.
Poor devil, what has that great prince, Akhilleus,
done for you? He must have told you often
as you were leaving and he stayed behind,
'Never come back to me, to the deepsea ships,
Patróklos, till you cut to rags
the bloody tunic on the chest of Hektor!'
That must have been the way he talked, and won
your mind to mindlessness."

                                        In a low faint voice,
Patróklos, master of horse, you answered him:

"This is your hour to glory over me,
Hektor. The Lord Zeus and Apollo gave you

the upper hand and put me down with ease.
They stripped me of my arms. No one else did.
Say twenty men like you had come against me,
all would have died before my spear.
No, Lêto's son and fatal destiny
have killed me; if we speak of men, Euphórbos.
You were in third place, only in at the death.
I'll tell you one thing more; take it to heart.
No long life is ahead for you. This day
your death stands near, and your immutable end,
at Prince Akhilleus' hands."

His own death

came on him as he spoke, and soul from body,
bemoaning severance from youth and manhood,
slipped to be wafted to the underworld.
Even in death Prince Hektor still addressed him:

"Why prophesy my sudden death, Patróklos?
Who knows, Akhilleus, son of bright-haired Thetis,
might be hit first; he might be killed by me."

At this he pulled his spearhead from the wound,
setting his heel upon him; then he pushed him
over on his back, clear of the spear,
and lifting it at once sought Automédôn,
companion of the great runner, Akhilleus,
longing to strike him. But the immortal horses,
gift of the gods to Pêleus, bore him away.

BOOK SEVENTEEN

Contending for a Soldier Fallen

LINES I–II

In the midst of the great fight
the eye of Meneláos, dear to the wargod,
had seen Patróklos brought down by the Trojans.
Now he came forward in his fiery bronze
through clashing men to stand astride the body—
protective as a heifer who has dropped
her first-born calf: she stands above it, lowing,
never having known birth-pangs before.
So, over dead Patróklos, Meneláos
planted his heels, with compact shield and spear
thrust out to kill whoever might attack him.
One whose heart leaped at Patróklos' fall
was the son of Pánthoös, Euphórbos.
Halting nearby, he said to Meneláos:

"Son of Atreus, nobly bred, Lord Marshal,
yield, leave the corpse, give up his bloody gear!
No Trojan hit Patróklos in the fight
before I hit him. Let me have my glory.
Back, or I'll take your sweet life with one blow."

Hot with anger, red-haired Meneláos
growled:

"Father Zeus, this vanity and bragging
offends the air! A lion or a leopard
could not be so reckless; or a boar,
baleful with pounding fury in his ribcage:
the sons of Pánthoös are bolder,
more headlong than these. But youth and brawn
brought no triumph or joy to Hyperênor,
when he sneered at me and fought me. Feeblest of all
Danääns he called me!

Never on his own feet, I swear,
did he return to gladden wife and kin.
Aye, and you—I'll break your fighting heart
if you stand up to me. Give way!
Don't challenge me, get back into the ruck
before something happens to you! Any fool
can see a thing already done."

The other
took no heed but answered:

"Now, by god,
you will give satisfaction for my brother,
the man you killed and boast of having killed,
leaving his bride lonely in her new chamber,
his parents harrowed by the loss!
I might become a stay against their grief
if I could put your head and shield and helm
in Pánthoös' hands, in the fair hands of Phrontis.
Come on, no more delay in fighting out
the test of this—we'll see who holds his ground,
who backs away."

And at these words he struck
the other's shield. The bronze point failed to break it,

bending at impact on the hard plate. Then
in his turn Meneláos made his lunge,
calling on Zeus. The spearhead pierced the young man's
throat at the pit as he was falling back,
and Meneláos with his heavy grip
drove it on, straight through his tender neck.
He thudded down, his gear clanged on his body,
and blood bathed his long hair, fair as the Graces',
braided, pinched by twists of silver and gold.
Think how a man might tend a comely shoot
of olive in a lonely place, well-watered,
so that it flourished, being blown upon
by all winds, putting out silvery green leaves,
till suddenly a great wind in a storm
uprooted it and cast it down: so beautiful
had been the son of Pánthoös, Euphórbos,
when Meneláos killed him and bent over
to take his gear.

                                  And as a mountain lion
cuts out a yearling from a grazing herd—
the plumpest one—clamping with his great jaws
upon her neck to break it, and then feeds
on blood and vitals, rending her; around him
dogs and herdsmen raise a mighty din
but keep away, unwilling to attack,
as pale dread takes possession of them all:
so not one Trojan had the heart to face
Meneláos in his pride. He might with ease
have borne Euphórbos' gear away, had not
Apollo taken umbrage and aroused
Hektor, peer of the swift wargod, against him.
In a man's guise, in that of Mentês, Lord
of Kikonês, Apollo said:

                                        "Lord Hektor,
here you are chasing what cannot be caught,
the horses of Akhilleus! Intractable
to mortal men they are, no one could train them
except their master, whom a goddess bore.
Meanwhile Meneláos, dear to Arês,
stands guard over Patróklos. He has killed
a princely Trojan, son of Pánthoös,

Euphórbos, putting an end to his audacity,
his high heart."

                Turning back, once more the god
entered the moil of men. But heavy pain
bore down on Hektor's darkened heart, and peering
along the ranks in battle he made out
one man loosing the armor of the other,
prone on the field, his gashed throat welling blood.
Then Hektor shouldered through the fight, his helmet
flashing, and his shout rose like the flame
of Hêphaistos' forge, unquenchable. It blasted
Meneláos, and cursing in his heart
the Akhaian said to himself:

                      "What now? If I
abandon this good armor, leave Patróklos,
who lies here for my honor's sake, I hope
no Danáäns may see me to my shame!
But if I fight alone in pride, they may
surround me, Hektor and the other Trojans—
god forbid—many against one man.
And now Hektor is leading the pack this way!
Why go on arguing with myself? To enter
combat when the will of god's against you—
to fight a man god loves—that's doom, and quickly.
No Danáän will lift his brows at me
for giving ground to Hektor: Hektor goes
under god's arm to war. If I could only spot
Aías anywhere, we two might brace
in joy of battle, and contend once more,
even against god's will, to bring the body
back to Akhilleus—somehow. That would be
making the best of it."

                  But while he pondered,
Trojan ranks came on, as Hektor led them.
Backward at last he turned, and left the body,
facing about at every step, the way
a bearded lion does when dogs and men
with spears and shouts repel him from a farmyard,

and hatred makes his great heart turn to ice
as he is forced from the cattle pen. Just so,
forced from Patróklos, tawny Meneláos
step by step retired, then stood fast
on reaching the main body of his men.
Meanwhile he kept an eye out for great Aías,
the son of Télamôn, and all at once
he saw him, on the far left of the battle,
cheering his men, to make them stand and fight,
for Apollo put wild fear into them all.
Meneláos ran to his side and said:

"Aías, come, good heart, we'll make a fight of it
near Patróklos, try to bring his body
back to Akhilleus, though he lies despoiled,
his gear in Hektor's hands."

                                        This call went straight
to the fighting heart of Aías, and he followed
Meneláos down the field.

                                                    Meanwhile

when he had stripped Patróklos of his armor,
Hektor pulled at the corpse: now to behead it
and give the trunk to Trojan dogs! But Aías
came up then, his great shield like a tower,
and Hektor fell back on the waiting ranks
to mount his car. The splendid arms of Akhilleus
he gave to soldiers to be borne to town,
his trophies, his great glory.

                                                    And still Aías,

extending his broad shield above Patróklos,
stood as a lion will above his cubs
when a hunting party comes upon the beast
in underbrush, leading his young; he narrows
eyes to slits, drawing his forehead down.
So Aías took his stand above Patróklos,
while Meneláos, dear to the wargod, stood
nearby and let his grief mount up.

                                                    Now Glaukos,

Hippólokhos' son, captain of Lykians,
glaring at Hektor, had harsh words for him:

"Hektor, you are a great man, by the look of you,
but in a fight you're far from great.
That's how it goes, a big name, and a craven!
Put your mind on how to save your town
with troops born here at Ilion, no others!
Not one Lykian goes into combat
after this for Troy! What have we gained,
battling without rest against hard enemies?
How would you save a lesser man in war,
you heartless fraud, if you could quit Sarpêdôn,
comrade in arms and guest as well, and leave him
to be the Argives' prey and spoil? In life
he was a great ally to you and Troy,
and yet to keep the scavenging dogs from him—
you had no heart for that! Here's what I say,
if any of the Lykians obey me,
we are for home, and let doom fall on Troy!
If the Trojans had spirit—had that unshakable
will that rightly comes to men who face
for their own land the toil and shock of war,
we'd pull Patróklos into Ilion quickly!
And were he brought in death to the great town
of Priam, if we dragged him from the fury,
the Argives would return Sarpêdôn's arms,
his body, too, for us to carry home
to Ilion in fair exchange.
For he who perished here was the dear friend
of a great prince, greatest by far of those
who hold the beach and their tough men-at-arms.
But as for you, you did not dare
meet Aías, face to face and eye to eye,
in the din of battle, or engage him. Why?
Because he is a better man than you are."

Hektor in his shimmering helmet frowned
and answered him:

                                "So young, and yet so insolent?
Old son, I had thought you a steady man,
coolest of those who live in Lykia.
Now I despise your thought. Nonsense to say

I would not meet huge Aías. When have I
shown fear of swordplay, or of trampling horses?
Strongest of all, though, is the mind of Zeus
who bears the stormcloud: he can turn back
a champion, and rob him of his triumph,
even when he incites the man. Come here,
my friend, stand by me, watch me in action. All
day long I'll be the coward you describe,
or else you'll see me stop the enemy cold
no matter how he fights to shield Patróklos."

To the Trojans now he gave a mighty shout:

"Trojans, Lykians, hard-fighting Dardanoi,
be men, old friends, remember your own valor,
while I put on Akhilleus' beautiful arms,
taken from Patróklos when I killed him."

Then in his shimmering helmet Hektor turned
to leave the deadly fight, and running hard
he caught up soon with his platoon of soldiers;
they were not far, bearing the great man's armor
up to the city. Hektor stood there then,
apart from all the dolorous war, and changed.
He who had given those arms to be carried back
into the proud town, to the folk of Troy,
now buckled on the bright gear of Akhilleus,
Pêleus' son—that gear the gods of heaven
granted his father. He, when old, bestowed it
on a son who would not wear it into age.
And Zeus who gathers cloud saw Hektor now
standing apart, in the hero's shield and helm,
and nodded, musing over him:

                                        "Ah, poor man,
no least presage of death is in your mind,
how near it is, at last. You wear the gear
of a great prince. Other men blanch before him.
It is his comrade, gentle and strong, you killed,
and stripped his head and shoulders of helm and shield
without respect. Power for the time being
I will concede to you, as recompense,

for never will Andrómakhê receive
Akhilleus' arms from you on your return."

He bent his great head, over his black brows,
and made the arms fit Hektor.

                                    Then fierce Arês
entered the man, his bone and sinew thrilled
with power and will to fight. Among his men
he shouldered forward with a mighty shout,
flashing in the armor of Akhilleus,
and stirred each man he came abreast of—
Mesthlês, Glaukos, Medôn, Thersílokhos,
Asteropaíos, Deisênôr, Hippóthoös,
Phorkys, Khromíos, and the seer of birds,
Ennomos. In a swift speech he urged them:

"Hear me, hosts of neighbors and allies,
not from desire for numbers or display
did I enlist you, bring you from your cities
here to Troy. You were to save our wives
and children from the Akhaians, our besiegers.
And I deprive my people to that end
with requisitioning for you—supplies,
to build your strength and strength of heart. Go forward,
every man, therefore, to meet destruction
or to come through: these are the terms of war.
Patróklos has been killed indeed. Whoever
pulls his body to our charioteers—
if Aías can be made to yield to him—
that man wins half our spoils
when I allot them. I myself take half,
so glory equal to my own is his."

At this they surged ahead and bore down hard
with lifted spears on the Danáäns. High hopes
they had of dragging off the corpse from Aías—
fools, for he took their lives, many, upon it.
To Meneláos, clarion in battle,
Aías now said:

                                    "Old-timer, Meneláos,
I see no hope for us of getting back,

all on our own, out of this fight. My fear
is less for the dead body of Patróklos—
glutting the dogs and birds he may be, soon—
than for my life and yours, in mortal peril.
Hektor's a battle-cloud, covering everything.
Our death looms in that cloud.
Call to our champions, if they can hear you."

Meneláos complied, and high and clear
made himself heard by the Danáäns:

                                              "Friends,

captains and lords of Argives, all who drink
with Agamémnon and with Meneláos
wine of the peers, and all those in command
of men-at-arms—glory from Zeus attend you—
I find it hard to pick out single men,
the action being so hot,
but let each one come forward on his own
against the shame of seeing Trojan dogs
sport with Patróklos!"

                                    Aías the runner, son

of Oïleus, heard distinctly and came first
through battle on the run; Idómeneus
came next, and his retainer, Meríonês,
peer of the murderous wargod. Then the rest;
and who could name so many in his mind,
who came up afterward to rouse the action.

Now the Trojans charged, all in a mass,
led by Hektor.

                              As at a river mouth

a big sea thunders in against the stream,
high banks resound, and spume blows from the surf,
so came the Trojans shouting. The Akhaians
formed a line in singleness of heart
around Patróklos, walled by brazen shields.
And Zeus the son of Krónos poured thick mist
about their shining helms, for in the past
 Patróklos never had offended him

while he lived on as the comrade of Akhilleus;
now he hated to see him prey to dogs
and stirred his friends to fight for him.

First, though,
the Trojan impetus bent the Akhaian line
back from the dead man, wavering, though not one
could Trojan spearmen kill, for all their passion.
Now they pulled at the corpse, but not for long
were the Akhaians to be parted from it:
Aías made them spring back, he whose bulk
and feats of war surpassed all the Akhaians
after Prince Akhilleus. Plunging ahead,
he broke the Trojans, valorous as a boar
in mountain land who scatters dogs and men
with ease, wheeling upon them in a glade.
Even so the son of Télamôn,
magnificent Aías, whirled about and broke
the clump of Trojans that had ringed Patróklos
thinking now surely to drag away the body
to their own town, and win acclaim for it.
Aye, the illustrious son of the Pelasgian
Lêthos, Hippóthoös, looping his swordbelt
around the tendons at the ankles, drew
the body backward on the field of war
to win favor with Hektor and the Trojans.
Black fate came to him; none could deflect it.
Aías leaping through the mêlée struck
his helm with brazen cheekplates; round the point
the ridge that bore the crest crumpled at impact,
cleft by a great spear in a massive hand.
His brains burst, all in blood, out of the wound
as far as the spearhead socket. On the spot
his life died out in him and from his hands
he let Patróklos' foot fall to the ground
as he pitched forward headfirst on the body,
far from Larisa's rich farmland; nor ever
would he repay his parents for their care,
his life being cut short by the spear of Aías.

There and then, with spearpoint flashing, Hektor
lunged at Aías; Aías saw it coming

and dodged the bronze point by a hair. Instead
the shock came to the son of Iphitos,
Skhedíos, a Phokian hero, who had lived
as lord of many in renowned Panopeus.
Now the spear caught him under the collarbone;
the bronze point cut through to his shoulder blade,
and down he crashed, his war-gear clanging on him.
For his part, Aías hit the son of Phainops,
veteran Phorkys, in the middle belly
just as he came up to Hippóthoös.
The spearhead broke his cuirass at the joint
and pierced his abdomen. Fallen in the dust,
he clutched the earth with hand outspread. His men
fell back, then; so did Hektor; and the Argives
gave a loud cry as they dragged off
the bodies of Phorkys and Hippóthoös,
ripping from their shoulders gear of war.

At that point, under pressure from Akhaians
and overcome by their own weakness, Trojans
might have re-entered Ilion; beyond
the limit set by Zeus the Argives might
have won the day by their own heart and brawn.
Not so: Apollo now inflamed Aineías,
taking the form of Epytos' son, Períphas,
a crier, and a kind man, who had aged
in the crier's duty, serving old Ankhísês.
In that disguise Apollo son of Zeus
said:

                              "How could men like you save Ilion,
Aineías, overriding heaven's will?
In other days I've seen men put their trust
in their own strength and manhood, or in numbers,
and hold their realms, beyond the will of Zeus.
And now in fact Zeus wills the victory
far more for us than for Danáäns. Amazing,
the way you shrink from battle!"

                                               Facing him,
Aineías recognized the archer, Apollo,
and shouted then to Hektor:

"Hektor! all
captains of Trojans and allies! what shame
to go back into Ilion, spent and beaten!
Here, standing near me, is a god who tells me
Zeus on high is our defender, Zeus,
master of battle! Come, we'll cut our way
through the Danáäns; and god forbid they take
Patróklos' corpse aboard ship at their leisure!"

At this he leapt ahead and took position
forward of his line: the rest swung round
and faced the Akhaians. With his spear Aineías
hit Arisbas' son, Leiókritos,
comrade of Lykomêdês, and the heart
of Lykomêdês grieved as he went down.
He moved in range, thrust out, and hit
Apisaôn Hippásidês, a captain,
in the liver under the ribs. His knees
buckled, and he who had come from Paionia,
the best at warfare after Asteropaíos,
fell to earth. Asteropaíos grieved
as he went down, and now with generous heart
he too attacked but failed to break the Danáäns,
whose line of shields made them a barrier,
spearpoints advanced, compact around Patróklos.

Aías it was who passed from man to man
saying:

                    "No one retreats a step; but no one
fights out of line, either, before the rest.
Close in around him, fight on, hand to hand."

These were great Aías' orders. Now the earth
grew stained with bright blood as men fell in death
close to one another: Trojans, allies,
and Danáäns, too, for they, too, bled,
although far fewer died—each one remembering
to shield his neighbor from the fatal stroke.
So all fought on, a line of living flame.

And safe, you'd say, was neither sun nor moon,
since all was darkened in the battle-cloud—
as were the champions who held and fought
around the dead Patróklos.

The main armies.

Trojans and Akhaians under arms,
were free to make war under the open sky
with sunlight sharp about them: not a cloud
appeared above the whole earth or the hills.
The armies fought, then rested, pulling back
to a good distance, out of range
of one another's arrows, quills of groaning.
Those in the center, though, endured the cloud
with toil of war; and they lost blood as well
to heartless bronze, those champions.

Two fine men,

Thrasymêdês and Antílokhos, famous both,
were unaware of Prince Patróklos' death,
thinking he still fought in the forward line.
Vigilant to deal with death and rout, these two
gave battle on the flank, as Nestor ordered,
urging them from the black ships into action.
For the other heroes all day long the bout
of bitter striving raged: fatigue and sweat,
with never a pause; all knees and shins and feet
and hands and eyes of fighters were bespattered,
around the noble friend of swift Akhilleus.
A man will give his people a great oxhide
to stretch for him, having it soaked in grease;
and grasping it, on all sides braced around it,
they pull it till the moisture goes, the oil
sinks in, with many tugging hands, and soon
the whole expanse is dry and taut. Just so,
this way and that way in a little space
both sides kept tugging at the body: Trojans
panting to drag it off toward Ilion,
Akhaians to the decked ships. Round about,
wild tumult rose. Arês, Frenzy of Soldiers,
would not have scorned that fight, nor would Athêna,
even in deadly rage, so murderous

the toil of men and chariots for Patróklos
that Zeus prolonged that day.

                            Not yet, remember,
had Prince Akhilleus word of his friend's death.
Far from the ships this action had gone on
under the Trojans' wall, and no foreboding
occurred to him: Patróklos would, he thought,
approach the gates but then turn back; he could not
hope alone to take the town by storm.
Often Akhilleus, listening in secret,
had learned things from his mother as she foretold
the will of mighty Zeus for him. This time
she gave no word to him of what calamity
had come, that his great friend had been destroyed.
But hour by hour the rest fought for the body,
gripping whetted spears, dealing out death.
And some Akhaian veteran might say:

"Old friends, no glory in our taking ship
again for home; sooner may black earth here
embed us all! That would be better far
than giving up this body to the Trojans,
a trophy for them, and a glory won!"

And of the Trojans there were some to say:

"Old friends, if in the end we are cut down
alongside this one—just like him—the lot of us,
still not a man should quit the fight!"

                                That way
the Trojans talked and cheered each other on.
And that was how that battle went—a din
of ironhearted men through barren air
rose to the sky all brazen.

                              Out of range,
the horses of Akhilleus, from the time
they sensed their charioteer downed in the dust
at the hands of deadly Hektor, had been weeping.
Automédôn, the son of Diorês,
laid often on their backs his flickering whip,

pled often in a low tone—or he swore at them—
but neither toward the shipways and the beach
by Hellê's waters would they budge, nor follow
Akhaians into battle. No: stock-still
as a gravestone, fixed above the tomb
of a dead man or woman, they stood fast,
holding the beautiful war-car still: their heads
curved over to the ground, and warm tears flowed
from under eyelids earthward as they mourned
their longed-for driver. Manes along the yoke
were soiled as they hung forward under yokepads.
Seeing their tears flow, pitying them, Lord Zeus
bent his head and murmured in his heart:

"Poor things, why did I give you to King Pêleus,
a mortal, you who never age nor die,
to let you ache with men in their hard lot?
of all creatures that breathe and move on earth
none is more to be pitied than a man.
Never at least shall Hektor, son of Priam,
ride behind you in your painted car.
That I will not allow. Is it not enough
that he both has the gear and brags about it?
I shall put fire in your knees and hearts
to rescue Automédôn, bear him away
from battle to the decked ships. Glory of killing,
even so, I reserve to his enemies
until they reach the ships, until sundown,
until the dusk comes, full of stars."

                                                                With this
he sent a fiery breath into the horses.
Shaking the dust to earth from their long manes,
they bore the war-car swiftly amid the armies.
Automédôn gave battle as he rode,
though grieving for his friend. Behind the horses
in foray like a hawk on geese, with ease
he doubled back, out of the Trojan din,
then quickly drove full tilt upon the mass,
but made no kills, though whipping in pursuit,
being singlehanded in his car—unable

to thrust well with a spear, needing both hands
to guide the horses.

One of his men at last
caught on: one Alkimédôn, son of Laërkês
Haimónidês: he halted just behind
and called out:

"Automédôn,
this futile plan of action—which of the gods
put you up to it? He took your wits away—
fighting alone like this against the Trojans,
and in the line!—though your companion fell,
and Hektor himself has got Akhilleus' arms
to swagger in."

And to this Automédôn,
son of Diorês, answered:

"Alkimédôn,
what other Akhaian has your knack
for guiding the divine fire of these horses?
Only Patróklos, matchless when he lived,
but destiny and death have come upon him.
Come then, take the whip and the bright reins,
while I step from the chariot into battle!"

Alkimédôn, mounting the swift war-car,
caught up whip and reins, and Automédôn
vaulted down. Hektor noticed all this,
and to Aineías, near at hand, he said:

"Counselor of the Trojans mailed in bronze,
I've seen that team, Akhilleus' team, re-enter
battle with poor drivers. I might hope
to capture it, if you, for one, were with me;
against the two of us, closing upon it,
they would not make a stand or dare give battle."

Ankhísês' noble son nodded, and both
went forward, shoulders cased in hardened oxhide
shields, all plated with a wealth of bronze,
and at their heels went Khromíos and Arêtos,

hoping to kill that pair of charioteers
and drive the haughty team away. But they were
fooled in this: from Automédôn's stroke
they would not come unbloodied. Calling on Zeus,
he felt new power surge about his heart,
and cried to Alkimédôn, his loyal friend:

"Not at a distance from me! Keep the team
close up, aye, keep them breathing on my back!
I do not think Hektor Priámidês
will quit until he mounts this car
behind the beautiful horses of Akhilleus,
killing us both, routing the Argive line;
else in the front line he must fall himself."

To those called Aías, and to Meneláos,
he shouted:

                    "Aías and Aías, captains of Argives,
and you, Meneláos: turn the body over
to your best men; let them stand by and hold
the enemy back. But come yourselves, defend
the living, too—the pair of us—ward off
our evil hour! Hektor and Aineías,
Trojan champions, have put their weight
into the painful battle.

                              Now, by heaven,
the issue lies upon the gods' great knees,
and as for me, I'll make my throw. Let Zeus
look after all the rest."

                                Rifling the spear
over its long slim shadow, he let fly
and hit Arêtos' circular shield. The surface
failed to hold, and the bronze point drove on
straight through his belt into the lower belly.
As when a rugged fellow with an ax
has cleft an ox behind the horns, and cut
through all the hump, so the beast rears and falls,
Arêtos reared and tumbled back, undone
by the long spear still quivering in his bowels.
Now with his spearhead flashing, Hektor cast

at Automédôn, who foresaw the cast
and doubled forward, dodging under the point.
The great shaft punched into the earth behind him,
sticking there, vibrating. Burly Arês
deprived it of its force there. Now with swords
the men made for each other, hand to hand,
but soon the two named Aías broke them apart,
shouldering at their friend's call through the press.
Flurried by these two, Hektor and Aineías,
Khromíos, too, backed off again,
leaving Arêtos lying there, his life
slashed out of him. Then Automédôn, peer
in speed of the wargod, took the dead man's armor,
and vaunting cried:

                              "By heaven now I've eased
my heart somewhat of anguish for Patróklos,
tearing out a man's guts; but no such man as he."

Lifting the bloodstained gear into his car,
he stepped aboard, his legs and forearms wet
with blood, like a lion sated on a bull.

Over Patróklos the rough combat widened,
loud with oaths and sobs; and from the sky
Athêna came, kindling the fight, for Zeus
who views the wide world, as his humor changed,
had sent her down to stiffen the Danáäns.
As when from storm-lit heaven he bends a rainbow,
omen of war to mortal men, or omen
of a chill tempest, pelting flocks and herds,
and ending the field work of countrymen,
so, folded in a ragged cloud of stormlight,
Athêna entered the Akhaian host.
She braced each soldier's will to fight, but first
to the son of Atreus, massive Meneláos,
she spoke, as he stood near to her. Her form
seemed that of Phoinix, her strong voice his voice:

"The shame of it will make you hang your head,
Meneláos, if glorious Akhilleus'

faithful friend is dragged under Troy wall
by ravening dogs! Call on your own strength,
and put fight in the army!"

                                                           Meneláos,
the deep-lunged man of battle, answered her:

"Phoinix, yes—old-timer, full of years—
and may Athêna give me force, may she
deflect the spears. My will is to defend
Patróklos. When he died, it touched my heart.
But Hektor is a devouring flame: he will not
pause, laying about him: Zeus exalts him!"

At this the grey-eyed goddess secretly
took pleasure, that of all the gods he chose
to make his prayer to her. Power in his shoulders
she instilled, and gristle in his knees,
and in his heart the boldness of a shad fly
fiercely brushed away, but mad to bite,
as human blood is ambrosial drink to him.
So furious daring swelled in Meneláos'
dark chest cave, and he regained his place
above Patróklos, leveling his spear.

There was a Trojan, son of Eëtíôn,
Podês by name, a rich and noble man,
whom Hektor honored most in all the realm
as his convivial friend. This was the fighter
tawny Meneláos hit in the belt
as he recoiled, and drove the spearhead through.
He went down with a crash. The son of Atreus
pulled his body from amid the Trojans
over to his own line.

                                                           Now Apollo
standing at Hektor's elbow spurred him on.
Phainops Asíadês he seemed, who came
from Ábydos and held first place with Hektor
of all his foreign friends. In this man's guise
the archer Apollo said:

                              "Would any Akhaian
fear you now? How openly you shrank

from Meneláos—in the past, at least,
no tough man with a spear! Just now, alone,
he carried off a dead man from the Trojans,
a faithful friend of yours whom he had killed,
a brave man in attack, Podês, the son
of Eëtíôn."

Then a cloud of pain
darkened the heart of Hektor. Amid attackers
he went forward, helmed in the fiery bronze.
And now the son of Krónos took in hand
the stormcloud with its fringe and fitful glare,
and hid in cloud Mount Ida. Flash on flash
he let his lightning fall, with rumbling thunder,
shaking the earth. To the Trojans now he gave
clean victory, and he routed the Akhaians.
First to panic was Pênéleos
the Boiotian: as he turned, face to the front,
he took a spear wound in the shoulder—just
a grazing wound, but one that nicked the bone—
from Poulýdamas' point, thrust close at hand;
and at close quarters Hektor wounded Lêïtos,
great Alektrýon's son, on the forearm
and put him out of action. He retreated,
thinking no longer with one useless hand
to fight the Trojans. And as Hektor chased him,
Idómeneus cast at the Trojan's cuirass,
hitting him near the nipple, but the shaft
broke off below the point. A cry went up
from the Trojan side, and Hektor threw in turn
at Idómeneus, the son of Deukálión,
mounted now in his chariot. By a hair
he missed him, but the spear brought down
Meríonês' friend and driver, Koíranos.
From Kretan Lyktos Koíranos had come
along with Meríonês. At first, that day,
Idómeneus had left the camp and ships
on foot, in peril, offering the Trojans
a triumph, had not Koíranos driven up
full speed and come abreast to be his savior,
shielding him from his evil hour. Koíranos

now lost his life to Hektor, killer of men,
who speared him under jaw and ear and pried
his teeth out, roots and all, splitting his tongue.
Down from his chariot he fell, dropping
the reins to earth. Meríonês bent to take them
in his own hands, then said to Idómeneus:

"Use your whip to make it to the camp!
You know as well as I, there's no fight left
in the Akhaians."

                                        Away, and toward the ships,
Idómeneus lashed his horses with long manes,
for fear had entered him at last.

                                                        Great Aías
and Meneláos were not blind: they saw
that Zeus accorded victory to the Trojans.
Telamônian Aías bowed before it.
"Damn this day," he said. "A fool would know
that Zeus had thrown his weight behind the Trojans.
All their stones and javelins hit the mark,
whoever flings them, good soldier or bad!
As for ourselves, no luck at all, our shots
are spent against the ground. We two, alone,
may think what's best to do—somehow to try
dragging the body back, as we ourselves
return alive to comfort friends of ours.
There they are, desperately looking toward us,
hopeless now of a pause in Hektor's rage,
his uncontainable handiwork: they see
he'll break in on our black ships. Now if only
there was a man to run for it, to bring word
to Pêleus' son! I think he can't have heard
the black report that his dear friend is dead.
I cannot anywhere see a runner, though,
in this cloud, covering men and chariots.
O Father Zeus, come, bring our troops from under
the dustcloud: make clear air: give back our sight!
Destroy us in daylight—as your pleasure is
to see us all destroyed!"

The Father pitied him,
seeing his tears flow. He dispersed the cloud,
rolled back the battle-haze, and sunlight shone,
so the whole fight became abruptly clear.
Then Aías said to Meneláos:

"Will you

use your eyes now, royal friend,
to spot, if you can, Antílokhos, Nestor's son
and a good fighter. Send him on the run
to tell Akhilleus of his dear friend's death."

Meneláos complied, but slowly, as a lion
goes from a farmyard, lagging, tired out
with worrying dogs and men who watched all night
to keep him from his choice of fatted cattle.
Avid for meat, he bounds in to attack
but has no luck: a hail of javelins
thrown by tough cowherds comes flying out at him,
and brands of flame from which he flinches, roaring.
At dawn he trails away with sullen heart.
So Meneláos, lord of the great warcry,
left Patróklos, hating to go, afraid
the panicking Akhaians would abandon him
to be their enemies' prey. He lingered long,
bidding Meríonês and the two named Aías:

"Remember poor Patróklos, each of you,
his warmth of heart. He had a way of being
kind to all in life. Now destiny and death
have overtaken him."

Then Meneláos

turned to search the field, keen as an eagle
who has, they say, of all birds under heaven
the sharpest eyes: even at a great height
he will not miss a swift hare gone to earth
under a shady bush; he plummets down
straight on him, catches him, and tears his life.
So your bright eyes, Prince Meneláos,
glanced everywhere amid the crowd of soldiers,
looking for Nestor's son, if he lived still.

And soon enough he found him, on the left flank,
cheering his men, sending them into action,
and as he reached him red-haired Meneláos
cried:

                              "Antílokhos, come here, young prince,
and hear sad news. Would god it had not happened!
You yourself have seen, I think, by now
that god sends ruin surging on our army.
Victory goes to the Trojans. Our best man,
Patróklos, fell—irreparable loss
and grief to the Danáäns.

                                        Here is your duty:
run to the ships, tell all this to Akhilleus,
in hope that he can make all haste to save
the disarmed corpse, and carry it aboard—
though Hektor has his armor."

                                        Hearing these words
appalled and sick at heart, Antílokhos
lost for a time his power of speech: his eyes
brimmed over, and his manly voice was choked.
Yet even so he heeded Meneláos,
handing over his armor to his friend,
Laódokos, who turned his team and chariot
near to him. Then he set off on the run.

And so in tears Antílokhos left the battle
with evil news for Akhilleus Pêleidês.
As for you, Meneláos, you did not
lend a hand to his friends, when he had gone,
leaving a great void for the men of Pylos.
Rather, Meneláos sent Thrasymêdês
and ran back to Patróklos. There he stood
by those named Aías telling them:

                                        "I found him.

Then I sent him shoreward. He will report
to our great runner, Akhilleus. But I doubt
Akhilleus will appear, even though he'll be
insane with rage at Hektor. Can he come
to make war on the Trojans without armor?

No, we had better plan it for ourselves,
how best to save the dead man, and how best
escape death in the hue and cry of Trojans."

Telamônian Aías answered:

                                                "All you say

is reasonable, excellency. Be quick,
you and Meríonês, get good leverage
under the body, lift it, and lug it back
out of the line. We two will stay behind
to engage the Trojans and Prince Hektor—being
alike in name and heart. Often in the past
we've waited side by side for slashing Arês."

At this Meneláos and Meríonês
got their arms under the dead man and gave
a great heave upward. From the Trojan mass
a cry broke out, as they perceived the Akhaians
lifting the body, and they set upon them
like a dog pack chasing a wounded boar
ahead of young men hunting. For a while
they stream out in full cry, ready to rend him,
but when he wheels to take them on, staking
everything on his own valor, they recoil
and swerve this way and that. The Trojans, too,
came harrying behind them in a pack
with cut and thrust of sword and bladed spear,
but when the two named Aías wheeled and stood
to menace them, their faces changed: not one
dared charge ahead for a contest over the body.
Guarded so, the bearers, might and main,
strove on to bring it to the ships. Around them
battle spread like a fire that seethes and flares
once it has broken out upon a city;
houses fall in with flame-bursts, as the wind
makes the great conflagration roar: so now
incessant din of chariots and spearmen
beset them on their way. Grim as a mule-team
putting their strong backs into hauling, down
a rocky footpath on a mountainside,
a beam or a ship's timber; and their hearts

are wearied out, straining with toil and sweat:
so these with might and main carried the body.
And, close behind, the two named Aías fought
their rearguard action. As a wooded headland
formed across a plain will stem a flood
and hold roiled currents, even of great rivers,
deflecting every one to wander, driven
along the plain; and not one, strongly flowing,
can wash it out or wear it down: just so
the two named Aías held the fighting Trojans
and threw them back. Still they pressed on, and most
of all Aineías Ankhisíadês
with brilliant Hektor. As a cloud of starlings
or jackdaws shrieking bloody murder flies
on seeing a hawk about to strike; he brings
a slaughter on small wingèd things: just so
under pursuit by Hektor and Aineías
Akhaian soldiers shrieked and fled, their joy
in combat all forgotten. Routed Akhaians'
gear of war piled up along the moat,
and there was never a respite from the battle.

BOOK EIGHTEEN

The Immortal Shield

LINES 1–13

While they were still in combat, fighting seaward
raggedly as fire, Antílokhos
ran far ahead with tidings for Akhilleus.
In shelter of the curled, high prows he found him
envisioning what had come to pass,
in gloom and anger saying to himself:

"Ai! why are they turning tail once more,
unmanned, outfought, and driven from the field
back on the beach and ships? I pray the gods
this may not be the last twist of the knife!
My mother warned me once that, while I lived,
the most admirable of Myrmidons
would quit the sunlight under Trojan blows.
It could indeed be so. He has gone down,
my dear and wayward friend!

Push their deadly fire away, I told him,
then return! You must not fight with Hektor!"

And while he called it all to mind,
the son of gallant Nestor came up weeping
to give his cruel news:

"Here's desolation,
son of Pêleus, the worst news for you—
would god it had not happened!—Lord Patróklos
fell, and they are fighting over his body,
stripped of armor. Hektor has your gear."

A black stormcloud of pain shrouded Akhilleus.
On his bowed head he scattered dust and ash
in handfuls and befouled his beautiful face,
letting black ash sift on his fragrant khiton.
Then in the dust he stretched his giant length
and tore his hair with both hands.

From the hut
the women who had been spoils of war to him
and to Patróklos flocked in haste around him,
crying loud in grief. All beat their breasts,
and trembling came upon their knees.

Antílokhos
wept where he stood, bending to hold the hero's
hands when groaning shook his heart: he feared
the man might use sharp iron to slash his throat.
And now Akhilleus gave a dreadful cry.

Her ladyship
his mother heard him, in the depths offshore
lolling near her ancient father. Nymphs
were gathered round her: all Nêrêïdês
who haunted the green chambers of the sea.
Glaukê, Thaleia, and Kymodokê,
Nesaiê, Speiô, Thoê, Haliê
with her wide eyes; Kymothoê, Aktaiê,
Limnôreia, Melitê, and Iaira,
Amphitoê, Agauê, Dôtô, Prôtô,
Pherousa, Dynaménê, Dexaménê,
Amphinomê, Kallianeira, Dôris,

Panopê, and storied Galateia,
Nêmertês and Apseudês, Kallianassa,
Klyméne, Ianeira, Ianassa,
Maira, Oreithyia, Amathyia,
and other Nêrëïdês of the deep sea,
filling her glimmering silvery cave. All these
now beat their breasts as Thetis cried in sorrow:

"Sisters, daughters of Nêreus, hear and know
how sore my heart is! Now my life is pain
for my great son's dark destiny! I bore
a child flawless and strong beyond all men.
He flourished like a green shoot, and I brought him
to manhood like a blossoming orchard tree,
only to send him in the ships to Ilion
to war with Trojans. Now I shall never see him
entering Pêleus' hall, his home, again.
But even while he lives, beholding sunlight,
suffering is his lot. I have no power
to help him, though I go to him. Even so,
I'll visit my dear child and learn what sorrow
came to him while he held aloof from war."

On this she left the cave, and all in tears
her company swam aloft with her. Around them
a billow broke and foamed on the open sea.
As they made land at the fertile plain of Troy,
they went up one by one in line to where,
in close order, Myrmidon ships were beached
to right and left of Akhilleus. Bending near
her groaning son, the gentle goddess wailed
and took his head between her hands in pity,
saying softly:

                                        "Child, why are you weeping?
What great sorrow came to you? Speak out,
do not conceal it. Zeus
did all you asked: Akhaian troops,
for want of you, were all forced back again
upon the ship sterns, taking heavy losses
none of them could wish."

                                    The great runner
groaned and answered:

                                    "Mother, yes, the master
of high Olympos brought it all about,
but how have I benefited? My greatest friend
is gone: Patróklos, comrade in arms, whom I
held dear above all others—dear as myself—
now gone, lost; Hektor cut him down, despoiled him
of my own arms, massive and fine, a wonder
in all men's eyes. The gods gave them to Pêleus
that day they put you in a mortal's bed—
how I wish the immortals of the sea
had been your only consorts! How I wish
Pêleus had taken a mortal queen! Sorrow
immeasurable is in store for you as well,
when your own child is lost: never again
on his homecoming day will you embrace him!
I must reject this life, my heart tells me,
reject the world of men,
if Hektor does not feel my battering spear
tear the life out of him, making him pay
in his own blood for the slaughter of Patróklos!"

Letting a tear fall, Thetis said:

                                                  "You'll be
swift to meet your end, child, as you say:
your doom comes close on the heels of Hektor's own."

Akhilleus the great runner ground his teeth
and said:

                                    "May it come quickly. As things were,
I could not help my friend in his extremity.
Far from his home he died; he needed me
to shield him or to parry the death stroke.
For me there's no return to my own country.
Not the slightest gleam of hope did I
afford Patróklos or the other men
whom Hektor overpowered. Here I sat,
my weight a useless burden to the earth,

and I am one who has no peer in war
among Akhaian captains—

                                                    though in council

there are wiser. Ai! let strife and rancor
perish from the lives of gods and men,
with anger that envenoms even the wise
and is far sweeter than slow-dripping honey,
clouding the hearts of men like smoke: just so
the marshal of the army, Agamémnon,
moved me to anger. But we'll let that go,
though I'm still sore at heart; it is all past,
and I have quelled my passion as I must.

Now I must go to look for the destroyer
of my great friend. I shall confront the dark
drear spirit of death at any hour Zeus
and the other gods may wish to make an end.
Not even Hêraklês escaped that terror
though cherished by the Lord Zeus. Destiny
and Hêra's bitter anger mastered him.
Likewise with me, if destiny like his
awaits me, I shall rest when I have fallen!
Now, though, may I win my perfect glory
and make some wife of Troy break down,
or some deep-breasted Dardan woman sob
and wipe tears from her soft cheeks. They'll know then
how long they had been spared the deaths of men,
while I abstained from war!
Do not attempt to keep me from the fight,
though you love me; you cannot make me listen."

Thetis, goddess of the silvery feet,
answered:

                                    "Yes, of course, child: very true.
You do no wrong to fight for tired soldiers
and keep them from defeat. But still, your gear,
all shining bronze, remains in Trojan hands.
Hektor himself is armed with it in pride!—
Not that he'll glory in it long, I know,
for violent death is near him.

                                      Patience, then.
Better not plunge into the moil of Arês
until you see me here once more. At dawn,
at sunrise, I shall come
with splendid arms for you from Lord Hêphaistos."

She rose at this and, turning from her son,
told her sister Nêrëïdês:

                                        "Go down
into the cool broad body of the sea
to the sea's Ancient; visit Father's hall,
and make all known to him. Meanwhile, I'll visit
Olympos' great height and the lord of crafts,
Hêphaistos, hoping he will give me
new and shining armor for my son."

At this they vanished in the offshore swell,
and to Olympos Thetis the silvery-footed
went once more, to fetch for her dear son
new-forged and finer arms.

                              Meanwhile, Akhaians,
wildly crying, pressed by deadly Hektor,
reached the ships, beached above Hellê's water.
None had been able to pull Patróklos clear
of spear- and swordplay: troops and chariots
and Hektor, son of Priam, strong as fire,
once more gained upon the body. Hektor
three times had the feet within his grasp
and strove to wrest Patróklos backward, shouting
to all the Trojans—but three times the pair
named Aías in their valor shook him off.
Still he pushed on, sure of his own power,
sometimes lunging through the battle-din,
or holding fast with a great shout: not one step
would he give way. As from a fresh carcass
herdsmen in the wilds cannot dislodge
a tawny lion, famished: so those two
with fearsome crests could not affright the son
of Priam or repel him from the body.
He might have won it, might have won unending

glory, but Iris running on the wind
came from Olympos to the son of Pêleus,
bidding him gird for battle. All unknown
to Zeus and the other gods she came, for Hêra
sent her down. And at his side she said:

"Up with you, Pêleidês, who strike cold fear
into men's blood! Protect your friend Patróklos,
for whom, beyond the ships, desperate combat
rages now. They are killing one another
on both sides: the Akhaians to defend him,
Trojans fighting for that prize
to drag to windy Ilion. And Hektor
burns to take it more than anyone—
to sever and impale Patróklos' head
on Trojan battlements. Lie here no longer.
It would be shameful if wild dogs of Troy
made him their plaything! If that body suffers
mutilation, you will be infamous!"

Prince Akhilleus answered:

                                          "Iris of heaven,
what immortal sent you to tell me this?"

And she who runs upon the wind replied:

"Hêra, illustrious wife of Zeus,
but he on his high throne knows nothing of it.
Neither does any one of the gods undying
who haunt Olympos of eternal snows."

Akhilleus asked:

                                          "And now how shall I go
into the fighting? Those men have my gear.
My dear mother allows me no rearming
until I see her again here.
She promises fine arms from Lord Hêphaistos.
I don't know whose armor I can wear,
unless I take Aías' big shield.
But I feel sure he's in the thick of it,
contending with his spear over Patróklos."

Then she who runs upon the wind replied:

"We know they have your arms, and know it well.
Just as you are, then, stand at the moat; let Trojans
take that in; they will be so dismayed
they may break off the battle, and Akhaians
in their fatigue may win a breathing spell,
however brief, a respite from the war."

                                                                    At this,

Iris left him, running downwind. Akhilleus,
whom Zeus loved, now rose. Around his shoulders
Athêna hung her shield, like a thunderhead
with trailing fringe. Goddess of goddesses,
she bound his head with golden cloud, and made
his very body blaze with fiery light.
Imagine how the pyre of a burning town
will tower to heaven and be seen for miles
from the island under attack, while all day long
outside their town, in brutal combat, pikemen
suffer the wargod's winnowing; at sundown
flare on flare is lit, the signal fires
shoot up for other islanders to see,
that some relieving force in ships may come:
just so the baleful radiance from Akhilleus
lit the sky. Moving from parapet
to moat, without a nod for the Akhaians,
keeping clear, in deference to his mother,
he halted and gave tongue. Not far from him
Athêna shrieked. The great sound shocked the Trojans
into tumult, as a trumpet blown
by a savage foe shocks an encircled town,
so harsh and clarion was Akhilleus' cry.
The hearts of men quailed, hearing that brazen voice.
Teams, foreknowing danger, turned their cars
and charioteers blanched, seeing unearthly fire,
kindled by the grey-eyed goddess Athêna,
brilliant over Akhilleus. Three great cries
he gave above the moat. Three times they shuddered,
whirling backward, Trojans and allies,
and twelve good men took mortal hurt

from cars and weapons in the rank behind.
Now the Akhaians leapt at the chance
to bear Patróklos' body out of range.
They placed it on his bed,
and old companions there with brimming eyes
surrounded him. Into their midst Akhilleus
came then, and he wept hot tears to see
his faithful friend, torn by the sharp spearhead,
lying cold upon his cot. Alas,
the man he sent to war with team and chariot
he could not welcome back alive.

                                                            Her majesty,

wide-eyed Hêra, made the reluctant sun,
unwearied still, sink in the streams of Ocean.
Down he dropped, and the Akhaian soldiers
broke off combat, resting from the war.
The Trojans, too, retired. Unharnessing
teams from war-cars, before making supper,
they came together on the assembly ground,
every man on his feet; not one could sit,
each being still in a tremor—for Akhilleus,
absent so long, had once again appeared.
Clearheaded Poulýdamas, son of Pánthoös,
spoke up first, as he alone could see
what lay ahead and all that lay behind.
He and Hektor were companions-in-arms,
born, as it happened, on the same night; but one
excelled in handling weapons, one with words.
Now for the good of all he spoke among them:

"Think well of our alternatives, my friends.
What I say is, retire upon the town,
instead of camping on the field till dawn
here by the ships. We are a long way
from our stone wall. As long as that man raged
at royal Agamémnon, we could fight
the Akhaians with advantage. I was happy
to spend last night so near the beach and think
of capturing ships today. Now, though, I fear
the son of Pêleus to my very marrow!
There are no bounds to the passion of that man.

He will not be contained by the flat ground
where Trojans and Akhaians share between them
raging war: he will strive on to fight
to win our town, our women. Back to Troy!
Believe me, this is what we face!
Now, starry night has made Akhilleus pause,
but when day comes, when he sorties in arms
to find us lingering here, there will be men
who learn too well what he is made of. Aye,
I daresay those who get away will reach
walled Ilion thankfully, but dogs and kites
of Troy will feed on many. May that story
never reach my ears! If we can follow
my battle plan, though galled by it, tonight
we'll husband strength, at rest in the market place.
Towers, high gates, great doors of fitted planking,
bolted tight, will keep the town secure.
Early tomorrow we shall arm ourselves
and man the walls. Worse luck then for Akhilleus,
if he comes looking for a head-on fight
on the field around the wall! He can do nothing
but trot back, after all, to the encampment,
his proud team in a lather from their run,
from scouring every quarter below the town.
Rage as he will, he cannot force an entrance,
cannot take all Troy by storm. Wild dogs
will eat him first!"

                                        Under his shimmering helmet
Hektor glared at the speaker. Then he said:

"Poulýdamas, what you propose no longer
serves my turn. To go on the defensive
inside the town again? Is anyone
not sick of being huddled in those towers?
In past days men told tales of Priam's city,
rich in gold and rich in bronze, but now
those beautiful treasures of our home are lost.
Many have gone for sale to Phrygia
and fair Mêïoniê, since Lord Zeus
grew hostile toward us.

                                   Now when the son of Krónos
Crooked Wit has given me a chance
of winning glory, pinning the Akhaians
back on the sea—now is no time to publish
notions like these to troops, you fool! No Trojan
goes along with you, I will not have it!
Come, let each man act as I propose.
Take your evening meal by companies;
remember sentries; keep good watch; and any
Trojan tired of his wealth, who wants
to lose everything, let him turn it over
to the army stores to be consumed in common!
Better our men enjoy it than Akhaians.
At first light we shall buckle armor on
and bring the ships under attack. Suppose
the man who stood astern there was indeed
Akhilleus, then worse luck for him,
if he will have it so. Shall I retreat
from him, from clash of combat? No, I will not.
Here I'll stand, though he should win; I might
just win, myself: the battle-god's impartial,
dealing death to the death-dealing man."

This was Hektor's speech. The Trojans roared
approval of it—fools, for Pallas Athêna
took away their wits. They all applauded
Hektor's poor tactics, but Poulýdamas
with his good judgment got not one assent.
They took their evening meal now, through the army,
while all night long Akhaians mourned Patróklos.

Akhilleus led them in their lamentation,
laying those hands deadly to enemies
upon the breast of his old friend, with groans
at every breath, bereft as a lioness
whose whelps a hunter seized out of a thicket;
late in returning, she will grieve, and roam
through many meandering valleys on his track
in hope of finding him; heart-stinging anger
carries her away. Now with a groan
he cried out to the Myrmidons:

"Ah, god,
what empty prophecy I made that day
to cheer Menoitios in his mégaron!
I promised him his honored son, brought back
to Opoeis, as pillager of Ilion
bearing his share of spoils.
But Zeus will not fulfill what men design,
not all of it. Both he and I were destined
to stain the same earth dark red here at Troy.
No going home for me; no welcome there
from Pêleus, master of horse, or from my mother,
Thetis. Here the earth will hold me under.
Therefore, as I must follow you into the grave,
I will not give you burial, Patróklos,
until I carry back the gear and head
of him who killed you, noble friend.
Before your funeral pyre I'll cut the throats
of twelve resplendent children of the Trojans—
that is my murdering fury at your death.
But while you lie here by the swanlike ships,
night and day, close by, deep-breasted women
of Troy, and Dardan women, must lament
and weep hot tears, all those whom we acquired
by labor in assault, by the long spear,
pillaging the fat market towns of men."

With this Akhilleus called the company
to place over the campfire a big tripod
and bathe Patróklos of his clotted blood.
Setting tripod and caldron on the blaze
they poured it full, and fed the fire beneath,
and flames licked round the belly of the vessel
until the water warmed and bubbled up
in the bright bronze. They bathed him then, and took
sweet oil for his anointing, laying nard
in the open wounds; and on his bed they placed him,
covering him with fine linen, head to foot,
and a white shroud over it.

So all that night
beside Akhilleus the great runner,
the Myrmidons held mourning for Patróklos.
Now Zeus observed to Hêra, wife and sister:

"You had your way, my lady, after all,
my wide-eyed one! You brought him to his feet,
the great runner! One would say the Akhaian
gentlemen were progeny of yours."

And Hêra with wide eyes replied:

                                       "Dread majesty,

Lord Zeus, why do you take this tone? May not
an ordinary mortal have his way,
though death awaits him, and his mind is dim?
Would anyone suppose that I, who rank
in two respects highest of goddesses—
by birth and by my station, queen to thee,
lord of all gods—that I should not devise
ill fortune for the Trojans whom I loathe?"

So ran their brief exchange. Meanwhile
the silvery-footed Thetis reached Hêphaistos'
lodging, indestructible and starry,
framed in bronze by the bandy-legged god.
She found him sweating, as from side to side
he plied his bellows; on his forge were twenty
tripods to be finished, then to stand
around his mégaron. And he wrought wheels
of gold for the base of each, that each might roll
as of itself into the gods' assembly,
then roll home, a marvel to the eyes.
The caldrons were all shaped but had no handles.
These he applied now, hammering rivets in;
and as he toiled surehandedly at this,
Thetis arrived.

                              Grace in her shining veil
just going out encountered her—that Grace
the bowlegged god had taken to wife. She greeted
Thetis with a warm handclasp and said:

"My lady Thetis, gracious goddess, what
has brought you here? You almost never honor us!
Please come in, and let me give you welcome."

Loveliest of goddesses, she led the way,
to seat her guest on a silver-studded chair,

elaborately fashioned, with a footrest.
Then she called to Hêphaistos:

                                                    "Come and see!
Thetis is here, in need of something from you!"

To this the Great Gamelegs replied:

"Ah, then we have a visitor I honor.
She was my savior, after the long fall
and fractures that I had to bear, when Mother,
bitch that she is, wanted to hide her cripple.
That would have been a dangerous time, had not
Thetis and Eurýnomê taken me in—
Eurýnomê, daughter of the tidal Ocean.
Nine years I stayed, and fashioned works of art,
brooches and spiral bracelets, necklaces,
in their smooth cave, round which the stream of Ocean
flows with a foaming roar: and no one else
knew of it, gods or mortals. Only Thetis
knew, and Eurýnomê, the two who saved me.
Now she has come to us. Well, what I owe
for life to her ladyship in her soft braids
I must repay. Serve her our choicest fare
while I put up my bellows and my tools."

At this he left the anvil block, and hobbled
with monstrous bulk on skinny legs to take
his bellows from the fire. Then all the tools
he had been toiling with he stowed
in a silver chest.

                        That done, he sponged himself,
his face, both arms, bull-neck and hairy chest,
put on a tunic, took a weighty staff,
and limped out of his workshop. Round their lord
came fluttering maids of gold, like living girls:
intelligences, voices, power of motion
these maids have, and skills learnt from immortals.
Now they came rustling to support their lord,
and he moved on toward Thetis, where she sat
upon the silvery chair. He took her hand
and warmly said:

"My Lady Thetis, gracious
goddess, why have you come? You almost never honor us.
Tell me the favor that you have in mind,
for I desire to do it if I can,
and if it is a thing that one may do."

Thetis answered, tear on cheek:

"Hêphaistos,

who among all Olympian goddesses
endured anxiety and pain like mine?
Zeus chose me, from all of them, for this!
Of sea-nymphs I alone was given in thrall
to a mortal warrior, Pêleus Aiákidês,
and I endured a mortal warrior's bed
many a time, without desire. Now Pêleus
lies far gone in age in his great hall,
and I have other pain. Our son, bestowed
on me and nursed by me, became a hero
unsurpassed. He grew like a green shoot;
I cherished him like a flowering orchard tree,
only to send him in the ships to Ilion
to war with Trojans. Now I shall never see him
entering Pêleus' hall, his home, again.
But even while he lives, beholding sunlight,
suffering is his lot. I have no power
to help him, though I go to him. A girl,
his prize from the Akhaians, Agamémnon
took out of his hands to make his own,
and ah, he pined with burning heart! The Trojans
rolled the Akhaians back on the ship sterns,
and left them no escape. Then Argive officers
begged my son's help, offering every gift,
but he would not defend them from disaster.
Arming Patróklos in his own war-gear,
he sent him with his people into battle.
All day long, around the Skaian Gates,
they fought, and would have won the city, too,
had not Apollo, seeing the brave son
of Menoitios wreaking havoc on the Trojans,
killed him in action, and then given Hektor
the honor of that deed.

On this account
I am here to beg you: if you will, provide
for my doomed son a shield and crested helm,
good legging-greaves, fitted with ankle clasps,
a cuirass, too. His own armor was lost
when his great friend went down before the Trojans.
Now my son lies prone on the hard ground in grief."

The illustrious lame god replied:

"Take heart.

No trouble about the arms. I only wish
that I could hide him from the power of death
in his black hour—wish I were sure of that
as of the splendid gear he'll get, a wonder
to any one of the many men there are!"

He left her there, returning to his bellows,
training them on the fire, crying, "To work!"
In crucibles the twenty bellows breathed
every degree of fiery air: to serve him
a great blast when he labored might and main,
or a faint puff, according to his wish
and what the work demanded.

Durable

fine bronze and tin he threw into the blaze
with silver and with honorable gold,
then mounted a big anvil in his block
and in his right hand took a powerful hammer,
managing with his tongs in his left hand.

His first job was a shield, a broad one, thick,
well-fashioned everywhere. A shining rim
he gave it, triple-ply, and hung from this
a silver shoulder strap. Five welded layers
composed the body of the shield. The maker
used all his art adorning this expanse.
He pictured on it earth, heaven, and sea,
unwearied sun, moon waxing, all the stars
that heaven bears for garland: Plêïadês,
Hyadês, Oríôn in his might,
the Great Bear, too, that some have called the Wain,

pivoting there, attentive to Oríôn,
and unbathed ever in the Ocean stream.

He pictured, then, two cities, noble scenes:
weddings in one, and wedding feasts, and brides
led out through town by torchlight from their chambers
amid chorales, amid the young men turning
round and round in dances: flutes and harps
among them, keeping up a tune, and women
coming outdoors to stare as they went by.
A crowd, then, in a market place, and there
two men at odds over satisfaction owed
for a murder done: one claimed that all was paid,
and publicly declared it; his opponent
turned the reparation down, and both
demanded a verdict from an arbiter,
as people clamored in support of each,
and criers restrained the crowd. The town elders
sat in a ring, on chairs of polished stone,
the staves of clarion criers in their hands,
with which they sprang up, each to speak in turn,
and in the middle were two golden measures
to be awarded him whose argument
would be the most straightforward.

                                        Wartime then;
around the other city were emplaced
two columns of besiegers, bright in arms,
as yet divided on which plan they liked:
whether to sack the town, or treat for half
of all the treasure stored in the citadel.
The townsmen would not bow to either: secretly
they armed to break the siege-line. Women and children
stationed on the walls kept watch, with men
whom age disabled. All the rest filed out,
as Arês led the way, and Pallas Athêna,
figured in gold, with golden trappings, both
magnificent in arms, as the gods are,
in high relief, while men were small beside them.
When these had come to a likely place for ambush,
a river with a watering place for flocks,
they there disposed themselves, compact in bronze.

Two lookouts at a distance from the troops
took their posts, awaiting sight of sheep
and shambling cattle. Both now came in view,
trailed by two herdsmen playing pipes, no hidden
danger in their minds. The ambush party
took them by surprise in a sudden rush;
swiftly they cut off herds and beautiful flocks
of silvery grey sheep, then killed the herdsmen.
When the besiegers from their parleying ground
heard sounds of cattle in stampede, they mounted
behind mettlesome teams, following the sound,
and came up quickly. Battle lines were drawn,
and on the riverbanks the fight began
as each side rifled javelins at the other.
Here then Strife and Uproar joined the fray,
and ghastly Fate, that kept a man with wounds
alive, and one unwounded, and another
dragged by the heels through battle-din in death.
This figure wore a mantle dyed with blood,
and all the figures clashed and fought
like living men, and pulled their dead away.

Upon the shield, soft terrain, freshly plowed,
he pictured: a broad field, and many plowmen
here and there upon it. Some were turning
ox teams at the plowland's edge, and there
as one arrived and turned, a man came forward
putting a cup of sweet wine in his hands.
They made their turns-around, then up the furrows
drove again, eager to reach the deep field's
limit; and the earth looked black behind them,
as though turned up by plows. But it was gold,
all gold—a wonder of the artist's craft.

He put there, too, a king's field. Harvest hands
were swinging whetted scythes to mow the grain,
and stalks were falling along the swath
while binders girded others up in sheaves
with bands of straw—three binders, and behind them
children came as gleaners, proffering
their eager armfuls. And amid them all

the king stood quietly with staff in hand,
happy at heart, upon a new-mown swath.
To one side, under an oak tree his attendants
worked at a harvest banquet. They had killed
a great ox, and were dressing it; their wives
made supper for the hands, with barley strewn.

A vineyard then he pictured, weighted down
with grapes: this all in gold; and yet the clusters
hung dark purple, while the spreading vines
were propped on silver vine-poles. Blue enamel
he made the enclosing ditch, and tin the fence,
and one path only led into the vineyard
on which the loaded vintagers took their way
at vintage time. Lighthearted boys and girls
were harvesting the grapes in woven baskets,
while on a resonant harp a boy among them
played a tune of longing, singing low
with delicate voice a summer dirge. The others,
breaking out in song for the joy of it,
kept time together as they skipped along.

The artisan made next a herd of longhorns,
fashioned in gold and tin: away they shambled,
lowing, from byre to pasture by a stream
that sang in ripples, and by reeds a-sway.
Four cowherds all of gold were plodding after
with nine lithe dogs beside them.

                                                    On the assault,
in two tremendous bounds, a pair of lions
caught in the van a bellowing bull, and off
they dragged him, followed by the dogs and men.
Rending the belly of the bull, the two
gulped down his blood and guts, even as the herdsmen
tried to set on their hunting dogs, but failed:
no trading bites with lions for those dogs,
who halted close up, barking, then ran back.

And on the shield the great bowlegged god
designed a pasture in a lovely valley,
wide, with silvery sheep, and huts and sheds
and sheepfolds there.

                                          A dancing floor as well
he fashioned, like that one in royal Knossos
Daidalos made for the Princess Ariadnê.
Here young men and the most desired young girls
were dancing, linked, touching each other's wrists,
the girls in linen, in soft gowns, the men
in well-knit khitons given a gloss with oil;
the girls wore garlands, and the men had daggers
golden-hilted, hung on silver lanyards.
Trained and adept, they circled there with ease
the way a potter sitting at his wheel
will give it a practice twirl between his palms
to see it run; or else, again, in lines
as though in ranks, they moved on one another:
magical dancing! All around, a crowd
stood spellbound as two tumblers led the beat
with spins and handsprings through the company.

Then, running round the shield-rim, triple-ply,
he pictured all the might of the Ocean stream.

Besides the densely plated shield, he made
a cuirass, brighter far than fire light,
a massive helmet, measured for his temples,
handsomely figured, with a crest of gold;
then greaves of pliant tin.

                                          Now when the crippled god
had done his work, he picked up all the arms
and laid them down before Akhilleus' mother,
and swift as a hawk from snowy Olympos' height
she bore the brilliant gear made by Hêphaistos.

BOOK NINETEEN

The Avenger Fasts and Arms

Dawn in her yellow robe rose in the east
out of the flowing Ocean, bearing light
for deathless gods and mortal men. And Thetis
brought to the beach her gifts from the god of fire.
She found her dear son lying beside Patróklos,
wailing, while his men stood by
in tears around him. Now amid that throng
the lovely goddess bent to touch his shoulder
and said to him:

                        "Ah, child, let him lie dead,
for all our grief and pain, we must allow it;
he fell by the gods' will.
But you, now—take the war-gear from Hêphaistos.
No man ever bore upon his shoulders
gear so magnificent."

And she laid the armor
down before Akhilleus, clanging loud
in all its various glory. Myrmidons
began to tremble at the sound, and dared not
look straight at the armor; their knees shook.
But anger entered Akhilleus as he gazed,
his eyes grown wide and bright as blazing fire,
with fierce joy as he handled the god's gifts.
After appraising them in his delight
he spoke out to his mother swiftly:

"Mother,
these the god gave are miraculous arms,
handiwork of immortals, plainly—far
beyond the craft of men. By heaven, I'll wear them!
Only, I feel the dread that while I fight
black carrion flies may settle on Patróklos'
wounds, where the spearheads marked him, and I fear
they may breed maggots to defile the corpse,
now life is torn from it. His flesh may rot."

But silvery-footed Thetis answered:

"Child,
you must not let that prey on you. I'll find
a way to shield him from the black fly hordes
that eat the bodies of men killed in battle.
Though he should lie unburied a long year,
his flesh will be intact and firm. Now, though,
for your part, call the Akhaians to assembly.
Tell them your anger against Agamémnon
is over and done with!
After that, at once
put on your gear, prepare your heart, for war!"

Her promise gave her son wholehearted valor.
Then, turning to Patróklos, she instilled
red nectar and ambrosia in his nostrils
to keep his body whole.

And Prince Akhilleus
passed along the surf-line with a shout
that split the air and roused men of Akhaia,

even those who, up to now, had stayed
amid the massed ships—navigators, helmsmen,
men in charge of rations and ship stores.
Aye, even these now headed for assembly,
since he who for so long had shunned the battle,
Akhilleus, now appeared upon the field.
Resolute Diomêdês and Odysseus,
familiars of the wargod, limped along,
leaning on spears, for both had painful wounds.
They made their way to the forefront and sat down,
and last behind them entered the Lord Marshal
Agamémnon, favoring his wound: he too
had taken a slash, from Antênor's son, Koôn.
When everyone had crowded in, Akhilleus,
the great battlefield runner, rose and said:

"Agamémnon, was it better for us
in any way, when we were sore at heart,
to waste ourselves in strife over a girl?
If only Artemis had shot her down
among the ships on the day I made her mine,
after I took Lyrnessos!
Fewer Akhaians would have died hard
at enemy hands, while I abstained in anger—
Hektor's gain, the Trojans' gain. Akhaians
years hence will remember our high words,
mine and yours. But now we can forget them,
and, as we must, forego our passion. Aye,
by heaven, I drop my anger now!
No need to smolder in my heart forever! Come,
send your long-haired Akhaians into combat,
and let me see how Trojans will hold out,
if camping near the beachhead's their desire!
I rather think some will be glad to rest,
provided they get home, away from danger,
out of my spear's range!"

                              These were his words,
and all the Akhaians gave a roar of joy
to hear the prince abjure his rage.
Lord Marshal Agamémnon then addressed them,

standing up, not in the midst of them,
but where he had been sitting:

                                        "Friends, fighters,
Danääns, companions of Arês: it is fair
to listen to a man when he has risen
and not to interrupt him. That's vexation
to any speaker, able though he may be.
In a great hubbub how can any man
attend or speak? A fine voice will be muffled.
While I open my mind to the son of Pêleus,
Argives, attention! Each man weigh my words!
The Akhaians often brought this up against me,
and chided me. But I am not to blame.
Zeus and Fate and a nightmare Fury are,
for putting savage Folly in my mind
in the assembly that day, when I wrested
Akhilleus' prize of war from him. In truth,
what could I do? Divine will shapes these things.
Ruinous Folly, eldest daughter of Zeus,
beguiles us all. Her feet are soft, from walking
not on earth but over the heads of men
to do them hurt. She traps one man or another.
Once indeed she deluded Zeus, most noble
of gods and men, they say. But feminine
Hêra with her underhanded ways
tricked him, the day Alkmênê, in high Thebes,
was to have given birth to Hêraklês.
Then glorying Zeus remarked to all the gods:
'Hear me, all gods and goddesses, I'll tell you
of something my heart dwells upon. This day
the childbirth goddess, Eileithyía, brings
into the light a man who will command
all those around him, being of the race of men
who come of my own blood!' But in her guile
the Lady Hêra said: 'You may be wrong,
unable to seal your word with truth hereafter.
Come, Olympian, swear me a great oath
he will indeed be lord of all his neighbors,
the child of your own stock in the race of men
who drops between a woman's legs today!'

Zeus failed to see her crookedness: he swore
a mighty oath, and mightily went astray,
for flashing downward from Olympos crest
Hêra visited Argos of Akhaia,
aware that the strong wife of Perseus' son,
Sthénelos, was big with child,
just entering her seventh month. But Hêra
brought this child into the world's daylight
beforehand by two months, and checked Alkmênê's
labor, to delay the birth of hers.
To Zeus the son of Krónos then she said:
'Zeus of the bright bolt, father, let me add
a new event to your deliberations.
Even now a superior man is born
to be a lord of Argives: Eurýstheus,
a son of Sthénelos, the son of Perseus,
of your own stock. And it is not unfitting
for him to rule the Argives.' This report
sharply wounded the deep heart of Zeus.
He picked up Folly by her shining braids
in sudden anger—swearing a great oath
that never to starred heaven or Olympos
Folly, who tricks us all, should come again.
With this he whirled her with one hand and flung her
out of the sky. So to men's earth she came,
but ever thereafter made Zeus groan to see
his dear son toil at labors for Eurýstheus.

So, too, with me: when in his shimmering helm
great Hektor slaughtered Argives near the ships,
could I ignore my folly, my delusion?
Zeus had stolen my wits, my act was blind.
But now I wish to make amends, to give
all possible satisfaction. Rouse for war,
send in your troops! I here repeat my offer
of all that Odysseus promised yesterday!
Stay if you will, though the wargod presses you.
Men in my service will unload the gifts
from my own ship, that you may see how richly
I reward you!"

Akhilleus answered:

"Excellency,
Lord Marshal Agamémnon, make the gifts
if you are keen to—gifts are due; or keep them.
It is for you to say. Let us recover
joy of battle soon, that's all!
No need to dither here and lose our time,
our great work still undone. When each man sees
Akhilleus in a charge, crumpling the ranks
of Trojans with his bronze-shod spear, let each
remember that is the way to fight his man!"

Replied Odysseus, the shrewd field commander:

"Brave as you are, and like a god in looks,
Akhilleus, do not send Akhaian soldiers
into the fight unfed! Today's mêlée
will not be brief, when rank meets rank, and heaven
breathes fighting spirit into both contenders.
No, tell all troops who are near the ships to take
roast meat and wine, for heart and staying power.
No soldier can fight hand to hand, in hunger,
all day long until the sun goes down!
Though in his heart he yearns for war, his legs
go slack before he knows it: thirst and famine
search him out, and his knees fail as he moves.
But that man stayed with victualing and wine
can fight his enemies all day: his heart
is bold and happy in his chest, his legs
hold out until both sides break off the battle!
Come, then, dismiss the ranks to make their breakfast.
Let the Lord Marshal Agamémnon
bring his gifts to the assembly ground
where all may see them; may your heart be warmed.
Then let him swear to you, before the Argives,
never to have made love to her, my lord,
as men and women by their nature do.
So may your heart be peaceable toward him!
And let him sate your hunger with rich fare
in his own shelter, that you may lack nothing

due you in justice. Afterward, Agamémnon,
you'll be more just to others, too. There is
no fault in a king's wish to conciliate
a man with whom he has been quick to anger!"

And the Lord Marshal Agamémnon answered:

"Glad I am to hear you, son of Laërtês,
finding the right word at the right time
for all these matters. And the oath you speak of
I'll take willingly, with all my heart,
and will not, before heaven, be forsworn.
Now let Akhilleus wait here, though the wargod
tug his arm; and all the rest of you
wait here assembled till the gifts have come
down from our quarters, and our peace is made.
For you, Odysseus, here is my command:
choose the finest young peers of all Akhaia
to fetch out of my ship those gifts we pledged
Akhilleus yesterday; and bring the women.
Let Talthýbios prepare for sacrifice,
in the army's name, a boar to Zeus and Hêlios."

Replied Akhilleus:

                                        "Excellency, Lord Marshal,
another time were better for these ceremonies,
some interval in the war, and when I feel
less passion in me. Look, those men lie dead
whom Hektor killed when Zeus allowed him glory,
and yet you two propose a meal! By god,
I'd send our soldiers into action now
unfed and hungry. Have a feast, I'd say,
at sundown, when our shame has been avenged!
Before that, for my part, I will not swallow
food or drink—my dear friend being dead,
lying before my eyes, bled white by spear-cuts,
feet turned to his hut's door, his friends in mourning
around him. Your concerns are none of mine.
Slaughter and blood are what I crave, and groans
of anguished men!"

                         But the shrewd field commander
Odysseus answered:

                                   "Akhilleus, flower and pride
of the Akhaians, you are more powerful
than I am—and a better spearman, too—
only in sizing matters up I'd say
I'm just as far beyond you, being older,
knowing more of the world. So bear with me.
Men quickly reach satiety with battle
in which the reaping bronze will bring to earth
big harvests, but a scanty yield, when Zeus,
war's overseer for mankind, tips the scales.
How can a fasting belly mourn our dead?
So many die, so often, every day,
when would soldiers come to an end of fasting?
No, we must dispose of him who dies
and keep hard hearts, and weep that day alone.
And those whom the foul war has left unhurt
will do well to remember food and drink,
so that we may again close with our enemies,
our dangerous enemies, and be tough soldiers,
hardened in mail of bronze. Let no one, now,
be held back waiting for another summons:
here is your summons! Woe to the man who lingers
beside the Argive ships! No, all together,
let us take up the fight against the Trojans!"

He took as escort sons of illustrious Nestor:
Phyleus' son Mégès, Thoas, and Meríonès,
and the son of Kreion, Lykomêdês, and
Melánippos, to Agamémnon's quarters.
No sooner was the work assigned than done:
they brought the seven tripods Agamémnon
promised Akhilleus, and the twenty caldrons
shining, and the horses, a full dozen;
then they conducted seven women, skilled
in housecraft, with Brisêis in her beauty.
Odysseus weighed ten bars of purest gold
and turned back, followed by his young Akhaians,
bearing the gifts to place in mid-assembly.

Now Agamémnon rose. Talthýbios
the crier, with his wondrous voice, stood near him,
holding the boar. The son of Atreus drew
the sheath knife that he carried, hung
beside the big sheath of his sword, and cut
first bristles from the boar. Arms wide to heaven
he prayed to Zeus, as all the troops kept still,
all sitting in due order in their places,
hearing their king. In prayer he raised his eyes
to the broad sky and said:

                                        "May Zeus, all-highest
and first of gods, be witness first, then Earth
and Hêlios and the Furies underground
who punish men for having broken oaths,
I never laid a hand on your Brisêis,
proposing bed or any other pleasure;
in my quarters the girl has been untouched.
If one word that I swear is false,
may the gods plague me for a perjured liar!"

He slit the boar's throat with his blade of bronze.
Then Talthýbios, wheeling, flung the victim
into the offshore water, bait for fish.
Akhilleus rose amid the Argive warriors,
saying:

                                "Father Zeus, you send mankind
prodigious follies. Never otherwise
had Agamémnon stung me through and through;
never would he have been so empty-headed
as to defy my will and take the girl!
No, for some reason Zeus had death at heart
for the Akhaians, and for many.

                                                          Well:
go to your meat, then we'll resume the fighting."

Thus he dismissed the assembly. All the men
were quick to scatter, each to his own ship.
As for the gifts, the Myrmidons took over
and bore them all to Akhilleus' ship, to stow

within his shelter. There they left the women
and drove the horses to the herd.

                                                    The girl
Brisêis, in her grace like Aphrodítê,
on entering saw Patróklos lying dead
of spear wounds, and she sank down to embrace him
with a sharp sobbing cry, lifting her hands
to tear her breast, soft throat, and lovely face,
this girl, shaped like the goddesses of heaven.
Weeping, she said:

                                        "Patróklos, very dear,
most dear to me, cursed as I am, you were
alive still when I left you, left this place!
Now I come back to find you dead, my captain!
Evil follows evil so, for me.
The husband to whom father and mother gave me
I saw brought down by spears before our town,
with my three brothers, whom my mother bore.
Dear brothers, all three met their day of wrath.
But when Akhilleus killed my lord, and sacked
the city of royal Mynês, not a tear
would you permit me: no, you undertook
to see me married to the Prince Akhilleus,
conveyed by ship to Phthía, given a wedding
among the Myrmidons. Now must I mourn
your death forever, who were ever gentle."

She wailed again, and women sobbed about her,
first for Patróklos, then for each one's grief.
Meanwhile Akhaian counselors were gathered
begging Akhilleus to take food. He spurned it,
groaning:

                                "No, I pray you, my dear friends,
if anyone will listen!—do not nag me
to glut and dull my heart with food and drink!
A burning pain is in me. I'll hold out
till sundown without food. I say I'll bear it."

With this he sent the peers away, except
the two Atreidai and the great Odysseus,

Nestor, Idómeneus, and old Lord Phoinix.
These would have comforted him, but none
could quiet or comfort him until he entered
the bloody jaws of war. Now pierced by memory,
he sighed and sighed again, and said:

                                                    "Ah, once

you, too, poor fated friend, and best of friends,
would set a savory meal deftly before us
in our field shelter, when the Akhaians wished
no time lost between onsets against Trojans.
Now there you lie, broken in battle. Ah,
lacking you, my heart will fast this day
from meat and drink as well. No greater ill
could come to me, not news of Father's death—
my father, weeping soft tears now in Phthía
for want of that son in a distant land
who wars on Troy for Helen's sake—that woman
who makes the blood run cold. No greater ill,
even should my son die, who is being reared
on Skyros, Neoptólemos, if indeed
he's living still. My heart's desire has been
that I alone should perish far from Argos
here at Troy; that you should sail to Phthía,
taking my son aboard your swift black ship
at Skyros, to introduce him to his heritage,
my wide lands, my servants, my great hall.
In this late year Pêleus may well be dead
and buried, or have few days yet to live,
beset by racking age, always awaiting
dire news of me, of my own death."

As he said this he wept. The counselors groaned,
remembering each what he had left at home;
and seeing them sorrow, Zeus took pity on them,
saying quickly to Athêna:

                                                    "Daughter,

you seem to have left your fighting man alone.
Should one suppose you care no more for Akhilleus?
There he sits, before the curving prows,
and grieves for his dear friend. The other soldiers

flock to meat; he thirsts and hungers. Come,
infuse in him sweet nectar and ambrosia,
that an empty belly may not weaken him."

He urged Athêna to her own desire,
and like a gliding sea hawk, shrilling high,
she soared from heaven through the upper air,
while the Akhaians armed throughout the ranks.
Nectar and ambrosia she instilled
within Akhilleus, that his knees be not
assailed by hollow famine; then she withdrew
to her mighty father's house. Meanwhile the troops
were pouring from the shipways to the field.
As when cold snowflakes fly from Zeus in heaven,
thick and fast under the blowing north wind,
just so, that multitude of gleaming helms
and bossed shields issued from the ships, with plated
cuirasses and ashwood spears. Reflected
glintings flashed to heaven, as the plain
in all directions shone with glare of bronze
and shook with trampling feet of men. Among them
Prince Akhilleus armed. One heard his teeth
grind hard together, and his eyes blazed out
like licking fire, for unbearable pain
had fixed upon his heart. Raging at Trojans,
he buckled on the arms Hêphaistos forged.
The beautiful greaves, fitted with silver anklets,
first he put upon his legs, and next
the cuirass on his ribs; then over his shoulder
he slung the sword of bronze with silver scabbard;
finally he took up the massive shield
whence came a radiance like the round full moon.
As when at sea to men on shipboard comes
the shining of a campfire on a mountain
in a lone sheepfold, while the gusts of nightwind
take them, loath to go, far from their friends
over the teeming sea: just so
Akhilleus' finely modeled shield sent light
into the heavens. Lifting his great helm
he placed it on his brows, and like a star
the helm shone with its horsetail blowing free,

all golden, that Hêphaistos had set in
upon the crest. Akhilleus tried his armor,
shrugging and flexing, making sure it fitted,
sure that his gleaming legs had play. Indeed
the gear sat on him light as wings: it buoyed him!
Now from a spear-case he withdrew a spear—
his father's—weighty, long, and tough. No other
Akhaian had the strength to handle it,
this great Pêlian shaft
of ashwood, given his father by the centaur
Kheirôn from the crest of Pêlion
to be the death of heroes.

                                                      Automédôn

and Álkimos with swift hands yoked his team,
making firm the collars on the horses,
placing the bits between their teeth, and pulling
reins to the war-car. Automédôn then
took in hand the shining whip and mounted
the chariot, and at his back Akhilleus
mounted in full armor, shining bright
as the blinding Lord of Noon. In a clarion voice
he shouted to the horses of his father:

"Xánthos and Balíos! Known to the world
as foals of great Podargê! In this charge
care for your driver in another way!
Pull him back, I mean, to the Danáäns,
back to the main body of the army,
once we are through with battle; this time,
no leaving him there dead, like Lord Patróklos!"

To this, from under the yoke, the nimble Xánthos
answered, and hung his head, so that his mane
dropped forward from the yokepad to the ground—
Hêra whose arms are white as ivory
gave him a voice to say:

                                        "Yes, we shall save you,
this time, too, Akhilleus in your strength!
And yet the day of your destruction comes,
and it is nearer. We are not the cause,
but rather a great god is, and mighty Fate.

Nor was it by our sloth or sluggishness
the Trojans stripped Patróklos of his armor.
No, the magnificent god that Lêto bore
killed him in action and gave Hektor glory.
We might run swiftly as the west wind blows,
most rapid of all winds, they say; but still
it is your destiny to be brought low
by force, a god's force and a man's!"

On this,

the Furies put a stop to Xánthos' voice.
In anger and gloom Akhilleus said to him:

"Xánthos, why prophesy my death? No need.
What is in store for me I know, know well:
to die here, far away from my dear father,
my mother, too. No matter. All that matters
is that I shall not call a halt today
till I have made the Trojans sick of war!"

And with a shout he drove his team
of trim-hooved horses into the front line.

BOOK TWENTY

The Ranging of Powers

Thus on the beachhead the Akhaians armed
with you, Akhilleus, avid again for war,
and Trojans faced them on the rise of plain.
Zeus meanwhile, from the utmost snowy height
of ridged Olympos, gave command to Themis
to call the gods together. Everywhere
she went about and bade them to his hall.
None of the rivers failed to come, not one
except the Ocean stream; none of the nymphs
who haunt cool greenwood groves and riverheads
and inland grassy meads. All made their way
to the hall of Zeus, lord of the clouds of heaven,
taking their chairs in sunlit courts, laid out
with all Hêphaistos' art in polished stone.

So these assembled. Then the god of earthquake
heeded the goddess; from the great salt sea
he came aloft to take his place among them,
asking his brother Zeus what he proposed:

"Lord of the bright bolt, why do you bring us here?
Something to do with Trojans and Akhaians,
now their lines are drawn, and the war flares?"

And Zeus who gathers cloud replied:

                                                    "You know

what plan I have in mind and why I called you,
why you are here. Men on both sides may perish,
still they are near my heart. And yet, by heaven,
here I stay, at ease upon a ridge.
I'll have an ample view here. But you others,
go into action, side with men of Troy
or with Akhaians, as each has a mind to.
Suppose Akhilleus takes the Trojans on
alone: not for a minute will they hold him.
In times past they used to shake to see him,
and now he's mad with rage for his friend's death,
I fear he'll break the wall down, sack the town,
before the time has come for it."

                                                    Lord Zeus

fell silent then, but kindled bitter war,
and the immortals entered it. They took
positions as they wished: Hêra, Athêna,
Poseidon, girdler of the earth, and Hermês,
most sharp-witted of them all; Hêphaistos,
proud and brawny but with tottery shanks:
these were the seaborne Akhaians' partisans.

For the Trojans, Arês in a flashing helm,
beside him long-haired Phoibos, Artemis,
Lêto and Xánthos, and the smiling goddess
Aphrodítê. Until the gods came near
the Akhaians gloried more, now that Akhilleus
again had joined the fight so long foregone.
Every Trojan felt his knees atremble,

seeing the great runner armed
and flashing like the deadly god of war.
When the Olympians joined the lines arrayed,
Strife came in power, goader of fighting men.
Then standing by the moat outside the wall
or on the shore of beating surf, Athêna
shrieked, and her adversary, Arês, yelled
across from her, like a pitch-black hurricane
roaring to Trojans from the heights of Troy,
or veering by the course of Simóeis
on Kallikolônê.

                                        So the gods in bliss
roused the contenders, hurled them into war,
and broke in massive strife among themselves.
Out of heaven the father of gods and men
thundered crack on crack; Poseidon heaving
underground made the wide mainland quake
even to craggy mountain peaks. On Ida,
white with watercourses, all the slopes
and crests were set atremble; so was the city,
Troy, and the grounded ships of the Akhaians.
Dread came in undergloom to Aïdôneus,
lord of shades: he bounded from his throne
and gave a cry, in fear that earth, undone
by Lord Poseidon's shaking, would cave in,
and the vile moldy kennels the gods hate
might stand revealed to mortals and immortals.
That was the measure of the shock
created by the onset of the gods.
And now, by heaven, against Lord Poseidon
Phoibos Apollo drew his feathered bolts;
against Enyálios the grey-eyed goddess
Athêna stood; and like a golden shaft
the archer, Artemis, of whistling arrows,
sister of Apollo, faced great Hêra.
Lêto was opposed by gracious Hermês,
wayfinder for souls, and the god of fire,
Hêphaistos, faced a mighty eddying river,
Xánthos to the gods, to men Skamánder.
These were the divine adversaries.

Akhilleus

went into that battle wild to engage
great Hektor, son of Priam, with whose blood
his heart and soul desired to glut the wargod.
Straight against him, though, Apollo drove
Aineías. He put courage in this man.
Taking Lykáôn's voice and look, he said:

"Counselor of Trojans, Prince Aineías, tell me:
what of your threats and promises, in wine,
before your peers, to face the son of Pêleus,
Akhilleus, in the battle?"

And Aineías

answered him:

"Lykáôn, son of Priam,
why demand this, when my heart's unready
to take that formidable fighter on?
It will not be the first time: once before
I met him, and he drove me with his spear
from Ida, when he raided herds of ours
and took Lyrnessos, plundered Pêdasos.
The Lord Zeus helped me out of it; he gave me
wind and legs to run, else I had fallen
under Akhilleus' and Athêna's blows.
She went ahead of him and cast her light
of glory on him, made him with his spear
defeat and strip the Lélegês and Trojans.
This is the point: no man can fight Akhilleus!
In every battle, one of the gods is there
to save him from destruction, while his weapon
flies unwavering till it bites its way
through some man's flesh. Would the god only bring
under equal strain both parties to the fight,
Akhilleus would not win so easily,
not though the man is bronze from head to foot."

And Lord Apollo, son of Zeus, replied:

"Come, sir, you too invoke the gods, the undying,
the ever young! One hears you are, yourself,

a child of Aphrodítê.
Akhilleus comes of a goddess not so high—
not, like yours, a daughter of Zeus, but born
to the sea's Ancient. Come, then, bear your point
straight forward, bronze unworn, unbloodied! Never
be turned aside by taunts or threats from him!"

He breathed into the captain's heart a glow
of fighting spirit, and Aineías shouldered
forward, helmed in fiery bronze. But Hêra
glimpsed Ankhísês' son on the attack,
hunting Akhilleus through the field. She called
her two confederates, saying:

                                        "Now take care,

Poseidon and Athêna, how this action
runs its course! There is Aineías, helmet
flashing, facing the son of Pêleus;
Phoibos Apollo forced him to attack.
Why do we not, all three of us, repel him,
turn him in his tracks? Or one of us
could back Akhilleus, give him the edge in power,
in stamina, in valor, let him know
the high immortals love him! Those who fought
for Trojans in past days of deadly war
were unavailing as the wind. We three
have come down from Olympos to engage
in this great battle, that he take no hurt
from Trojans on this day. In time he'll suffer
all that his destiny, on his life's thread,
spun for him when his mother gave him birth.
But lacking intimation of these things—
dream-voice of gods—Akhilleus may feel dread
when some god comes against him in the combat.
Gods take daunting shapes when they appear."

At this the god who makes the mainland quake,
Poseidon, said:

                                "No need for senseless anger.
Why should we be quick to embroil ourselves
as adversaries of the others, being

far more powerful than they are? Come,
we'll move out of the trampled plain and take
some lookout post on high. Let men make war!
Only if Arês fights, or Lord Apollo,
or if they keep Akhilleus from the combat,
then the clang of battle will begin
between us on the spot—
with a quick outcome, I predict: they'll be
so battered by our arms, they must fall back
on the Olympian conclave."

And Poseidon
led them to the Wall of Hêraklês,
an earthwork, built for the mighty man by Pallas
Athêna and the Trojans in times past,
as cover for him when the sea-monster
drove him from beach to plain. Now Lord Poseidon
took his ease there, followed by the others,
shoulders mantled in unbroken cloud.

On Kallikolônê's brow, opposing gods
were seated around Arês, breacher of walls,
with you, Archer Apollo. Resting so,
both companies were thoughtful: neither cared
to take the initiative toward wounds and war,
but Zeus from his high throne ruled over all.

The whole plain now filled up with troops and flashed
with bronze of men and chariots, as the earth
reverberated under their feet. Two fighters,
far and away the best, between the armies
made for each other, both on edge for combat,
Aineías Ankhisíadês and Akhilleus.
Aineías had gone forward first
and nodded, menacing, with heavy helm.
Well forward of his chest he held his shield,
and shook his bronze-shod spear. Opposing him
Akhilleus now came up like a fierce lion
that a whole countryside is out to kill:
he comes heedless at first, but when some yeoman
puts a spear into him, he gapes and crouches,

foam on his fangs; his mighty heart within him
groans as he lashes both flanks with his tail,
urging his valor on to fight; he glares
and bounds ahead, hoping to make a kill
or else himself to perish in the tumult.
That was the way Akhilleus' heart and spirit
drove him to meet Aineías. As they closed,
Akhilleus, prince and formidable runner,
spoke first:

                                "Why are you out of line so far,
Aineías? Moved to challenge me in battle?
Hoping to lord it over Trojan horsemen,
heir to Priam's dignity as king?
Ha! Even if you kill me, not for that
will Priam put his honor in your hands!
Has he not sons, is he not sound, is he
so bird-witted? Or have the Trojans parceled
gardenland, their choicest, in your name,
vineyard and plowland, rich, for you to tend
in case you kill me? Rough work that will be,
let me predict. At spearpoint once before
I think I made you skip. Don't you remember
the time I chased you from your herd, alone
down Ida's hills, fast as your legs would take you?
You ran without a backward look, ran on
into Lyrnessos; but I broke that town
in one charge, with Athêna and Lord Zeus,
making its women spoil, taking their day
of freedom from them. As for you, Zeus moved
to save your life; so did the other gods,
but there will be no saving you this time,
I think, though luck like that is what you pray for.
Now enough. Here's my command: retire
on your own people, make no pass at me,
or you'll be hurt. A child or fool can see
what's done when it is done."

                                    Aineías answered:

"Son of Pêleus, use words to frighten
a small boy, not me. I am well able

to bandy cutting words and insults too.
Each knows about the other's birth and parents
from the old tales of mortals that we've heard;
you'll never see my parents nor I yours.
Royal Pêleus' son, you are said to be,
and the salt-sea goddess Thetis was your mother.
My own claim is that I was born the son
of Ankhísês, the hero, and my mother
is Aphrodítê. Of these four, one pair
will mourn a son today—as not by bragging
can this quarrel be resolved, I'd say,
so that we two may be relieved of battle.
But if you wish to learn such things as well,
to know the story of our race, already
known to many soldiers: Zeus, cloud-master,
fathered Dárdanos and built the town
Dardániê, since Ilion's stronghold
was not yet walled or peopled on the plain,
and men still made their home on Ida's hills.
Dárdanos begot King Erikhthónios,
richest of mortals in his time: he owned
three thousand mares that grazed his pastureland
and gloried in their frisking colts. These mares
Boreas the north wind loved even as they grazed,
and in the likeness of a black-maned stallion
chose his brood-mares. They conceived and bore
twelve colts, that in their gallop over farmland
ran without trampling on the tips of grain,
and running on the sea's broad back they clipped
the whitecaps doffing foam on grey salt water.
Erikhthónios was the father of Trôs,
lord of the Trojans. Three fine sons he had:
Ilos, Assárakos, and Ganymêdês,
handsomest of mortals, whom the gods
caught up to pour out drink for Zeus and live
amid immortals for his beauty's sake.
Ilos begot Laomédôn, Laomédôn
Tithonos, Priam, Lampós, Klytios,
and Hikeráôn, wild sprig of the wargod.
Assárakos fathered Kapys, he Ankhísês,
Ankhísês fathered me. Priam begot

Prince Hektor. These are the blood-lines I claim.
But Zeus gives men more excellence or less
as he desires, being omnipotent.
Come, no more childish talk, here at the heart
of a great battle. Each side has a mass
of bitter words to say: no deepsea ship
could take that load, even a hundred-bencher.
Men have twisty tongues, and on them speech
of all kinds; wide is the grazing land of words,
both east and west. The manner of speech you use,
the same you are apt to hear. By what necessity
must we goad one another face to face
with provocations? like two city women
ruffling into the middle of a street
to wrangle, bitten by rage,
with many a true word—and some false, for anger
calls out those as well. My mind is set
on honor. Words of yours cannot throw me off,
not till our spears have crossed. Come, on with it!
We'll have a taste of one another's bronze!'"

At this he drove hard with his massive spear
against the marvelous shield: a great clang
resounded at the impact of the spearhead.
Akhilleus with his big fist held the shield
at arm's length, instinctively, for fear
Aineías' shaft might cleave it and come through—
a foolishness; he had not learned as yet
how slim the chance is that the splendid gifts
of gods will crack or yield to mortal fighters.
In fact, this time Aineías' well-aimed spear-thrust
could not breach the shield. The firegod's plate
of gold contained it. Though it pierced two layers,
there were three more: the bandy-legged smith
had wrought five all together, two of bronze,
two inner ones of tin, and the gold plate
by which the ashwood spear was now contained.
Akhilleus in his turn rifled his spear
and hit Aineías' round shield near the rim
where bronze was thinnest, and the bull's hide thinnest.
Straight through drove the Pêlian ash. The plate

gave way screeching. Down Aineías crouched
and held his shield away from him in fear.
The spearshaft cleared his back and then stuck fast
in the battlefield, hurled with such force; it broke
asunder two disks of the covering shield.
But he ducked under it, then stood, and pain
in a rush came over him, clouding his eyes,
for dread of the spear implanted close at hand.
Akhilleus closed with him, drawing his sword,
with a wild warcry. But Aineías bent
for a boulder, a huge weight, that, as men are
in our day, two men could not carry: this
he hefted easily alone. Aineías
might have smashed his lunging adversary
either on the helm or on the shield
that had protected him from rending death;
Akhilleus with his sword stroke at close quarters
might have slashed the other's life away,
had not Poseidon's sharp eye caught the danger.
Instantly to his immortal friends
he said:

                    "Here's trouble for Aineías' sake!
He goes to dark Death at Akhilleus' hands
and soon: being gullible he listened
to Apollo, but that god will not protect him
against a foul close. Why must the blameless man
be hurt to no good end, for the wrongs of others?
His gifts were always pleasing to the gods
who hold wide heaven.

                    Come now, we ourselves
may take him out of danger, and make sure
that Zeus shall not be angered by his death
at Akhilleus' hands. His fate is to escape,
to ensure that the great line of Dárdanos
may not unseeded perish from the world.
For Zeus cared most for Dárdanos, of all
the sons he had by women, and now Zeus
has turned against the family of Priam.
Therefore Aineías and his sons, and theirs,
will be lords over Trojans born hereafter."

The Lady Hêra answered with wide eyes:

"Earthshaker, put your own mind on Aineías,
whether to save him or to let him die.
By heaven, Pallas and I have taken oath
before the immortals many times: we shall not
keep the evil day from any Trojans,
even when all Troy catches fire, with flames
the fighting Akhaians light!"

On hearing this,

Poseidon, shaker of the earth, made off
along the battle line, through press of spears,
until he reached Aineías and Akhilleus.
Instantly over Akhilleus' eyes he cast
a battle-haze, and pulled his ashwood shaft
out of the round shield of Aineías; then
he laid the spear down at Akhilleus' feet,
but swept Aineías off the ground and upward.
Lifted aloft by the god's hand, he soared,
traversing many lines of men and chariots,
until he reached the flank of the wild field
where the Kaukônês entered combat.

There

Poseidon swiftly said into his ear:

"Aineías, what god has commanded it—
this recklessness of challenging Akhilleus,
a man more powerful than you are, dearer
to the immortal gods? No, no,
stay clear of meeting him, or else you'll drop
before your time into the house of Death.
Remember, after Akhilleus meets his doom
you may be daring; then go forward, then
take on the leaders, for there is no other
Akhaian who can slay you on the field."

With this, since all was said, he left him there,
and from Akhilleus' eyes he blew away
the magic battle-haze. With all his might
the man stared, and then full of bitterness
said to himself:

"By god, here is a wonder
wrought before my eyes! Here on the ground
my spear lies, and there's no man to be seen
where one stood and I made my cast to kill him!
Aineías has been dear to the gods then, sure
enough, though I had thought his boasts were wind.
To hell with him! He'll never have the heart
to stand up to me now, glad as he was
to slip away from death. Come on, I'll lead
Danääns who love war; we'll press the fight
against the rest, to see what they are made of!"

At this he bounded back on the first line,
calling on every fighter:

"Soldiers, Akhaians,
no more waiting out of range of Trojans!
Every man make up his mind to fight
and move on his enemy! Strong as I am,
it's hard for me to face so many men
and fight with all at once. Not even Arês,
god though he is, immortal, nor Athêna
could face the opening jaws of such a battle
and bear the toil alone. And yet I will,
so far as I have power in arms and legs,
and stamina. I'll not ease off, I swear,
not for an instant. No. I'll break their line.
I think no Trojan crossing spears with me
will burn with joy for it!"

So he cheered them on.
And splendid Hektor shouted to the Trojans
to go against Akhilleus:

"Trojans, fighters,
have no fear of the son of Pêleus. Using
words, I too could fight the gods. The test
is harder with a spear: gods are far stronger.
Akhilleus cannot accomplish all he says.
One thing he'll do, another leave half done.
I'll face him, though he thrusts like fire, bladed
fire, and though he has a heart like iron!"

He cheered the Trojans, and they lifted spears
against Akhilleus, all in a clump, in valor
closing ranks, while a battlecry went up.

And then at Hektor's side Apollo said:

"Do not attack Akhilleus yet: wait for him
deep in the mass, out of the front line shouting,
else he may down you with his long shaft thrown
or with a sword-cut close at hand."

                                                        Once more
afraid when he had heard the god's voice speaking,
Hektor drew back amid the crowded troops.
Akhilleus rushed upon them in his might
with a bloodcurdling shout, and first he killed
the son of Otrynteus, brave Iphitîôn,
born by a naiad to the raider of cities
under snow-covered Tmôlos, in the fertile
townland of Hydê. As this young man strove
to meet him, Prince Akhilleus struck his head
square in the middle, and it split in two.
He thudded down. Akhilleus then sang out:

"Terror of all soldiers, there you lie!
Here is your place of death! So far away
your birthplace, near Gygaiê lake, and there
your father's royal parkland on the trout-stream
Hyllos and the eddying Hermos river!"

So he exulted, while the other's eyes
were veiled in night. Then chariots of Akhaians
cut the body asunder with sharp wheels
in the advancing battle. And Akhilleus
killed a second man, Dêmoleôn,
Antênor's son, a good defensive fighter.
He hit him on the temple through the helmet
fitted with bronze cheek-pieces, and the metal
could not hold; the driven
spearhead cleft it, broke the temple-bone,
so that his brains were spattered in the helm.
For all his fighting heart, Akhilleus downed him.
Then Hippodámas: he had left his car

to run before Akhilleus, but the Akhaian
speared him in the back. He gasped his life out,
bellowing, like a bull dragged up before
Poseidon, lord of Hélikê, by boys
who yank his halter—and the god of earthquake
takes joy watching them. Bellowing so,
the rugged soul left Hippodámas' bones.
Akhilleus turned his spear on Polydôros,
Priam's son. The father had refused
permission to this boy to fight, as being
youngest of all his sons and dearest, one
who could outrun the rest.

> Just now, in fact,
out of pure thoughtlessness, showing his speed,
he ran the front line till he met his end.
The great battlefield runner, Prince Akhilleus,
hit him square in the back as he flashed by—
hit where the golden buckles of his belt
and both halves of his cuirass linked together.
Passing through the man, out at the navel
the spearhead came, and on his knees he fell
with a loud cry. The blinding cloud of death
enveloped him as he sprawled out, his entrails
held in his hands before him. Hektor saw
his brother Polydôros fallen aside
against the earth, his entrails in his hands;
and mist of death veiled Hektor's eyes as well.
He could not hang at a distance any longer,
but shook his spear and ran upon Akhilleus
like a wild flame. When the Akhaian saw him
he gave a start and prayed:

> "The man is near
who most has hurt my heart; he took the life
of the friend I had so cherished. May we two
not shrink from one another any longer
upon the open ground of war!"

> He glared
under his brows at Hektor and gave a shout:

"Come on, come on straight! You will make it
all the sooner to the edge of doom!"

But Hektor answered without fear:

"Akhilleus,
why suppose you can frighten me with words
like a small boy? I, too, have some gift
for jeers and insults. You are strong, I know,
and I am far from being a match for you.
But on the gods' great knees these matters lie.
Poorest of men, compared to you, by heaven,
I still may take your life with one spear-cast.
My spearhead, too, has had its cutting power!"

Even as he spoke he hefted and let fly,
and with a puff of wind Athêna turned
the spearhead from Akhilleus in his glory—
a windpuff like a sigh. The spear came back
to Hektor, falling at his feet. Akhilleus
put all his heart into a lunge to kill him,
raising a wild cry. But Apollo caught
the Trojan up, god-fashion, with great ease
and hid him in a white cloud. Then three times
the great battlefield runner, Prince Akhilleus,
lunged with his spear, three times he cleft the cloud,
but when, beside himself, he lunged a fourth time,
then he vented a blood-chilling cry:

"You got away from death again, you dog!
The evil hour came near you, but Apollo
saved you again: I'm sure you pray to him
on entering spear-play. Even so, I'll kill you
later, on sight, if I too have a god
beside me. I can tackle others now,
whatever Trojan I may find."

With this,
he jabbed and wounded Dryops in the neck,
then left him, fallen at his feet, and turned
on Dêmoukhos, Philêtor's rugged son,
whom he checked with a spear-thrust at the knees,
then killed with a swinging blow of his long sword.
Next he took on Laógonos and Dárdanos,
Bías' sons, and forced them from their chariot,

one with a spear-cast, one slashed by the sword.
Then Trôs, Alástôr's son, sank at his knees
and begged the Akhaian to take him prisoner,
to spare a man his own age, not to kill
but pity him. How witless, to imagine
Akhilleus could be swayed! No moderate temper,
no mild heart was in this man, but harsh
and deadly purpose. Trôs embraced his knees,
beseeching him, but with his blade he opened
a wound below the liver. Out it slipped,
with red blood flowing downward from the wound,
filling his lap. Then darkness veiled his eyes
and spirit failed him. But Akhilleus moved
toward Moulios and hit him with a spear-thrust
square on the left ear; the bronze point at once
punched through and out the ear on the right side.
Then he chopped Ekheklos, Agênor's son,
with his long, hilted sword, straight through his head,
and all the blade grew hot with blood, as dusky
death and destiny overcame the man.
Deukálión next he speared, where elbow tendons
held together, and the spearpoint pierced
through the man's arm. Standing with arm inert,
Deukálión waited, seeing death before him.
Akhilleus aimed a sword-cut at his neck
and knocked both head and helmet far away.
The fluid throbbed out of his vertebrae
as he lay stretched upon the earth. Akhilleus
turned to the noble son of Peirês, Rhigmos,
one who had come from the rich land of Thrace.
He jabbed him in the belly, and the spearhead
stuck in his bowels; he dropped from his chariot.
Just as his driver swung the team around
Akhilleus hit him with his spear between
the shoulder blades, jolting him from the car
as the horses panicked.

                                        A forest fire will rage
through deep glens of a mountain, crackling dry
from summer heat, and coppices blaze up
in every quarter as wind whips the flame:

so Akhilleus flashed to right and left
like a wild god, trampling the men he killed,
and black earth ran with blood. As when a countryman
yokes oxen with broad brows to tread out barley
on a well-bedded threshing floor, and quickly
the grain is husked under the bellowing beasts:
the sharp-hooved horses of Akhilleus just so
crushed dead men and shields. His axle-tree
was splashed with blood, so was his chariot rail,
with drops thrown up by wheels and horses' hooves.
And Pêleus' son kept riding for his glory,
staining his powerful arms with mire and blood.

BOOK TWENTY-ONE

The Clash of Man and River

As they came down to a ford in the blue Xánthos,
eddying and running, god-begotten
wondrous river, there Akhilleus drove
amid the rout and split them, left and right—
scattering half toward Troy over the plain
where yesterday Akhaians broke and ran
when Hektor raged. Now Trojans ran that way,
and Hêra spread a cloud ahead to slow them.
The other half were forced into the stream
now running high with foam on whirlpools. Down
they plunged, smacking the water, and the banks
and gullied beds echoed their hurly-burly.
This way and that they swam, shouting, spun round
and round by eddies. As when locusts flitter

before a prairie fire into a river,
tireless flames, leaping abruptly higher,
scorch them, and they crumple into the water:
so the currents rushing before Akhilleus
now grew choked with men and chariot-teams.

He left his spear propped on a tamarisk
by the riverbank, then like a wild god
he leapt in savagely for bloody work
with sword alone, and struck to right and left,
as cries and groans went up from men he slashed
and dark blood flushed the stream.

                                   As darting fish,
in flight before a dolphin, crowd the bays
of a great roadstead, terrified, for he
engorges all he catches: so the Trojans
cowered down the dangerous river's course
and under overhanging banks. Arm-wearied
by butchery, Akhilleus from the stream
picked twelve young men alive to pay the price
for dead Patróklos. He led these ashore,
startled as fawns, and bound their hands behind them,
using the well-cut thongs they wore as belts
round braided combat-shirts. He turned them over
to men of his command to be led back
to the decked ships, then launched himself again
on furious killing.

                                   At this point he met
a son of Priam, Prince Lykáôn,
scrambling from the river. Akhilleus once
on a night raid had captured this young man,
forced him out of his father's orchard, where
with a bronze knife he had been cutting boughs
of a wild fig for chariot rails: the raider
came like a ghost upon him, unforeseen.
That time Akhilleus sold him overseas
to Lemnos. Iêson's son had purchased him,
but he was freed by an old family friend,
Eëtíôn of Imbros, who gave passage
to the fair town Arísbê, whence in flight
he reached his father's hall. Being come again

from Lemnos, he enjoyed eleven days
with friends at home. On the twelfth day a god
returned him to the rough hands of Akhilleus,
who would dispatch him to the realm of Death.
The great battlefield runner, Prince Akhilleus,
found the man disarmed: he had no helm,
no shield, not even a spear; all were thrown down
when heat and sweat oppressed him as he toiled
to leave the stream, his knees sapped by fatigue.
Taken aback, grimly Akhilleus said
in his great heart:

                                        "God, here is a strange thing
to have before my eyes! Trojans I've killed
will stand up in the western gloom of death
if this one could return, his evil day
behind him—after I sold him, shipped him out
to Lemnos island. The great grey salt sea
that balks the will of many could not stop him.
Well, let him taste our spearhead now. Let me
absorb the answer: can it be he'll come
back from the grave, or will the fertile earth
detain him, as it does the strongest dead?"

Thus he reflected, waiting, and the other
came in a rush to clasp his knees, confused,
but mad with hope to escape the pain of death
and the black shape of destiny. Akhilleus
raised his long spear aiming to run him through.
Lykáôn ducked and ran and took his knees
even as the driven spear passed over, starved
for blood and raw manflesh, and stuck in earth.
Grasping one knee, the unarmed man held on
with his left hand to the spearshaft of Akhilleus,
and pled with him:

                                        "I come before your knees
Akhilleus: show respect, and pity me.
Pleader and plea are worth respect, your grace.
You were the first Akhaian at whose hands
I tasted the bruised barley of Dêmêtêr,
upon that day when, among orchard trees,

you captured me, then shipped me out to Lemnos
away from father and friends. I earned for you
a hundred bulls' worth. Triple that I'll bring
as ransom, this time. Twelve days have gone by
since I returned from my hard life abroad
to Ilion. But now sinister fate
has put me in your hands a second time:
in hate, somehow, Zeus guided me to you.
A man of short life—so my mother bore me,
Laóthoê, daughter of old Altês, lord
of the fighting Lélegês, who holds the rock
of Pêdasos upon the Satnióeis.
Priam, lover of many, loved his daughter,
and two of us were born of her; both men
you will have slaughtered. Aye, you killed my brother
amid foot soldiers, noble Polydôros—
brought him down with a spear-throw. And here
my evil hour has come. I see I cannot
get away from you; the will of heaven
forced us to meet. But think of one thing more:
don't kill me, since the belly where I grew
never held Hektor, never held the man
who killed your friend, that gentle and strong soldier."

In these terms Priam's son pled for his life,
but heard a voice of iron say:

"Young fool, don't talk to me of what you'll barter.
In days past, before Patróklos died
I had a mind to spare the Trojans, took them
alive in shoals, and shipped them out abroad.
But now there's not a chance—no man that heaven
puts in my hands will get away from death
here before Ilion—least of all a son
of Priam. Come, friend, face your death, you too.
And why are you so piteous about it?
Patróklos died, and he was a finer man
by far than you. You see, don't you, how large
I am, and how well-made? My father is noble,
a goddess bore me. Yet death waits for me,
for me as well, in all the power of fate.

A morning comes or evening or high noon
when someone takes my life away in war,
a spear-cast, or an arrow from a bowstring."

At this the young man's knees failed, and his heart;
he lost his grip upon the spear
and sank down, opening his arms. Akhilleus
drew his sword and thrust between his neck
and collarbone, so the two-edged blade went in
up to the hilt. Now face down on the ground
he lay stretched out, as dark blood flowed from him,
soaking the earth. Akhilleus picked him up
by one foot, wheeled, and slung him in the river
to be swept off downstream. Then he exulted:

"Nose down there with fishes. In cold blood
they'll kiss your wound and nip your blood away.
Your mother cannot put you on your bed
to mourn you, but Skamánder whirling down
will bear you to the sea's broad lap,
where any fish that jumps, breaking a wave,
may dart under the dark wind-shivered water
to nibble white fat of Lykáôn. Trojans,
perish in this rout until you reach,
and I behind you slaughtering reach, the town!
The god-begotten river swiftly flowing
will not save you. Many a bull you've offered,
many a trim-hooved horse thrown in alive
to Xánthos' whirlpools. All the same, you'll die
in blood until I have avenged Patróklos,
paid you back for the death-wounds of Akhaians
cut down near the deep-sea-going ships
far from my eyes."

                                        On hearing this, the river
darkened to the heart with rage. He cast
about for ways to halt prodigious Akhilleus'
feats of war and keep death from the Trojans.
Meanwhile the son of Pêleus took his spear
and bounded straight for Asteropaíos,
burning to kill this son of Pêlegôn,

whom the broad river Áxios had fathered
on Periboia, eldest of the daughters
of Akessámenos. Whirling, deep-running
river that he was, Áxios loved her.
And now Akhilleus made for Asteropaíos,
who came up from the stream-bed to confront him,
holding two spears. And Xánthos, in his anger
over all the young men dead, cut down
by Akhilleus pitilessly in the stream,
gave heart to this contender. As they drew near,
the great runner and prince was first to speak:

"Who are you, soldier? Where do you come from,
daring to challenge me? Grief comes to all
whose sons meet my anger."

Pêlegôn's
brave son replied:

"Heroic son of Pêleus,
why do you ask my birth? I am a native
of rich farmland, Paiônia; Paiônês
are the spearmen I command. Today the eleventh
dawn came up since I arrived at Ilion.
My line began, if you must know, with Áxios,
mover of beautiful water over land,
who fathered the great spearman, Pêlegôn,
and Pêlegôn is said to have fathered me.
But now again to battle, Lord Akhilleus."

That was his prideful answer. Then Akhilleus
lifted his Pêlian ash. His enemy,
being ambidextrous, cast both spears at once
and failed. With one he hit Akhilleus' shield
but could not pierce it, for the gold plate held,
the god's gift; with his other spear he grazed
the hero's right forearm. Dark blood ran out,
but, craving manflesh still, the spear passed on
and fixed itself in earth. In turn, Akhilleus,
putting his heart into the cast to bring down
Asteropaíos, rifled his ashwood spear.
He missed him, hitting the high bank of the river,

where the long shaft punched in to half its length.
The son of Pêleus, drawing sword from hip,
lunged forward on his enemy, who could not
with his big fist work the spear loose: three times
he tried to wrench it from the arching bank,
three times relaxed his grip, then put his weight
into a fourth attempt to break the shaft,
and bent it; but Akhilleus closed
and killed him with a sword stroke. Near the navel
he slashed his belly; all his bowels dropped out
uncoiling to the ground. He gasped, and darkness
veiled his eyes. Upon his chest Akhilleus
mounted, and then bent to strip his armor,
gloating:

                "This way you'll rest. It is rough work
to match yourself with children of Lord Zeus,
river's offspring though you are. You claimed
descent from a broad river; well, I claim
descent from Zeus almighty. My begetter,
lord over many Myrmidons, was Pêleus,
the son of Aíakos, a son of Zeus.
Zeus being stronger than the seaward rivers,
so are his offspring than a river's get!
Here's a big river for you, flowing by,
if he had power to help you. There's no fighting
Zeus the son of Krónos. Akhelôïos
cannot rival him; neither can the might
of the deep Ocean stream—from whom all rivers
take their waters, and all branching seas,
all springs and deep-sunk wells. And yet he too
is terrified by the lightning flash of Zeus
and thunder, when it crashes out of heaven."

With this he pulled from the bank's overhang
his bronze-shod spear, and, having torn the life
out of the body, left it there, to lie
in sand, where the dark water lapped at it.
Then eels and fish attended to the body,
picking and nibbling kidney fat away.

As for Akhilleus, he ran onward, chasing
spearmen of Paiônia in their rout
along the eddying river: these had seen
their hero vanquished by the hand and blade
and power of Akhilleus. Now he slew
Thersílokhos, Mydôn, and Astýpylos,
Mnêsos, Thrásios, Ainios, Ophelestês,
and would have killed far more, had not the river,
cold with rage, in likeness of a man,
assumed a voice and spoken from a whirlpool:

"O Akhilleus, you are first in power
of all men, first in waywardness as well,
as gods forever take your side. If Zeus
has given you all Trojans to destroy,
destroy them elsewhere, do your execution
out on the plain! Now my blue watercourses
back up, filled with dead; I cannot spend
my current in the salt immortal sea,
being dammed with corpses. Yet you go on killing
wantonly. Let be, marshal of soldiers."

Akhilleus the great runner answered:

                                        "Aye,
Skamánder, child of Zeus, as you require,
the thing shall be. But as for killing Trojans,
arrogant enemies, I take no rest
until I back them on the town and try out
Hektor, whether he gets the best of me
or I of him."

                        At this he hurled himself
upon the Trojans like a wild god. The deep
and swirling river then addressed Apollo:

"All wrong, bow of silver, child of Zeus!
You have not worked the will of Zeus. How often
he made you free to take the Trojan side!
You could defend them until sunset comes,
till evening darkens grainland."

                                        As he spoke,
the great spearman Akhilleus in a flash

leapt into midstream from the arching bank.
But he, the river, surged upon the man
with all his currents in a roaring flood,
and swept up many of the dead, who jostled
in him, killed by Akhilleus. He ejected
these to landward, bellowing like a bull,
but living men he kept in his blue streams
to hide them in deep places, in backwaters.
Then round Akhilleus with an ominous roar
a wave mounted. It fell against his shield
and staggered him, so that he lost his footing.
Throwing his arms around a leafy elm
he clung to it; it gave way, roots and all,
and tore the bank away, and dipped its branches
in the clear currents, damming up the river
when all had fallen in. The man broke free
of swirling water, turned into the plain
and ran like wind, in fear. But the great god
would not be shaken off: with his dark crest
he reared behind to put the Prince Akhilleus
out of action and protect the Trojans.
Akhilleus led him by a spear-throw, running
as fast as the black eagle, called the hunter,
strongest and swiftest of all birds: like him
he flashed ahead, and on his ribs the bronze
rang out with a fierce clang. At a wide angle
he fled, and the river with tremendous din
flowed on behind. Remember how a farmer
opens a ditch from a dark reservoir
to water plants or garden: with his mattock
he clears away the clods that dam the stream,
and as the water runs ahead, smooth pebbles
roll before it. With a purling sound
it snakes along the channel, going downhill,
outrunning him who leads it: so the wave
sent by the river overtook Akhilleus
momently, in spite of his great speed,
as gods are stronger than men are. Each time
the great battlefield runner, Prince Akhilleus,
turned to make a stand—to learn if all
the immortal gods who own the sweep of heaven
chased him—every time, the rain-fed river's

crest buffeted his back, and cursing
he leapt high in the air. Across his knees
the pressure of swift water tired him,
and sand was washed away under his feet.
Lifting his eyes to heaven, Akhilleus cried:

"Father Zeus, to think that in my travail
not one god would save me from the river—
only that! Then I could take the worst!
None of the gods of heaven is so to blame
as my own mother, who beguiled me, lying,
saying my end would come beneath Troy's wall
from flashing arrows of Apollo. Ah,
I wish Hektor had killed me; he's their best.
Then one brave man would have brought down another.
No, I was fated to ignoble death,
whelmed in a river, like a swineherd's boy
caught by a winter torrent as he crosses."

Now as he spoke, Poseidon and Athêna,
taking human form, moved near and stood,
and took his hands to tell him what would calm him.
Poseidon was the speaker:

                              "Son of Pêleus,
do not be shaken overmuch or fearful,
seeing what gods we are, your two allies,
by favor of Zeus—myself and Pallas Athêna.
The river is not destined to pull you down.
He will fall back, and you will soon perceive it.
Meanwhile here's good counsel, if you'll take it.
Do not allow your hands to rest from war—
from war that treats all men without distinction—
till you have rolled the Trojan army back
to Ilion, every man of them who runs,
and shut them in the wall. Then when you've taken
Hektor's life, retire upon the ships.
We give you glory; it is yours to win."

At this the two went off to join the gods.
Akhilleus, as their great directive stirred him,
crossed the plain, filled with flood water now,

where beautiful gear of slain men was afloat
and corpses, too. With high and plunging strides
he made his way in a rush against the current,
and the broad flooded river could not check him,
fired as he was with power by Athêna.
Skamánder, though, did not give up; his rage
redoubled, and he reared his foaming crest
with a hoarse shout to Simóeis:

                              "My own brother,
if we both try, can we not hold this man?
If not, he'll storm Lord Priam's tower soon;
the Trojans all in tumult won't resist him.
Give me a hand now, fill your channels up
with water from the springs, make dry beds brim,
and lift a wall of water: let it grind
and thump with logs and stones; we'll halt this madman,
powerful at the moment though he is,
with his intent to match the gods. I say
neither his great brawn nor his splendid form
will pull him through, nor those magnificent arms.
They will be sunk in mud under flood water.
As for the man, I'll roll him up in sand
and mound a ton of gravel round about him.
Akhaians who would gather up his bones
will have no notion how, in all the slime
I'll pack him in. And that will be his tomb;
no need for them to heap a barrow for him
when soldiers make his funeral."

                                        Now Xánthos
surged in turbulence upon Akhilleus,
tossing his crest, roaring with spume and blood
and corpses rolling, and a dark wave towering
out of the river fed by heaven swept
downward to overwhelm the son of Pêleus.
Hêra cried aloud in dread for him
whom the great raging stream might wash away,
and called to her dear son Hêphaistos:

                                            "Action,
Gamelegs, my own child! We thought you'd be

a match for whirling Xánthos in the battle.
Lend a hand, and quickly. Make your fire
blaze up. I'll be raising from the sea
a rough gale of the west wind and the south wind,
able to carry flames to burn the heads
and armor off the Trojans. Kindle trees
by Xánthos' banks, hurl fire at the river,
and do not let him put you off with threats
or honeyed speech. No slackening your fury!
Only when I call out, with a long cry,
withhold your living fire then."

                                        Hêphaistos

brought heaven's flame to bear: upon the plain
it broke out first, consuming many dead men
there from the number whom Akhilleus killed,
while all the plain was burned off and the shining
water stopped. As north wind in late summer
quickly dries an orchard freshly watered,
to the pleasure of the gardener, just so
the whole reach of the plain grew dry, as fire
burned the corpses. Then against the river
Hêphaistos turned his bright flame, and the elms
and tamarisks and willows burned away,
with all the clover, galingale, and rushes
plentiful along the winding streams.
Then eels and fish, in backwaters, in currents,
wriggled here and there at the scalding breath
of torrid blasts from the great smith, Hêphaistos,
and dried away by them, the river cried:

"Hêphaistos, not one god can vie with you!
Neither would I contend with one so fiery.
Break off the quarrel: let the Prince Akhilleus
drive the Trojans from their town. Am I
a party to that strife? Am I their savior?"

He spoke in steam, and his clear current seethed,
the way a caldron whipped by a white-hot fire
boils with a well-fed hog's abundant fat
that spatters all the rim, as dry split wood

turns ash beneath it. So his currents, fanned
by fire, seethed, and the river would not flow
but came to a halt, tormented by the gale
of fire from the heavenly smith, Hêphaistos.
Turning in prayer to Hêra, Xánthos said:

"Hêra, why did your son pick out my stream
from others to attack? You know
I merit this less than the other gods
who intervened for Trojans. Yet by heaven
if you command it, I'll give up the fight;
let the man, too, give up, and in the bargain
I swear never to interpose between
the Trojans and their day of wrath, that day
when all Troy blazes with consuming fire
kindled by the warriors of Akhaia."

Hêra whose arms are white as ivory
listened to this, then told her son Hêphaistos:

"Hold now, splendid child. It will not do
to vex an immortal river, for men."

At this Hêphaistos quenched his heavenly fire,
and back in its blue channels ran the wave.
And now that Xánthos had been overcome,
the two gods dropped their combat: Hêra, still
angry, checked them. Heavy and harsh strife,
however, came upon the rest, whose hearts
grew stormy on both sides against each other.
Now they attacked in uproar. The broad earth
resounded, and great heaven blared around them,
and Zeus, who heard from his Olympian seat,
laughed in his heart for joy, seeing the gods
about to meet in strife. And not for long
were they apart, now Arês the shield-cleaver
led them; first he lunged against Athêna,
gripping his bronze-shod spear and roaring at her:

"Why do you drive the gods to quarrel once more,
dogfly, with your bold and stormy ways,
and the violent heart that sets you on? Remember

telling Diomêdês to hit me hard?
Remember: you yourself, taking the spear
quite openly, made a thrust at me, and gashed
my noble flesh? Now in your turn, for that
and all you've done, I think you'll have to pay!"

With this he struck hard at the stormcloud shield
that trails the rain of heaven: even a bolt
from Zeus will not undo it. Blood-encrusted
Arês hit it with his giant spear.
Recoiling, in her great hand she picked up
a boulder lying there, black, jagged, massive,
left by the men of old as a boundary stone,
and hurling it hit Arês' neck. His knees
gave way and down he went on seven hundred
feet of earth, his long mane in the dust,
and armor clanged upon him. Laughing at him,
Athêna made her vaunt above him:

                                                    "Fool,
you've never learned how far superior
I'm glad to say I am. Stand up to me?
Lie there: you might fulfill your mother's curse,
baleful as she is, incensed at you,
because you switched to Trojans from Akhaians."

Now Aphrodítê, Zeus's daughter, taking
Arês' hand, began to help him away,
as he wheezed hard and fought to get his breath.
But Hêra saw her. She called out to Athéna:

"Daughter of Zeus the Stormking, what a couple!
There that dogfly goes, escorting Arês,
bane of mankind, out of the deadly war
amid the battle din. Go after them!"

Athêna followed, in a flash, with joy,
and from the side struck Aphrodítê's breast
with doubled fist, so that her knees went slack,
her heart faint, and together she and Arês
lay in a swoon upon the earth. Athêna
said derisively:

"If only
all the gods who would assist the Trojans
came to fight the Argives with such power!
If only they were bold as these, and tough
as Aphrodítê was, rescuing Arês
under my nose! In that case, long ago
we should have dropped the war—for long ago
we should have carried Ilion by storm."

At this Queen Hêra smiled. And the Earthshaker
said to Apollo:

                              "Phoibos, must we two
stay out of it? That isn't as it should be,
when others enter into action. More's
the pity if we go back without fighting
to Olympos, to the bronze doorsill of Zeus.
You take the lead, you are younger: it would be
awkward of me, since I was born before you,
know more than you do.

                              Idiot, but how
forgetful you have been! Don't you remember
even now, what troubles over Ilion
we alone among the gods have had,
when from the side of Zeus we came to serve
the strong man Laomédôn all one year
for a stated wage? Then he assigned our work,
no trifle for my own: I walled the city
massively in well-cut stone, to make
the place impregnable. You herded cattle,
slow and dark amid the upland vales
of Ida's wooded ridges. When the seasons
happily brought to an end our term of hire,
barbaric Laomédôn kept all wages
from us, and forced us out, with vile threats:
to bind us hand and foot, he said, and send us
in a slave ship to islands overseas—
but first to crop our ears with a bronze knife!
So we departed, burning inwardly
for payment he had promised and not made.
For this you coddle his people now? You are not

willing, like the rest of us, to see
the Trojans in their pride, with wives and children,
come utterly to ruin and to grief."

The lord of distant archery, Apollo,
answered:

                              "Lord of earthquake, sound of mind
you could not call me if I strove with you
for the sake of mortals, poor things that they are.
Ephemeral as the flamelike budding leaves,
men flourish on the ripe wheat of the grainland,
then in spiritless age they waste and die.
We should give up our fighting over men.
Let men themselves contend with one another."

On this he turned away. He would not face
his father's brother, hand to hand.
And now he was derided by his sister,
Lady Artemis, huntress of wild beasts,
who had her stinging word:

                              "In full retreat
are you, yielding victory to Poseidon,
making him pay nothing for his glory.
Idiot, why do you have your useless bow?
I'll never let you brag again
in Father's hall, among the gods,
that you'll oppose Poseidon in the battle."

To this, Archer Apollo made no answer,
but Hêra, Zeus's consort, did, in anger:

"How can you think to face me, shameless bitch?
A hard enemy I'll be for you, although
you carry a bow, and Zeus has made of you
a lioness to women. You have leave
to put to death any you choose. No matter:
better to rend wild beasts on mountainsides,
and woodland deer, than fight a stronger goddess.
If you want lessons in war, then you can learn
how I excel you, though you face me—"

                                                    Here
she took hold of the wrists of Artemis
in her left hand; with her right hand she snatched
her quiver and bow and boxed her ears with them,
smiling to see her duck her head, as arrows
showered from the quiver. Artemis
ran off in tears, as a wild dove, attacked
by a diving hawk, will fly to a hollow rock,
a narrow cleft where she cannot be taken.
So, weeping, she took flight and left her bow.
Then Hermês the Wayfinder said to Lêto:

"I would not dream of fighting you, so rough
seem the Cloudmaster's wives in fisticuffs.
No, you may make your boast quite happily
to all the immortal gods that you have beaten me!"

Lêto retrieved the bow of Artemis
and picked her arrows up where they had veered
and landed in a flurrying of dust.
Then she retired with her daughter's weapons.
Artemis reached Olympos, crossed the bronze
doorsill of Zeus, and at her father's knees
sank down, a weeping girl, her fragrant gown
in tremors on her breast. Her father hugged her,
asking with a mild laugh:

                                        "Who in heaven
injured you, dear child? Pure willfulness!
As though for a naughty act!"

                                        To this the mistress
of baying packs, her hair tied back, replied:

"Your lady, Hêra, buffeted me, father.
She of the snow-white arms, by whom the gods
are plagued with strife and bickering."

                                        While these two
conversed, Phoibos Apollo entered Ilion,
concerned for the wall, to keep the Danáän men
from storming it this day, before their time.
The other deathless ones went to Olympos,

some in anger, others enjoying triumph,
and took their chairs beside their father, lord
of stormcloud. But Akhilleus all that time
wrought havoc with the Trojans and their horses.
As a smoke column from a burning town
goes heavenward, propelled by the gods' anger,
grief to many a townsman, toil for all,
Akhilleus brought the Trojans harrowing grief.

Erect on Troy's great tower, aging Priam
gazed at huge Akhilleus, before whom
Trojans in tumult fled, and no defense
materialized. Then groaning from the tower
Priam descended. For the gatekeepers,
known as brave soldiers, he had urgent words:

"Keep the gates open, hold them, till the troops
retiring from battle are in the town.
There is Akhilleus, harrying them. Too near.
I fear we'll have a slaughter. When our soldiers
crowd inside the wall to get their breath,
close both your timbered gates, bolt them again.
I fear this murderous man may leap the wall."

At this they pushed the bolts, opening the gates,
and the gateway made a refuge. Then Apollo
flashed out to avert death from the Trojans,
headed as they were for the high wall,
men grown hoarse in thirst, covered with dust
out of the plain where they had run. Akhilleus,
wrought to a frenzy, pressed them with his spear,
all his great heart bent on winning glory.
Troy of the high gates might have fallen now
to the Akhaian soldiers, but Apollo
stirred the Prince Agênor, strong and noble
son of Antênor. Into this man's heart
the god sent courage, and stood near him, leaning
on an oak tree, concealed in heavy mist,
to guard him from the shapes and weight of death.
Agênor halted when he saw the raider
of cities, Akhilleus, and his heart grew large

as he awaited him, saying to himself
grimly:

                        "This is the end of me. If I break
and run before Akhilleus like the others,
he'll take me, even so: I'll have my throat
cut like a coward for my pains. What if
I let them go in panic toward the town
ahead of him, while I run at a tangent
leaving the wall, to cross the plain
until I reach the mountain slopes of Ida,
taking cover in undergrowth? This evening
after a river bath to cleanse my sweat,
I might return to Ilion. Why say it?
God forbid he sees me cutting away
from Troy into the open; in one sprint
he'll have me. After that, there's no escape
from my last end of death, so powerful
the man is, far beyond us all. Suppose
I meet him here, on the west approach to Troy?
Surely his body, even his, can be
wounded by sharp bronze; he can live but once;
men say he's mortal, though the son of Krónos,
Zeus, awards him glory."

                                     Even as he spoke,
he pulled himself together to face Akhilleus,
blood surging to his heart before the fight.
And as a panther out of underbrush
will go to meet a hunter, and have no fear,
and never falter when it hears the hounds;
and even though the hunter draw first blood,
the beast trailing the spear that wounded it
will not give up, until it close with him
or else go down: just so the Prince Agênor,
son of Antênor, would not now retreat
until he put Akhilleus to the test.
With round shield held before him, and his spear
aimed at the man, he gave a battle shout
and cried:

                        "You hoped today at last to storm
the city of the Trojans. A rash hope.

Grief and wounds are still to be suffered for her.
Inside there, we are many fighting men.
For our dear parents, wives, and sons, we'll hold
the city and defend it. You come here
to meet your doom, prodigious though you are,
sure as you are in warfare."

                                        He let fly

the sharp spear from his heavy hand and struck
the shin below the kneecap square and hard.
Around his leg the new shinguard of tin
rang out deafeningly; back from the point
of impact sprang the spearhead, piercing nothing,
buffeted back by the god's gift.

                              Then Akhilleus

struck in turn at his princely enemy,
Agênor, but Apollo
would not let him win this glory now.
He whisked away Agênor, hid him in mist,
and quietly removed him from the war.
By trickery then he kept the son of Pêleus
away from Trojan soldiers: taking Agênor's
likeness to the last detail, he halted
within range of Akhilleus, who set off
to chase him. For a long time down the plain
of grainland he pursued him, heading him
along Skamánder, as the god kept a bare lead—
for so Apollo teased him on; Akhilleus
thought to catch his quarry with a sprint.
Meanwhile the other Trojans in their panic
reached the walled town, thanking heaven, and all
the city filled up, jammed with men. They dared not
wait outside the wall for one another,
to learn who died in battle, who came through,
but all whose legs had saved them now took cover,
in hot haste entering the city.

BOOK TWENTY-TWO

Desolation Before Troy

Once in the town, those who had fled like deer
wiped off their sweat and drank their thirst away,
leaning against the cool stone of the ramparts.
Meanwhile Akhaians with bright shields aslant
came up the plain and nearer. As for Hektor,
fatal destiny pinned him where he stood
before the Skaian Gates, outside the city.

Now Akhilleus heard Apollo calling
back to him:

                              "Why run so hard, Akhilleus,
mortal as you are, after a god?
Can you not comprehend it? I am immortal.
You are so hot to catch me, you no longer
think of finishing off the men you routed.

They are all in the town by now, packed in
while you were being diverted here. And yet
you cannot kill me; I am no man's quarry."

Akhilleus bit his lip and said:

"Archer of heaven, deadliest
of immortal gods, you put me off the track,
turning me from the wall this way. A hundred
might have sunk their teeth into the dust
before one man took cover in Ilion!
You saved my enemies with ease and stole
my glory, having no punishment to fear.
I'd take it out of you, if I had the power."

Then toward the town with might and main he ran,
magnificent, like a racing chariot horse
that holds its form at full stretch on the plain.
So light-footed Akhilleus held the pace.
And aging Priam was the first to see him
sparkling on the plain, bright as that star
in autumn rising, whose unclouded rays
shine out amid a throng of stars at dusk—
the one they call Oríôn's dog, most brilliant,
yes, but baleful as a sign: it brings
great fever to frail men. So pure and bright
the bronze gear blazed upon him as he ran.
The old man gave a cry. With both his hands
thrown up on high he struck his head, then shouted,
groaning, appealing to his dear son. Unmoved,
Lord Hektor stood in the gateway, resolute
to fight Akhilleus.

                              Stretching out his hands,
old Priam said, imploring him:

                                        "No, Hektor!
Cut off as you are, alone, dear son,
don't try to hold your ground against this man,
or soon you'll meet the shock of doom, borne down
by the son of Pêleus. He is more powerful
by far than you, and pitiless. Ah, were he
but dear to the gods as he is dear to me!

Wild dogs and kites would eat him where he lay
within the hour, and ease me of my torment.
Many tall sons he killed, bereaving me,
or sold them to far islands. Even now
I cannot see two sons of mine, Lykáôn
and Polydôros, among the Trojans massed
inside the town. A queen, Laóthoê,
conceived and bore them. If they are alive
amid the Akhaian host, I'll ransom them
with bronze and gold: both I have, piled at home,
rich treasures that old Altês, the renowned,
gave for his daughter's dowry. If they died,
if they went under to the homes of Death,
sorrow has come to me and to their mother.
But to our townsmen all this pain is brief,
unless you too go down before Akhilleus.
Come inside the wall, child; here you may
fight on to save our Trojan men and women.
Do not resign the glory to Akhilleus,
losing your own dear life! Take pity, too,
on me and my hard fate, while I live still.
Upon the threshold of my age, in misery,
the son of Krónos will destroy my life
after the evil days I shall have seen—
my sons brought down, my daughters dragged away,
bedchambers ravaged, and small children hurled
to earth in the atrocity of war,
as my sons' wives are taken by Akhaians'
ruinous hands. And at the end, I too—
when someone with a sword-cut or a spear
has had my life—I shall be torn apart
on my own doorstep by the hounds
I trained as watchdogs, fed from my own table.
These will lap my blood with ravenous hearts
and lie in the entranceway.

                                    Everything done
to a young man killed in war becomes his glory,
once he is riven by the whetted bronze:
dead though he be, it is all fair, whatever
happens then. But when an old man falls,
and dogs disfigure his grey head and cheek

and genitals, that is most harrowing
of all that men in their hard lives endure."

The old man wrenched at his grey hair and pulled out
hanks of it in both his hands, but moved
Lord Hektor not at all. The young man's mother
wailed from the tower across, above the portal,
streaming tears, and loosening her robe
with one hand, held her breast out in the other,
saying:

                              "Hektor, my child, be moved by this,
and pity me, if ever I unbound
a quieting breast for you. Think of these things,
dear child; defend yourself against the killer
this side of the wall, not hand to hand.
He has no pity. If he brings you down,
I shall no longer be allowed to mourn you
laid out on your bed, dear branch in flower,
born of me! And neither will your lady,
so endowed with gifts. Far from us both,
dogs will devour you by the Argive ships."

With tears and cries the two implored their son,
and made their prayers again, but could not shake him.
Hektor stood firm, as huge Akhilleus neared.
The way a serpent, fed on poisonous herbs,
coiled at his lair upon a mountainside,
with all his length of hate awaits a man
and eyes him evilly: so Hektor, grim
and narrow-eyed, refused to yield. He leaned
his brilliant shield against a spur of wall
and in his brave heart bitterly reflected:

"Here I am badly caught. If I take cover,
slipping inside the gate and wall, the first
to accuse me for it will be Poulýdamas,
he who told me I should lead the Trojans
back to the city on that cursed night
Akhilleus joined the battle. No, I would not,
would not, wiser though it would have been.
Now troops have perished for my foolish pride,

I am ashamed to face townsmen and women.
Someone inferior to me may say:
'He kept his pride and lost his men, this Hektor!'
So it will go. Better, when that time comes,
that I appear as he who killed Akhilleus
man to man, or else that I went down
before him honorably for the city's sake.
Suppose, though, that I lay my shield and helm
aside, and prop my spear against the wall,
and go to meet the noble Prince Akhilleus,
promising Helen, promising with her
all treasures that Aléxandros brought home
by ship to Troy—the first cause of our quarrel—
that he may give these things to the Atreidai?
Then I might add, apart from these, a portion
of all the secret wealth the city owns.
Yes, later I might take our counselors' oath
to hide no stores, but share and share alike
to halve all wealth our lovely city holds,
all that is here within the walls. Ah, no,
why even put the question to myself?
I must not go before him and receive
no quarter, no respect! Aye, then and there
he'll kill me, unprotected as I am,
my gear laid by, defenseless as a woman.
No chance, now, for charms from oak or stone
in parley with him—charms a girl and boy
might use when they enchant each other talking!
Better we duel, now at once, and see
to whom the Olympian awards the glory."
These were his shifts of mood. Now close at hand
Akhilleus like the implacable god of war
came on with blowing crest, hefting the dreaded
beam of Pêlian ash on his right shoulder.
Bronze light played around him, like the glare
of a great fire or the great sun rising,
and Hektor, as he watched, began to tremble.
Then he could hold his ground no more. He ran,
leaving the gate behind him, with Akhilleus
hard on his heels, sure of his own speed.
When that most lightning-like of birds, a hawk

bred on a mountain, swoops upon a dove,
the quarry dips in terror, but the hunter,
screaming, dips behind and gains upon it,
passionate for prey. Just so, Akhilleus
murderously cleft the air, as Hektor
ran with flashing knees along the wall.
They passed the lookout point, the wild figtree
with wind in all its leaves, then veered away
along the curving wagon road, and came
to where the double fountains well, the source
of eddying Skamánder. One hot spring
flows out, and from the water fumes arise
as though from fire burning; but the other
even in summer gushes chill as hail
or snow or crystal ice frozen on water.
Near these fountains are wide washing pools
of smooth-laid stone, where Trojan wives and daughters
laundered their smooth linen in the days
of peace before the Akhaians came. Past these
the two men ran, pursuer and pursued,
and he who fled was noble, he behind
a greater man by far. They ran full speed,
and not for bull's hide or a ritual beast
or any prize that men compete for: no,
but for the life of Hektor, tamer of horses.
Just as when chariot-teams around a course
go wheeling swiftly, for the prize is great,
a tripod or a woman, in the games
held for a dead man, so three times these two
at full speed made their course round Priam's town,
as all the gods looked on. And now the father
of gods and men turned to the rest and said:

"How sad that this beloved man is hunted
around the wall before my eyes! My heart
is touched for Hektor; he has burned thigh flesh
of oxen for me often, high on Ida,
at other times on the high point of Troy.
Now Prince Akhilleus with devouring stride
is pressing him around the town of Priam.
Come, gods, put your minds on it, consider

whether we may deliver him from death
or see him, noble as he is, brought down
by Pêleus' son, Akhilleus."

                              Grey-eyed Athêna
said to him:

                                    "Father of the blinding bolt,
the dark stormcloud, what words are these? The man
is mortal, and his doom fixed, long ago.
Would you release him from his painful death?
Then do so, but not all of us will praise you."

Zeus who gathers cloud replied:

                                          "Take heart,
my dear and honored child. I am not bent
on my suggestion, and I would indulge you.
Act as your thought inclines, refrain no longer."

So he encouraged her in her desire,
and down she swept from ridges of Olympos.
Great Akhilleus, hard on Hektor's heels,
kept after him, the way a hound will harry
a deer's fawn he has startled from its bed
to chase through gorge and open glade, and when
the quarry goes to earth under a bush
he holds the scent and quarters till he finds it;
so with Hektor: he could not shake off
the great runner, Akhilleus. Every time
he tried to sprint hard for the Dardan gates
under the towers, hoping men could help him,
sending missiles down, Akhilleus loomed
to cut him off and turn him toward the plain,
as he himself ran always near the city.
As in a dream a man chasing another
cannot catch him, nor can he in flight
escape from his pursuer, so Akhilleus
could not by his swiftness overtake him,
nor could Hektor pull away. How could he
run so long from death, had not Apollo

for the last time, the very last, come near
to give him stamina and speed?

                                        Akhilleus

shook his head at the rest of the Akhaians,
allowing none to shoot or cast at Hektor—
none to forestall him, and to win the honor.
But when, for the fourth time, they reached the springs,
the Father poised his golden scales.

                                        He placed

two shapes of death, death prone and cold, upon them,
one of Akhilleus, one of the horseman, Hektor,
and held the midpoint, pulling upward. Down
sank Hektor's fatal day, the pan went down
toward undergloom, and Phoibos Apollo left him.
Then came Athêna, grey-eyed, to the son
of Pêleus, falling in with him, and near him,
saying swiftly:

                                        "Now at last I think

the two of us, Akhilleus loved by Zeus,
shall bring Akhaians triumph at the ships
by killing Hektor—unappeased
though he was ever in his thirst for war.
There is no way he may escape us now,
not though Apollo, lord of distances,
should suffer all indignity for him
before his father Zeus who bears the stormcloud,
rolling back and forth and begging for him.
Now you can halt and take your breath, while I
persuade him into combat face to face."

These were Athêna's orders. He complied,
relieved, and leaning hard upon the spearshaft
armed with its head of bronze. She left him there
and overtook Lord Hektor—but she seemed
Dêíphobos in form and resonant voice,
appearing at his shoulder, saying swiftly:

"Ai! Dear brother, how he runs, Akhilleus,
harrying you around the town of Priam!
Come, we'll stand and take him on."

To this,
great Hektor in his shimmering helm replied:

"Dêíphobos, you were the closest to me
in the old days, of all my brothers, sons
of Hékabê and Priam. Now I can say
I honor you still more
because you dared this foray for my sake,
seeing me run. The rest stay under cover."

Again the grey-eyed goddess Athêna spoke:

"Dear brother, how your father and gentle mother
begged and begged me to remain! So did
the soldiers round me, all undone by fear.
But in my heart I ached for you.
Now let us fight him, and fight hard.
No holding back. We'll see if this Akhilleus
conquers both, to take our armor seaward,
or if he can be brought down by your spear."

This way, by guile, Athêna led him on.
And when at last the two men faced each other,
Hektor was the first to speak. He said:

"I will no longer fear you as before,
son of Pêleus, though I ran from you
round Priam's town three times and could not face you.
Now my soul would have me stand and fight,
whether I kill you or am killed. So come,
we'll summon gods here as our witnesses,
none higher, arbiters of a pact: I swear
that, terrible as you are,
I'll not insult your corpse should Zeus allow me
victory in the end, your life as prize.
Once I have your gear, I'll give your body
back to Akhaians. Grant me, too, this grace."

But swift Akhilleus frowned at him and said:

"Hektor, I'll have no talk of pacts with you,
forever unforgiven as you are.
As between men and lions there are none,

no concord between wolves and sheep, but all
hold one another hateful through and through,
so there can be no courtesy between us,
no sworn truce, till one of us is down
and glutting with his blood the wargod Arês.
Summon up what skills you have. By god,
you'd better be a spearman and a fighter!
Now there is no way out. Pallas Athêna
will have the upper hand of you. The weapon
belongs to me. You'll pay the reckoning
in full for all the pain my men have borne,
who met death by your spear."

                             He twirled and cast
his shaft with its long shadow. Splendid Hektor,
keeping his eye upon the point, eluded it
by ducking at the instant of the cast,
so shaft and bronze shank passed him overhead
and punched into the earth. But unperceived
by Hektor, Pallas Athêna plucked it out
and gave it back to Akhilleus. Hektor said:

"A clean miss. Godlike as you are,
you have not yet known doom for me from Zeus.
You thought you had, by heaven. Then you turned
into a word-thrower, hoping to make me lose
my fighting heart and head in fear of you.
You cannot plant your spear between my shoulders
while I am running. If you have the gift,
just put it through my chest as I come forward.
Now it's for you to dodge my own. Would god
you'd give the whole shaft lodging in your body!
War for the Trojans would be eased
if you were blotted out, bane that you are."

With this he twirled his long spearshaft and cast it,
hitting his enemy mid-shield, but off
and away the spear rebounded. Furious
that he had lost it, made his throw for nothing,
Hektor stood bemused. He had no other.
Then he gave a great shout to Dêíphobos

to ask for a long spear. But there was no one
near him, not a soul. Now in his heart
the Trojan realized the truth and said:

"This is the end. The gods are calling deathward.
I had thought
a good soldier, Dêíphobos, was with me.
He is inside the walls. Athêna tricked me.
Death is near, and black, not at a distance,
not to be evaded. Long ago
this hour must have been to Zeus's liking
and to the liking of his archer son.
They have been well disposed before, but now
the appointed time's upon me. Still, I would not
die without delivering a stroke,
or die ingloriously, but in some action
memorable to men in days to come."

With this he drew the whetted blade that hung
upon his left flank, ponderous and long,
collecting all his might the way an eagle
narrows himself to dive through shady cloud
and strike a lamb or cowering hare: so Hektor
lanced ahead and swung his whetted blade.
Akhilleus with wild fury in his heart
pulled in upon his chest his beautiful shield—
his helmet with four burnished metal ridges
nodding above it, and the golden crest
Hêphaistos locked there tossing in the wind.
Conspicuous as the evening star that comes,
amid the first in heaven, at fall of night,
and stands most lovely in the west, so shone
in sunlight the fine-pointed spear
Akhilleus poised in his right hand, with deadly
aim at Hektor, at the skin where most
it lay exposed. But nearly all was covered
by the bronze gear he took from slain Patróklos,
showing only, where his collarbones
divided neck and shoulders, the bare throat
where the destruction of a life is quickest.
Here, then, as the Trojan charged, Akhilleus

drove his point straight through the tender neck,
but did not cut the windpipe, leaving Hektor
able to speak and to respond. He fell
aside into the dust. And Prince Akhilleus
now exulted:

> "Hektor, had you thought
that you could kill Patróklos and be safe?
Nothing to dread from me; I was not there.
All childishness. Though distant then, Patróklos'
comrade in arms was greater far than he—
and it is I who had been left behind
that day beside the deepsea ships who now
have made your knees give way. The dogs and kites
will rip your body. His will lie in honor
when the Akhaians give him funeral."

Hektor, barely whispering, replied:

"I beg you by your soul and by your parents,
do not let the dogs feed on me
in your encampment by the ships. Accept
the bronze and gold my father will provide
as gifts, my father and her ladyship
my mother. Let them have my body back,
so that our men and women may accord me
decency of fire when I am dead."

Akhilleus the great runner scowled and said:

"Beg me no beggary by soul or parents,
whining dog! Would god my passion drove me
to slaughter you and eat you raw, you've caused
such agony to me! No man exists
who could defend you from the carrion pack—
not if they spread for me ten times your ransom,
twenty times, and promise more as well;
aye, not if Priam, son of Dárdanos,
tells them to buy you for your weight in gold!
You'll have no bed of death, nor will you be
laid out and mourned by her who gave you birth.
Dogs and birds will have you, every scrap."

Then at the point of death Lord Hektor said:

"I see you now for what you are. No chance
to win you over. Iron in your breast
your heart is. Think a bit, though: this may be
a thing the gods in anger hold against you
on that day when Paris and Apollo
destroy you at the Gates, great as you are."

Even as he spoke, the end came, and death hid him;
spirit from body fluttered to undergloom,
bewailing fate that made him leave his youth
and manhood in the world. And as he died
Akhilleus spoke again. He said:

"Die, make an end. I shall accept my own
whenever Zeus and the other gods desire."

At this he pulled his spearhead from the body,
laying it aside, and stripped
the bloodstained shield and cuirass from his shoulders.
Other Akhaians hastened round to see
Hektor's fine body and his comely face,
and no one came who did not stab the body.
Glancing at one another they would say:

"Now Hektor has turned vulnerable, softer
than when he put the torches to the ships!"

And he who said this would inflict a wound.
When the great master of pursuit, Akhilleus,
had the body stripped, he stood among them,
saying swiftly:

                              "Friends, my lords and captains
of Argives, now that the gods at last have let me
bring to earth this man who wrought
havoc among us—more than all the rest—
come, we'll offer battle around the city,
to learn the intentions of the Trojans now.
Will they give up their strongpoint at this loss?
Can they fight on, though Hektor's dead?

But wait:
why do I ponder, why take up these questions?
Down by the ships Patróklos' body lies
unwept, unburied. I shall not forget him
while I can keep my feet among the living.
If in the dead world they forget the dead,
I say there, too, I shall remember him,
my friend. Men of Akhaia, lift a song!
Down to the ships we go, and take this body,
our glory. We have beaten Hektor down,
to whom as to a god the Trojans prayed."

Indeed, he had in mind for Hektor's body
outrage and shame. Behind both feet he pierced
the tendons, heel to ankle. Rawhide cords
he drew through both and lashed them to his chariot,
letting the man's head trail. Stepping aboard,
bearing the great trophy of the arms,
he shook the reins, and whipped the team ahead
into a willing run. A dustcloud rose
above the furrowing body; the dark tresses
flowed behind, and the head so princely once
lay back in dust. Zeus gave him to his enemies
to be defiled in his own fatherland.
So his whole head was blackened. Looking down,
his mother tore her braids, threw off her veil,
and wailed, heartbroken to behold her son.
Piteously his father groaned, and round him
lamentation spread throughout the town,
most like the clamor to be heard if Ilion's
towers, top to bottom, seethed in flames.
They barely stayed the old man, mad with grief,
from passing through the gates. Then in the mire
he rolled, and begged them all, each man by name:

"Relent, friends. It is hard; but let me go
out of the city to the Akhaian ships.
I'll make my plea to that demonic heart.
He may feel shame before his peers, or pity
my old age. His father, too, is old,
Pêleus, who brought him up to be a scourge

to Trojans, cruel to all, but most to me,
so many of my sons in flower of youth
he cut away. And, though I grieve, I cannot
mourn them all as much as I do one,
for whom my grief will take me to the grave—
and that is Hektor. Why could he not have died
where I might hold him? In our weeping, then,
his mother, now so destitute, and I
might have had surfeit and relief of tears."

These were the words of Priam as he wept,
and all his people groaned. Then in her turn
Hékabê led the women in lamentation:

"Child, I am lost now. Can I bear my life
after the death of suffering your death?
You were my pride in all my nights and days,
pride of the city, pillar to the Trojans
and Trojan women. Everyone looked to you
as though you were a god, and rightly so.
You were their greatest glory while you lived.
Now your doom and death have come upon you."

These were her mournful words. But Hektor's lady
still knew nothing; no one came to tell her
of Hektor's stand outside the gates. She wove
upon her loom, deep in the lofty house,
a double purple web with rose design.
Calling her maids in waiting,
she ordered a big caldron on a tripod
set on the hearthfire, to provide a bath
for Hektor when he came home from the fight.
Poor wife, how far removed from baths he was
she could not know, as at Akhilleus' hands
Athêna brought him down.

                       Then from the tower
she heard a wailing and a distant moan.
Her knees shook, and she let her shuttle fall,
and called out to her maids again:

                             "Come here.
Two must follow me, to see this action.

I heard my husband's queenly mother cry.
I feel my heart rise, throbbing in my throat.
My knees are like stone under me. Some blow
is coming home to Priam's sons and daughters.
Ah, could it never reach my ears! I die
of dread that Akhilleus may have cut off Hektor,
blocked my bold husband from the city wall,
to drive him down the plain alone! By now
he may have ended Hektor's deathly pride.
He never kept his place amid the chariots
but drove ahead. He would not be outdone
by anyone in courage."

                                        Saying this, she ran
like a madwoman through the mégaron,
her heart convulsed. Her maids kept at her side.
On reaching the great tower and the soldiers,
Andrómakhê stood gazing from the wall
and saw him being dragged before the city.
Chariot horses at a brutal gallop
pulled the torn body toward the decked ships.
Blackness of night covered her eyes; she fell
backward swooning, sighing out her life,
and let her shining headdress fall, her hood
and diadem, her plaited band and veil
that Aphrodítê once had given her,
on that day when, from Eëtíôn's house,
for a thousand bridal gifts, Lord Hektor led her.
Now, at her side, kinswomen of her lord
supported her among them, dazed and faint
to the point of death. But when she breathed again
and her stunned heart recovered, in a burst
of sobbing she called out among the women:

"Hektor! Here is my desolation. Both
had this in store from birth—from yours in Troy
in Priam's palace, mine by wooded Plakos
at Thêbê in the home of Eëtíôn,
my father, who took care of me in childhood,
a man cursed by fate, a fated daughter.
How I could wish I never had been born!

Now under earth's roof to the house of Death
you go your way and leave me here, bereft,
lonely, in anguish without end. The child
we wretches had is still in infancy;
you cannot be a pillar to him, Hektor,
now you are dead, nor he to you. And should
this boy escape the misery of the war,
there will be toil and sorrow for him later,
as when strangers move his boundary stones.
The day that orphans him will leave him lonely,
downcast in everything, cheeks wet with tears,
in hunger going to his father's friends
to tug at one man's cloak, another's khiton.
Some will be kindly: one may lift a cup
to wet his lips at least, though not his throat;
but from the board some child with living parents
gives him a push, a slap, with biting words:
'Outside, you there! Your father is not with us
here at our feast!' And the boy Astýanax
will run to his forlorn mother. Once he fed
on marrow only and the fat of lamb,
high on his father's knees. And when sleep came
to end his play, he slept in a nurse's arms,
brimful of happiness, in a soft bed.
But now he'll know sad days and many of them,
missing his father. 'Lord of the lower town'
the Trojans call him. They know, you alone,
Lord Hektor, kept their gates and their long walls.
Beside the beaked ships now, far from your kin,
the blowflies' maggots in a swarm will eat you
naked, after the dogs have had their fill.
Ah, there are folded garments in your chambers,
delicate and fine, of women's weaving.
These, by heaven, I'll burn to the last thread
in blazing fire! They are no good to you,
they cannot cover you in death. So let them
go, let them be burnt as an offering
from Trojans and their women in your honor."

Thus she mourned, and the women wailed in answer.

BOOK TWENTY-THREE

A Friend Consigned to Death

That was the way they grieved at Troy. Retiring
shoreward to the beach and Hellê's waters,
each to his ship, Akhaians turned away,
but not the Myrmidons. Akhilleus held them
undismissed, and spoke among these fighters:

"Chariot-skirmishers, friends of my heart,
we'll not unharness our good horses now
but in our war-cars filing near Patróklos
mourn him in line. That is fit honor paid
to a captain fallen. When we've gained relief
in lamentation, we can free the teams
and take our evening meal here."

                                              With one voice
they all cried out in sorrow, and he led them,

driving their teams with wind-blown manes three times
around the body, weeping, and among them
Thetis roused their longing to lament.
The sandy field, the gear of men grew wet
with salt tears, for they missed him bitterly,
the man who turned the battle-tide. Akhilleus
led them in repeated cries of grief,
laying his deadly hands upon his friend:

"Patróklos, peace be with you in the dark
where Death commands, aye, even there. You see
I shall have soon done all I promised you:
I dragged Hektor this far, to give wild dogs
his flesh and let them rend it among themselves,
and I have brought twelve radiant sons of Troy
whose throats I'll cut, to bloody your great pyre,
such fury came upon me at your death."

Shameless abuse indeed he planned for Hektor,
and laid the body face down in the dust
beside Patróklos' bed of death. His soldiers
now unbuckled all their brazen gear,
freed the whinnying horses of their harness,
and sat down, in their hundreds, all before
Akhilleus' ship. Then to their heart's desire
he made the funeral feast. Sleek oxen, many,
bellowed and fell slack on the iron blade
in slaughter; many sheep and bleating goats
and tuskers ruffed in fat. These beasts were singed,
then held out spitted in Hêphaistos' flame,
and blood ran streaming down around the body.

Akhaian peers induced Akhilleus now—
barely prevailing on his grief and rage—
to visit the Lord Agamémnon;
and when they came up to the Marshal's hut
they bade the clear-voiced criers there
set out a tripod caldron on the fire,
thinking Akhilleus might wash off the blood
that stained his body. He would not hear of it,
but swore:

"By Zeus, I will not! By that god
best and all-highest, it is not in order
to bring hot water near me, till I lay
Patróklos on his pyre, and heap his barrow,
and shear my hair. No burden like this grief
will come a second time upon my heart,
while I remain among the living.

                                                    Now,

by heaven, we'll consent to the grim feast.
At first light turn the men out, my Lord Marshal,
to bring in all the firewood required
that the dead man may reach the gloomy west;
then let strong fire hide and consume the corpse;
and let the troops return to duty."

So he spoke, and they listened and obeyed him,
busied themselves with dinner, took their meat,
and no one lacked his portion of the feast.
When they had put their hunger and thirst away,
the rest retired, each man to his hut,
but on the sea beach near the wash and ebb
Akhilleus lay down groaning among his men,
his Myrmidons, on a bare open place
where breakers rolled in spume upon the shore.
Pursuing Hektor around windy Troy
he had worn out his legs. Now restful floods
of sleep, dissolving heartache, came upon him,
and soon forlorn Patróklos' shade came near—
a perfect likeness of the man, in height,
fine eyes, and voice, and dressed in his own fashion.
The image stood above him and addressed him:

"Sleeping so? Thou hast forgotten me,
Akhilleus. Never was I uncared for
in life but am in death. Accord me burial
in all haste: let me pass the gates of Death.
Shades that are images of used-up men
motion me away, will not receive me
among their hosts beyond the river. I wander
about the wide gates and the hall of Death.
Give me your hand. I sorrow.

When thou shalt have allotted me my fire
I will not fare here from the dark again.
As living men we'll no more sit apart
from our companions, making plans. The day
of wrath appointed for me at my birth
engulfed and took me down. Thou too, Akhilleus,
face iron destiny, godlike as thou art,
to die under the wall of highborn Trojans.
One more message, one behest, I leave thee:
not to inter my bones apart from thine
but close together, as we grew together,
in thy family's hall. Menoitios
from Opoeis had brought me, under a cloud,
a boy still, on the day I killed the son
of Lord Amphídamas—though I wished it not—
in childish anger over a game of dice.
Pêleus, master of horse, adopted me
and reared me kindly, naming me your squire.
So may the same urn hide our bones, the one
of gold your gracious mother gave."

                                                    Akhilleus
spoke in answer, saying:

                                            "Dear old friend,
why comest hither, and why these demands?
I shall bring all to pass for thee; I shall
comply with all thy bidding. Only stand
nearer to me. For this little time
may we embrace and take our fill of tears."

He stretched his arms out but took hold of nothing,
as into earth Patróklos' shade like smoke
retreated with a faint cry. Then Akhilleus
rose in wonderment and clapped his hands,
and slowly said:

                                        "A wisp of life remains
in the undergloom of Death: a visible form,
though no heart beats within it. All this night
the shade of poor Patróklos bent above me

grieving and weeping, charging me with tasks.
It seemed to the life the very man."

                                                            At this
the Myrmidons were stirred again to weep.
Then Dawn with rose-red fingers in the east
began to glow upon them as they mourned
around the pitiful body.

                                                            Agamémnon
ordered out mules and men from every hut
to forage firewood. As overseer
went that good man Meríonês, lieutenant
of staunch Idómeneus. The troops filed out
with loggers' axes and tough plaited rope,
while mules plodded ahead of the working party.
Up hill and down, and cutting across the slopes,
they tramped until they came to Ida's valleys.
There at once they pitched in, hewing hard
with whetted axes at the towering oaks
until they came down crashing. The Akhaians
trimmed and split the trunks and lashed the logs
on muleback. Laden mules broke up the ground
and trod out paths through underbrush, descending
eagerly to the plain, while all the axmen
carried logs as well; Meríonês
had so commanded. On the shore they stacked
their burdens in a woodpile, where Akhilleus
planned Patróklos' barrow and his own;
then, having heaped a four-square mass of timber,
all sat down together. Now Akhilleus
ordered his veteran Myrmidons to arm
and yoke their horses to the chariots.
They rose and put their gear on. Chariot fighters
mounted with drivers in the cars, and these
moved out ahead; behind, a cloud of infantry
followed. In between, his old companions
bore Patróklos, covering the corpse
with locks of hair they sheared off and let fall.
Akhilleus held the head in grief; his friend
he would consign now to the world of Death.
When they had reached the place Akhilleus chose

they put the body down and built the pyre
of timber, high as they could wish. Akhilleus
turned to another duty now. Apart
from the pyre he stood and cut the red-gold hair
that he had grown for the river Sperkheios.
Gazing over the winedark sea in pain,
he said:

                     "Sperkheios, Pêleus my father's vow
to you meant nothing, that on my return
I'd cut my hair as an offering to you,
along with fifty sheep ungelded, slain
at your headwaters, where your park and altar
fragrant with incense are. The old man swore it,
but you would not fulfill what he desired.
Now, as I shall not see my fatherland,
I would confer my hair upon the soldier
Patróklos."

                     And he closed his dear friend's hands
upon it, moving all to weep again.
The sun would have gone down upon their weeping
had not Akhilleus quickly turned and said
to Agamémnon:

                     "Sir, troops act at once
on your command. Men may grow sick of tears.
Dismiss these from the pyre to make a meal,
and we who are closest to the dead will care
for what is to be done now. Let each captain
stay with us here."

                     On hearing this, the Marshal
Agamémnon made the troops disperse
at once to their own ships. Close friends remained.
They added timber and enlarged the pyre
to a hundred feet a side. On top of it
with heavy hearts they laid the dead man down.
Sheep and shambling cattle, then, in droves
they sacrificed and dressed before the pyre.
Taking fat from all, splendid Akhilleus
sheathed the body head to foot. He piled

flayed carcasses around it. Amphorae
of honey and unguent he arranged in order,
tilted against the bier. He slung the bodies
of four fine horses on the pyre, and groaned.
Nine hunting dogs had fed at the lord's table;
upon the pyre he cut the throats of two,
but as for the noble sons of Troy, all twelve
he put to the sword, as he willed their evil hour.
Then in the midst he thrust the pitiless might
of fire to feed upon them all, and cried
upon his dead companion:

                                        "Peace be with you
even in the dark where Death commands, Patróklos.
Everything has been finished as I promised.
Fire will devour twelve noble sons of Troy
along with you, but I will not restore
Hektor to Priam; he shall not be eaten
by fire but by wild dogs."

                                        That was his boast,
but no dogs nosed at Hektor: Zeus's daughter
Aphrodítê kept them from his body
night and day, anointing it with oil
ambrosial, rose-fragrant, not to let
rough dragging by Akhilleus rip the skin.
Phoibos Apollo, too, from heaven sent down
a black cloud to the plain, shading the spot
the body lay on—that the power
of burning sun should not invade and parch
the flesh of limbs and sinews.

                                        And now, too,
Patróklos' pyre would not flame up. Akhilleus
thought of another way. He drew apart
and prayed to the two winds of the north and west,
assuring them of sacrificial gifts.
Then from a golden cup he made libation
copiously, praying the two to come,
so that the dead might quickly be consumed
by conflagration of the great logs. Iris
heard his prayers and went to tell the winds,

at that time gathered indoors, in the home
of the blustering west wind, for a drinking bout.
Iris ran down to stand upon the doorstone,
and, when they saw her, all the winds uprose
with invitations, each one for himself.
But she refused and said:

                                                    "I must not stay;
I'm bound onward, across the streams of Ocean,
to the country of the Sunburned: hekatombs
they'll make the gods; I must attend the feast.
Akhilleus begs the winds of north and west
to blow toward him; he promises fine offerings
if you will fan and set aflame the pyre
Patróklos lies on, mourned by all Akhaians."

That said, she soared away. The north and west winds
issued with a wondrous cry, both driving
cloud before them. Over open sea
they blew in a rush and took their gusty way,
as seas grew rough under the galewind wailing.
Then to the fertile plain of Troy they came
and fell upon the pyre. The flame roared,
blazing up terribly, and all night long
they joined to toss the crest of fire high
with keening blasts. And all night long Akhilleus
dipped up wine from a golden bowl and poured
his double cupfuls down, soaking the earth,
and calling Patróklos' feeble shade. He mourned him
as a father mourns a newly married son
whose death is anguish to his kin. Just so
Akhilleus mourned his friend and gave his bones
to the great flame to be devoured; with dragging
steps and groans he moved about the pyre.
Now when the star of morning eastward rose
to herald daylight on the earth, and Dawn
came after, yellow-robed, above the sea,
the pyre died down, the flame sank, and the winds
departed, veering homeward once again
by sea for Thrace, as the ground swell heaved and foamed.

Akhilleus left the pyre and lay down spent,
and sweet sleep overtook him at a bound.

But when the rest returned round Agamémnon,
voices and trampling feet awoke the sleeper.
Up he sat, then spoke out:

                                     "Son of Atreus,

noblemen of Akhaia's host, begin
by wetting down the pyre with tawny wine
to quench whatever fire hangs on. Then come,
we'll comb the ashes for Patróklos' bones!
They will be easy to pick out: he lay
alone, in the pyre's middle, and the rest
were burnt apart from him, around the edge,
all jumbled in no order, men and horses.
Then we'll pack his bones in a golden urn
with sheepfat in a double fold, to keep
until I too go hid in undergloom.
No heavy labor at a heavy tomb
I ask—only a fitting one; in due course
build it wide and high, you who are left
behind me in the long ships of the oarsmen."

They did his will: dampened the pyre with wine
in every part where flame had licked its way
and a bed of ashes fallen. Shedding tears
for their mildhearted friend they gathered up
his bones into a golden urn and added
a double fold of fat, then withindoors
they set the urn and veiled it with fine linen.
Next they drew a circle for a mound
around the pyre, and laid stones on the line,
and made a mound of earth. When they had done,
they were all ready to be gone, but now
Akhilleus held the troops upon the spot
and seated them, forming a wide arena.
Prizes out of the ships, caldrons and tripods,
horses and mules and oxen he supplied,
and softly belted girls, and hoary iron.
First for charioteers he set the prizes:

a girl adept at gentle handicraft
to be taken by the winner, and a tripod
holding twenty-six quarts, with handle-rings.
For the runner-up he offered a six-year-old
unbroken mare, big with a mule foal.
For third prize a fine caldron of four gallons,
never scorched, bright as on casting day,
and for the fourth two measured bars of gold;
for fifth, a new two-handled bowl.

He stood erect and spoke to all the Argives:

"Son of Atreus, soldiers of Akhaia,
these rewards await the charioteers
in this arena. If our competition
were held in honor of another man,
I'd carry off the first prize in this race.
You know how far my team outpoints the rest
in form and breeding, being divine: Poseidon
gave them to Pêleus, he in turn to me.
But I am out of it, so are my horses,
now they have lost their splendid charioteer,
the kind man, who so often glossed their manes
with oil when he had scrubbed their bodies down.
Now where they stand they droop their heads for him,
their manes brushing the ground, and grieve at heart.
Get ready, any others of the army
confident in your teams and rugged cars!"

Akhilleus finished, and the drivers gathered,
first of all Admêtos' dear son, Lord
Eumêlos, best at management of horses;
then powerful Diomêdês, son of Tydeus,
yoking the Trojan horses he had taken
from Aineías when Apollo saved the man.
After him tawny-headed Meneláos,
Atreus' noble son, with his fast team,
his own Podárgos, Agamémnon's Aithê—
a mare that Ekhepôlos Ankhisíadês
gave Agamémnon, to avoid the toil
of serving under him at windy Troy,

and to enjoy his days at home. For Zeus
had made him wealthy, living at Sikyôn
where dancing floors are spacious. Meneláos
harnessed the mare, all quivering for the run.
Antílokhos, the fourth, readied his team—
resplendent son of the heroic Lord
Nestor Nêlêïadês. Horses of Pylos
drew his war-car. At his elbow now
his father halted, with a word to the wise:

"Antílokhos, by heaven, even as a youngster
Zeus and Poseidon cared for you and taught you
every kind of horsemanship. No need
for me to add instruction, when you know
so well the trick of making turns. However,
these are slow horses, and they may turn in
a second-rate performance. The other teams
are faster. But the charioteers
know no more racing strategy than you do.
Work out a plan of action in your mind,
dear son, don't let the prize slip through your fingers.
Astuteness makes a forester, not brawn,
and by astuteness on the open sea
a helmsman holds a ship on the right course
though roughed by winds. One driver beats another
thinking it out beforehand. Many a one
will trust his team and chariot so far
that he wheels wide on turns, and carelessly,
to one side, then the other, and his horses
careen over the track, not kept in hand.
But a skilled charioteer with slower horses,
keeping his eye on the turning post,
will cling to it as he takes the curve, remembering
to give his horses rein into the stretch
but with a sure hand, watching the front-runner.
As to the mark, it stands out; you can't miss it:
a dry stump, a man's height above the ground,
of oak or pine, not rotted by the rain,
where the outward course turns home. Around this mark
there is smooth footing. It may be a memorial
of a man dead long ago, or a turning post

built in the old days. Now the Prince Akhilleus
makes it our halfway mark. As you drive near it,
hug it with car and horses; you yourself
in the chariot basket lean a bit to the left
and at the same time lash your right-hand horse
and shout to him, and let his rein run out.
Your left-hand horse should graze the turning post
so that your wheelhub seems to scrape the edge.
But mind there's no collision with the stump:
you'll hurt the horses and destroy the car,
and that will bring joy to your adversaries,
humiliation to you. No, son, be cool and watchful.
If on the turn you overtake and pass,
there's not a chance of someone catching you—
not if he drove the great horse of Adrêstos,
fleet Aríon, born of the gods, or those
of Laomédôn, splendid ones bred here."

When he had told his son the ultimate arts
of charioteering, Nestor sat down again.
The fifth to enter was Meríonês,
and he now yoked his team. All drivers mounted,
then the pebbles marked by each were dropped
in a helmet, and Akhilleus churned it round
till one bounced out: the token of Antílokhos,
second, that of Eumêlos, as it chanced,
then came the master-spearman Meneláos,
then in the line-up came Meríonês,
and Diomêdês, greatest of them all,
came last of all in order of the start.
Reining in line they waited, while Akhilleus
showed the mark far off on the flat plain
and stationed near it, as a referee,
Phoinix, the lord companion of his father,
to judge the race and to report the truth.
All the drivers raised their whips at once
above their teams, then lashed, with reins as well,
and cheered the horses as they broke away.
Over the plain they covered distance quickly,
running at full stretch, leaving the ships behind,
as dust rose under the barrels of the horses

like a cloud raised by a whirlwind, and their manes
flew backward in the windstream as they ran.
The cars went rocketing, now on the level field,
now through the air on rises. Charioteers
kept their feet, and each man's heart beat hard
with passion to be first. All cheered their teams,
and horses raised a dustcloud in their flight.
Now when they turned into the homestretch
back to the grey sea, each man's quality
appeared as the horses went all out. The mares
of Pherês' son had pulled ahead; behind him
Diomêdês' Trojan horses kept the pace
and not a length behind, but hard upon him.
Always about to mount his car, they seemed,
and his broad back and shoulders felt their breath
in warm gusts, as they seemed at every stride
to rest their heads upon him. Diomêdês
would have passed him now, or pulled up even,
had not Apollo in a fit of anger
struck the flashing whip out of his hands.
Now Diomêdês' eyes welled tears of rage.
He saw the mares ahead still, going away,
as running without a lash his team slowed down.
Athêna, though, had noticed how Apollo
cheated him. She darted after him
to give the whip back, and revive his horses,
then in anger overtook Eumêlos
and cracked his yoke in two. The horses parted,
swerving on the track; the chariot pole
swung earthward; and the man himself was thrown
out of his car to roll beside the wheel.
His elbows, mouth, and nose were skinned,
his forehead battered at his brows, his eyes
clouded with tears, his big voice choked.
But Diomêdês passed him wide and drove
in a spurt ahead of all the rest. Athêna
fired his team and awarded him the glory.
After him, tawny-headed Meneláos
now ran second. As for Antílokhos,
he called to his father's horses:

"Move, you two!

Stretch yourselves, and do it now! By god,
I don't expect you to contest the lead
of Diomêdês' team: Athêna gave them
speed, gave him his glory. Only catch
Meneláos' horses, don't be left behind!
Will Aithê put you both to shame, a filly?
Why eat her dust, you champions?
Here's what I promise, and it will be done:
You'll get no grooming and no feed from Nestor;
far from it; he'll butcher you on the spot
if you lose form and we bring up the rear.
Press that chariot, and put on speed.
I'll manage it, I know the way to pass
at the narrow point ahead: I can't go wrong."

Stung to fear by their master's angry voice,
the team put on a burst of speed, and suddenly
Antílokhos saw the narrowing track ahead.
A gully ran there, where storm-water massed
had broken off the edge and made a landslide.
Driving for the passage, Meneláos
tried to keep his wheels clear, but Antílokhos
swung to one side to pass, and drove his team
outside the track, sheering a little toward him.
Then Meneláos was afraid. He yelled:

"Antílokhos, you're driving like a madman!
Pull up! The track's too narrow here. Ahead
it widens, you can pass there! Keep away,
or you'll collide and wreck us both!"

                                          Antílokhos

only drove harder, lashing at his team,
like a man deaf and blind. About as far
as a discus flies, whirled out from wheeling shoulders,
when a young athlete tries his form, so far
the two teams raced each other. Then Meneláos'
mares fell back; he leaned back on the reins,
not to let the chariots lock wheels
and overturn and pile up on the track,

while drivers, mad to win, sprawled in the dust.
His opponent passed, and tawny Meneláos
growled at him:

                              "Antílokhos, no man
in the world is a more dangerous pest than you are.
Pass, and be damned to you. The rest of us
were wrong to think you had a grain of sense.
But you can't have the prize this way, unless
you take oath for it."

                              And he called his horses:

"Don't hold back, don't falter, moping there.
The others' knees and fetlocks will be tired
before your own: they have no youth like yours."

Fearing their master's tone, his horses now
recovered speed, and gained upon the others.

Meanwhile the Argives on the measured field
sat watching as the chariots coursed the plain,
raising plumes of dust. The Kretan captain
Idómeneus caught sight of the horses first,
headed for home; he sat outside the field
high up, on a lookout point. Hearing a shout
from someone far away, he knew the voice
and recognized the stallion in the lead—
all chestnut-colored, save that on his forehead
he wore a blaze of white, round as the moon.
Up stood Idómeneus and shouted down:

"Friends, lords and captains of the Argives, am I
the only one who can make out the horses,
or do you too? A new team has the lead,
as I see it, another charioteer
is coming into view. Eumêlos' horses
must have been hurt along the way: they had
the edge on the outward lap.
By god, the ones I saw rounding the turn
I cannot see now anywhere, though I
have strained my eyes to scan the plain of Troy.

The driver lost his reins, couldn't control
his team full circuit, so he failed the turn.
His chariot broke down, he must have fallen,
and the stampeded mares ran off. Stand up
and look, the rest of you! I can't be sure
I recognize him, but he seems that man,
Aitolian by birth and lord of Argives,
son of Tydeus, rugged Diomêdês!"

A rude reply he got from the runner, Aías,
Oïleus' son, who said:

                                      "Idómeneus,
why this rash talk too soon? Those running horses
are still far off and have the plain to cover.
Not by a long shot are you youngest here
or the one who has the best eyes in his head.
But you always have to say something. No point
in blurting it out now; sharper men are here.
The leading team is the one that led before:
Eumêlos' team, and he's the one who rides
behind and holds the reins."

                                      The Kretan captain
answered him in anger:

                                      "No one like you
for picking fights and giving foolish counsel;
otherwise you rank last among the Argives,
having a mind like a hoof. Here, let me wager
a tripod or a caldron and appoint
Agamémnon arbiter between the two of us
as to which team is first. You'll know, all right,
when you have to pay!"

                                      Aías got up at once
in hot anger, to make a rough reply,
and more and louder bickering was in prospect,
had not Akhilleus towered up and said:

"No more of this, no railing back and forth,
Aías, Idómeneus! Not on this occasion!
If someone else behaved so, you'd resent it.

Sit down, both of you, and watch the race.
The chariot-teams are coming this way fast,
whipped on to win. Before long, you will know
who's first and who's behind."

                                                    Even as he spoke,
Diomêdês came on racing for the finish,
laying on his whip with shoulder strokes,
so that his horses lifted their hooves high
at every furious track-devouring stride.
A constant spray of dust rained on the man
as the chariot, overlaid with gold and tin,
ran on the horses' heels. Behind the tires
no deep wheelmark was left in the fine dust.
The team stormed to the finish. He pulled up
in the arena, as a bath of sweat
poured to the ground from horses' necks and chests.
Then he swung from the glittering car and propped
his long whip on the yoke. And his lieutenant,
Sthénelos, took the prizes without delay.
He handed the woman over to his men
and let them carry the tripod by its rings,
while he unyoked the team. In second place
Antílokhos Nestóridês drove in,
by guile, not speed, outrunning Meneláos,
who finished, even so, close on his heels:
close as a chariot wheel to a horse that pulls
his master at a dead run on the plain:
tips of his tail hairs whisk at the wheel rim
as he runs just ahead, with no expanse
between, and all the plain beyond to cover.
Just so close, Meneláos came in behind
Antílokhos. At first by a discus throw
he had been outrun, but then he caught up fast,
helped by the valor of Agamémnon's mare,
silken-coated Aithê. A longer race
and Meneláos would have passed, to win
decisively, and no dead heat. In fourth place
Meríonês, Idómeneus' right-hand man,
came after Meneláos by a spear-cast.
His were the slowest horses of them all,

and he least fit for driving on a racecourse.
Last of all the son of Admêtos came,
on foot, pulling his car, driving his horses
before him at a walk. And beholding him
swift Prince Akhilleus felt a pang of pity.
Sharply he spoke out, standing amid the Argives:

"The best man is the last to bring his team in.
Come, we'll award him second prize, in fairness.
Let Diomêdês have the first."

Then all the soldiers shouted "Aye" to this,
and as they had approved, he would have given
the prize mare to Eumêlos; but Antílokhos
made his claim in protest:

"O Akhilleus,

I'll be enraged if you carry out this thing
you have announced! You mean to take my prize,
considering that his chariot and team
were hurt, and he, too, the brave fellow. Well,
he should have prayed the immortals! If he had,
he would have finished far from last. Granted
that you are sorry for him, fond of him,
there's gold aplenty in your hut, and bronze,
and you have cattle, serving maids, and horses.
Take some later; give him a greater prize;
or take them here and now. You'll have the Akhaians'
praise for it. *I will not yield the mare.*
And any man who cares to fight for her
can try me, hand to hand."

At this

the Prince Akhilleus, the great runner, smiled,
enjoying Antílokhos, as he liked the man.
He warmly answered him:

"Antílokhos,

if you invite me to find something else
to award Eumêlos, I'll be glad to do it.
The cuirass that I took from Asteropaíos,
bronze with a casting of bright tin around it:
that he shall have, and worth a great sum, too."

He told his close companion, Automédôn,
to bring the cuirass from the hut. He did so,
and Akhilleus handed it over to Eumêlos,
who took it gladly.

                                                    But now Meneláos

faced them all, still sore at heart, his anger
grimly set against Antílokhos. A herald
handed him a staff and called for silence.
Then he spoke among them as a king:

"Antílokhos, you were clearheaded once.
How have you acted now? Mocked at my skill
and fouled my horses, pushing your own ahead,
though they were inferior by far.
Come now, lords and captains of the Argives,
judge between us—and no favoring me.
Never let any Akhaian soldier say:
'Meneláos got the upper hand by lies
against Antílokhos; he takes the prize,
because although his horses were slower far
he himself prevailed by power and rank.'
Here: I'll conduct the case, and not one man
will take exception; it will be justly done.
Antílokhos, come here, sir, as good discipline
requires; stand there before your team and car.
Pick up the slim whip that you used in driving;
touch your horses; by the god of earthquake
swear you did not mean to foul my car."

Clearheaded Antílokhos answered:

                                                    "Wait a bit, sir.

Surely I'm younger far than you, my Lord
Meneláos; you stand higher in age and rank.
You know a young man may go out of bounds:
his wits are nimble, but his judgment slight.
Be patient, then. The mare I won I'll give you,
and any other and greater thing of mine
you might request I'd wish to give at once,
rather than fall in your esteem, my lord,
for all my days, and live as an offender
before the unseen powers."

When he had spoken,
the son of Nestor led the mare across
and put the bridle in Meneláos' hands.
And Meneláos was refreshed at heart
as growing grain is, when ears shine with dew,
and the fields ripple.

So the heart within you,
Meneláos, was refreshed. And happily
the older man said to the younger:

"Now,

Antílokhos, I am coming round to you,
after my anger. You were never thoughtless
before this. Youth prevailed over your good sense.
The next time, have a care not to pull tricks
on higher officers. Truly, no other
Akhaian could so quickly win me over,
but you've fought hard, and toiled long years,
as your father and brave brother have, for me.
I shall comply with what you asked at first
and give the mare to you, though she is mine,
so these men too may know
my temper is not cruel and overbearing."

Then to Noêmon, squire of Antílokhos,
he gave the mare to lead away, and took
instead the shining caldron. Meríonês,
as fourth to cross the finish line, picked up
the measured bars of gold. But the fifth prize,
the bowl with handles on both sides, remained.
Akhilleus carried it across the field
to make a gift of it to Nestor, saying:

"Here is a keepsake, venerable sir,
for you, too, from Patróklos' funeral day.
You'll never see him again among the Argives.
Prize though it is, I give this bowl, since you
will not contend in boxing or in wrestling,
nor will you enter for the javelin throw
or run the quarter mile. Stiffness of age
encumbers you even now."

And he gave the bowl.
Nestor received it and was pleased. He said:

"You've put the matter very well, my son.
My legs are strong no longer, as you say;
I am not fast on my feet; my hands no longer
move out fast to punch or throw. Would god
I had my young days back, my strength entire,
as when the Epeioi buried Amarýngkeus
at Bouprasíon, and his sons
held contests in his honor. That day, no one
gave me a match—no man of the Epeioi,
Pylians, or brave Aitolians.
In boxing I defeated Klytomêdês,
the son of Enops; in the wrestling bout
I threw my man, Angkaios the Pleurônian;
in the quarter mile I beat an excellent runner,
Íphiklos; and in the javelin-throw
I out-cast both Phyleus and Polydôros.
Only in chariot racing, Aktor's sons
pulled out ahead. By being two against one
they pushed their team in front, hating to see me
win again when the greatest prize remained.
Those two were twins: one held the reins alone—
the reins alone—while the other used the whip.
That was the man I was. Now let the young
take part in these exertions: I must yield
to slow old age, though in my time I shone
among heroic men.

                                          Well, carry on
the funeral of your friend with competitions.
This I take kindly, and my heart is cheered
that you remember me as well disposed,
remembering, too, the honor that is due me
among Akhaians. May the gods
in fitting ways reward you for it all."

Akhilleus bent his head to Nestor's praise
and then returned across the field of Akhaians.
Now as first prize for the bruising fist fight
he led a mule to tie it in the ring,

a beast of burden, six years old, unbroken,
that would be hard to break. And for the loser
he set out a two-handled cup, then stood
and said to the Argives:

                    "Excellency, Agamémnon,
and other Akhaians under arms, I call
on two of our most powerful men to try
for these awards in boxing.
The one Apollo helps to keep his feet—
if all Akhaians will concede the winner—
may take this working animal for his own,
while a two-handled cup goes to the loser."

At this a huge man got to his feet at once,
huge but compact, clever with his fists,
Epeiós, a son of Panopeus.
He laid hold of the stubborn mule and said:

"Step up, one of you men, and take the cup!
I think no other here will take the mule
by whipping me. I'm best, I don't mind saying.
Enough to admit I'm second-rate at war;
no man can be a master in everything.
Here is my forecast, and it's dead sure.
I'll open his face and crack his ribs. His friends
should gather and stand by to take him off
after my left and right have put him down."

At this they all grew silent. Eurýalos
alone stood up to face him, well-built son
of Lord Mêkisteus Talaïonidês,
who in the old days came to Thebes when Oidipous
had found his grave. At that time, Mêkisteus
defeated all the Kadmeíans. His son
had Diomêdês to attend him now
and cheer him on, wishing him victory.
First he cinched around him a fighter's belt
and then bound rawhide strips across his knuckles.
Both men, belted, stepped into the ring
and, toe to toe, let fly at one another,
hitting solid punches. Heavy fists

then milled together as they worked in close
with a fierce noise of grinding jaws. Their bodies
ran with sweat. Then Epeiós leapt out
with a long left hook and smashed the other's cheek
as he peered out through puffed eyes. He could keep
his feet no longer, but his legs gave way
and down he went—the way a leaping fish
falls backward in the offshore sea when north wind
ruffles it down a beach littered with seawrack:
black waves hide him. So the man left his feet
and dropped at the blow. Gallantly Epeiós
gave him a hand and pulled him up; his friends
with arms around him helped him from the ring,
scuffing his feet and spitting gouts of blood,
his head helplessly rolling side to side.
They sat him down, addled, among themselves,
and took charge of the double-handled cup.

Akhilleus now at once put on display
before the troops a third array of prizes—
those for the grinding wrestling bout. The winner
was to acquire a fire-straddling tripod
valued at twelve oxen by the Akhaians.
As for the loser, in their midst Akhilleus
placed a woman versatile at crafts,
whose value was four oxen. Standing there,
he said to the Argives:

                                        "Up with you, the pair
who will contend for this one."

                                                        Up they stood,
huge Aías Telamônios, then Odysseus,
the calculating and resourceful man.
Wearing their belts, the two leaned toward each other
in the arena, and with oaken hands
gripped one another's elbows. Think of timbers
fitted at a steep angle for a roof
a master-builder makes to break the winds!
The bones in each man's back creaked at the strain
put on him by their corded thews, and sweat

ran down in rills. Around their ribs and shoulders
welts were raised by the holds they took, all scarlet
where the blood gathered. Without pause they strove
to win the tripod: neither could Odysseus
throw his man and pin him, nor could Aías,
countered by Odysseus' brawn. At last
when the tied match began to bore the soldiers,
Aías muttered:

                    "Son of Laërtês, royal
Odysseus, master mariner and soldier,
hoist me, or I'll hoist you. What happens then
is god's affair."

                    At this he heaved him up.
But Odysseus had his bag of tricks: he kicked
behind the knee, knocking his legs from under him,
and down went Aías backward, as Odysseus
dropped on his chest. The onlookers came alive,
looked hard and marveled at the fall. The wrestlers
got to their feet for a fresh try, and Odysseus
heaved in turn, but could not budge the big man
even a half inch off the ground. He bent
his knee behind him, and then both went down
locked together: both got coats of dust.
They would have roused and tried for a third fall,
had not Akhilleus held them back. He said:

"No more of this bone-cracking bout.
The victory goes to both. Take equal prizes.
Off with you, so the rest here can compete."

They broke and turned away as he commanded,
wiped off the dust, and pulled their khitons on.

For the next event, the quarter mile, Akhilleus
offered a silver winebowl of six gallons.
Never a mixing bowl in all the world
could match its beauty: artisans of Sidon
had lavished art upon it. Phoinikians
had brought it out by sea and, mooring ship
in a roadstead, had conferred the bowl on Thoas.

Eunêos, son of Iêson, later gave it
as ransom to Patróklos for Lykáôn,
son of Priam. Now at his old friend's funeral
Akhilleus put the bowl down, as first prize,
for that man who should prove the fastest runner.
Second prize he made a giant ox,
and, for the hindmost, half a bar of gold.
Towering there, he gave the word to Argives:

"Step up, if you will try for this award."

Aías the runner, son of Oïleus,
at once came forward; then that canny man,
Odysseus, and then Nestor's son, Antílokhos,
fastest man of them all among the young.
They toed the line, Akhilleus showed the finish,
then from the starting line the race began,
and Aías quickly took the lead. Beside him
noble Odysseus pressed him hard. As close
as to a weaving woman's breast the bar
of warp is drawn, when accurately she passes
shuttle and spool along the meshing web
and holds to her breast one weighted bar, so close
in second place Odysseus ran: his feet
came sprinting in the other's tracks before
the dust fell, and on Aías' nape he blew
hot breath as he ran on. All the Akhaians
cheered for Odysseus, the great contender,
and called to him as he ran with laboring heart.
But entering the last hundred yards, Odysseus
prayed in his heart to the grey-eyed one, Athêna:

"Hear me, goddess: come, bless me with speed!"

That was his prayer, and Pallas Athêna heard him,
lightened his legs, lightened his feet and arms,
and when they all came fighting for the finish
Aías on the dead run slipped—Athêna
tripped him—at a point where dung had dropped
from lowing oxen that Akhilleus killed
in honor of Patróklos. Aías' mouth
and nose were plastered, plugged with muck.

But Prince Odysseus, the long-enduring,
bore off the winebowl, having finished first,
while Aías took the ox. He stood a moment,
holding the beast's horns in his hands, and spat
the dung out of his mouth before he said:

"Damn the luck: she did for me, that goddess
always beside him, like a coddling mother!"

At this the crowd laughed at him, full of glee.
Antílokhos took the last prize with a smile
and said to the Argives:

                              "Every man here knows,
but anyway I'll say it, friends: the immortals
honor the older men as much as ever.
Aías has it over me in age
by only a few years, but the captain here
belongs to an earlier generation of men.
Fresh in age, they call him. He's a tough one
for any runner to match himself against,
except Akhilleus."

                              By these final words
he gave due honor to the son of Pêleus.
Akhilleus in return said:

                              "Antílokhos,
that word of praise will not go unrewarded.
I'll add another half bar to your prize."

This he bestowed, and the young man took it gladly.

Then Akhilleus brought a battle spear,
a shield and helm, and laid them on the field—
the armor of Sarpêdôn, which Patróklos
took for spoil. He stood and told the Argives:

"Now I invite two men to fight for these—
two of our bravest, in full battle-gear,
equipped with cutting weapons, too. They are
to take one another on before the crowd.
And that one of the two who first shall hit

the good flesh of the other, draw his blood,
making a stroke through helm or shield—to him
I'll give this handsome broadsword, silver-hilted,
Thracian, that I took from Asteropaíos.
The armor shall belong to both in common,
and in our hut we'll make them a good feast."

Huge Aías rose, the son of Télamôn,
and rugged Diomêdês rose as well.
On one side and the other of the crowd
they put their gear on, then paced to the center,
hot for combat, glaring, while a hush
of admiration ran through all the troops.
As they came near, with lightning feints three times
they all but charged each other, and then Aías
hit Diomêdês hard on the round shield.
He came short of his body, as the breastplate
safely enclosed it. Over the tower shield
Diomêdês now with flickering point at play
endangered Aías' throat, and in commotion,
fearing for Aías, the Akhaians cried:

"Break off this duel, and pick up equal prizes!"

Akhilleus, though, awarded the big sword,
scabbard, and well-cut belt to Diomêdês.
Then he set out a meteorite, a missile
Eëtíôn in power used to hurl—
before Akhilleus brought him down and took
this fused iron with plunder in his ships.
Now he stood and told the men:

                                        "Step forward,
those who will try for this one. A man's fields
may lie far from his town, but five long years
this lump will last: neither shepherd nor plowman
need go up to town for want of iron,
he'll be supplied at home."

                            Then Polypoitês,
a man who stood his ground in battle, rose,
then stalwart, sturdy-hearted Leonteus,

then Aías Telamônios and Epeiós
moved into place. Epeiós took the iron,
and heaved it—and the crowd of Akhaians laughed.
The good fighter, Leonteus, made his try,
and then, as third man, Telamônian Aías
hurled the iron from his massive hand
beyond the others. But when Polypoitês
took the lump in turn, he made it hurtle
as far as a herdsman throws a cattle staff,
rifling it clear across a herd: so far
beyond the ring he hurled it, and the soldiers
roared applause. Men of his company
carried the royal prize down to the ships.

Wrought iron for the archers now—ten axheads
double-bladed, ten with single blades—
Akhilleus laid in order in the ring.
He set a mast up from a black-hulled ship
at the sand's edge, and tethered by a cord
around one foot a rockdove.

                                                    "Shoot at that!"
said he. "The man who hits the fluttering dove
may carry all the double axes home.
If someone cuts the cord he'll miss the bird:
call it a poor shot! Second prize for him!"

At this the kingly archer Teukros rose,
followed by Idómeneus' lieutenant,
staunch Meríonês. And choosing lots
they rolled them in a helmet. Teukros' pebble
had the luck: he drew and shot his arrow
without a pause, also without a vow
of rams in hekatomb to Lord Apollo.
He missed the bird, begrudged him by Apollo,
hitting instead the cord that tethered her.
The cutting arrowhead parted the cord,
and skyward the bird flew, as the frayed length
of cord dangled to earth. All the Akhaians
breathed a mighty sigh—but in one motion
Meríonês whipped the bow out of his hands.

He held an arrow ready for his shot
and now vowed to Apollo, archer of heaven,
to offer first-born lambs in hekatomb.
Aloft, dark against cloud, he saw the dove,
and as she wheeled he shot her through the body
under the wing. His arrow, passing through,
plummeted back and stuck before his feet.
The wounded rockdove settled on the mast
with hanging head and drooping wings, and soon,
as life throbbed from her body, she fell down
far from the bowman. All the troops looked on
and marveled at the shooting. Then Meríonês
picked up the double blades, Teukros the single,
to carry to the ships.

                                        Finally, Akhilleus
furnished a throwing spear and a new caldron
chased with floral figures, worth an ox.
The javelin-throwers advanced: first Agamémnon,
ruler of the great plains, then Meríonês,
lieutenant to Idómeneus. But Akhilleus
had a proposal for them.

                                        "Son of Atreus,
considering that you excel us all—
and by so much—in throwing power, I'd say
that you should simply carry off this prize.
We'll give the spear, though, to Meríonês,
if you agree. That is what I propose."

Lord Marshal Agamémnon gave consent,
so the bronze-shod spear went to Meríonês.
Then to his crier, Talthýbios,
Agamémnon entrusted the beautiful caldron.

BOOK TWENTY-FOUR

A Grace Given in Sorrow

LINES 1–13

The funeral games were over. Men dispersed
and turned their thoughts to supper in their quarters,
then to the boon of slumber. But Akhilleus
thought of his friend, and sleep that quiets all things
would not take hold of him. He tossed and turned
remembering with pain Patróklos' courage,
his buoyant heart; how in his company
he fought out many a rough day full of danger,
cutting through ranks in war and the bitter sea.
With memory his eyes grew wet. He lay
on his right side, then on his back, and then
face downward—but at last he rose, to wander
distractedly along the line of surf.
This for eleven nights. The first dawn, brightening
sea and shore, became familiar to him,

as at that hour he yoked his team, with Hektor
tied behind, to drag him out, three times
around Patróklos' tomb. By day he rested
in his own hut, abandoning Hektor's body
to lie full-length in dust—though Lord Apollo,
pitying the man, even in death,
kept his flesh free of disfigurement.
He wrapped him in his great shield's flap of gold
to save him from laceration. But Akhilleus
in rage visited indignity on Hektor
day after day, and, looking on,
the blessed gods were moved. Day after day
they urged the Wayfinder to steal the body—
a thought agreeable to all but Hêra,
Poseidon, and the grey-eyed one, Athêna.
These opposed it, and held out, since Ilion
and Priam and his people had incurred
their hatred first, the day Aléxandros
made his mad choice and piqued two goddesses,
visitors in his sheepfold: he praised
a third, who offered ruinous lust.
Now when Dawn grew bright for the twelfth day,
Phoibos Apollo spoke among the gods:

"How heartless and how malevolent you are!
Did Hektor never make burnt offering
of bulls' thighbones to you, and unflawed goats?
Even in death you would not stir to save him
for his dear wife to see, and for his mother,
his child, his father, Priam, and his men:
they'd burn the corpse at once and give him burial.
Murderous Akhilleus has your willing help—
a man who shows no decency, implacable,
barbarous in his ways as a wild lion
whose power and intrepid heart
sway him to raid the flocks of men for meat.
The man has lost all mercy;
he has no shame—that gift that hinders mortals
but helps them, too. A sane one may endure
an even dearer loss: a blood brother,
a son; and yet, by heaven, having grieved

and passed through mourning, he will let it go.
The fates have given patient hearts to men.
Not this one: first he took Prince Hektor's life
and now he drags the body, lashed to his car,
around the barrow of his friend, performing
something neither nobler in report
nor better in itself. Let him take care,
or, brave as he is, we gods will turn against him,
seeing him outrage the insensate earth!"

Hêra whose arms are white as ivory
grew angry at Apollo. She retorted:

"Lord of the silver bow, your words would be
acceptable if one had a mind to honor
Hektor and Akhilleus equally.
But Hektor suckled at a woman's breast,
Akhilleus is the first-born of a goddess—
one I nursed myself. I reared her, gave her
to Pêleus, a strong man whom the gods loved.
All of you were present at their wedding—
you too—friend of the base, forever slippery!—
came with your harp and dined there!"

                                Zeus the stormking
answered her:

                                "Hêra, don't lose your temper
altogether. Clearly the same high honor
cannot be due both men. And yet Lord Hektor,
of all the mortal men in Ilion,
was deárest to the gods, or was to me.
He never failed in the right gift; my altar
never lacked a feast
of wine poured out and smoke of sacrifice—
the share assigned as ours. We shall renounce
the theft of Hektor's body; there is no way;
there would be no eluding Akhilleus' eye,
as night and day his mother comes to him.
Will one of you now call her to my presence?
I have a solemn message to impart:

Akhilleus is to take fine gifts from Priam,
and in return give back Prince Hektor's body."

At this, Iris who runs on the rainy wind
with word from Zeus departed. Midway between
Samos and rocky Imbros, down she plunged
into the dark grey sea, and the brimming tide
roared over her as she sank into the depth—
as rapidly as a leaden sinker, fixed
on a lure of wild bull's horn, that glimmers down
with a fatal hook among the ravening fish.
Soon Iris came on Thetis in a cave,
surrounded by a company of Nereids
lolling there, while she bewailed the fate
of her magnificent son, now soon to perish
on Troy's rich earth, far from his fatherland.
Halting before her, Iris said:

                                            "Come, Thetis,
Zeus of eternal forethought summons you."

Silvery-footed Thetis answered:

                                            "Why?

Why does the great one call me to him now,
when I am shy of mingling with immortals,
being so heavyhearted? But I'll go.
Whatever he may say will have its weight."

That loveliest of goddesses now put on
a veil so black no garment could be blacker,
and swam where windswift Iris led. Before them
on either hand the ground swell fell away.
They rose to a beach, then soared into the sky
and found the viewer of the wide world, Zeus,
with all the blissful gods who live forever
around him seated. Athêna yielded place,
and Thetis sat down by her father, Zeus,
while Hêra handed her a cup of gold
and spoke a comforting word. When she had drunk,
Thetis held out the cup again to Hêra.
The father of gods and men began:

"You've come
to Olympos, Thetis, though your mind is troubled
and insatiable pain preys on your heart.
I know, I too. But let me, even so,
explain why I have called you here. Nine days
of quarreling we've had among the gods
concerning Hektor's body and Akhilleus.
They wish the Wayfinder to make off with it.
I, however, accord Akhilleus honor
as I now tell you—in respect for you
whose love I hope to keep hereafter. Go, now,
down to the army, tell this to your son:
the gods are sullen toward him, and I, too,
more than the rest, am angered at his madness,
holding the body by the beaked ships
and not releasing it. In fear of me
let him relent and give back Hektor's body!
At the same time I'll send Iris to Priam,
directing him to go down to the beachhead
and ransom his dear son. He must bring gifts
to melt Akhilleus' rage."

Thetis obeyed,

leaving Olympos' ridge and flashing down
to her son's hut. She found him groaning there,
inconsolable, while men-at-arms
went to and fro, making their breakfast ready—
having just put to the knife a fleecy sheep.
His gentle mother sat down at his side,
caressed him, and said tenderly:

"My child,

will you forever feed on your own heart
in grief and pain, and take no thought of sleep
or sustenance? It would be comforting
to make love with a woman. No long time
will you live on for me: Death even now
stands near you, appointed and all-powerful.
But be alert and listen: I am a messenger
from Zeus, who tells me the gods are sullen toward you
and he himself most angered at your madness,

holding the body by the beaked ships
and not releasing it. Give Hektor back.
Take ransom for the body."

Said Akhilleus:

"Let it be so. Let someone bring the ransom
and take the dead away, if the Olympian
commands this in his wisdom."

So, that morning,

in camp, amid the ships, mother and son
conversed together, and their talk was long.
Lord Zeus meanwhile sent Iris to Ilion.

"Off with you, lightfoot, leave Olympos, take
my message to the majesty of Priam
at Ilion. He is to journey down
and ransom his dear son upon the beachhead.
He shall take gifts to melt Akhilleus' rage,
and let him go alone, no soldier with him,
only some crier, some old man, to drive
his wagon team and guide the nimble wagon,
and afterward to carry home the body
of him that Prince Akhilleus overcame.
Let him not think of death, or suffer dread,
as I'll provide him with a wondrous guide,
the Wayfinder, to bring him across the lines
into the very presence of Akhilleus.
And he, when he sees Priam within his hut,
will neither take his life nor let another
enemy come near. He is no madman,
no blind brute, nor one to flout the gods,
but dutiful toward men who beg his mercy."

Then Iris at his bidding ran
on the rainy winds to bear the word of Zeus,
until she came to Priam's house and heard
voices in lamentation. In the court
she found the princes huddled around their father,
faces and clothing wet with tears. The old man,
fiercely wrapped and hooded in his mantle,

sat like a figure graven—caked in filth
his own hands had swept over head and neck
when he lay rolling on the ground. Indoors
his daughters and his sons' wives were weeping,
remembering how many and how brave
the young men were who had gone down to death
before the Argive spearmen.

                                                    Zeus's courier,
appearing now to Priam's eyes alone,
alighted whispering, so the old man trembled:

"Priam, heir of Dárdanos, take heart,
and have no fear of me; I bode no evil,
but bring you friendly word from Zeus,
who is distressed for you and pities you
though distant far upon Olympos. He
commands that you shall ransom the Prince Hektor,
taking fine gifts to melt Akhilleus' rage.
And go alone: no soldier may go with you,
only some crier, some old man, to drive
your wagon team and guide the nimble wagon,
and afterward to carry home the body
of him that Prince Akhilleus overcame.
Put away thoughts of death, shake off your dread,
for you shall have a wondrous guide,
the Wayfinder, to bring you across the lines
into the very presence of Akhilleus.
He, for his part, seeing you in his quarters,
will neither take your life nor let another
enemy come near. He is no madman,
no blind brute, nor one to flout the gods,
but dutiful toward men who beg his mercy."

Iris left him, swift as a veering wind.
Then Priam spoke, telling the men to rig
a four-wheeled wagon with a wicker box,
while he withdrew to his chamber roofed in cedar,
high and fragrant, rich in precious things.
He called to Hékabê, his lady:

                                                    "Princess,
word from Olympian Zeus has come to me

to go down to the ships of the Akhaians
and ransom our dead son. I am to take
gifts that will melt Akhilleus' anger. Tell me
how this appears to you, tell me your mind,
for I am torn with longing, now, to pass
inside the great encampment by the ships."

The woman's voice broke as she answered:

                                        "Sorrow,
sorrow. Where is the wisdom now that made you
famous in the old days, near and far?
How can you ever face the Akhaian ships
or wish to go alone before those eyes,
the eyes of one who stripped your sons in battle,
how many, and how brave? Iron must be
the heart within you. If he sees you, takes you,
savage and wayward as the man is,
he'll have no mercy and no shame. Better
that we should mourn together in our hall.
Almighty fate spun this thing for our son
the day I bore him: destined him to feed
the wild dogs after death, being far from us
when he went down before the stronger man.
I could devour the vitals of that man,
leeching into his living flesh! He'd know
pain then—pain like mine for my dead son.
It was no coward the Akhaian killed;
he stood and fought for the sweet wives of Troy,
with no more thought of flight or taking cover."

In majesty old Priam said:

                                        "My heart
is fixed on going. Do not hold me back,
and do not make yourself a raven crying
calamity at home. You will not move me.
If any man on earth had urged this on me—
reader of altar smoke, prophet or priest—
we'd say it was a lie, and hold aloof.
But no: with my own ears I heard the voice,
I saw the god before me. Go I shall,

and no more words. If I must die alongside
the ships of the Akhaians in their bronze,
I die gladly. May I but hold my son
and spend my grief; then let Akhilleus kill me."

Throwing open the lids of treasure boxes
he picked out twelve great robes of state, and twelve
light cloaks for men, and rugs, an equal number,
and just as many capes of snowy linen,
adding a dozen khitons to the lot;
then set in order ten pure bars of gold,
a pair of shining tripods, four great caldrons,
and finally one splendid cup, a gift
Thracians had made him on an embassy.
He would not keep this, either—as he cared
for nothing now but ransoming his son.

And now, from the colonnade,
he made his Trojan people keep their distance,
berating and abusing them:

                                                        "Away,

you craven fools and rubbish! In your own homes
have you no one to mourn, that you crowd here,
to make more trouble for me? Is this a show,
that Zeus has crushed me, that he took the life
of my most noble son? You'll soon know what it means,
as you become child's play for the Akhaians
to kill in battle, now that Hektor's gone.
As for myself, before I see my city
taken and ravaged, let me go down blind
to Death's cold kingdom!"

                                                Staff in hand,

he herded them, until they turned away
and left the furious old man. He lashed out
now at his sons, at Hélenos and Paris,
Agathôn, Pammôn, Antíphonos,
Polítês, Dêíphobos, Hippóthoös,
and Dios—to these nine the old man cried:

"Bestir yourselves, you misbegotten whelps,
shame of my house! Would god you had been killed

instead of Hektor at the line of ships.
How curst I am in everything! I fathered
first-rate men, in our great Troy; but now
I swear not one is left: Mêstôr, Trôilos,
laughing amid the war-cars; and then Hektor—
a god to soldiers, and a god among them,
seeming not a man's child, but a god's.
Arês killed them. These poltroons are left,
hollow men, dancers, heroes of the dance,
light-fingered pillagers of lambs and kids
from the town pens!

                              Now will you get a wagon
ready for me, and quickly? Load these gifts
aboard it, so that we can take the road."

Dreading the rough edge of their father's tongue,
they lifted out a cart, a cargo wagon,
neat and maneuverable, and newly made,
and fixed upon it a wicker box; then took
a mule yoke from a peg, a yoke of boxwood
knobbed in front, with rings to hold the reins.
They brought out, too, the band nine forearms long
called the yoke-fastener, and placed the yoke
forward at the shank of the polished pole,
shoving the yoke-pin firmly in. They looped
three turns of the yoke-fastener round the knob
and wound it over and over down the pole,
tucking the tab end under. Next, the ransom:
bearing the weight of gifts for Hektor's person
out of the inner room, they piled them up
on the polished wagon. It was time to yoke
the mule-team, strong in harness, with hard hooves,
a team the Mysians had given Priam.
Then for the king's own chariot they harnessed
a team of horses of the line of Trôs,
reared by the old king in his royal stable.
So the impatient king and his sage crier
had their animals yoked in the palace yard
when Hékabê in her agitation joined them,
carrying in her right hand a golden cup
of honeyed wine, with which, before they left,

they might make offering. At the horses' heads
she stood to tell them:

> "Here, tip wine to Zeus,
the father of gods. Pray for a safe return
from the enemy army, seeing your heart is set
on venturing to the camp against my will.
Pray in the second place to Zeus the stormking,
gloomy over Ida, who looks down
on all Troy country. Beg for an omen-bird,
the courier dearest of all birds to Zeus
and sovereign in power of flight,
that he appear upon our right in heaven.
When you have seen him with your own eyes, then,
under that sign, you may approach the ships.
If Zeus who views the wide world will not give you
vision of his bird, then I at least
cannot bid godspeed to your journey,
bent on it though you are."

> In majesty

Priam replied:

> "My lady, in this matter
I am disposed to trust you and agree.
It is an excellent thing and salutary
to lift our hands to Zeus, invoking mercy."

The old king motioned to his housekeeper,
who stood nearby with a basin and a jug,
to pour clear water on his hands. He washed them,
took the cup his lady held, and prayed
while standing there, midway in the walled court.
Then he tipped out the wine, looking toward heaven,
saying:

> "Zeus, our Father, reigning from Ida,
god of glory and power, grant I come
to Akhilleus' door as one to be received
with kindliness and mercy. And dispatch
your courier bird, the nearest to your heart
of all birds, and the first in power of flight.

Let him appear upon our right in heaven
that I may see him with my own eyes
and under that sign journey to the ships."

Zeus all-foreseeing listened to this prayer
and put an eagle, king
of winged creatures, instantly in flight:
a swamp eagle, a hunter, one they call
the duskwing. Wide as a doorway in a chamber
spacious and high, built for a man of wealth,
a door with long bars fitted well, so wide
spread out each pinion. The great bird appeared
winging through the town on their right hand,
and all their hearts lifted with joy to see him.
In haste the old king boarded his bright car
and clattered out of the echoing colonnade.
Ahead, the mule-team drew the four-wheeled wagon,
driven by Idaíos, and behind
the chariot rolled, with horses that the old man
whipped into a fast trot through the town.
Family and friends all followed weeping
as though for Priam's last and deathward ride.
Into the lower town they passed, and reached
the plain of Troy. Here those who followed after
turned back, sons and sons-in-law. And Zeus
who views the wide world saw the car and wagon
brave the plain. He felt a pang for Priam
and quickly said to Hermês, his own son:

"Hermês, as you go most happily
of all the gods with mortals, and give heed
to whom you will, be on your way this time
as guide for Priam to the deepsea ships.
Guide him so that not one of the Danáäns
may know or see him till he reach Akhilleus."

Argeiphontês the Wayfinder obeyed.
He bent to tie his beautiful sandals on,
ambrosial, golden, that carry him over water
and over endless land on a puff of wind,
and took the wand with which he charms asleep—

or, when he wills, awake—the eyes of men.
So, wand in hand, the strong god glittering
paced into the air. Quick as a thought
he came to Hellê's waters and to Troy,
appearing as a boy whose lip was downy
in the first bloom of manhood, a young prince,
all graciousness.

After the travelers

drove past the mound of Ilos, at the ford
they let the mules and horses pause to drink
the running stream. Now darkness had come on
when, looking round, the crier
saw Hermês near at hand. He said to Priam:

"You must think hard and fast, your grace;
there is new danger; we need care and prudence.
I see a man-at-arms there—ready, I think,
to prey on us. Come, shall we whip the team
and make a run for it? Or take his knees
and beg for mercy?"

Now the old man's mind

gave way to confusion and to terror.
On his gnarled arms and legs the hair stood up,
and he stared, breathless. But the affable god
came over and took his hand and asked:

"Old father,

where do you journey, with your cart and car,
while others rest, below the evening star?
Do you not fear the Akhaians where they lie
encamped, hard, hostile outlanders, nearby?
Should someone see you, bearing stores like these
by night, how would you deal with enemies?
You are not young, your escort's ancient, too.
Could you beat off an attacker, either of you?
I'll do no hurt to you but defend you here.
You remind me of my father, whom I hold dear."

Old Priam answered him:

"Indeed, dear boy,

the case is as you say. And yet some god

stretched out his hand above me, he who sent
before me here—and just at the right time—
a traveler like yourself, well-made, well-spoken,
clearheaded, too. You come of some good family."

The Wayfinder rejoined:

                                    "You speak with courtesy,
dear sir. But on this point enlighten me:
are you removing treasure here amassed
for safety abroad, until the war is past?
Or can you be abandoning Ilion
in fear, after he perished, that great one
who never shirked a battle, your own princely son?"

Old Priam replied:

                        "My brave young friend, who are you?
Born of whom? How nobly you acknowledge
the dreadful end of my unfortunate son."

To this the Wayfinder replied:

                                            "Dear sir,
you question me about him? Never surmise
I have not seen him with my very eyes,
and often, on the field. I saw him chase
Argives with carnage to their own shipways,
while we stood wondering, forbidden war
by the great anger that Akhilleus bore
Lord Agamémnon. I am of that company
Akhilleus led. His own ship carried me
as one of the Myrmidons. My father is old,
as you are, and his name's Polyktôr; gold
and other wealth he owns;
and I am seventh and last of all his sons.
When I cast lots among them, my lot fell
to join the siege against Troy citadel.
Tonight I've left the camp to scout this way
where, circling Troy, we'll fight at break of day;
our men are tired of waiting and will not stand
for any postponement by the high command."

Responded royal Priam:

"If you belong
to the company of Akhilleus, son of Pêleus,
tell me this, and tell me the whole truth:
is my son even now beside the ships?
Or has Akhilleus by this time dismembered him
and thrown him to the wild dogs?"

The Wayfinder
made reply again:

"Dear sir,
no dogs or birds have yet devoured your son.
Beside Akhilleus' ship, out of the sun,
he lies in a place of shelter. Now twelve days
the man has lain there, yet no part decays,
nor have the blowfly's maggots, that devour
dead men in war, fed on him to this hour.
True that around his dear friend's barrow tomb
Akhilleus drags him when dawn-shadows come,
driving pitilessly; but he mars him not.
You might yourself be witness, on the spot,
how fresh with dew he lies, washed of his gore,
unstained, for the deep gashes that he bore
have all closed up—and many thrust their bronze
into his body. The blest immortal ones
favor your prince, and care for every limb
even in death, as they so cherished him."

The old king's heart exulted, and he said:

"Child, it was well to honor the immortals.
He never forgot, at home in Ilion—
ah, did my son exist? was he a dream?—
the gods who own Olympos. They in turn
were mindful of him when he met his end.
Here is a goblet as a gift from me.
Protect me, give me escort, if the gods
attend us, till I reach Akhilleus' hut."

And in response Hermês the Wayfinder
said:

"You are putting a young man to the test,
dear sir, but I may not, as you request,
accept a gift behind Akhilleus' back.
Fearing, honoring him, I could not lack
discretion to that point. The consequence, too,
could be unwelcome. As for escorting you,
even to Argos' famous land I'd ride
a deck with you, or journey at your side.
No cutthroat ever will disdain your guide."

With this, Hermês who lights the way for mortals
leapt into the driver's place. He caught up
reins and whip, and breathed a second wind
into the mule-team and the team of horses.
Onward they ran toward parapet and ships,
and pulled up to the moat.

                                          Now night had fallen,
bringing the sentries to their supper fire,
but the glimmering god Hermês, the Wayfinder,
showered a mist of slumber on them all.
As quick as thought, he had the gates unbarred
and open to let the wagon enter, bearing
the old king and the ransom.

                                          Going seaward
they came to the lofty quarters of Akhilleus,
a lodge the Myrmidons built for their lord
of pine trees cut and trimmed, and shaggy thatch
from mowings in deep meadows. Posts were driven
round the wide courtyard in a palisade,
whose gate one crossbar held, one beam of pine.
It took three men to slam this home, and three
to draw the bolt again—but great Akhilleus
worked his entryway alone with ease.
And now Hermês, who lights the way for mortals,
opened for Priam, took him safely in
with all his rich gifts for the son of Pêleus.
Then the god dropped the reins, and stepping down
he said:

                                          "I am no mortal wagoner,
but Hermês, sir. My father sent me here
to be your guide amid the Akhaian men.

Now that is done, I'm off to heaven again
and will not visit Akhilleus. That would be
to compromise an immortal's dignity—
to be received with guests of mortal station.
Go take his knees, and make your supplication:
invoke his father, his mother, and his child;
pray that his heart be touched, that he be reconciled."

Now Hermês turned, departing for Olympos,
and Priam vaulted down. He left Idaíos
to hold the teams in check, while he went forward
into the lodge. He found Akhilleus, dear
to Zeus, there in his chair, with officers
at ease across the room. Only Automédôn
and Álkimos were busy near Akhilleus,
for he had just now made an end of dinner,
eating and drinking, and the laden boards
lay near him still upon the trestles.

                                                            Priam,
the great king of Troy, passed by the others,
knelt down, took in his arms Akhilleus' knees,
and kissed the hands of wrath that killed his sons.

When, taken with mad Folly in his own land,
a man does murder and in exile finds
refuge in some rich house, then all who see him
stand in awe.
So these men stood.

                                                            Akhilleus
gazed in wonder at the splendid king,
and his companions marveled too, all silent,
with glances to and fro. Now Priam prayed
to the man before him:

                                    "Remember your own father,
Akhilleus, in your godlike youth: his years
like mine are many, and he stands upon
the fearful doorstep of old age. He, too,
is hard pressed, it may be, by those around him,
there being no one able to defend him
from bane of war and ruin. Ah, but he
may nonetheless hear news of you alive,

and so with glad heart hope through all his days
for sight of his dear son, come back from Troy,
while I have deathly fortune.

                                        Noble sons

I fathered here, but scarce one man is left me.
Fifty I had when the Akhaians came,
nineteen out of a single belly, others
born of attendant women. Most are gone.
Raging Arês cut their knees from under them.
And he who stood alone among them all,
their champion, and Troy's, ten days ago
you killed him, fighting for his land, my prince,
Hektor.

                            It is for him that I have come
among these ships, to beg him back from you,
and I bring ransom without stint.

                                        Akhilleus,

be reverent toward the great gods! And take
pity on me, remember your own father.
Think me more pitiful by far, since I
have brought myself to do what no man else
has done before—to lift to my lips the hand
of one who killed my son."

                                    Now in Akhilleus
the evocation of his father stirred
new longing, and an ache of grief. He lifted
the old man's hand and gently put him by.
Then both were overborne as they remembered:
the old king huddled at Akhilleus' feet
wept, and wept for Hektor, killer of men,
while great Akhilleus wept for his own father
as for Patróklos once again; and sobbing
filled the room.

                        But when Akhilleus' heart
had known the luxury of tears, and pain
within his breast and bones had passed away,
he stood then, raised the old king up, in pity
for his grey head and greybeard cheek, and spoke
in a warm rush of words:

"Ah, sad and old!
Trouble and pain you've borne, and bear, aplenty.
Only a great will could have brought you here
among the Akhaian ships, and here alone
before the eyes of one who stripped your sons,
your many sons, in battle. Iron must be
the heart within you. Come, then, and sit down.
We'll probe our wounds no more but let them rest,
though grief lies heavy on us. Tears heal nothing,
drying so stiff and cold. This is the way
the gods ordained the destiny of men,
to bear such burdens in our lives, while they
feel no affliction. At the door of Zeus
are those two urns of good and evil gifts
that he may choose for us; and one for whom
the lightning's joyous king dips in both urns
will have by turns bad luck and good. But one
to whom he sends all evil—that man goes
contemptible by the will of Zeus; ravenous
hunger drives him over the wondrous earth,
unresting, without honor from gods or men.
Mixed fortune came to Pêleus. Shining gifts
at the gods' hands he had from birth: felicity,
wealth overflowing, rule of the Myrmidons,
a bride immortal at his mortal side.
But then Zeus gave afflictions too—no family
of powerful sons grew up for him at home,
but one child, of all seasons and of none.
Can I stand by him in his age? Far from my country
I sit at Troy to grieve you and your children.
You, too, sir, in time past were fortunate,
we hear men say. From Makar's isle of Lesbos
northward, and south of Phrygia and the Straits,
no one had wealth like yours, or sons like yours.
Then gods out of the sky sent you this bitterness:
the years of siege, the battles and the losses.
Endure it, then. And do not mourn forever
for your dead son. There is no remedy.
You will not make him stand again. Rather
await some new misfortune to be suffered."

The old king in his majesty replied:

"Never give me a chair, my lord, while Hektor
lies in your camp uncared for. Yield him to me
now. Allow me sight of him. Accept
the many gifts I bring. May they reward you,
and may you see your home again.
You spared my life at once and let me live."

Akhilleus, the great runner, frowned and eyed him
under his brows:

                                   "Do not vex me, sir," he said.
"I have intended, in my own good time,
to yield up Hektor to you. She who bore me,
the daughter of the Ancient of the sea,
has come with word to me from Zeus. I know
in your case, too—though you say nothing, Priam—
that some god guided you to the shipways here.
No strong man in his best days could make entry
into this camp. How could he pass the guard,
or force our gateway?

                                   Therefore, *let me be.*
Sting my sore heart again, and even here,
under my own roof, suppliant though you are,
I may not spare you, sir, but trample on
the express command of Zeus!"

                                   When he heard this,
the old man feared him and obeyed with silence.
Now like a lion at one bound Akhilleus
left the room. Close at his back the officers
Automédôn and Álkimos went out—
comrades in arms whom he esteemed the most
after the dead Patróklos. They unharnessed
mules and horses, led the old king's crier
to a low bench and sat him down.
Then from the polished wagon
they took the piled-up price of Hektor's body.
One khiton and two capes they left aside
as dress and shrouding for the homeward journey.
Then, calling to the women slaves, Akhilleus

ordered the body bathed and rubbed with oil—
but lifted, too, and placed apart, where Priam
could not see his son—for seeing Hektor
he might in his great pain give way to rage,
and fury then might rise up in Akhilleus
to slay the old king, flouting Zeus's word.
So after bathing and anointing Hektor
they drew the shirt and beautiful shrouding over him.
Then with his own hands lifting him, Akhilleus
laid him upon a couch, and with his two
companions aiding, placed him in the wagon.
Now a bitter groan burst from Akhilleus,
who stood and prayed to his own dead friend:

                                        "Patróklos,
do not be angry with me, if somehow
even in the world of Death you learn of this—
that I released Prince Hektor to his father.
The gifts he gave were not unworthy. Aye,
and you shall have your share, this time as well."

The Prince Akhilleus turned back to his quarters.
He took again the splendid chair that stood
against the farther wall, then looked at Priam
and made his declaration:

                                        "As you wished, sir,
the body of your son is now set free.
He lies in state. At the first sight of Dawn
you shall take charge of him yourself and see him.
Now let us think of supper. We are told
that even Niobê in her extremity
took thought for bread—though all her brood had perished,
her six young girls and six tall sons. Apollo,
making his silver longbow whip and sing,
shot the lads down, and Artemis with raining
arrows killed the daughters—all this after
Niobê had compared herself with Lêto,
the smooth-cheeked goddess.

                                        She has borne two children,
Niobê said, How many have I borne!
But soon those two destroyed the twelve.

Besides,

nine days the dead lay stark, no one could bury them,
for Zeus had turned all folk of theirs to stone.
The gods made graves for them on the tenth day,
and then at last, being weak and spent with weeping,
Niobê thought of food. Among the rocks
of Sipylos' lonely mountainside, where nymphs
who race Akhelôïos river go to rest,
she, too, long turned to stone, somewhere broods on
the gall immortal gods gave her to drink.

Like her we'll think of supper, noble sir.
Weep for your son again when you have borne him
back to Troy; there he'll be mourned indeed."

In one swift movement now Akhilleus caught
and slaughtered a white lamb. His officers
flayed it, skillful in their butchering
to dress the flesh; they cut bits for the skewers,
roasted, and drew them off, done to a turn.
Automédôn dealt loaves into the baskets
on the great board; Akhilleus served the meat.
Then all their hands went out upon the supper.
When thirst and appetite were turned away,
Priam, the heir of Dárdanos, gazed long
in wonder at Akhilleus' form and scale—
so like the gods in aspect. And Akhilleus
in his turn gazed in wonder upon Priam,
royal in visage as in speech. Both men
in contemplation found rest for their eyes,
till the old hero, Priam, broke the silence:

"Make a bed ready for me, son of Thetis,
and let us know the luxury of sleep.
From that hour when my son died at your hands
till now, my eyelids have not closed in slumber
over my eyes, but groaning where I sat
I tasted pain and grief a thousandfold,
or lay down rolling in my courtyard mire.
Here for the first time I have swallowed bread
and made myself drink wine.

Before, I could not."

Akhilleus ordered men and servingwomen
to make a bed outside, in the covered forecourt,
with purple rugs piled up and sheets outspread
and coverings of fleeces laid on top.
The girls went out with torches in their hands
and soon deftly made up a double bed.
Then Akhilleus, defiant of Agamémnon,
told his guest:

                                    "Dear venerable sir,
you'll sleep outside tonight, in case an Akhaian
officer turns up, one of those men
who are forever taking counsel with me—
as well they may. If one should see you here
as the dark night runs on, he would report it
to the Lord Marshal Agamémnon. Then
return of the body would only be delayed.
Now tell me this, and give me a straight answer:
How many days do you require
for the funeral of Prince Hektor?—I should know
how long to wait, and hold the Akhaian army."

Old Priam in his majesty replied:

"If you would have me carry out the burial,
Akhilleus, here is the way to do me grace.
As we are penned in the town, but must bring wood
from the distant hills, the Trojans are afraid.
We should have mourning for nine days in hall,
then on the tenth conduct his funeral
and feast the troops and commons;
on the eleventh we should make his tomb,
and on the twelfth give battle, if we must."

Akhilleus said:

                                    "As you command, old Priam,
the thing is done. I shall suspend the war
for those eleven days that you require."

He took the old man's right hand by the wrist
and held it, to allay his fear.

Now crier
and king with hearts brimful retired to rest
in the sheltered forecourt, while Akhilleus slept
deep in his palisaded lodge. Beside him,
lovely in her youth, Brisêis lay.
And other gods and soldiers all night long,
by slumber quieted, slept on. But slumber
would not come to Hermês the Good Companion,
as he considered how to ease the way
for Priam from the camp, to send him through
unseen by the formidable gatekeepers.
Then Hermês came to Priam's pillow, saying:

"Sir, no thought of danger shakes your rest,
as you sleep on, being great Akhilleus' guest,
amid men fierce as hunters in a ring.
You triumphed in a costly ransoming,
but three times costlier your own would be
to your surviving sons—a monarch's fee—
if this should come to Agamémnon's ear
and all the Akhaian host should learn that you are here."

The old king started up in fright, and woke
his herald. Hermês yoked the mules and horses,
took the reins, then inland like the wind
he drove through all the encampment, seen by no one.
When they reached Xánthos, eddying and running
god-begotten river, at the ford,
Hermês departed for Olympos. Dawn
spread out her yellow robe on all the earth,
as they drove on toward Troy, with groans and sighs,
and the mule-team pulled the wagon and the body.
And no one saw them, not a man or woman,
before Kassandra. Tall as the pale-gold
goddess Aphrodítê, she had climbed
the citadel of Pergamos at dawn.
Now looking down she saw her father come
in his war-car, and saw the crier there,
and saw Lord Hektor on his bed of death
upon the mulecart. The girl wailed and cried
to all the city:

"Oh, look down, look down,
go to your windows, men of Troy, and women,
see Lord Hektor now! Remember joy
at seeing him return alive from battle,
exalting all our city and our land!"

Now, at the sight of Hektor, all gave way
to loss and longing, and all crowded down
to meet the escort and body near the gates,
till no one in the town was left at home.
There Hektor's lady and his gentle mother
tore their hair for him, flinging themselves
upon the wagon to embrace his person
while the crowd groaned. All that long day
until the sun went down they might have mourned
in tears before the gateway. But old Priam
spoke to them from his chariot:

                                        "Make way,
let the mules pass. You'll have your fill of weeping
later, when I've brought the body home."

They parted then, and made way for the wagon,
allowing Priam to reach the famous hall.
They laid the body of Hektor in his bed,
and brought in minstrels, men to lead the dirge.
While these wailed out, the women answered, moaning.
Andrómakhê of the ivory-white arms
held in her lap between her hands
the head of Hektor who had killed so many.
Now she lamented:

                                "You've been torn from life,
my husband, in young manhood, and you leave me
empty in our hall. The boy's a child
whom you and I, poor souls, conceived; I doubt
he'll come to manhood. Long before, great Troy
will go down plundered, citadel and all,
now that you are lost, who guarded it
and kept it, and preserved its wives and children.
They will be shipped off in the murmuring hulls
one day, and I along with all the rest.

You, my little one, either you come with me
to do some grinding labor, some base toil
for a harsh master, or an Akhaian soldier
will grip you by the arm and hurl you down
from a tower here to a miserable death—
out of his anger for a brother, a father,
or even a son that Hektor killed. Akhaians
in hundreds mouthed black dust under his blows.
He was no moderate man in war, your father,
and that is why they mourn him through the city.
Hektor, you gave your parents grief and pain
but left me loneliest, and heartbroken.
You could not open your strong arms to me
from your deathbed, or say a thoughtful word,
for me to cherish all my life long
as I weep for you night and day."

                                                Her voice broke,
and a wail came from the women. Hékabê
lifted her lamenting voice among them:

"Hektor, dearest of sons to me, in life
you had the favor of the immortal gods,
and they have cared for you in death as well.
Akhilleus captured other sons of mine
in other years, and sold them overseas
to Samos, Imbros, and the smoky island,
Lemnos. That was not his way with you.
After he took your life, cutting you down
with his sharp-bladed spear, he trussed and dragged you
many times round the barrow of his friend,
Patróklos, whom you killed—though not by this
could that friend live again. But now I find you
fresh as pale dew, seeming newly dead,
like one to whom Apollo of the silver bow
had given easy death with his mild arrows."

Hékabê sobbed again, and the wails redoubled.
Then it was Helen's turn to make lament:

"Dear Hektor, dearest brother to me by far!
My husband is Aléxandros,

who brought me here to Troy—God, that I might
have died sooner! This is the twentieth year
since I left home, and left my fatherland.
But never did I have an evil word
or gesture from you. No—and when some other
brother-in-law or sister would revile me,
or if my mother-in-law spoke to me bitterly—
but Priam never did, being as mild
as my own father—you would bring her round
with your kind heart and gentle speech. Therefore
I weep for you and for myself as well,
given this fate, this grief. In all wide Troy
no one is left who will befriend me, none;
they all shudder at me."

                                                        Helen wept,

and a moan came from the people, hearing her.
Then Priam, the old king, commanded them:

"Trojans, bring firewood to the edge of town.
No need to fear an ambush of the Argives.
When he dismissed me from the camp, Akhilleus
told me clearly they will not harass us,
not until dawn comes for the twelfth day."

Then yoking mules and oxen to their wagons
the people thronged before the city gates.
Nine days they labored, bringing countless loads
of firewood to the town. When Dawn that lights
the world of mortals came for the tenth day,
they carried greathearted Hektor out at last,
and all in tears placed his dead body high
upon its pyre, then cast a torch below.
When the young Dawn with finger tips of rose
made heaven bright, the Trojan people massed
about Prince Hektor's ritual fire.
All being gathered and assembled, first
they quenched the smoking pyre with tawny wine
wherever flames had licked their way, then friends
and brothers picked his white bones from the char
in sorrow, while the tears rolled down their cheeks.

In a golden urn they put the bones,
shrouding the urn with veiling of soft purple.
Then in a grave dug deep they placed it
and heaped it with great stones. The men were quick
to raise the death-mound, while in every quarter
lookouts were posted to ensure against
an Akhaian surprise attack. When they had finished
raising the barrow, they returned to Ilion,
where all sat down to banquet in his honor
in the hall of Priam king. So they performed
the funeral rites of Hektor, tamer of horses.

NOTE

Line numbers at the top of each right-hand page refer to the Greek text. A few lines that seem wrong or out of place have been omitted from the translation. These are:

Book One, line 296.
Book Eight, lines 73 and 74, 550 through 552.
Book Nine, line 416.
Book Ten, lines 191, 409 through 411, 497, 531.
Book Twelve, line 372.
Book Fourteen, line 269.
Book Fifteen, line 481.
Book Sixteen, lines 614 and 615.

The translator gratefully acknowledges help in the form of fellowship grants from the Bollingen Foundation, the John Simon Guggenheim Memorial Foundation, and the National Endowment for the Humanities. Sally Fitzgerald was a close and invaluable critic of the entire work in progress. Until his death in 1968, Dudley Fitts gave the translation his strict and exhilarating attention. Penelope Laurans' taste and discernment enhanced the quality of the final manuscripts. The enthusiasm of the translator's children, and their observations, cheered him often.

Of friends who commented on drafts of the work, Cedric and Anne Whitman read and listened to strategic sections and were munificent with their learning and love of Homer; Mason and Florence Hammond were hospitable auditors and critics throughout; George Lord made helpful notes on several books. The translator is greatly indebted to other friends whose kindness to him and faith in his work sustained him.

On the part of the publisher, Anne Freedgood, William Whitehead, and Carolyn Hart were invariably sympathetic and attentive. The translation could not have been undertaken or carried on without the support of the English and Comparative Literature Departments of Harvard University.

ABOUT THE TRANSLATOR

ROBERT FITZGERALD was Boylston Professor of Rhetoric and Oratory Emeritus at Harvard University until his death in 1985. He was a member of the National Academy of Arts and Sciences and a Chancellor of the Academy of American Poets. In 1984 he was named the poet of the Library of Congress. He published four volumes of his own poetry, and translations, with Dudley Fitts, of *Alcestis*, *Antigone*, and *Oedipus Rex*, in addition to his *Iliad*, *Aeneid*, and *Oedipus at Colonus*.

ABOUT THE INTRODUCER

GREGORY NAGY is Francis Jones Professor of Classical Greek Literature and Professor of Comparative Literature at Harvard University. His most recent publications are *Pindar's Homer: The Lyric Possession of an Epic Past* and *Greek Mythology and Poetics*.

TITLES IN EVERYMAN'S LIBRARY

Everyman's Library, founded in 1906 and relaunched in 1991, aims to offer the most enduring library in the English language of the world's classics. Each volume is printed in a classic typeface on acid-free, cream-wove paper with a sewn full cloth binding.

883.01   Homer.
HOM
         The Iliad.

$20.00

DATE			